Resistance and Contradiction:
Miskitu Indians and the Nicaraguan State,
1894–1987

Charles R. Hale

RESISTANCE AND CONTRADICTION

Miskitu Indians and the Nicaraguan State,

1894–1987

Stanford University Press, Stanford, California

Stanford University Press
Stanford, California
© 1994 by the Board of Trustees of the
Leland Stanford Junior University
Printed in the United States of America

CIP data are at the end of the book

Stanford University Press publications
are distributed exclusively by Stanford
University Press within the United States,
Canada, Mexico, and Central America;
they are distributed exclusively by
Cambridge University Press throughout
the rest of the world.

Original printing 1994
Last figure below indicates year of this printing:
05   04   03   02   01   00   99   98   97   96

For Amalia

Acknowledgments

THIS BOOK HAS been a central focus of my life for so long that these few paragraphs seem an inadequate means to thank the people and institutions that have been of help along the way. I hope that what is written here merits the considerable trust placed in me and the help I have received. In addition, I hope the text conveys a sense of the best principles and ideals of the Sandinista revolution, which provided much of the inspiration for what I did, and which have left an indelible influence on my thinking about the relationship between political activism and academic anthropology. Though the standard line about the responsibility being mine alone holds as well, my debt to the revolution is to have learned that much more is—or at least should be—at stake in our work than accountability for possible errors or ineptitude in a written text.

I was extremely fortunate to have the opportunity to work for nearly five years as a CIDCA investigator. Galio Gurdián, CIDCA's director, provided full institutional backing for my research on the Atlantic Coast and was a constant source of friendship and intellectual dialogue on Coast culture and politics. I also wish to thank the many others in CIDCA with whom I have worked since 1981, especially those of the Bluefields office.

A number of Bluefields regional government and Sandinista leaders placed confidence in me, which made it possible for me to work in Sandy Bay. In particular, I would like to thank Harry Chavez, Carlos Castro, and Comandante Lumberto Campbell. Work and informal discussions with them and many other Sandinistas also taught me much about the Atlantic Coast and the revolution. I am deeply grateful to scores of townspeople from Sandy Bay and other Río Grande communities, who welcomed me into their lives with extraordinary warmth, and especially to those who served as research assistants and CIDCA-sponsored "community researchers." Of the abundant knowledge that they shared with me, I learned most from their sharp, perceptive critique of the Sandinista revolution. I trust they would approve of my summary of that lesson: such movements of social change do not come without serious contradictions, which are ignored at great cost, and which might be better understood, even overcome, by listening more attentively to those who resist from within. These community members go unnamed here, as in the rest of the book, as a gesture of respect for their privacy. Among the Miskitu intellectuals who were co-workers in CIDCA, I owe special thanks to Hazel Law and Jorge Matamoros.

While in Bluefields I relied enormously on the friendship of Edmundo Gordon and Daisy Garth; in large part thanks to their hospitality, along with that of Miss Elma Archibold, Bluefields quickly became a place that felt like home.

Many of the ideas in this book emerged from discussions and collective endeavors with Mundo. His knowledge of the Atlantic Coast, theoretical insights into race/ethnic politics, and principled commitment to an anthropology of liberation have exerted a deep and lasting influence on my own thinking. I am very grateful to Martin Diskin, who read the manuscript for Stanford University Press with care and thoroughness well beyond the call of duty. Both his thoughtful criticisms and his strong encouragement helped me immensely as I began the final round of revisions. Many others read early drafts of parts of what is written here, and I gratefully acknowledge their comments, especially those of Richard Adams, Philippe Bourgois, Philip Dennis, Les Field, Smadar Lavie, Carol Smith, Orin Starn, Susan Stokes, John Walton, and Katherine Yih.

During one phase of revisions, I benefited greatly from a semester at the University of Texas and participation in the Ethnicity Colloquium of the Institute of Latin American Studies. For making that experience productive and enjoyable, my thanks go to Richard Adams, Richard Reed, and Ramón Fogel. For an equally productive affiliation with the Latin American Studies program at the University of Washington, I thank Charles Bergquist. My research assistant there, Jeff Cowie, helped enormously at a crucial phase of manuscript preparation. I also thank Rev. Vernon Nelson, director of the Moravian Archives in Bethlehem, Pennsylvania, for the photos and written materials that he made available.

This book had an earlier form as a dissertation, which was much improved by the help of my teachers at Stanford. My principal adviser, William H. Durham, gave me constant support and wise advice from my first day at Stanford in 1982 through the final days of writing. In advising my graduate studies and my work on the dissertation, Bill always insisted on the highest of standards, while at the same time placing full confidence in me to develop the project as I saw fit. Especially now, as I begin to experience that relationship from the opposite perspective, I am admiring of and grateful for Bill's unusual talents as a teacher. G. William Skinner also has been critically engaged with the project since its inception, providing rigorous intellectual guidance and warm support, first as a dissertation committee member, and then as a colleague at U.C. Davis. I also was very fortunate to receive a close reading of and valuable comments on the dissertation from Richard Fagen. While I was writing my dissertation, Bolivar House at Stanford provided me with an office and otherwise eased the difficulties of my return from Nicaragua. For this I thank George Collier, Sharon Phillips, Jutta Mohr, and, especially, my friend and office mate Mauricio Tenorio.

My parents have provided constant support throughout my years of work in Nicaragua, support on which I depend so implicitly that it too often goes unacknowledged. In addition, my father has been a critical reader, a source of wise advice, an example to whom I look for inspiration, and a partner in an ongoing intellectual exchange that I value deeply.

Financial support for research, writing, and revisions came from the following sources, all of which are gratefully acknowledged: National Science Foundation (Dissertation Improvement Grant), Whiting Fellowship (Stanford University Dean's Office), Harry Frank Guggenheim Foundation, SSRC/MacArthur Post-Doctoral Fellowship in International Peace and Security, and U.C. Davis Faculty Research Grant.

My editors at Stanford University Press—Lynn Stewart, Trudie Calvert, Nancy Lerer, and Julia Johnson Zafferano—all of sharp eye and considerable expertise, contributed much to making this book readable and technically competent.

Finally, my most enduring gratitude is to Meliss, for her love, companionship, sharp judgment, and an infallible ability always to know what matters most.

                                                                    C.R.H.

Contents

Figure, Tables, and Maps

Photographs appear on pp. 95 and 177 and following pp. 46 and 162

Note to the Reader

QUOTED PASSAGES in this book come from one of three sources. The first is published material, which is noted in the standard manner. The second is taped interviews, which I conducted myself unless otherwise indicated. Excerpts from these interviews are enclosed in double quotation marks. The third source is informal discussions and interviews, later reconstructed in my fieldnotes. Excerpts from this source are enclosed in single quotation marks. For additional details on interview methods, see Appendixes A and B.

I conducted nearly all the interviews in the speaker's first language (Miskitu, Spanish, or Creole English), and all translations from the Miskitu and Spanish are my own. The only important exception is a taped interview with Manuel Rodriguez, a native Miskitu speaker, conducted in Creole English and cited frequently in Chapter 3. For the sake of clarity, I have transcribed the text using Standard English orthography. The reader should bear in mind, however, that this rendering obscures significant differences in pronunciation between Creole and Standard English.

It is difficult to start a revolution, more difficult to sustain it, and still more difficult to win it. But it is later, when we have won, that the real difficulties will begin.

—Ben M'Hidi, leader of the FLN, as depicted in Gillo Pontecorvo's film, *The Battle of Algiers* (1966)

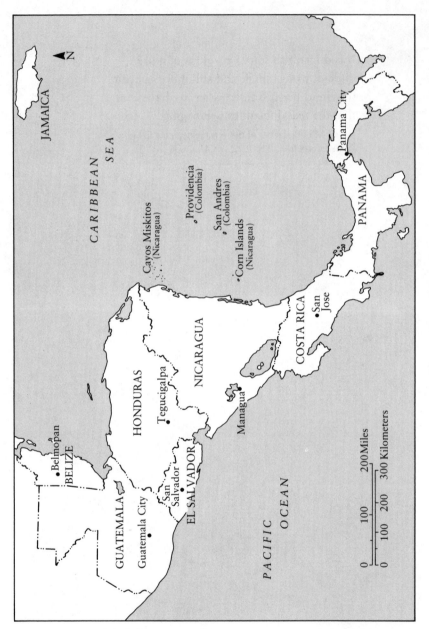

MAP 1. Central America

Introduction

THE DAYS ARE OVER when a cultural anthropologist from the West can travel to the Third World, with pretenses of living for a few years as an objective observer or detached scientist, and then return to write up the research. At least in Nicaragua and in the other parts of Latin America that I know, the conditions of field research have become deeply politicized. Although anthropology has been enmeshed in politics and power relations since its inception, there is a difference now: to a much greater extent the subjects of research now hold anthropologists accountable for what we do. When this occurs, one cannot avoid consciously taking on a dual role of researcher and political actor. These certainly were the ground rules under which I worked on the Atlantic Coast between 1985 and 1988. Although I did and still do subscribe to them out of conviction, they are best understood as existing irrespective of my own preferences. Because this dual role in turn influenced the methods, theoretical concerns, and analysis of this study, it is best specified from the outset.

During a year's work in Nicaragua in 1981–82, I caught the last part of the wave of euphoria that swept over the country after July 19, 1979. Popular insurrection against the Somoza dictatorship had given rise to an extraordinary burst of collective political energy: literacy and health campaigns, intense popular organizing in the city and countryside, hopeful initiatives of economic reconstruction. By early 1985, when I returned to begin dissertation research, this spontaneous energy had subsided, replaced by political resolve for many and by resignation or disillusionment for others. Ronald Reagan had just been reelected president in the United States, and the U.S.-backed *contra* war against Nicaragua was reaching a crescendo. Political slogans now focused on "defense of the revolution" and the implementation of a "survival economy." I quickly came to share the widespread sense of foreboding.

Ironically, one of the few glimmers of hope on the horizon came from the region where political strife and military conflict had first arisen. Just a year after coming to power, the revolutionary government had confronted serious political unrest in the Caribbean or Atlantic Coast region. By mid-1981 a number of prominent Miskitu Indian leaders had left the country, made contact with the incipient contra movement, and declared themselves in armed struggle against the government. For a period, Miskitu Indian opposition even became the Reagan administration's cause célèbre, providing alleged proof of the Nicaraguan government's totalitarian bent and justification for covert aid to the contras. In late 1984, however, the government announced its commitment to recognize Coast peoples' rights to autonomy and entered into negotiations with MISURASATA (MIskitu, SUmu, RAma, and Sandinista, Asla, TAkanka [working together]), one of the Miskitu contra organizations.[1] By January 1985, these two initiatives had generated cautious optimism for a return to peace on the war-torn Atlantic Coast.

During 1981–82 I worked as an analyst in the Center for Research and Documentation on the Atlantic Coast (CIDCA), a Nicaraguan organization that does applied social science research. Founded in mid-1981, CIDCA occupied a complex political space that combined firm support for the revolution's guiding principles with sharp criticism of government policies toward the Coast. By the time I began work with CIDCA, political turmoil on the Coast was too severe for me to acquire permission for extended field research. Living in Managua, with occasional trips to the Coast, I nevertheless became thoroughly engaged with the problem. What had gone wrong? Even if one accepted the view from Managua, which gave primacy to the U.S. role as provocateur, it was still necessary to explain why provocation had been so successful there and not elsewhere. How could a revolutionary government, committed to meeting the urgent material needs of its Indian population, become so quickly embroiled in profound and widespread ethnic conflict?

Originally, I proposed to address these questions through research in the agroindustrial center of Kukra Hill (see Map 2). During the war years (1982–84) many Miskitu refugees had resettled in Kukra Hill, finding work as sugarcane cutters or field laborers, at the bottom of the labor hierarchy. A microcosm of the regionwide economic structure, this place seemed well suited to a study of the interrelations of class, ethnic identity, and political consciousness. Kukra Hill had another advantage as well. It was the only community of the southern Atlantic Coast (apart from Bluefields) with a sizable Miskitu population that had not been attacked, put under siege, or otherwise engulfed in the war during 1983 and 1984. In the first months of 1985, I met people in Kukra Hill, learned to cut sugarcane, and began fieldwork in this muddy, grimy, depressed sugar mill town.

Broad political changes under way throughout the Coast, however, led me to adopt a new research plan. In May 1985, Nicaraguan government

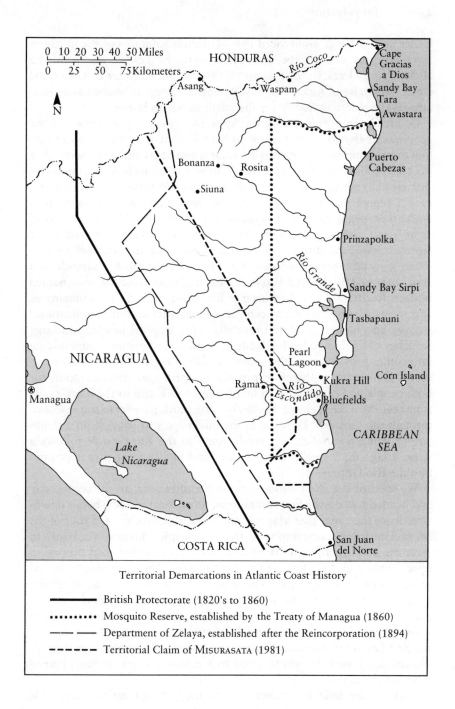

Territorial Demarcations in Atlantic Coast History

———— British Protectorate (1820's to 1860)
•••••••••• Mosquito Reserve, established by the Treaty of Managua (1860)
— — — Department of Zelaya, established after the Reincorporation (1894)
– – – – – Territorial Claim of MISURASATA (1981)

leader Tomás Borge announced that Miskitu inhabitants of the northern Río Coco area, who had been evacuated in the heat of the war, would be allowed to go back to their communities. Within a matter of weeks, the ethnic hierarchy of Kukra Hill lost its bottom rung, as boatloads of Miskitu residents left anxiously for the north to return home.

Of greater importance still, on April 26, 1985, MISURASATA and the government signed an agreement to "cease offensive actions" and to allow the resumption of services to areas affected by the war. Soon after the truce took hold, the opportunity arose for me to join a commission that would visit the five communities of the Río Grande zone and prepare a report to recommend how government and private institutions could best begin to meet townspeople's needs. On May 5 a team of eight—two doctors, two agricultural extension workers, a Red Cross representative, the director of special projects for the regional government, a social worker, and me—left Bluefields for the Río Grande in a boat chartered by the Red Cross. A Miskitu leader from the zone named Manuel Rodriguez, who had been in Bluefields, agreed to accompany us and serve as interlocutor between the communities and the commission.[2]

Over 200 inches of annual rainfall, dense tropical jungle, and large stretches of easily flooded lowlands have prevented people from building intercommunity roads in the southern coastal region. Wooden inboard-motor fishing boats therefore provide the principal transportation for both people and cargo. In such boats, the 75-mile trip to the Río Grande zone takes two days, chugging slowly northward, parallel to the seacoast, through the "inside." Dredged in the mid-1970's to provide an alternative to going out to sea, the inside route to the Río Grande follows a river, a lagoon, a creek, more lagoon, and finally a canal that empties into the Río Grande.

We reached the Río Grande early in the afternoon on the second day and headed toward the first community, Kara, located a few bends downriver from the canal (see Map 3). As we approached, the red roof of the Moravian church came into view, then the people who lined the banks to meet the boat, then, as we drew nearer still, a group of men dressed in olive green, with long hair and automatic rifles. My companions looked grim. No one had expected to meet directly with the contras. When the boat stopped at the banks of Kara, Manuel Rodriguez took charge. He got off, shook hands with the contra officer, spoke to him for a while in Miskitu, and then translated for a brief exchange between the officer and the Red Cross representative, who headed our commission.[3] He then indicated that it was all right to go on to Karawala, where we had planned to spend the night.

Back on the boat Rodriguez assured us, "There's no problem." He

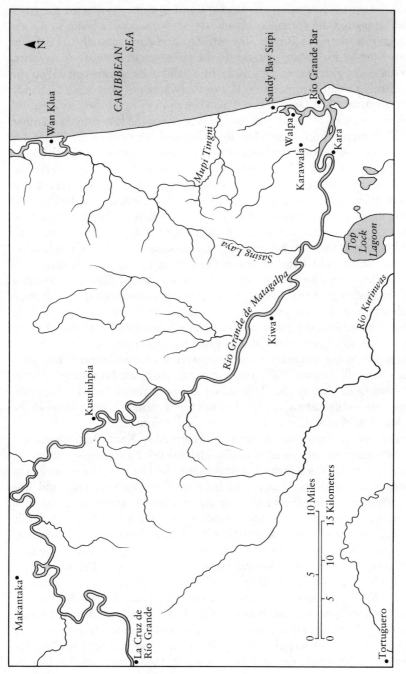

MAP 3. Río Grande zone

said the men belonged to MISURASATA and that they respected the truce and supported the commission's efforts. Only then did I begin to understand how deeply contested the Río Grande zone actually was. From Kara upriver for about 60 miles to the government outpost of La Cruz, MISURASATA exerted military authority. Sandinista troops controlled the three other main communities: Karawala (where we were headed), Sandy Bay Sirpi, and Río Grande Bar. I also began to grasp Rodriguez's central role in the incipient peace process: he was one of the few who could move easily between both sides. Finally, I learned a new Miskitu term: for Rodriguez, these contras were *wan unta wahmika nani*—"our bush boys."

The soldiers in the Sandinista *tropa* stationed in Karawala greeted us warmly. Spanish-speaking Mestizos from the Pacific, they were a few years older, on the average, than the bush boys. These men and (a few) women were not professional soldiers but civilians, who had been carefully chosen by the government to form part of a political-military brigade charged with advancing the peace process in the Río Grande communities. We held a meeting with the officers to explain our objectives and to hear their analysis of the communities' needs. They began with a frank diagnosis of the reasons for people's estrangement from the revolution and affinities with MISURASATA, which included sharp criticism of abuses committed by previous army detachments and acknowledgment that Sandinista government policies had been in error. For these officers, the MISURASATA combatants in Kara were no longer contras but *alzados*—"people in arms." The two forces communicated regularly by letter or envoy and were gradually building a base of mutual trust. These officers were surely among the revolution's finest cadres: keenly aware of the political nature of their mission, principled, committed.

The next morning our commission returned to Kara. Before the community meeting, we talked with the MISURASATA bush people, asking the same questions posed to the Sandinistas the night before. The MISURASATA spokesman, who could not have been over twenty years old and was slightly nervous, gave a brief response in Miskitu, which someone then translated. He detailed the same concerns that we would hear repeatedly during the rest of the week: people were sick, without adequate clothing, lacking supplies necessary to resume production, abandoned by the government, destitute since the war began three years ago. The needs were many, he concluded, and he pledged full support for the commission's work. After our meeting with the community, while the two doctors distributed medicine and saw patients, I took the chance to use my still rudimentary Miskitu and talk more with the bush people. Receptive to my questions, they answered patiently. They were fighting for "Miskitu autonomy," they explained, for their rights to the "riches" of the Atlantic

Coast. They expressed the pride and self-confidence of people who finally had stood up to resist long-standing subjugation.

During the trip back to Karawala I felt overwhelmed by the complexity of these political conditions but exhilarated by the potential—indeed the necessity—for reconciliation. Despite all that kept them apart, the two military forces clearly shared a broad common ground, and both had the political will for a settlement. The thought of them going back to war against each other seemed a sickening tragedy. Possibilities for a return to peace appeared greater still as we got to know Thomas Hammond, the newly assigned Sandinista Front for National Liberation (FSLN) representative to the zone. A Creole[4] from the nearby community of Pearl Lagoon, Hammond had already begun to learn Miskitu and to move easily among townspeople. He spoke in an energetic way about progress in making the revolution respond to Río Grande people's needs and about the many plans for the future. Having a Coast person like Hammond in this position of political leadership, I thought, was bound to defuse ethnic tensions and to confirm the sincerity of the government's commitment to autonomy.

The next community that we visited was Sandy Bay Sirpi, located a few miles northeast of Karawala on the Caribbean seacoast. We held a meeting in the Moravian church. Women and men filed in and sat, according to custom, on opposite sides of the aisle. Manuel Rodriguez, Sandy Bay's headman, presided and encouraged people to speak their minds. Although similar in content to those of the other communities, their complaints had a more critical edge: the government had denied them permission to travel to distant farms, forced them to depend on donated food, made promises that went unfulfilled. I talked further with a group of them afterward. They acknowledged that the government troops treated them much better than previous ones had, readily confirmed their sympathies with the bush people, offered a few shuddering descriptions of the war, and expressed the utmost desire that the truce not be broken. Sandy Bay's 800 inhabitants, the most politically assertive in the zone, had been active in the antigovernment mobilization and would surely play a pivotal role in the reconciliation process. This community, I decided, would be the ideal site for my study.

The excitement that had been building over those four days, stimulated by evident prospects for a negotiated settlement to the conflict and by the thought of this new research plan, suddenly dissolved in a matter of hours. Upon returning to Karawala, we heard bad news. The previous day, the community nurse, a Karawala native named Mildred Gomez, had been summoned to Kara to attend to a sick person. Soon after she arrived, for reasons that were never fully clarified, a MISURASATA officer killed her in cold blood. In addition, Hammond informed us that Marshall Point, a community to the south, had been attacked and that the Nicaraguan army, in pursuit of the perpetrators, had exchanged fire with some MISURASATA combatants. The repercussions from these events seemed sure to include a breakdown of the truce. Karawala turned gloomy as townspeople mourned Gomez's death and tense as Hammond and tropa leaders prepared for the possibility of renewed combat. Rodriguez, clearly distraught, reported that a dissident faction of MISURASATA, which had repudiated the truce and joined the Nicaraguan Democratic Forces (FDN), was now present in Kara.[5] He claimed that these dissidents had been responsible for the two acts. Depressed and pessimistic, we returned to Bluefields by sea to avoid the fighting that had broken out along the inside route.

Over the following weeks the truce did indeed break down. On May 18 a combined force of the Revolutionary Democratic Alliance (ARDE) and MISURASATA attacked Bluefields.[6] A day later, MISURASATA attacked the community of Pearl Lagoon. Thomas Hammond, home by chance for a visit, was caught by surprise in the middle of the night and killed before he could get out of bed. In the fourth round of talks held in Colombia on May 26 the FSLN denounced these and other violations of the truce, and MISURASATA leader Brooklyn Rivera responded with counteraccusations. The talks ended in an impasse and were suspended indefinitely. Over the next few months a sense of vulnerability and apprehension settled over Bluefields. We often heard nearby machine-gun and mortar fire at night; rumors abounded of plans for another attack. Travel to outlying communities was unthinkable until more was known about the results of government efforts to preserve the cease-fire through local-level negotiations with MISURASATA field commanders. It was three months before CIDCA received permission from the government for me to return to Sandy Bay to carry out a first month of fieldwork.

In the meantime I devoted my energy to helping make CIDCA-Bluefields operate as an efficient, productive research center, which in early 1985 was a full-time job. There was a new office to set up, research assistants to supervise, two new microcomputers that people had to be trained to use, and ongoing research related to the autonomy process that demanded attention. Even when a return trip to the Río Grande did become possible, my research had to be justified to the government as part of CIDCA's broader objectives and political contribution. Initially this was easy enough. After the first trip I wrote a brief sociocultural sketch of the community: kinship, community politics, people's reasons for distrusting the government and supporting the bush people, their aspirations for autonomy. Because Sandy Bay had been a war zone during the previous three years, the Sandinistas had barely a clue about the community; they were fascinated by my report. But they had much less interest in return trips, preferring research that would produce similar sketches of other communities in the region or that would address one of the many urgent problems of the day. When CIDCA argued for the value of long-term research, some government leaders were convinced, but others remained skeptical.

Moreover, each trip required special permission from State Security because the Río Grande area was still considered a war zone. Often these permits were delayed or granted less time than I requested; when war-related problems arose or were anticipated, State Security closed the area completely. On each of my eight trips to the Río Grande I was fully aware that it might be my last. To make matters worse, some people connected with State Security began to suspect that my interest in Miskitu people with "contra" sympathies had ulterior motives. That was all the more reason to spend a few months in Bluefields after each trip, giving suspicions a chance to subside.

Being unable to live for an extended period in the community that became my field site was initially a source of concern and anxiety. After all, that is what anthropologists were supposed to do. Would I miss too much of daily events in Sandy Bay? Would I fail fully to understand the process of political change as the inhabitants experienced and perceived it? In retrospect I credit these constraints—despite their unpleasant aspects—with having generated the methodological innovation on which this study is based. From the outset I was committed to achieving a grasp of the conflict from both sides. Yet if it had been possible, I probably would have worked mainly in Sandy Bay, staying for long, uninterrupted stretches, as anthropological fieldworkers generally do. This would not have precluded hearing Sandinista voices because I could always talk with the Sandinista soldiers stationed there. But it would have seriously attenuated the dual perspective that I gradually acquired. As it happened, repeatedly, I would be just beginning to settle in, to move with the rhythms of Sandy Bay's daily life, when my time ran out and I would be compelled to return to Bluefields, unable to pick up the thread until two, three, or four months later.

Although this truncation of community-based fieldwork surely deprived me of important insights, what I gained in return was even more valuable. It forced on me a repeated shift in standpoint. While in Bluefields, I talked, worked, and passed time as a quasi-insider within what might be called the revolutionary establishment. I thus gained much insight into the workings of the Sandinista party and state, as well as a view of the state's relations with Miskitu communities from the Sandinista perspective. More important still was the brute reality of daily life in a city and a country under siege—of living among friends and acquaintances who, literally by virtue of where we stood, felt deeply at risk from a common external threat. On May 18, 1985, I woke up in Bluefields to the sound of machine-gun fire and watched neighbors head off, rifles in hand, to defend the city from attack. Later that year, my closest friends and their infant son were riding in a civilian boat down the Escondido River toward Bluefields when the contras opened fire from the banks. Several passengers were badly wounded; my friends barely escaped unharmed. The contrast between this standpoint and the one associated with everyday life in Sandy Bay could not have been greater. There nearly everyone assumed, based on ample experience of the past three years, that renewed combat would result in harm to loved ones from Sandinista bullets. Gradually, these crossings back and forth between two radically different versions of reality grew from a necessary inconvenience into the backbone of my research method.

To be sure, broader changes in political and military conditions made the method possible. From 1982 through 1984 Sandy Bay Sirpi—like many Miskitu communities throughout the Coast—was engulfed in war. The fighting precluded virtually all nonmilitary presence, not to mention field research by a foreign anthropologist. Prior steps toward a negotiated settlement were therefore a precondition for this study. Moreover, with the introduction of autonomy in 1984, CIDCA's role as a research organization acquired greater importance and viability, which in turn generated interest in and political support for work such as my own.

At least through 1988, however, peaceful coexistence—not to mention complete reconciliation—was far from assured. Tensions frequently ran high, and at every juncture over the three years the potential for a return to armed conflict in the Sandy Bay area was manifest. The experience of moving back and forth made it painfully clear that each side remained far from coming to accept or even fully understand basic elements of the other's perspective. This allowed privileged analytical insight into the conflict but also generated tensions and discomfort in relation to both sides.

The Sandinistas' view of me was shaped by the well-established category for foreigners who worked in solidarity with the revolution: the *internacionalistas*. The expectation was that internacionalistas acted in accordance with cadres' assessments of the revolution's needs and priorities, rarely dissented, and in the case of political disagreement always deferred. The more immersed in my research I became, the more these assumptions began to chafe. Miskitu of Sandy Bay had a trajectory of past collective actions and an array of ongoing political demands that confronted the revolution with a radical critique. When it became clear that autonomy, despite its impressive achievements and potential, would not neatly resolve the entire problem, this Miskitu critique became an embarrassment to the Sandinista portrayal of steady progress toward reconciliation. Because my research was intended to validate as well as understand the Miskitu standpoint, it came to be viewed by some within the state and party as provocative, even subversive. Fortunately, a few key high-ranking Sandinistas were unusually open-minded and continued to acknowledge the value of my work, which explains why my research permission was not revoked. It also helped that the line between raising questions from within and challenging the revolutionary framework was hazy, especially when the latter was in the process of change. But my work never ceased to be controversial and stood increasingly at odds with what was generally expected from an *internacionalista*.

The Miskitu of Sandy Bay welcomed me with open arms. They also had an established category for people like me: I was a *Miriki*. Translated literally as "American," the term was packed with politically charged meanings. Missionaries, company bosses and workers, participants in a University of Wisconsin health promotion program funded by the U.S. Agency for International Development (USAID), and other North American fieldworkers all had a part in shaping the content of this term in community members' minds, thereby contributing to their preformed image of me.[7] Even before developing personal ties, I reaped the benefits of their glowing associations with all the white North Americans who had preceded me. In some ways, I met their expectations. I learned to speak Miskitu with reasonable fluency, talked at length with people about things that concerned them most, participated in the activities of their daily lives. Occasionally, through the auspices of CIDCA, I was even able to help resolve one or another trouble that afflicted them. As for my admiration, respect, and fondness for Sandy Bay people, I trust that the content of this book will speak for itself.

Yet there were facets of this privileged welcome—and of the underlying meaning of Miriki—that I found deeply troubling. People accepted me so willingly in part because of their affinities with Anglo culture, which resulted from a history of Anglo-American hegemony on the Atlantic Coast. Moreover, I am sure that my being a Miskitu-speaking white North American mitigated their perceptions of my connections with the Nicaraguan government. Everyone knew that I and CIDCA worked with the government and that we actively supported the government-backed autonomy process. For a few this connection merited mistrust, but the great majority quickly overcame their suspicions. They developed confidence in me, to the point of speaking openly about politically sensitive issues. Such confidence would have been nearly impossible for a Mestizo

Nicaraguan to achieve (for a discussion of the methodological implications of Miskitu Anglo affinity, see Appendix A).

Anthropologists invariably pride themselves on their ability to fit in,
develop close ties, communicate with fluidity, and achieve the trust of the
people with whom they work. I am not immune from such vanities, and
if I had conducted fieldwork only in Sandy Bay, I might easily have been
lulled into understanding my relations with people largely in those terms.
Yet each trip back to Bluefields quickly cured me of such illusions. Sandinistas admired my linguistic skills and my ability to thrive in the rustic
(and at times dangerous) conditions, but their main explanation for my
success came with the half-joking, half-serious remark: "Those Miskitu
sure do love gringos." I had to admit they were right.

These inclinations of dissent from both cultural categories established
for me were mirror images of each other. Although they arose in part
from ideas and values that I brought with me to Nicaragua, they were
also shaped and reinforced by the research method I chose to follow.
Paradoxically, that method also came to entail the best response—
however partial and contradictory—I could muster to deal with the discomfort. To Miskitu townspeople, the Sandinistas' crucial distinction
between the (imperialist) government and the (solidary) people of the
United States meant next to nothing. They (we) were all Miriki. Though
I tried, whenever the opportunity arose, to reiterate my opposition to the
Reagan-Bush policies, such protestations rarely had much impact.[8] To
the contrary, for the Miskitu I was a walking refutation of the Sandinistas' anti-imperialism. In a single line of thought they would often scoff at
condemnations of the "Yankees," contrast my Miskitu language skills
with the lame attempts of Sandinista soldiers stationed in the community
to learn a few words, and end by evoking fond memories of Parson so-
and-so, a North American Moravian missionary of years past who also
had become fluent in Miskitu.

After a period of time in the role of Miriki, it was a great relief to
reaffirm my affinity with the Sandinistas, my solidarity with the principles
that animated the revolution. As soon as I crossed the cultural/political
line and resumed my identity as an *internacionalista*, my anti-imperialist
convictions were again largely assumed. Yet it would not take long for
the discomfort to begin again. Depreciation of Miskitu culture and the
vanguardist premise that "we know what's best for them" were both
fairly near the surface in Sandinista discourse, even after the onset of
autonomy. I remember talking about my research with two officers, who
expressed their approval: "I think what you're doing is great," and then
lowered their voices to add, "but remember, Miskitu people are born
liars. They won't even tell you what their real names are." I could not

help fancying those two as colonial administrators, muttering about the natives' deceptive ways. A similar reaction would come from reading party documents that commonly referred to the need for "political-ideological work" that gets the "people to assume the tasks of the Revolution as their own."[9] After a period of such experiences I wanted nothing more than to return to Sandy Bay to align myself with the townspeople's struggle to overcome this internal colonial legacy.

This inevitably tension-ridden research endeavor was made feasible by the existence of CIDCA. Challenging in any case, the logistics of daily life would have been a bureaucratic nightmare without such an affiliation. With CIDCA's backing, my residency papers and the rarely granted permission to live in the volatile coastal region passed through the Managua bureaucracy with little delay. More important, CIDCA-Bluefields embodied an imagined political space of reconciliation: defending the Miskitu struggle as far as possible, especially in relation to Mestizo dominance, without undermining the Nicaraguan state's sovereignty, especially in relation to U.S. government aggression. We worked closely with the FSLN yet maintained a stance that was consistently critical in fundamental ways. We established parallel relations with Miskitu communities, demonstrating our commitment to research that served their interests, yet made clear our resolve to work within rather than against the revolution.[10] Although far from homogeneous, people who worked in CIDCA generally shared this standpoint and forged ties with others of like minds. With these people I developed both personal friendships and a crucial sense of being part of a broader political effort. Without such ties, quite apart from the institutional support CIDCA provided, I am sure that this study would never have been completed.

The final and most important reason my political commitments became inextricable from scholarly objectives was the interventionist policies of my own government. The only way to avoid these conditions of inextricability would have been to conduct research elsewhere. The Inter-American Foundation, to which I applied for research support, encouraged me to do exactly that: it awarded me a fellowship provided that I carry out the study in Bolivia. My decision to turn down that offer was ultimately a political decision. I wanted to defy U.S. government policies of aggression against the Nicaraguan revolution and to work in support of the process of conflict resolution under way on the Atlantic Coast. I hope this book demonstrates that politically positioned research of this sort is not only possible, but capable of generating practical, analytical, and theoretical insights that would otherwise be impossible to achieve.

1 Ethnicity and the State in Revolutionary Nicaragua

> [Peoples' reactions to experiences] of subordination and dehumanization . . . [consist] in a complex admixture of tacit (even uncomprehending) accommodation to the hegemonic order at one level and diverse expressions of symbolic and practical resistance at another. . . . The point may be extended to colonialism at large: a critical feature of the colonization of consciousness among the Tswana, and others like them, was the process by which they were drawn unwittingly into the dominion of European "civilization" while at the same time often contesting its presence and the explicit content of its worldview.
> —Jean and John Comaroff, *Of Revelation and Revolution*, 1991

> The repertoire of activities and institutions conventionally identified as 'the State' are cultural forms. . . . States define, in great detail, acceptable forms and images of social activity and individual and collective identity; they regulate, in empirically specifiable ways, much—very much, by the twentieth century—of social life. In this sense 'the State' never stops talking.
> —Philip Corrigan and Derek Sayer, *The Great Arch*, 1985

THE MISKITU PEOPLE, with a few exceptions, passed the Sandinista insurrection against the Somoza dictatorship as detached observers of a distant political drama. Less than two years later they became protagonists in a rebellion that convulsed the coastal region and garnered nearly unanimous support. By 1985, at the height of the war in western Nicaragua, these same communities throughout the Coast became active participants in a process of negotiated return to peace and transition to autonomy. This chapter introduces the theoretical ideas that guided my analysis of these three moments in Miskitu history: from relative quiescence, to mobilization, and back again.

Easy explanations for the Miskitu-Sandinista conflict were always readily available in the anti-Sandinista analysis that came mainly from outside Nicaragua, particularly the United States. With varying degrees of sophistication, scholars and pundits, conservatives and "disenchanted liberals"[1] blamed the Sandinistas for problems imposed upon them, imbued every mistake with cynical or sinister motives, and took every reform initiative as evidence of the revolution's fundamental flaws. From my standpoint—a commitment to study and work on Miskitu politics from within the revolution—these responses appeared both analytically deficient and ethically unacceptable. They assumed what needed to be explained, and they formed part of precisely what the revolution was meant to contest. The driving force behind Sandinista politics was a passionate defiance of U.S. imperialism in all its manifestations: economic, military, diplomatic, and, equally important, the imperial prerogative of distant critics to draw conclusions and cast judgments that deeply influence the fate of the poor and powerless, without taking responsibility for those consequences. In contrast, my work has been predicated on the legitimacy of the Sandinistas' mobilization in defense of sovereignty and self-determination. This made the questions that animated my research all the more urgent: Why did that endeavor and the equally legitimate Miskitu quest for self-determination come so directly into conflict? Under what conditions could a just and enduring resolution be achieved?

Although introduced with emphasis on precedents and continuities, Sandinista leaders' announced commitment to autonomy in late 1984 involved a sharp break with the past. The process of reflection and political change that followed had two distinct points of reference. First, the announcement sent a clear message that previous understandings of the "ethnic question" had been in error, thereby opening political space for new theoretical approaches to class and ethnicity, consciousness and action. Although much of the new analysis went no further than a rejection of the "economism"—or class reductionism—endemic to Marxism, the opening also legitimated research, theory, and political practice of a more radical bent. Developing an account of the conflict based on the perspectives of Miskitu protagonists forced me to call into question fundamental elements of the Sandinista discourse. I began to see economism as a symptom of a broader problem: the deeply ingrained internal colonial relations between Mestizo Nicaraguans and Miskitu people. These relations fused structural inequity with cultural oppression, which ensured that the Miskitu would be treated as objects (of both study and policy), rather than active, knowing, fully constituted subjects. At the same time, the more time I spent with the Miskitu the more convinced I became of the validity of the Sandinistas' principal critical insight. Miskitu consciousness did include hegemonic premises associated with the Anglo-American cultural world; they espouse what I call "Anglo affinity." I began to rethink ethnicity theory to make room for these two insights, which became central to my analysis of Miskitu people's collective action.

Second, by setting in motion this sweeping policy change, the Sandinistas necessarily focused attention on contradictions within the revolutionary state and ideology. They of course tried constantly to limit the scope and depth of this inward reflection—admitting mistakes, while in the same breath stating assuredly that the "problem" had been "solved." They also argued—much more convincingly—that the very emergence of autonomy stood as eloquent evidence of the state's commitment to social justice and capacity for pragmatic reform. Nonetheless, the changes invited more critical scrutiny: Why had "participatory democracy" among the Miskitu failed almost from the outset? In what ways had state policies contributed directly to the conflict? Could these irritants be completely eliminated, or would they limit what autonomy could achieve? These questions drew me into a second area of theoretical discussion, of democracy and revolutionary change in multiethnic societies.

This study does not follow the established practice of detached, "objective" social science research. Rather, my interest in supporting efforts toward conflict resolution led me to an activist or politically engaged research method, described in detail in the Introduction. In some respects my stance coincides with that which has led many to proclaim a crisis in anthropological research and writing.[2] I hope to have incorporated some of the sophisticated and intelligent insights put forth in the name of anthropology's crisis, but I do not engage in that discussion here. The reason derives from the primary purpose I have defined for this study, though such a decision surely reflects deeper theoretical and political differences as well. For example, I fully endorse the critical thrust of Trinh Minh-ha's (1989: 64) portrayal of anthropology as a "conversation . . . of the white man with the white man about the primitive-native man." Yet I find Trinh's essay, and much of the writing in this "crisis-in-the-discipline" genre, to be limited to an inward-looking conversation among critical intellectuals about anthropological texts.

In contrast, I am most interested in exploring the analytical and theoretical rewards of a particular approach to research and writing on ethnic conflict. Briefly, this involved an effort to move back and forth, listening carefully to both Miskitu and Sandinista perspectives, avoiding collusion with their reductionist portrayals of each other while learning from their mutual critiques. This method encouraged a theoretical balance: the view from within yielded analysis of both as knowledgeable, motivated, fully constituted social actors, while the critical distance revealed contradictions that their respective cultures and consciousness entailed. I use the term "contradictory consciousness"—borrowed loosely from Antonio Gramsci and applied to both the Sandinistas and the Miskitu—to encapsulate this parallel analytical finding. Both were cultures of resistance, imbued with premises that limited their liberating potential and brought them squarely into conflict. If this analysis contributes productively to the dialogue among activists and intellectuals concerned with problems of building progressive, multicultural political movements in Central America and beyond, the book's primary goal will be achieved.

Ethnicity Theory and Miskitu Collective Action

It is unfortunate, though understandable, that Miskitu people's mobilization against the state, and not their subsequent return to peace, has been the focus of international scholars' energies in the 1980's. As I hope this study will demonstrate, the post-1984 period both raises complex analytical questions and contains important lessons for resolution of ethnic conflict elsewhere, which deserve more than the fleeting attention they have received. Nevertheless, precisely because of the intense, if ephemeral, interest generated by the conflict, it offers a useful place to start in this assessment of ethnicity theory. Across the political and analytical spectrum, accounts of the Miskitu mobilization have suffered from pervasive deficiencies, which are symptomatic of the broader problems that have led many to decry the "crisis of coherence" in ethnicity theory.

A flood of literature meant to explain Miskitu Indians' conflict with the Sandinistas poured forth between 1981 and 1985. One group of analysts emphasized structural factors, focusing either on the intrusive, repressive character of the Sandinista state or on the interventionist policies of the United States, whose operatives founded, funded, and orchestrated the anti-Sandinista contra movement. A second group emphasized Miskitu people's motivations, portraying them as a peace-loving tribal group, fiercely defending its "traditional" lifeways and fighting for autonomy, a people whose "moral economy" had been violated.[3]

These two emphases were not mutually exclusive; indeed they depended on each other, and the more sophisticated analysts made gestures toward their synthesis. Yet for the most part explanations remained confined to one side or the other of this divide. Structural analysis offered at best a vague and deductive sense of what Miskitu people understood themselves to be doing. Accounts that began from the "Indian perspective" tended to caricature the structural determinants of the conflict, to portray Miskitu culture in a vacuum, and to neglect how structural conditions had shaped Miskitu people's consciousness. These two emphases do not neatly correspond to political points of view. Structural analyses from opposite ends of the political spectrum (invoking imperialism and Sandinista repression, respectively, as the cause of the conflict) were equally neglectful of Miskitu consciousness; the tendency to set culture apart from political economic conditions has a long tradition in the social sciences among both apologists for colonialism and advocates for colonized peoples.

This dual barrier to a full understanding of Miskitu politics is symptomatic of a problem that confronts social theory more generally. For example, in her review of theory in anthropology, Sherry Ortner (1984) heralds a new analytical paradigm associated with the term "practice," which was to provide anthropological theory with a unifying focus and to correct some of its persistent deficiencies. Most important, practice theory purportedly incorporated the best of political economic analysis, while maintaining an emphasis on individual human actors, their motivations and consciousness, and the ways their actions shape the "system." Acknowledging the potential for "voluntarism" if such emphasis goes too far, Ortner concludes with a plea to retain the "dialectic" between human agency and the powerfully constraining effects of structural conditions. That conclusion echoes Anthony Giddens's broader critique of Western social theory, which he argues has suffered from a "deeply entrenched conceptual divide" between "voluntaristic and deterministic types of theory . . . a dualism of individual and society . . . subject and object" (1979: 4).

In an otherwise comprehensive review, Ortner is dismissive of the "burgeoning ethnicity industry," a literature she describes as "too vast and too amorphous for me to do more than nod to here" (1984: 142). With that omission—especially odd in light of the dramatic increase in ethnic-national conflict throughout the world—Ortner missed an opportunity to drive home her general point. The desultory growth of the "ethnicity industry," I contend, is related to the same conceptual problem that she, Giddens, and others have argued runs throughout social theory, namely, a disjuncture between structural and actor-centered analysis. I defend this contention with a brief review of theories on either side of this divide; I then propose a Gramscian "bridge" that can help resolve the problem.

Primordial Sentiments Versus Instrumental Choice

Until recently, considerable work on this topic was devoted to a debate between proponents of "primordial" and "instrumental" theories of ethnicity. The first refers to the view of ethnicity as a bundle of "primordial attachments" (kinship, religion, language, and the like), which acquire political salience as people respond to the disruptive change associated with efforts to forge modern postcolonial states. Summaries of this position invariably invoke Clifford Geertz's early essay on the "integrative revolution" (1973 [1963]), which casts primordialism in the now largely discredited framework of modernization theory.

Because few still defend primordialism as an explanatory scheme,[4] the position is best characterized today as having evolved into an overall approach to culture theory. Again following Geertz (1973), proponents of this approach seek to dissolve the separation between human behavior and culture. Through social action, Geertz argues, individuals reproduce the "webs of significance" that constitute both their culture and their subsequent behavior. The theoretical message to students of ethnic politics is clear. Before "explaining" a given ethnic mobilization, as if its meaning and purpose were largely self-evident, we must first break into and understand this "web of significance" for which ethnicity (or primordial attachments) is just our semantic marker.

"Instrumentalist" theory, in contrast, is concerned not with the "deep meaning" of culture but with the way shared cultural attributes—whatever their meaning may be—get used politically. Primordial attachments, by this line of argument, become relevant because they allow ethnic elites to communicate a message, forge a sense of unity, and galvanize political action. Cultural symbols retain importance because they motivate individuals to take political action, but they explain little about the underlying logic of the action itself. If symbols with meanings conducive to ethnic mobilization are not readily available, elites will invent them. Thus instrumental theorists reverse the causal relationship: emotionally packed primordial ties are the result, not the cause, of collective political action.

The crux of the instrumentalist challenge to Geertzians is the claim that human behavior has an objective logic that allows it to be observed and explained without having to make sense of the "hermeneutic web." This logic revolves around some notion of basic human needs or interests, which individuals pursue by rational means. An unconvincing application of the thesis focuses on elite strategies and relaxes the premise of rationality for the rest (e.g., Rothschild 1981).[5] In its more internally consistent form, instrumentalism converges with "rational choice" theory, which applies the assumptions to all social actors and makes an astoundingly broad claim regarding ethnic politics. As Michael Hechter explains, once we have established the individuals' "preferred goals," we can "predict the conditions under which ethnic collective action will arise." After making a "benefit/cost calculation," ethnic group members will choose to mobilize only when they "estimate that by doing so they will receive a net individual benefit" (1986: 271).

Understood in its original terms, the debate eventually reached an impasse because theorists found a way to reconcile the two positions. They could affirm the importance of primordial ties as meaningful cultural forms, while maintaining that elites make use of and transform these ties in the course of ethnic mobilization (e.g., Keyes 1981, Rothschild 1981). A parallel effort is under way for the more substantive version of the debate—between hermeneutics and rational choice. The entrée for such a synthesis, according to David Laitin, is rational choice theorists' need to establish the "preference schedule" by which individuals make choices. Only through a hermeneutic analysis of cultural symbols, Laitin contends, "can one adduce cultural preferences without tautologically claiming that preferences can be derived from the behavior of actors who are assumed to be rational" (1986: 16).

Although this second synthesis can never be fully achieved,[6] the effort highlights a fundamental similarity in these two seemingly disparate positions. Both focus on individual consciousness, culture, and action, neglecting the structural dimension of the problem. Geertz claims to have embedded a theory of society in his notion that culture resides not in "people's heads" but in "public symbols," created and reinforced through social interaction. But this still does not help us to understand how structures of inequality and oppression impinge on these interactions and thereby leave their imprint on the cultural production that results.[7]

Regarding rational choice theory, Hechter admits that "structural factors" obviously constrain individual actors and, further, that at present they cannot be convincingly accounted for by the theory itself.[8] Thus rational choice theory's present claim to "explain" ethnic mobilization rests on a basic dichotomy. The analyst first determines the constraining structures and the individual preference schedules through "detailed case studies" (1986: 277). Having established these parameters, he or she can then employ the methodology. While hermeneutic analysis may be helpful for determining the preference schedules, we are still left with a theoretical statement that assigns structural inequities the mere role of "parameters." Neither version of the actor-oriented analysis captures the dynamic, mutually constitutive impact of structure and individual action in the consciousness of subordinated ethnic group members.

Even theorists who acknowledge the logic of this critique tend to remain confined to one side of Giddens's conceptual divide. Consider, for example, Carter Bentley's effort to rise above the primordial-instrumental debate to a "more universal plane of explanation" through a "practice theory" of ethnic identity and change (1987: 26). The key to his argument is that both sides of this debate share a common flaw: neither specifies "how people recognize the commonalities (of interest or sentiment) underlying claims to common [ethnic] identity" (p. 24). The key lies in everyday practices through which individuals acquire a set of "generative schemes" (common sense, dispositions, unarticulated premises)—what Pierre Bourdieu calls "habitus"—that orient their subsequent thought and action. Habitus can account for ethnic affiliation without portraying it as either mysteriously "primordial" or fully goal-oriented and rational. Instead, Bentley locates the rationale for ethnic-based actions in the mental schemes created by ethnic group members themselves, while emphasizing that these actions can have unintended and unforeseen consequences.

Although this constitutes a clear advance in the debate, Bentley's resolution ultimately leaves the analytical divide between structural forces and individual consciousness intact. His discussion of "habitus and domination," for example, is limited to class divisions within an ethnic group, leaving the whole group's relationship to class society untheorized. Similarly, his explanation for ethnic mobilization is predicated on a sharp dichotomy between the ethnic group, on the one hand, and exogenous societal forces, on the other. Bentley argues that "rapid economic and political change" disrupts the "habitus" associated with an existing regime of domination, often creating "crises in ethnic identity," which in turn are an impetus for people to mobilize (p. 43). Though this causal sequence may be plausible, the original (structural) catalyst remains obscure while the actor's consciousness receives all the attention.

Because the primordial-instrumental debate remained on one side of the divide, it was bound to produce dissatisfying results. Conversely, on the structuralist side, theories ranging from Parsonian functionalism to the Marxism of Louis Althusser suffer from the opposite problem. They are characterized by what Giddens calls a "conceptual elimination" of the individual as a social actor who knows a great deal about, and actively shapes, the society of which he or she forms a part. This insight applies to a second corpus of ethnicity theory that has emphasized the structural determinants of ethnic mobilization.

Parsonian Functionalism Versus Structural Marxism

Talcott Parsons exerted a profound influence on all facets of the study of human societies, including theories of ethnic politics. Lurking beneath Geertz's early statement of the primordialist position was a Parsonian notion of the "normative integration" that had to occur if postcolonial societies were to become fully "modern."[9] This is only one of numerous variations on the "developmental" thesis inspired by Parsons's framework: with "modernization" people gradually assimilate society's universal norms, and ethnicity gives way to a plurality of less divisive civic affiliations.[10]

Prompted by extensive contradictory evidence, such as ethnic revivals in developed countries and obvious barriers to this "integration" in the Third World, analysts proposed modifications in the scheme. Most notably, the "plural society" theorists (e.g., M. G. Smith 1969) attributed lack of "political integration" in many Third World countries to the "systematic disassociation" of distinct ethnic or racial groups. They live under the same political rule, Smith observed, but otherwise have no basis for cultural interaction with one another. Under such conditions, it could be expected that one cultural group would rule through "regulation" and "asymmetrical relations" rather than democratic forms of government (p. 32). Concretely, the plural society thesis suggested—in keeping with Parsons's original formulation—that strong ethnic/racial mobilization and conflict occurred because cultural groups lived "separately" from one another, which prevented "normative integration."

Substantive and well-deserved critiques of Parsons's work (and derivative theories) came from Marxists, who replaced the notion of social equilibrium with that of classes inherently in conflict and reinterpreted "normative integration" as ideological domination of the capitalist class. From the Marxist perspective, the class and power relations that make up society set the course of ethnic politics. Michael Hechter, in his much-cited study of "internal colonialism" in Great Britain (1975 [conducted before his shift to rational choice theory]), took only a faltering step toward this Marxist challenge of Parsons. His explanation for the development of a reactive Celtic consciousness within the internal colony revolves around a relationship between ethnic groups ("a cultural division of labor"), detached from class structure in the colony itself.[11] Hechter ultimately remained trapped by the Parsonian bent for cultural analysis, which he intended to be reacting against.

Structural Marxism has contributed distressingly little to our understanding of ethnic mobilization, considering the obvious importance of the topic. Many theorists of ethnic or racial politics more solidly in the Marxist tradition (e.g., Barrera 1979, Gordon 1972, Bonacich 1979, and Reich 1972) seem concerned mainly with how capitalism gives rise to racial (or ethnic) inequality and racism, rather than with the specifics of oppressed groups' political responses. Edna Bonacich's "split labor market theory" (1976, 1979), a forcefully stated and persuasive argument, is a case in point. The central focus of Bonacich's analysis is the process of class struggle involving three groups: capitalists, white workers whose labor is high-priced, and workers of the minority ethnic or racial group whose labor (for historical reasons) has a lower market price. When the capitalists begin to employ minorities, white workers struggle to defend themselves against displacement, and racism or ethnic antagonism become prominent. Bonacich is critical of "functionalist" Marxism and emphasizes the need for "careful historical analysis" to determine how class struggle is related to racism in each particular case. But her argument is firmly structural: "Race [and ethnicity]," she contends, "are political constructs . . . important only so long as [they are] rooted in class processes" (1979: 19, 35).

Despite the enormous gulf between Parsonian functionalism and structural Marxism, the theories of ethnic politics that each inspires are similar in one important respect. Neither includes a well-developed focus on individual people: their consciousness, knowledge of society, and rationale for social action. Moreover, the role of individual action in the reproduction of social structure is left obscure. Both the developmental and plural society theories portray a process whereby individuals merely assimilate and enact norms that reside within society itself.[12] Bonacich's theory contains a parallel problem. However persuasive her argument for the structural determinants of racism and racial conflict, it relies on deductive assumptions (tending toward economic reductionism) regarding people's motives for action and lacks a systematic concern for the reproduction of ethnic consciousness outside the specific context of class struggle.[13]

In an effort to reformulate ethnicity theory, Philippe Bourgois (1988, 1989) seems to identify the problem I have described. His study of the highly politicized ethnic relations on a Costa Rican banana plantation is situated theoretically within a growing tendency to view ethnicity in the context of power relations. He devotes detailed attention to class structure and the productive process but rejects any simplistic causal relation between class and ethnic politics. Rather, his central theoretical plea is to abandon the sterile debate over "the relative determinacy of ideology and material reality" and to understand class and ethnicity as "social processes that define one another." Toward this end he coins the phrase "conjugated oppression," a situation in which "class . . . conflates with ideology . . . to create an experience of oppression which is more than merely the sum of economic exploitation and ethnic discrimination" (1988: 328–31). Conjugated oppression, Bourgois contends, helps to explain the particular forms of racism that prevail on the plantation (especially that afflicting the Guaymi Indians) and the patterns of political mobilization that result.

By arguing that political conflict both expresses and defines the content of ethnicity, Bourgois goes beyond structural determination to focus on

real interactions between individuals. The notion of "conjugated oppression," however, refers ultimately to a convergence of societal forces (both
ideological and economic) from which the consciousness of oppressed
ethnic group members is deduced. Thus he can explain Guaymi people's
responses to this oppression—for example, viewing it in primarily ethnic
terms, mobilizing around millenarian leaders (1988: 344)—without elu-
cidating their own premises, perceptions, and reasoning processes. Although "conjugated oppression" and a focus on the "material-social
process" help dispense with the sterile base-superstructure dichotomy,
neither concept embodies a theoretical approach to the analysis of human
agency.[14]

Beyond the Divide: Gramscian Theory and Ethnic Politics

The insights of Bentley and Bourgois need to be developed further, toward an approach that devotes simultaneous analytical attention to ethnic consciousness and to the constraining, constitutive impact of structure. Giddens's attempt to bridge this divide—"structuration theory"—is
expressed in such abstract terms that it cannot be considered a concrete
alternative (e.g., 1984: 282–84). But his critique is instructive in explaining the past failures of ethnicity theory and in charting a new course.
Specifically, he shifts our attention to the everyday practices of ethnic
group members: how they confront the multifaceted conditions of subordination, how they resist, accommodate, or otherwise fashion a response, and in so doing create cultural forms that guide their subsequent
thought and action. Culture, as Paul Gilroy puts it, is "a mediating space
between agents and structures in which their reciprocal dependency is
created and secured" (1987: 16). Efforts to privilege cultural analysis in
this way, while remaining broadly within a Marxist framework, owe a
primary debt to the theoretical legacy of Antonio Gramsci.

A growing number of analysts have applied Gramsci's ideas to the
study of racial and ethnic politics, often building on the perceptive
summaries and programmatic statements of Stuart Hall (1980, 1983,
1986).[15] Indeed, the last decade has seen an explosion of empirical studies
and theoretical expositions with a Gramscian orientation. They encompass a broad array of at times starkly divergent interpretations, arising
from the fragmentary, heavily censored, and preliminary nature of his
principal work, published as the *Prison Notebooks* (1971 [1929–35]).
Rather than attempt to review this work, much less evaluate the debates
that have ensued, I borrow liberally from his ideas to create a framework
that will be analytically useful to the problems at hand.

Subordinate ethnic group members—by the very definition of the term
"ethnic"—are not isolated social groups. They do assert boundaries—as

Fredrik Barth's (1969) classic essay confirms—but in so doing they draw to some degree on a shared cultural system that emanates from dominant actors and institutions. They experience, make sense of, and respond to structural inequities through means of this shared culture. There are exceptions. The Saramakan maroons, for example, mobilized against slavery with outright rejection, and frontal resistance, and for a certain period they were able to withdraw completely from the system (Price 1990). But this degree of militancy in effect severs the very basis of an ethnic identity—a relationship with others, structured in society. More commonly, subordinate ethnic group members' responses to oppression are multivalent, combining rejection with partial acceptance, resisting through efforts to appropriate and subvert the cultural symbols of the dominant order. As a result, they create a cultural form, in part actively resistant, in part expressing the "commonsense" premises that come directly from dominant actors and institutions, and in part consisting of symbols whose meanings remain undefined, ambiguous. That cultural form is never static or completely resolved, always subject to renegotiation. In this view, the struggle over cultural meanings is integral to the logic of collective action, constituting people's motivations to act, their understanding of what they are doing, and the conclusions they draw from the results.

Many analysts have observed the hybrid consciousness that tends to result from such struggle on the part of oppressed people and have used various terms to describe it. Sociologist Paul Willis (1981a), in a pioneering ethnography of working-class high school "lads" of Britain, analyzes the culture of resistance they create in response to an authoritarian, class-bound education.[16] When the lads apprehend and interpret their life conditions, Willis argues, they display striking "penetrations": sharp appraisals of the workings of society, including a critical analysis of the reasons for their subordinate position within it. Yet the appraisals are accompanied by "limitations": cultural premises associated with the dominant institutions that define the lads' everyday existence. These limitations act to neutralize or derail the lads' potentially radical insights. By emphasizing both elements, Willis can portray the lads as actively creating their own cultural form, which both vents their opposition to class society and leads them to life choices that ensure their confinement to the working class.[17] Jean and John Comaroff (1991), in a historical study of colonialism in South Africa, provide another eloquent statement of this effect, using the term "colonization of consciousness." These formulations can all be traced directly to Gramsci's distinction between "good sense" and "common sense," which he found often to coexist and together to form the basis of what he called a "contradictory consciousness" (1971: 333). Once its unnecessary and obscure baggage is discharged and its meaning rigorously defined, this concept can generate great insights into processes of ethnic mobilization.

Critics have complained—not completely without textual support from Gramsci's writing—that the distinction between good and common sense derives from a reductionist view of society, whereby "good sense" arises spontaneously from proletarians' material life conditions, and "common sense" is bourgeois ideological domination.[18] There are two objections here: that Gramsci's writings were ultimately anchored in class reductionist premises regarding society and social change, and that hegemony implies the imposition of dominant ideas on passive recipients who act but do not think.

In response to the first objection, I do use a broadly conceived class or structural analysis to situate people and institutions as dominant and subordinate within a given society. But I find Gramsci's ideas especially valuable in preventing this structuralist starting point from yielding a reductionist outcome. His notion of "historic bloc," for example, refers to a heterogeneous alliance whose members act according to a culturally mediated "collective will"; the emphasis on cultural mediation gives license for detailed attention to diverse identities, social sectors, and axes of inequity that cannot be reduced to class. As for the second objection, the great achievement of Willis's (1981a) study is to have definitively refuted the equation of the hegemony idea with the "dominant ideology thesis." He has cleared the way for the dual claim that subordinated people are conscious, creative, resistant social actors *and* that they often incorporate hegemonic premises into their cultural forms.

These ideas constitute a framework intended not to replace or supersede existing theories of ethnic-based collective action, but rather to train a bright light on their neglected or underdeveloped features. Predicated on the absence of a well-theorized bridge between structural determination and human action, it demonstrates how a critical, differentiated cultural analysis can help us address that problem. It dictates careful examination of subordinate people's cultural forms, asking whether they contain hegemonic premises, ideas, or symbols, which the people have embraced without successfully subverting or transforming their content. If so, then the notion of contradictory consciousness applies. This general process has even greater resonance when oppression encompasses multiple spheres of inequity. Each sphere may generate a combination of resistance and accommodation, but it also is common for people to focus their resistance on one sphere while largely accepting the premises on which the other is based. Thus subordinate members of an ethnic-based movement may neglect intraethnic class differentiation while resisting cultural oppression; women participants in movements of resistance to class oppression may unwittingly endorse and reproduce premises of gender inequality. In the case explored here, Miskitu people were subordinate to both the Nicaraguan state and the institutions of Anglo-American neocolonialism. They resisted the former, while largely accepting the hegemonic premises of the latter. The notion of contradictory consciousness places this particular Miskitu response in a broader theoretical context and yields a series of analytical implications.

Consider first the problem of quiescence or, more precisely, the range of collective actions that have the effect of accommodation with the existing order. This framework instructs us to be skeptical of explanations that focus solely on the constraining, coercive effects of power inequalities. Rather, it suggests that as group members responded to such conditions in a prior historical moment, they embraced premises that now dampen or divert their inclination to resist. This emphasis tends to collapse the sharp distinction between the constraining and constitutive effects of structure, between the physical and symbolic facets of coercion. People remain quiescent not only because, as James C. Scott argues, "frontal assaults are precluded by the realities of power" (1990: 191), but also because hegemonic ideas, present in people's consciousness, have rendered these "realities" natural or inevitable. People have not turned passive; rather their resistance takes forms that dominant actors can contain through negotiation or adjustment, leaving the structural underpinnings of their power intact.[19]

To guide explanations of ethnic mobilization, the framework does not preclude consideration of exogenous structural factors, which may induce a level of misery that makes rebellion (whatever the odds) an act of sheer necessity and, conversely, may create an opening that offers great advantage at little risk. Rather, it opens two additional explanatory avenues, related to the internal complexities of subordinated ethnic group members' consciousness. First, we must examine what Willis calls "penetrations"—the practical knowledge and associated acts of resistance (however "petty") that entail a sharply critical analysis of subordination—or what I have called in the Miskitu case "ethnic militancy." When that militancy deepens—through external influences or new internally generated understandings of oppression—the propensity for collective action increases. Second, this framework advances the idea that analysis must focus not only on penetrations or militancy but also on the role of hegemonic premises within group members' consciousness. Mobilization can result when these premises are directly challenged or undermined—for example, by new expressions of group solidarity, political organization, or critical education—and also when societal conditions change so that these premises, though unaltered, reverberate in ways that yield new rationales for action. The study of contemporary Miskitu politics sug-

gests a third assertion that combines these first two. When *both* the hegemonic ideas and a deepening militancy orient people toward mobilization, the results are truly explosive.

✳ ✳ ✳

Let us look ahead briefly, to anticipate how this argument will unfold.
In Chapter 2 I analyze the evolution of Miskitu people's consciousness
over the last century, documenting the results of their interactions with
two interconnected but largely distinct spheres: the Nicaraguan state's
political rule and the North American–dominated economy and civil society. To simplify an argument presented in full there, Miskitu people's
response entailed constant everyday resistance and occasional direct protest against the first sphere, combined with accommodation of the second. They developed a consciousness that fused "ethnic militancy" with
"Anglo affinity," terms that I define more fully in Chapter 3, where I
present Sandy Bay Miskitu people's collective memories of their past and
recent political history. The antinomy between ethnic militancy and
Anglo affinity, strikingly present in this narrative, is key to my explanations for their relative quiescence before 1979 and their explosive mobilization afterward, presented in Chapters 5 and 6 respectively. In Chapter 7 we turn to a third phase of Coast politics—the post-1984 return to
peace and autonomy. With the introduction of autonomy, the Nicaraguan state developed an unprecedented capacity for persuasion rather
than merely coercive rule; state officials could finally make a plausible
call for Miskitu people's consensual participation in national politics.
Sandy Bay townspeople responded to this policy shift by participating
actively in autonomy, while harboring skepticism of the Sandinistas and
a deep commitment to demands beyond what the state was willing to
concede. The hegemony idea is again crucial in my analysis of this dual
response. Accommodation resulted in part because the state made major
concessions while maintaining a coercive presence that raised the cost
of resistance. But another factor, I contend, is that Miskitu people came
to endorse commonsense premises, vigorously promoted by Sandinista
leaders and cadres, that made the negotiated settlement appear the only
reasonable alternative. This analysis of incipient Sandinista hegemony
helps to account for the return to peace and draws attention to the
persisting inequities that autonomy did not—and perhaps could not—
eliminate.

Democracy and Revolutionary Change in a Multiethnic Society

Since 1894 the nature of the Nicaraguan state's presence on the Coast
has undergone great change, from "Liberal" dictatorship, to centralist

revolutionary government, and finally, to the partial devolution of power through the transition to autonomy. Such changes highlight the need to develop further the other side of the analytical framework, thus far mentioned only in passing. Although the state can be viewed as part of the structural conditions at one point, this will not help us to explain its evolution, understand the rationale behind its policies, or assess the impact of these changes on Miskitu people.[20] Moreover, the need for focusing theoretical attention on the state follows directly from the second part of this study's dual mandate: to take seriously the Sandinistas' representations of themselves and their political vision, to give voice to their critique of Miskitu consciousness.

Making the revolutionary state a principal subject of analysis brings two key historical junctures to the fore. The first came early in 1981. After pursuing moderate, conciliatory policies for eighteen months—concessions, overtures, attempts to draw Miskitu people into the revolutionary alliance—in February 1981 the state enacted a swift and radical change in policy. Security forces arrested Indian leaders and disbanded their organization. For the next three and a half years, state officials justified nearly every action toward Coast people by invoking threats to "state security" and assigned little or no legitimacy to Miskitu people's demands as Indians. Then, in late 1984, came a radical shift toward the broad recognition of Miskitu and other Coast people's rights to autonomy. Although concerns about state security persisted—indeed, the autonomy process began just as the war reached the height of intensity—a distinctly nonmilitary political reasoning emerged, proved efficacious, and steadily gained acceptance among state and party officials concerned with the Coast. By the end of 1987, the once formidable military challenge posed by Miskitu antigovernment combatants had receded dramatically, and the ethnic question had returned largely to the civic arena.

We can understand the logic of these two policy changes, I contend, by examining the content of Sandinista ideology as expressed by both high-level leaders and local cadres.[21] In part, this focus is an outgrowth of my own vantage point and of the information available. It is also amply justified by the recent turn among theorists of the state, who emphasize the cultural underpinnings of political order and change. The new wave of "state-centered" research—catalyzed by Theda Skocpol's (1979) authoritative study—while generally important and salutary, has come under increasing criticism. Of particular pertinence here, a number of theorists have reacted against the overly structuralist frame with which Skocpol and others have "brought the state back in." John Walton, in a recent historical study of struggles between rural folk and the state in southern California, emphasizes that each phase of the conflict revolved centrally around notions of legitimacy. These struggles were decided not only by brute strength or coercion, he concludes, but by the fate of shared cultural symbols, which state institutions mobilized to maintain order, and social movements appropriated to justify opposition and protest (1992: 307).[22] Similarly, William H. Sewell (1985) has argued that Skocpol's analysis suffers from a neglect of state ideology as "constitutive of social order" and, by extension, as a factor in revolutionary change. Parallel ideas have motivated revisionist theories of nationalism. Benedict Anderson (1983), for example, has analyzed nationalism as a cultural form that expresses political elites' sense of community and affinity with one another, thereby putting forth a homogeneous standard of identity that distinguishes "loyal" citizens from marginals, subversives, or misfits.[23] These insights converge on a methodological tenet that guides my analysis here. The discourse of Sandinista leaders and cadres contains a series of premises that reveal the underlying rationale for their policies and their evolving expectations for the terms on which Miskitu people would join the newly constituted state and nation.

By departing slightly from Gramsci's original scheme, we can analyze Sandinista ideology in a manner consistent with the framework developed for the Miskitu. Gramsci uses the term "contradictory consciousness" in reference only to the unorganized "subaltern." He implies that contradictions do not persist when people forge an effective "counter-hegemonic" ideology. They become unified, he seems to assume, as a consequence of the common structural inequities that they face. In the Nicaraguan case this assumption cannot be sustained. As the Sandinista movement advanced and achieved state power, it faced two distinct contradictions regarding Miskitu people. The first was related to the great sociocultural heterogeneity of the movement's composition, a problem relevant, but by no means limited, to the ethnic diversity on Nicaragua's Atlantic Coast. The second contradiction arose specifically from the dominant culture's premises toward Indians, which many Sandinistas continued to espouse and which remained present in their ideology and guided their political practice.

Pluralism, Democracy, and Vanguard Politics

Opposition to the dictatorship came from highly differentiated sectors of Nicaraguan society, unified only by their disdain for Somoza and general support for the Sandinistas. FSLN leaders assumed responsibility for preserving the harmony of this unwieldy alliance by finding common political ground, forging compromises, and drawing the line between political expediency and inviolable principles of the "revolutionary project." Several theorists have identified this political role of the vanguard party, rather than a specific pattern of economic transformation, as the principal distinguishing feature of transition to socialism in underdeveloped, peripheral countries.[24] According to this view, the guarantee that diverse forms of popular consciousness and demands will contribute to socialist transition lies not in their intrinsic content but rather in their articulation with a revolutionary alliance under the leadership of the party.

The complexity of this relationship between vanguard party and popular organization has been lost in many analyses of postrevolutionary Nicaraguan politics. Right-wing scholars have portrayed the party as rigidly authoritarian, connected to the base by a top-down chain of command. What the Sandinistas called participatory democracy, in these critics' view, was little more than a facade or, at best, a shallow expression of consent guaranteed in advance by outright coercion and ideological control.[25] Scholars sympathetic to the revolution, in contrast, tended to downplay the role of the party and to emphasize the autonomy of popular (or mass-based) organizations on which Nicaragua's participatory democracy was based. For example, Gary Ruchwarger (1987) provides rich, convincing evidence of democratic participation within the five principal mass-based organizations, but he then proceeds as if this portrayal exhausted the issue. His study leaves the impression that all members of a given sector were adequately represented by their respective organizations and that each organization fully endorsed the Sandinista leadership, caring only about "conjunctural" questions of emphasis, pace of change, and the like.[26] His study does not square with the much deeper tensions that participatory democracy confronted in relation to nearly every political sector, quite apart from ethnic conflict on the Coast.[27] It obscures the enormous political power of the party, which in other socialist societies led to bureaucratization and to an attenuated (or nonexistent) democratic relationship with the base.

A more complex and penetrating view of the relationship between vanguard and people comes from Nicaraguan theorists who were at once analysts of and participants in the process.[28] Such sources have the added advantage of offering insight into how Sandinistas themselves conceived these problems. According to Orlando Nuñez Soto, the transition to socialism in Nicaragua rests on a fundamental distinction between the revolutionary (or "proletarian") project, on the one hand, and the heterogeneous popular classes that make up the vast majority of the country's population, on the other. The FSLN both assures the implementation of the "project" and defines its content, which Nuñez summarizes in two components: "destruction of the (bourgeois and pro-imperialist) ruling political system" and socioeconomic transformation toward the interests of the majority (1986: 240).[29] Resolute defense of this long-term vision is what gives the FSLN and the state a revolutionary character, not the class background of their leaders or the specific content of their policies.

This last point is critical. The revolution faces enormous obstacles, such as military aggression, underdevelopment, and political resistance from remnants of the bourgeoisie. To confront these obstacles, "the revolutionary leadership will oscillate between maintaining and defending its power and advancing and carrying out the revolutionary project" (p. 244). An emphasis on "defending the power" entails a message from the FSLN to its supporters: Defer your immediate demands to safeguard the project, to which the vanguard is firmly committed. People agree to defer at least in part because they helped to shape the project in the first place and believe it embodies their interests.

Yet the "people" are by no stretch of the imagination a well-defined proletariat with uniform perceptions of short- or long-term interests. Nuñez divides them into two groups. First there is the working class, defined as people whose political consciousness closely coincides with the FSLN's notion of the project. This, Nuñez admits, is a relatively small group. Second, there is the (somewhat inappropriately termed) "residual bloc," which "may be the majority." It is composed of "both economic groups (peasants, artisans and merchants) and technical-ideological groups (professionals, technicians, government officials, administrators . . .) . . . also [members of] special movements (youth, student, feminist, ethnic . . .) formed under the previous systems that are motivated ideologically to favor the immediate interests of their particular group" (p. 241). Here the FSLN faces its critical challenge because "if [the residual bloc] is not won over politically by the [vanguard] it will undoubtedly be won over by the bourgeoisie, which has been less than scrupulous when choosing its allies" (p. 242).

The FSLN "wins them over" by means of participatory democracy. Each sector is represented by a mass organization, which has a mandate to promote and defend the particular interests of its members. The relationship between mass organization and vanguard rests on a basic contract: the FSLN is responsive to the organization's demands and, in return, the organization vows to defend the revolution. This opens considerable political space in which democratic ferment—even struggle—between the mass organizations and authorities in the state or party regularly occurs.[30] The vanguard retains the last word, however, defining the project's content, determining when it is in danger, and deciding how to defend it. As long as the "residual sectors" accept these prerogatives, they maintain democratic relations with the state. In Nuñez's words: "The state is a combined form of dictatorship and democracy: intransigent toward those who oppose or endanger the proletarian project, but democratic in implementing that project. Its challenge is to . . . govern with increasing consensus until people's power is fully realized" (p. 247).

Here lies the problem. In the last instance, the FSLN defines the project and has recourse to the coercive power of the state to enforce its definition. As long as popular sectors embrace that definition as well and their demands focus exclusively on "conjunctural" issues, coercion remains largely unnecessary. The relationship develops in an exemplary democratic form, which indeed often was the case, especially in the revolution's early years. But what happened when popular sectors contested these ground rules? At times, usually in response to militant opposition, the FSLN agreed to renegotiate them. In other cases, the FSLN stood firm and acted to close discussion on the issue. In a 1986 speech, President Daniel Ortega defended the prerogative to take such action, arguing: "People can express any opinions they want, they can enter into contradictions with the FSLN, that is no crime. . . . But whoever goes outside the institutional framework and allies themselves with those who are attacking Nicaragua, then, that is different. . . . Whoever promotes a national unity that goes outside the institutional framework, whoever does not accept its premises, might as well declare themselves and go over to the side of the contras."[31] As an affirmation of resolve to fend off U.S.-backed aggression, the distinction is certainly justifiable. But it is not hard to imagine how the repressive face of the "institutional framework" could come into play.

To summarize the source of the first contradiction: the vanguard retains the prerogative to lead the revolutionary alliance and define the project, yet has to contend with popular sectors that are supposed to form part of that alliance but do not share the vanguard's vision of liberation. Historically, leftist movements have resolved this contradiction with recourse to a flawed premise of class essentialism. Having granted the working class an "ontological privilege" as subjects of history, they merely transferred that privilege from the workers to the political leadership of the mass movement. As Ernesto Laclau and Chantal Mouffe (1985: 56) correctly conclude, this solution seals the transition to authoritarian vanguardism. The FSLN did not blindly follow this flawed historical pattern. For example, Nuñez and Roger Burbach (1987: 49) acknowledge the problem explicitly and suggest that it can be resolved by replacing an a priori (i.e., ontological) definition of the proletarian project with a political program that embodies the sum of aspirations, freely expressed by each sector that the revolution purports to represent. Still, they do not explain how the transition to such a program might be achieved while maintaining a socialist vision intact, and their claim that the FSLN succeeded in such a feat is clearly overstated.[32]

A more convincing version of the Nuñez and Burbach position—which I suspect these authors and many other Sandinista analysts espoused privately—omits the latter claim and rests the case on a more pragmatic appeal. The contradiction persists, the argument goes, but progress toward its resolution has occurred, and at each phase the goal of eliminating the contradiction must be balanced with that of defending the revolution against external threats, especially U.S. imperialism. I am sympathetic to that perspective; indeed, it formed part of my own position as an analyst. It also highlights the point at which I part paths with Laclau and Mouffe: by completely abandoning structural analysis, they invalidate political efforts like the Sandinista revolution without offering a viable alternative principle by which leadership might be exercised and unity among oppressed peoples forged.[33] The great potential of *Sandinismo*, in contrast, was to seek a middle ground between the atomization inherent in this wholesale rejection of class politics and the authoritarian curtailment of democracy inherent in vanguardist solutions. Many examples of such renegotiation can be found in the relations between the FSLN and various western Nicaraguan mass organizations, especially the National Union of Farmers (UNAG). FSLN leaders' willingness to conceive and enact these fundamental changes in their revolutionary vision, I contend, was crucial in assuring the resilience of their popular support and limiting the extent of what Rudolf Bahro (1977) calls "bureaucratic ossification."

That sanguine appraisal, however, cannot suffice. There was also a second contradiction, unique to the FSLN's relationship with Indians, that was much less susceptible to the assertion that gradual progress would resolve the problem.

Dominant Culture Ideas and Sandinista Ideology

The difficulties of democratizing the vanguard in western Nicaragua were magnified many fold on the Atlantic Coast. The most apparent but in reality least serious problem was that of representation. The FSLN grew from a handful of militants in 1961 to the nationwide leadership of an insurrectionary movement that ousted Somoza, with minimal participation of the Miskitu people. Yet this neglect could easily be explained by the political and military exigencies of the struggle and could promptly be remedied. Indeed, in the first months after the Sandinista victory, the full range of Sandinista organizations—from the militia to the trade unions to the party itself—actively encouraged Miskitu membership. Some heeded the call. The majority demanded their own organization, and the Sandinistas agreed (albeit reluctantly), expecting it to become a vehicle for Miskitu participation in the "revolutionary alliance." This was not, in any overt sense, a politics of exclusion.

The issue grows more complex, however, if we shift attention toward the cultural underpinnings of Sandinismo. In their very efforts to put forth a political vision, to fashion what Gramsci called a "collective will," the FSLN incorporated explicit and implicit premises that had the effect of marginalizing Miskitu people, even though including them in name. This assertion must be clearly distinguished from problems of "cultural insensitivity" or "incomprehension of Atlantic Coast reality," which became standard in retrospective Sandinista explanations of the conflict. However great their impact may have been and however important their implied remedy (more sensitivity, comprehension, and so on), this line of argument does not exhaust the issue. Rather, the very premises that were integral to the Sandinistas' success in unifying the vast majority of Nicaraguans—encapsulating their demands, forging a broadly endorsed vision of social change, and rallying support for the increasingly urgent efforts to resist the onslaught of counterrevolutionary aggression—directly excluded the Miskitu. Put bluntly, the FSLN forged a counterhegemonic ideology that invalidated central facets of Miskitu Indians' deeply rooted ethnic militancy.

The theoretical basis for this assertion runs parallel to that developed above in relation to Miskitu resistance. The Sandinistas' unifying discourse had incorporated cultural elements from the dominant social and political institutions they opposed. Key premises toward Indians, deeply embedded in Nicaraguan political culture during the Somoza era, became neatly fused with the militantly anti-Somoza tenets of Sandinismo. To substantiate this argument I subject Sandinista ideology to the same analytical scrutiny devoted to the Miskitu. Chapter 2 reviews the past century of state presence in the coastal region, with an eye to the legacy of power-laden premises that the Sandinistas would inherit when they gained state power. Chapter 4 examines the place of Indians in contemporary Sandinista ideology, as expressed by both local cadres and national elites. It traces the trajectory of those "old regime" premises to discover which the Sandinistas abandoned, which they transformed, and which survived largely intact in the course of their struggle to create a new society, state, and nation. For example, I show that despite their newly developed emphasis on democratic participation and empowerment, Sandinistas did not dispense with a deeply ingrained association of Miskitu consciousness, identity, and demands with cultural backwardness. And despite great commitment to egalitarian economic change, they found it little easier than their Somocista predecessors to fathom

Indian economic organization as anything more than traditional forms badly in need of modernization. Most important, in my view, a radically new version of Nicaraguan nationalism—emphasizing sovereignty, self-sufficiency, and equality with other states—retained a Mestizo standard of cultural homogeneity to which all citizens were expected to conform. Thus the mobilization of nationalist indignation at U.S. intervention had a dual effect. It was undoubtedly crucial to the revolution's resolve for defiance and, indeed, its very survival. Yet it also helped to lock the Sandinistas into a spiral of ethnic conflict in which to identify as Miskitu became virtually synonymous with being counterrevolutionary.

*   *   *

The notion of contradictory consciousness—broadly understood as the fusion of "commonsense" premises adopted from the dominant order and "good sense" premises of critical understanding of and resistance to that order—therefore proves useful in analyzing both sides of the conflict. I contend that the coexistence of ethnic militancy and Anglo affinity holds a key to Miskitu people's collective action, both their relative quiescence and their mobilization. Sandinista ideology melded commonsense premises about Indians with a broad vision of liberation for the Nicaraguan nation. Tensions quickly reached a point where Sandinista leaders could not defend the revolution without suppressing Miskitu people's democratic expression and could not allow this expression without legitimating demands that they viewed as inimical to state security. Applied to the post-1984 return to peace, this analysis affirms the great achievements of autonomy and the persisting contradictions. There is much unfinished business in the Miskitu people's struggle for decolonization—of their territory and their consciousness—and in the Sandinistas' vision for a truly egalitarian and multiethnic Nicaragua.

2 Nation Building, Resistance, and Hegemony: Historical Roots of Ethnic Conflict, 1894–1960

We will be in the hands of a government and people who have not the slightest interests, sympathy, or good feeling for the inhabitants of the Mosquito Reservation; and as our manners, customs, religion, laws and language are not in accord, there can never be a unity. We most respectfully beg . . . your Majesty . . . to take back under your protection the Mosquito nation and people, so that we may become a people of your Majesty's Empire.
—Petition to Queen Victoria, submitted by residents of Bluefields, March 8, 1894

The national conscience should also be satisfied, because here [we have] a great mission to fulfill. . . . There must be commenced at once the slow but efficacious work of assimilating the indigenous element, and rendering it one of the sources of strength of the country.
—Rigoberto Cabezas, governor of the newly annexed Mosquito Reserve, January 1, 1895

RIGOBERTO CABEZAS LED the Nicaraguan campaign of early 1894 to annex the Mosquito Reserve. Within days of military occupation, residents of Bluefields and surrounding communities had registered vigorous protest and called on foreign powers to protect them. But their petitions and their later more militant resistance were to little avail. By December of that year the region had become part of Nicaraguan national territory. Cabezas was named its first governor. His words expressed frank acknowledgment that Indians stood outside the nation, complete certainty that they belonged inside, and confidence (although with a hint of doubt) that they soon would make the transition. The petitioners, by contrast, let it be known how painful and contested this transition would be.

Though laced with rhetoric, these two statements point to a central theme in the last century of Atlantic Coast political history. An ex-

pansionist state asserted territorial sovereignty over a culturally heterogeneous peripheral region and justified annexation through a national
myth that portrayed the new boundaries as natural and self-evident.
Even the term Spanish-speaking Nicaraguans chose to mark the event—
Reincorporation—contains the crucial prefix "Re," which refers to an
unspecified previous historical moment when the national territory had
been intact. Coast people who signed the petition to Queen Victoria, in
contrast, would probably have used the term "overthrow." They resisted
through diverse means, affirmed and renegotiated their distinct ethnic
identities in response to state oppression, and thereby influenced the
course of state formation in the region. This interplay of state penetration
and ethnic resistance figures prominently in the historical narrative that
follows: the overt racism and subtle politics of exclusion inherent in Nicaraguan state and nation building, contested by Coast peoples' protonationalist identity; the state's centralized control over the region's political
and economic affairs, in tension with Coast peoples' tenacious demands
for autonomy.

Further scrutiny of the juxtaposed quotations, however, should make
it clear that an analysis focused solely on this interplay cannot suffice.
Cabezas surely had read the Bluefields residents' petition when he made
his exhortation; what gave the drive for nationalization so much urgency
was the opponents' appeals for aid from such powerful allies. Likewise,
the petitioners' urgent plea for a return to the rule of their colonial masters raises difficult questions: Was it a feigned obsequiousness that disguised more strategic goals? A choice for the lesser of two evils? A genuine expression of cultural and political affinity? These questions highlight
the need to understand how the state's relations with Coast people were
influenced by the multifaceted Anglo-American presence in the coastal
region.

There are two pervasive interpretations of Miskitu history, each linked
to one side of the polarized course of this historical experience. The first,
closely associated with the ideology of Nicaraguan nationalism, brings
the U.S. role sharply into focus but understates the oppressive presence
of the nation-state. The second has the opposite strengths and weak-
nesses, vividly portraying the Miskitu culture of resistance to the state,
but giving inadequate attention to the impact of U.S. hegemony. Focusing
on three key historical periods, I offer an analysis that mediates between
these two, avoids the sharp dichotomy between accommodation and resistance, and lays the foundation for a fuller understanding of contemporary Miskitu consciousness.

A closer look at the petition quoted above will serve as an introduction
to this analysis. Petitioners appealed to Queen Victoria because formally

they were still subjects of the British Crown. From the early seventeenth century, British colonists ruled what is now the Caribbean coast of Nicaragua and Honduras, in defiance of Spanish pretensions to control the entire isthmus. Around 1680 the British crowned a Miskitu leader as king, giving rise to an institution known as the Mosquito Kingdom, which became the linchpin of British indirect rule for the next 200 years. Once established as intermediaries, Miskitu leaders developed a fierce loyalty to their sponsors. They supported British military campaigns, endorsed the colonial economic presence, and fully affirmed British sovereignty, even considering themselves subjects of the Crown. With British trade goods (particularly firearms and metal tools) and political backing, the Miskitu grew rapidly in number and territorial presence, achieving political-military dominion over the other indigenous groups inhabiting the region.[1]

In 1787 Britain withdrew from the Mosquito Shore, ceding the region to the Spanish, who initiated their own colonization plans. These efforts failed miserably, partly because of determined Miskitu resistance. In 1790 Miskitu forces attacked the southern community of Bluefields and plundered the holdings of a British landholder who, in order to remain on the Mosquito Shore, had pledged allegiance to the Spanish Crown. Ten years later a Miskitu contingent destroyed the Spanish fort at Black River, on the northern periphery of the region. For a brief period—roughly between 1790 and 1820—successive Miskitu kings and their chieftains dominated native inhabitants and exercised unprecedented political autonomy.[2] By the 1840's, however, renewed economic and geopolitical interests had brought the British back to the Mosquito Shore and to their previous role of unquestioned dominance within the Mosquito government. They now faced not Spanish but Nicaraguan resistance, which could have been summarily dismissed if not for the rise of a new imperial superpower, the United States.

Two principal factors shaped the intense and growing U.S. interest in the Mosquitia after the mid-nineteenth century. First, the San Juan River, which formed Nicaragua's southern border, had all the geographic attributes to be the favored transisthmus canal route. The prospect of having to negotiate canal rights with both the Mosquitian and the Nicaraguan governments complicated these plans immensely, especially because of the former's ties with Britain, a rival imperial power. Second, North American capitalists and commercial enterprises controlled an increasing proportion of the burgeoning economic activities in the Mosquitia. In rapid succession the Atlantic Coast underwent booms in the extraction of rubber (1860's and 1870's), mahogany (1880's), and minerals (1890's); in addition, banana production began in the early 1880's along the Escondido River, which soon turned Bluefields into a bustling commercial center.

Although many of these activities were begun by Coast natives, Spanish-speaking Nicaraguans from the west, British, or other Europeans, by 1890 North Americans reigned supreme, controlling 90 percent of the total investment, valued at over $10 million (Laird 1970: 26). In short, although Coast people responded to the annexation by following the customary (and formally correct) practice of appealing to the British, the region's future was already in the hands of the North Americans.

The petitioners' allusion to religious differences separating them from the Nicaraguans signals another key area of complexity. They refer not to an autochthonous religious tradition but rather to a European Protestant missionary church that had risen to prominence in their own lifetimes. Two Moravian missionaries from Germany founded a church in the town of Bluefields in 1849 and set out to convert its "heathen" inhabitants to the Christian faith. These missionaries gradually increased in number—reaching eleven by 1894—as did the mission stations, expanding first to Pearl Lagoon and Rama Cay in the 1850's and then to communities farther north.[3] After three decades of relentless toil with meager returns, a movement of mass conversion began in the 1880's, eulogized by church historians as the "Great Awakening" (e.g., Borhek 1949). Coast people approached missionaries by the hundreds, proclaiming their newfound Christian faith and at times even relocating their communities to be near established mission stations.[4] Meanwhile, the Moravian church also achieved a foothold in the higher echelons of the Mosquito Reserve government in Bluefields. Missionaries converted and educated successive Miskitu kings (known as chiefs after 1860), cultivated close ties with foreign residents and colonial authorities, and occupied the key post of treasurer in the Mosquito Council of Government. Though always professing strictly religious motives and political neutrality, by 1894 the Moravian church wielded considerable institutional power throughout the Reserve.

Finally, the petitioners' plea on behalf of one "people" and one "nation" is a gloss on the region's mosaic of ethnic groups, whose members lived in hierarchical relations with one another and who surely did not speak with a unified political voice. Indeed, most of the signatories in this case, and most of those who organized militant opposition to the Reincorporation, were not Miskitu Indians but Afro-Caribbean people known as Creoles. Descendants of African slaves brought directly to the Mosquitia and black immigrants from other parts of the Caribbean, Creoles gained prominence during the 40-year interregnum following the British withdrawal in 1787. Although the Creoles probably remained subject to Miskitu authority during this period, once the British returned in the 1820's they assumed the role of privileged intermediaries between the colonial power and the rest of Coast society.⁵ Close association with the Moravian missionaries further enhanced the Creoles' status; they were the first group to receive a Moravian education and to occupy the prestigious positions of native pastors and teachers within the church. The Creoles' Christian education (with a heavy emphasis on the Protestant work ethic) and ability to communicate in English⁶ placed them in a position to benefit from the economic boom of the 1880's. They became shop owners, middle-level employees of North American companies, and small-scale producers (mainly of bananas). Members of this same cultural and economic elite played key roles in the Mosquito Chief's Council, the entity responsible for managing the daily political affairs of the Reserve. Although the king (or chief) was always of Miskitu descent, the council— composed of Creoles, North Americans, and British—exercised de facto political power.⁷ Miskitu people's subordinate status within the kingdom that bore their name, I suggest, helps to explain their otherwise perplexing stance toward the Reincorporation.

The Reincorporation of 1894

On February 12, 1894, Nicaraguan troops under the command of General Rigoberto Cabezas occupied the town of Bluefields and declared a state of siege throughout the Coast. Although the central government had disputed the Mosquito Reserve's autonomous status since its creation in 1860, no Nicaraguan president had taken definitive action by the time José Santos Zelaya came to power in 1893.⁸ Lured by a potential bonanza of tariff revenues and spurred on by tacit consent from U.S. diplomats, Zelaya ordered Cabezas to "occupy Bluefields militarily: dispose the Mosquito Chief and leave the consequences to me."⁹ The original pretext for sending troops—a border clash with Honduras—soon gave way to a more definitive and inflammatory rationale: "The Treaty [of Managua, which established the Reserve in 1860] has lost its juridical validity, since it was created for the protection of Mosquito Indians . . . who have withdrawn deep into the jungle . . . while the Reserve Government has become a contemptible fiction under the control of black usurpers [*negros usurpadores*]."¹⁰

On March 8, 1894, Mosquito Chief Robert Henry Clarence delivered a petition to the British consul. The warship HMS *Cleopatra* landed in Bluefields in March to offer "police protection," but the petitioners' request for decisive military action fell on deaf ears. Although local British authorities, especially one Vice-Consul Hatch stationed in Bluefields, sympathized with the Mosquito government, they had instructions from the Foreign Office not to become embroiled in local affairs. Their most forceful step was to press for withdrawal of the majority of Nicaraguan troops, which occurred in early May. The British, however, did not obstruct Cabezas's plans to disband the Chief's Council and place the region fully under central government control.[11]

When U.S. Consul Lewis Baker traveled from Managua to Bluefields in April to investigate the problems, he approvingly described the town as "American to the core."[12] Not only did North Americans control most of the booming Bluefields economy, but they also had assumed a dominant role in the Chief's Council. A U.S. Navy captain stationed in Bluefields explained the expatriates' reasoning: "[They] found the Mosquito Government dominated by Jamaica negroes so inefficient and ignorant and unequal to keep pace with the growth of the place that they were greatly dissatisfied. As there was . . . no means for protecting commercial interests in a legal way . . . [they] felt it necessary for their own protection . . . to sit in on the council."[13]

Ironically, this economic and political involvement placed North American residents of Bluefields at odds with their own government's policy. Although disenchantment with the council members' "ignorance" led some initially to favor the annexation, the occupation itself quickly convinced them that Nicaraguan rule would not be good for business. Fearing instability, increased taxation, and loss of their substantial political and economic power, they petitioned the U.S. consul, "with all due deference to [Nicaraguan] sovereign rights," to make some arrangement of "local self-government" for the Bluefields area.[14] Secretary of State Walter Q. Gresham ignored these demands, having already determined that the annexation would advance the broader objective of securing rights to a canal passage through Nicaraguan territory. His instructions to Consul Baker claimed high moral ground: "Recognizing, as this Government does, the paramount rights of the Republic of Nicaragua [over the Mosquitia], it ill becomes the reputation of the U.S. to interfere [with] the Nicaraguan Government's exercise of these sovereign rights. . . . Take care to say nothing . . . to encourage pretensions to autonomous rights [within the Mosquito territory] inconsistent [with Nicaraguan sovereignty]."[15]

After the Nicaraguan troops withdrew from Bluefields in May, opponents of the annexation grew more courageous. On July 5 violence broke out between Creole residents and the few soldiers that had remained as Cabezas's police force. It quickly escalated into outright rebellion and spread from Bluefields to the nearby port of Bluff,[16] where a contingent of Nicaraguan soldiers was stationed, and then to Corn Island and Prinzapolka, where Creoles violently deposed Nicaraguan authorities and vowed allegiance to Clarence and the British Crown. Temporarily outnumbered, Cabezas left for the town of Rama on July 11. Meanwhile, the rebels reinstated the Mosquito Chief's Council, and Bluefields braced itself for a counterattack. The *Bluefields Messenger* applauded the residents' courage: "The [Mosquito chief's] administration is gathering volunteers, so if the Nicaraguan troops invade this city again, they will be received differently from the first time. Bluefields alone can provide 500 men, more than enough to resist 1,500 Nicaraguans sent to fight against us." [17] Yet the article also noted that people "anxiously awaited" the arrival of a British warship to back them up. Judging from the composition of the reinstated council, foreigners must also have assumed that external support was forthcoming. In addition to Creoles, six foreign residents (four North Americans and two British) accepted positions,[18] and the Moravian warden resumed his role as the council treasurer.[19]

Nicaraguan authorities returned with 500 soldiers on August 3. After receiving explicit consent from the U.S. occupation forces, they disembarked and took control of Bluefields without firing a shot. Disheartened by U.S. and British refusal to intervene on their behalf, Bluefields residents lost their resolve to resist. Over the next few months Zelaya's government renamed the vast Atlantic Coast region the Department of Zelaya, named Cabezas governor, sent Mosquito Chief Clarence into exile, and formed a Bluefields municipal government composed of residents amenable to annexation.[20] Creoles repeatedly boycotted Cabezas's efforts to form a municipal council in Bluefields and bitterly denounced the one accommodating Creole council member as a traitor (Wunderich and Rossbach 1985: 41). It therefore was especially crucial for Cabezas to achieve the Miskitu Indians' "voluntary incorporation" into the Nicaraguan state and nation. This would undermine Creole opposition and formally relieve Britain of prior treaty obligations to the Mosquito government.[21]

On November 20, 1894, some 80 Miskitu delegates arrived in Bluefields to attend a three-day convention that sealed the fate of the Mosquitia. They signed the Decree of Reincorporation that Cabezas had drawn up in advance, affirming the Nicaraguan state's full sovereign rights to the region. The government published celebratory descriptions of Miskitu delegates' role in the convention:

The natives spoke with ease, and some of them even with eloquence. . . . The usurpers had taken good care to foster in their minds an instinct almost of terror toward the people of Nicaragua, and on finding themselves amongst [Nicaraguans] deliberating freely, and choosing their own lot, they broke out at last, full of confidence, in bitter complaints of the past. They begged for protection . . . against the servitude of work; protection against the horrible servitude of ignorance; they asked to be free men, and not slaves.[22]

The other common genre of retrospective description is fundamentally at odds with the first:

Cabezas, by the aid of the "Mosquito Traitors," succeeded in bribing a few Indians from the Coast and had them brought to Bluefields. An act was drawn up in Spanish, read before the Indians who understood not a word (besides having been made drunk by Cabezas) and after a false interpretation of this Act was given the Indians [their names] were affixed to the document.[23]

＊　　　＊　　　＊

What are we to make of these polarized and contradictory accounts? The first smacks of racist propaganda, but there are good reasons to be skeptical of the second as well. If the Miskitu felt so vehemently, it seems odd that they would have been tricked into signing away their rights. They clearly acted under coercion. Yet Creoles, under similar conditions, exerted considerable resistance. Miskitu delegates to the convention, including some recognized community leaders, signed the decree without reported protest, and Miskitu communities remained largely tranquil during 1894.[24]

Neither of these diametrically opposed interpretations of this pivotal event—the one that emphasizes the state's brute coercion of Miskitu delegates or the one that portrays the delegates acting of their own free will—tells the whole story. Evidence less tainted by political motives than Cabezas's propaganda seems to confirm that the Miskitu were genuinely alienated from the government that bore their name. An observer noted in 1892, for example:

The Indian . . . hates [the machinery of government] because he feels the pressure of its iron heel when he disobeys its regulations. Instead of seeking to control [the government] by constitutional means, [the Indian] speculates as to methods for out-witting it, or for crushing it. The negroes, on the contrary, respond with enthusiasm to the call for conventions . . . and so, when the sense of the meeting is taken, it is found to be wholly African. . . . As a result . . . the government falls easily into the hands of the mixed population, which . . . operates further to make that class arrogant toward the Mosquitos. . . . The strife at times reaches a high tension.[25]

To summon delegates to the Mosquito convention, Nicaraguan authorities played heavily on this tension, and their methods seemed to rely more on persuasion than overt coercion. Traveling to Miskitu communities in the company of Andrew Hendy, a widely recognized Miskitu leader from the Río Coco, the Nicaraguans laced their rhetoric with promises: "The [Indians] were to have their own laws and customs and be free from taxes; the Government would provide school and church for them; their new chief should rule as in olden time from Black River (Truxillo) down to Greytown; all of the headmen of villages would get a good salary paid every six months."[26] If Cabezas had planned to achieve the annexation through brute force, such promises would have been superfluous.

Yet the fact remains that Miskitu headmen, apprehensive about the prospect of Nicaraguan rule, did attach their signatures to the Creole-initiated petitions and submit ones of their own in a similar vein. They complained explicitly of Nicaraguan state oppression, especially the forced exile of their leader, Chief Clarence.[27] Such complaints make Cabezas's rhetoric ring hollow and compel us seriously to consider the possibility that Miskitu delegates signed because they did not, or thought they did not, have a choice.

Rather than purporting definitively to resolve this historical question, I first want to emphasize that the event marks the contemporary origins of two political narratives whose broad contours and "significant silences" have persisted to this day.[28] Cabezas's rhetoric set the tone for the Mestizo nationalist discourse toward the Coast, which ever since has tended to portray Coast people's identities and demands as legitimate only if they did not threaten the national project. The convention also became a pivotal event in the discourse of ethnic militancy that developed subsequently. This was when Miskitu people lost their rights to autonomy, which they have been struggling to recover ever since.

If the convention was indeed the point of origin of these two contemporary political discourses, then one cannot explain what happened there assuming that the discourses were already fully in place. Perhaps Miskitu antipathy for the Nicaraguans was still incipient enough to be outweighed by both the allure of promises and their alienation from the Creole-controlled Mosquito government. Ethnic militancy would have been a much less prominent component of their consciousness; it would deepen only after they began fully to experience state oppression. In this case, it is plausible to suggest that they opted both to register protest with their old allies the British and to give the Nicaraguans' promises a try. In the absence of convincing evidence of brute coercion by Cabezas, this may be the only way to account for the convention's outcome without implicitly portraying the Miskitu delegates as passive victims of deception.[29]

Under Two Masters: Nicaraguan Rule and Anglo Hegemony

By the beginning of the twentieth century, Miskitu people contended daily with the opportunities, demands, and constraints of two masters. The Nicaraguan state made vigorous, if inept and largely ineffectual, attempts to exert sovereign control over the newly annexed territory. State officials imposed taxes, usurped Indian lands, established local structures of political rule, and imposed strict prohibitions on education in languages other than Spanish. Simultaneously, "Anglo" institutions penetrated the Coast economy, polity, and civil society to an astounding degree. In this era the Moravian church grew from a beleaguered handful of missionaries and faithful to a dynamic, powerful, Coastwide religious institution, and North American transnational companies turned the Coast economy into a bustling enclave of production and commerce. In 1909, when President José Santos Zelaya's nationalist pretensions began to pose a threat to these growing U.S. interests, the United States backed a rebellion to oust him. Armed conflict broke out and U.S. Marines occupied key urban centers. For the next sixteen years the strong hand of U.S. Marine occupation kept unpopular Conservative politicians in power while the state's predatory, centralist, and ethnocentric relations with the Coast remained unchanged.

How did Miskitu people respond to the predicament of being subject to these two spheres of authority? Accounts of this phase of Miskitu history are again polarized. One version, squarely within the tradition of Mestizo nationalism, tends to downplay Miskitu resistance to the state and stress the overwhelming influence of U.S. imperialism on the course of Coast history. The other emphasizes Miskitu resistance and adaptation, understating the constitutive influence of U.S. hegemony. The contrast applies to both central issues of the period: protest against the state for rights to land and sovereignty, and accommodation of Anglo-American presence in the form of Protestant missionaries and North American companies.

Mobilization for Rights to Land and Sovereignty

Whatever Miskitu people might have thought about the Reincorporation, they quickly became disillusioned with Nicaraguan rule. Foreign-owned productive and commercial concerns continued to prosper during the decade after 1894, but Indians were increasingly burdened by taxes, government military presence, and threats to their community lands from Mestizo politicians and entrepreneurs. Miskitu headmen turned to British authorities for help, presenting lists of grievances such as the following in mid-1898:

We the undersigned, desire of you your kind counsel on several subjects. . . . It is merely to ask of you about the promises made to us by Nicaragua. That we were slaves, and they would free us. Instead, we found their yoke heavier than it was. They promise that our children would be properly looked after. We find it is the contrary. . . . And the only thing we have to live by is rubber; that is also to be stopped. . . . We would like of you to learn something of our Chief, whether he will return or not.[30]

Glass slide from Moravian mission slide show, with the caption, "A typical heathen girl (showing primitive skirt)" (circa 1930). Moravian Archives, Bethlehem, Penn.

Glass slide from Moravian mission slide show, with the caption, "A Christian Sumu [Indian] family at Magdala, Pearl Lagoon, Nic." Moravian Archives, Bethlehem, Penn.

Parson Karl Bregenzer and his volunteer church workers in Karawala (circa 1929). The original photo belongs to the Moravian church in Karawala.

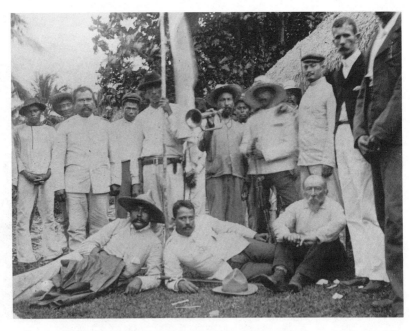

Glass slide from Moravian mission slide show, with the caption (in German), "In commemoration of the Sam Pitts Affair, 7 July 1906." Gathered are military and civilian officials of the Nicaraguan government on the Atlantic Coast. Moravian Archives, Bethlehem, Penn.

More militant actions followed. In 1900 a gathering of Miskitu head-men selected Sam Pitts, a leader from the northern community of Yulu, as their envoy to go to Jamaica to place Miskitu demands before British authorities. Pitts failed to gain support, returned to the Coast, continued to agitate against the government, and by 1906 had begun to organize an armed movement. All that is known about his program is that he declared himself the new Miskitu king, sought an end to Nicaraguan rule, and persisted in futile hopes for British intervention. Evidence that "Pitts gathered a good many Indians around him" comes from the Moravian missionaries, who, despite their antipathy for Zelaya, denounced and firmly opposed the movement. Pitts had begun to pose a challenge to the missionaries' authority in Miskitu communities, and they feared that ret-ribution might be directed against the church.[31] When government forces killed Pitts in November 1907, the movement collapsed. Without support from Creoles, either imperial power, or the Moravian church, his rebel-lion was doomed from the start.[32]

Within a few years Miskitu communities were again in turmoil, this time over the question of land rights. Under the Mosquito government Miskitu communities had not received land titles. Their rights had been defined by usufruct, while foreigners (and to a lesser extent Creoles) ac-quired legal titles, often on extremely favorable terms.[33] Before 1894 few overt conflicts over land occurred because the Coast was sparsely popu-lated and foreigners used land mainly for resource extraction (e.g., rub-ber and mahogany), which did not violently dislocate the Indian com-munities. Many Indians resettled to be near these foreign enterprises, attracted by the cash and consumer goods available from company commissaries.[34]

Mestizo elites who moved to the Bluefields area after the Reincorpora-tion used their newfound political clout to take advantage of the native inhabitants' vulnerable legal position. Zelaya made enormous grants of "unclaimed" Atlantic Coast land to reward supporters and mollify oppo-nents. In addition, petty government officials, whose salaries came irregu-larly if at all from Managua, taxed and plundered Indian lands as a means to secure their livelihood. Indians could acquire titles to usufruct lands only by petitioning the same government officials who posed the greatest threat. The case of a Rama Indian named Frederick Thomas is indicative:

In 1888 [he] cleared 4 manzanas of land the possession of which he enjoyed up to 1896—this special piece of land is now the property of one Bolaños. In 1897 the same Frederick Thomas cleared another patch of land, again 4 manzanas and held the same up to 1906 when General Estrada took possession of the same. This man Thomas each time denounced the land, had it measured etc., filled all the requirements of the law.[35]

In response to such obvious government connivance, Indians turned to British authorities with desperate pleas for assistance.

Hoping to withdraw definitively from prior treaty obligations and to end the deluge of petitions from Creoles and Indians, Britain negotiated the Harrison-Altamirano Treaty with Nicaragua. Ratified in 1906, the treaty recognized full Nicaraguan sovereignty over the Coast and established a procedure for the legal recognition of lands. Because abuses continued (indeed increased) after 1906 and virtually no titles were granted,[36] the treaty had the unintended consequence of dragging Britain further into the controversy. The British consul in Bluefields urged a more active role on the premise that "the Indians harbour the deepest distrust of all Nicaraguans, and for the present could not be persuaded to deal directly with any [Nicaraguan] lawyer. . . . It is impracticable to propose any other arrangement than that the amounts they subscribe and the claims they formulate . . . shall be transmitted to the lawyer by the intermediary of the British Consulate."[37] The Foreign Office consented reluctantly in 1914 and sent veteran diplomat H. O. Chalkley to revive and coordinate efforts of the Land Titles Commission. With Chalkley publicly in charge, the Indians responded to the commission with a groundswell of enthusiasm, in great contrast to their attitude over the previous nine years. The Miskitu understood Chalkley's involvement as a sign that Britain finally had decided to intervene on their behalf, perhaps even to back their demands for independence. When Chalkley tried to correct these misconceptions, community members expressed "unconcealed disappointment and some incredulity."[38] Miskitu communities throughout the Coast sent delegations to Bluefields to meet with Chalkley and discuss their claims. On Chalkley's request, headmen carried out detailed community censuses and collected contributions from each adult to defray the cost of lawyers' and surveyors' fees. Although the treaty stipulated an individual allotment of land for each Miskitu and Creole family, Chalkley considered this approach infeasible and convinced the headmen to present their claims as a block.[39] By early 1916, the commission had surveyed and granted some 30 collective titles, which guaranteed the lands of all Indians who lived inside the boundaries of the old Mosquito Reserve. Indians outside those boundaries had no recourse to the commission and had no land titles until the 1960's (see Map 2).

Ascendancy of the Moravian Church

Moravian church records contain abundant evidence that, especially at first, the missionaries found their jobs exceedingly difficult. They met great resistance to their edicts, engaged in intense power struggles with those who threatened church authority, and showed utter disdain for the traditional elements of Miskitu culture that were responsible for this obstinacy. In the church's *Periodical Accounts* missionaries described non-Christian Miskitu as pitiful "heathens" and, even after some were converted, gave stern admonishments about the slow pace of the "civilizing" process: they "are still like children," one reported, "complete moral bankrupts, [with] no feeling of shame." Missionaries also fought with the zeal of crusaders to rid the traditional Miskitu healers, or *sukias*, of their authority and to quash the syncretic religious movements that arose "where the decay of the heathen religion was not followed at once by effective missionary occupation."[40] Station diaries make for lurid reading of the missionaries' righteous campaigns to regulate community members' sexual mores and practices:

I explained to Evelina Evans that although she had always denied having had unlawful intercourse with Nathan, I had now proofs of it. So I told her she would be excluded and her sin be spoken of to the Congregation, although Evans had said, he would kill her and him also who should betray her to me. Such threats one cannot heed.

Parson told Josiah and Adeline if they would not stop having "la kumi" (i.e., friendly relations) with Reynaldo who is living in fornication, they would be put under 3rd degree discipline.[41]

Frequent references in these diaries to frustrations and setbacks confirm that the missionaries confronted considerable resistance, especially in the early stages of their work.

Yet they did ultimately prevail to a remarkable extent. By 1910 the church had an active presence in more than 50 Indian communities; by 1960 nearly half the Miskitu population were church members, including many who held positions of authority in the community. This success can be attributed in part to the church's institutional power and pervasive role in Coast civil society. As well as doing conventional religious work, missionaries and their native assistants ran stores, taught day school, provided health care, and became intimately involved in the daily affairs of community life. The Moravians offered Miskitu townspeople substantial benefits from participation in and support of the church and had the institutional power to make life very unpleasant for those who resisted. A second crucial reason for the Moravians' success was that the church bolstered Miskitu people's defiance of Nicaraguan government rule. Converting Miskitu people to Protestantism, educating them in Moravian schools, and promoting their own language reinforced their identity and enhanced their sense of being different from "Spaniards" (as Spanish-speaking Nicaraguans were commonly called). As church institutions conformed an entire civil society in the coastal region, they created alternative bases of economic welfare, social status, and even political power, largely outside the Nicaraguan state's sphere of influence.

Yet the Sam Pitts debacle highlights the contradictory consequences of this influence. No militancy could exist that directly challenged or even remotely threatened the institutional power of the church. As the church became ever more entrenched in Coast society, Miskitu identity and values gradually evolved to become harmonious complements of the Moravian standard. The sukia remained active as a traditional healer but without the spiritual and political authority previously assigned to him in Miskitu culture. People still routinely committed "fornication" and other "sins," but they no longer questioned that their morality would be judged by Moravian rules. As this convergence deepened, the Moravian church contributed immensely to the growth of Miskitu identity and ethnic militancy.

*   *   *

Nicaraguan anthropologist Jorge Jenkins Molieri, whose historical analysis is characteristic of the Mestizo nationalist perspective, hardly mentions the Sam Pitts affair and dismisses Miskitu resistance to the state as insignificant. In his interpretation, the mobilization for community land rights is more important for the concessions the state finally granted than for the resistance it entailed. On the other hand, he considers the Moravian missionaries' proselytization as little more than a cultural expression of U.S. imperialism. The Moravians "conformed" Miskitu consciousness, he argues, making it "alien to the social reality of Nicaragua" (1986: 83). Mary W. Helms, a leading ethnographer and ethnohistorian of the Miskitu, interprets this extraordinary Moravian influence in a very different way. She attributes the missionaries' success to "similarities and lack of serious conflict between traditional Miskitu behavioral standards and those of the Church" (1971: 172). Both Moravians and "traditional" Miskitu, she argues, placed a high value on kin relations; Moravians therefore left unchallenged many of the "traditional" organizational tenets of Miskitu society (p. 214). Miskitu people converted to the Moravian religion through a process of reciprocity, the argument goes, whereby missionaries respected, even deferred to, a preexisting Miskitu identity.

The same analytical divergence governs interpretations of the impact of U.S. companies on Miskitu consciousness. Jenkins Molieri essentially concludes that the Miskitu were fooled into mistaking the American companies' exploitation and oppression for beneficence (e.g., 1986:

113). Theodore MacDonald, in an argument closely parallel to Helms's, has pointed to a preexisting Miskitu "moral economy" that the North American companies did not violate. Thus Miskitu could gain access to consumer goods through intermittent wage labor, while their "subsistence security" and their "broad religious concepts of . . . land and resource rights" remained basically intact. Given this symbiosis, MacDonald concludes, it should come as no surprise that Miskitu welcomed the companies' presence and bemoaned their departure (1988: 111–22).[42]

A full understanding of Miskitu history must begin by overcoming the dichotomy between these two opposing views. The Miskitu mobilization for sovereignty and community land rights expressed both a deep defiance of Nicaraguan government authority and renewed hopes for independence under the protection of Britain. The land titles that communities achieved after 1911 took on great political importance as evidence of current rights as well as historic ties with Great Britain.[43] Miskitu people persisted in such associations at least in part because those ties conjured up images of political autonomy, freedom from taxes, and the absence of abusive government officials. Whether or not the British responded (they mostly did not), these images unified the Miskitu in the struggle against their principal adversaries: the "Spaniards." This hearkening back to the era of British colonialism expressed and advanced Miskitu resistance, at the cost of a reinforced sense of dependence on a powerful external actor and affinity with the values of Anglo civilization.

The same holds for Miskitu responses to Moravian missionaries and U.S. companies. Oral histories from Sandy Bay Sirpi suggest that as Miskitu people grew more involved with company production and market relations, they took on values that justified the companies' presence. They embraced a new definition of subsistence that included access to such consumer goods as flour, sugar, oil, and coffee and that could only be achieved through company work. It was probably during this time that they began to use the word *pawanka* (development) to describe admiringly the wages and consumer goods that companies brought. To claim that such an array of values formed part of a "moral economy" unconducive to resistance is reasonable, but only with the understanding that contact with the companies profoundly shaped the content of these values in the first place.

This argument is even more clearly documented in the case of Moravian ascendancy. Miskitu people first resisted, then actively chose to become Moravians. By embracing Moravian norms, they gained an institutional base from which to defend their separate identity and demands. But they also assimilated the image of Europeans as godly, powerful, and omniscient, premises of white superiority that were inextricable from the content of Moravian doctrine. Miskitu people soon vehemently defended the church as their own, and in so doing expressed and deepened an antinomy in their consciousness between militant rejection of Nicaraguan state ideology and affinity with premises that formed the underpinnings of Anglo-American hegemony.

Sandino and the Miskitu: A Challenge to the Antinomy

U.S. military forces that had been sent to Nicaragua in 1909 to "protect American lives and property" were still there fifteen years later. After 1912, when marines engaged in combat to quash an armed rebellion led by Benjamín Zeledón, the methods of U.S. occupation turned less violent, though hardly less direct. Control over Nicaragua's principal ports, railroads, and external finances enabled the United States to exert decisive influence while only rarely resorting to brute force. In 1916 the Conservative Emiliano Chamorro became president in elections in which, according to embassy correspondence, "only Conservatives voted" because the United States had pressured the Liberal candidates to withdraw.[44] Chamorro's uncle Diego Chamorro took power in 1921 under similar conditions, heightening already widespread discontent and antipathy for the Americans. Seeking to defuse the impending conflict, the United States then promoted a coalition government—Carlos Solórzano (a Conservative) for president and Juan Sacasa (a Liberal) for vice-president—which won handily in the elections of October 1924.

The coalition fell apart within a year. Emiliano Chamorro initiated a purge of Liberal cabinet members from the government, which led Solórzano to resign and Sacasa to flee the country. The United States condemned Chamorro but sought to maintain control by giving Adolfo Díaz, a loyal friend and ally, the chance to govern. A group of leading Liberal figures led by J. M. Moncada responded by initiating a revolution against the Díaz regime in favor of the "constitutional" president, Sacasa. The first act of rebellion occurred in May 1926, when Moncada seized the town of Bluefields. Marines landed to declare Bluefields a neutral zone, forcing the revolutionary headquarters northward to Puerto Cabezas, which the marines promptly occupied as well. In telling contrast to 1909, the United States obliged insurgents to remain outside these neutral zones and turned over customs duties collected at these ports to the Díaz government (Karnes 1977: 195).

Creoles played an active role in support of this Constitutional Revolution and for a short time espoused a remarkably critical stance toward U.S. intervention. Miskitu also generally sided with the revolution[45] and served as foot soldiers in the Liberal army (see, for example, the account of Mauro Salazar in Chapter 3). But unlike the case of the Creoles, there are few signs of enthusiastic and willing Miskitu involvement. By the Moravians' account, they often were pressed into service: "Our Indians were often called upon to serve as paddlers and carriers, to dig trenches and to do other work. . . . Never safe from the danger of being forced to assist one or another of the armies, many idled their time away in hiding. The villages were occupied by troops, and the people were compelled to share what little food they had with soldiers billeted upon them."[46] The missionaries professed neutrality and claimed to have counseled their parishioners similarly, yet they clearly opposed the Conservative government (Adams 1987: 54). Thus the Miskitu seem to have taken a stance consistent with that of the church: avoiding the conflict while siding passively with the Liberals.[47]

Fearing a long-term military engagement on the losing side of the war, in April 1927 the United States sent Henry Stimson as a special emissary to Nicaragua to achieve a negotiated agreement. Most Liberal generals were amenable, indeed remarkably receptive, to mediation by the United States despite its well-known partiality in the conflict. Upon signing the Espino Negro Pact that stipulated his surrender, Moncada expressed "confidence" in the United States, declaring that "Liberals cannot believe that the U.S. government . . . [would] give a promise which it will not fulfill." The promise apparently included assurances that Moncada would soon become president, which may help to explain his eagerness to cooperate. Although Moncada's government left Coast peoples' demands for greater autonomy unsatisfied,[48] having a U.S.-backed Liberal in power raised their hopes and defused their critical stance toward the United States.[49]

One Liberal general, Augusto César Sandino, did not submit to the Stimson accords. Sandino demanded the complete withdrawal of the marines, respect for Nicaragua's national sovereignty, and a government that represented the interests of the majority. In July 1927, U.S. Marine General Hatfield gave Sandino "one more opportunity to surrender with honor," informing him (rather brashly) that "Nicaragua has had its last Revolution."[50] Sandino refused, formed a guerrilla army, and waged a highly successful five-year campaign against the U.S. Marines and the newly formed Nicaraguan National Guard. Although Sandino operated mainly among Mestizo peasants in the northern departments of the Jinotega and Nuevo Segovia, his army also made numerous incursions into the Atlantic Coast.

Sandino's presence confronted Miskitu inhabitants of the Northeast with a choice between a nationalist army of peasant extraction and an occupying military force from the United States. Especially given the situation's striking similarity to the contemporary configuration of forces, evidence of extensive Miskitu support for Sandino's army is perplexing. Sandino espoused staunch anti-imperialism and Mestizo nationalism, both in direct contrast with the premises of ethnic militancy and Anglo affinity that Miskitu people espoused. How then do we account for their support? Did coercion or manipulation by either of the two military forces play a role? Or do the assertions about the content of Miskitu consciousness developed thus far need to be revised?

In March 1928, less than a year after the war began, U.S. Marine officials sent Major-General M. A. Edson on a reconnaissance trip up the Río Coco. He found Miskitu inhabitants to be generally in sympathy with the guerrilla army and to express a decided lack of receptivity toward his own forces. In two subsequent forays up the Coco later that year, despite concerted efforts to attract local support, Edson won few converts and even resorted to impressment to keep his boats manned by Miskitu oarsmen.[51] Between 1929 and 1933, Sandinista columns operated extensively throughout the northeastern region, aided by a well-organized network of Miskitu collaborators.[52] When the marines finally pulled out of Nicaragua early in 1933, Sandino had achieved a virtual liberated zone along the upper Río Coco, with headquarters in the predominantly Indian community of Bocay. Sandinistas provided schools, health care, and agricultural assistance and moved with ease among the native population.[53]

There were several keys to Sandino's success. First, he worked through local leaders such as Abraham Rivera and Adolfo Cockburn, who spoke Miskitu, enjoyed widespread popular support, and were sensitive to local demands. These intermediaries were involved in most well-documented cases of active Miskitu participation in the war.[54] Deteriorating economic conditions throughout the Coast, especially after 1929, may also have strengthened the Sandinistas' hand. American companies sharply reduced their payrolls, giving the Sandinistas' anti-American discourse greater resonance and generating recruits from among the economically disaffected.[55] Finally, Sandino sought to meet the material needs of local people. Unlike the two "revolutionary" armies that had swept through the Atlantic Coast in the previous twenty years, his commitment to the region went far beyond viewing it as a platform from which to take power in Managua.[56]

The marines, in contrast, acted in a way that could not have endeared them to the Miskitu. Although Edson may have been—as David Brooks (1989) depicts him—a nonracist and friendly man with an anthropological bent, others in the contingent displayed less exemplary behavior. At the time of Edson's incursions, Moravian missionaries complained of a "half crazy [marine lieutenant] by the name of Carrol, who was molesting the [Indian] girls and old women" in upriver Río Coco communities. Further, they report that marines stationed in the community of Andris in 1928 were "not of the best sort. Women could not walk near or pass the house they camped in after dark. When they were drunk they even attacked women in their houses. . . . The 'gentlemen' also . . . helped themselves to the people's orange trees without one cent in compensation." [57] After Edson's ground troops were pulled out in 1929, the marines abandoned efforts to win over the local population. They continued to fight along the Río Coco by strafing and bombing suspected guerrilla positions, which often were civilian communities as well (Brooks 1989: 335; MacCaulay 1967: 208).

*   *   *

Once again, accounts of Miskitu responses to Sandino line up along the divide of the narratives that emerged with the annexation. Jenkins Molieri celebrates the Miskitu people's extensive participation in Sandino's campaign, portraying it as a result of a largely self-evident convergence of interests (1986: chap. 3). Helms, in contrast, reports that Miskitu of the upper Río Coco uniformly remembered Sandino as a "bandit" who killed local people and plundered their property indiscriminately (1971: 113). Her strong implication that any Miskitu who supported Sandino must have been subjected to brute coercion is subtly reinforced in the work of historian David Brooks (1989). By describing Sandino's recruitment tactics with terms like "propaganda" and "psychological warfare" (borrowed from the marine diaries that are his principal sources), Brooks leaves the reader to infer that Miskitu people joined Sandino against their better interests. [58]

The course of events during this period of revolutionary turmoil (1926–33) had the potential radically to transform the pervasive antinomy in Miskitu people's consciousness. To lend active support to the guerrilla army, they must have shared some of its basic justifying ideas and demands and, correspondingly, developed an incipient critique of U.S. presence, symbolized by the unruly marines. If these trends had continued and Sandino had not been assassinated, a radically different version of Miskitu identity might well have emerged. There is, however, no reason to believe that the tensions accompanying such multiethnic alliances had been eliminated or even fully confronted. Just before his death Sandino told a reporter: "Now we will see if the [Miskitu] are intelligent. They have been completely abandoned. They are 100,000 people, without means of communication, schools, without any kind of government. That's where I want to go, with a colonization project to raise them up, and make real men out of them." [59] Although he showed great concern for Miskitu people's material welfare, Sandino had little receptivity to demands for autonomy. His stated objective, rather, was to "incorporate" the Miskitu into the nation (Román 1983: 105).

Finally, one wonders why the Moravian missionaries did not more effectively discourage and thwart Miskitu sympathies. The Moravians dreaded and vehemently opposed Sandino, especially after March 1931, when a Sandinista column accused missionary Karl Bregenzer of being an American spy and had him summarily executed. Bregenzer's death sent waves of panic through the Moravian ranks and convinced them beyond a doubt that Sandino and his men were ruthless bandits (Wunderich 1989: 67–84). Their fervent anti-Sandinista campaign raises the intriguing possibility that Miskitu support for Sandino was strongest precisely where successful proselytization had not yet occurred.[60] In the absence of Moravian church influence, Miskitu adherence to Anglo affinity would have been less pronounced and their ethnic demands less militant. They would have had much more in common with the Mestizo peasants whose demands Sandino's program was designed to address.

Even on the upper Río Coco, where Miskitu support had been the strongest, however, positive memories of Sandino quickly faded. Soon after his death, the missionaries initiated a "redemption campaign," urging those who had supported the "bandits" to confess, publicly declare their remorse, and reaffirm their belief in the "word of Jesus Christ" (Wunderich 1989: 134–35). Such efforts surely help to account for the anti-Sandino sentiments that Helms later heard and recorded. Just as the Miskitu's past resistance to Moravian teachings gradually receded in their memories, their images of Sandino changed from ally to bandit.[61]

Conclusions and a Look Forward

The annexation of 1894 marked the contemporary origins of two polarized narratives of Miskitu history, though one could certainly find earlier indications of the pattern. In 1894, the discourse of Nicaraguan national sovereignty over the Coast became intense and urgent, strongly encouraging Miskitu people to "join" the nation, rigidly intolerant of Miskitu thought and actions that did not conform to these plans. Anglo presence in the region and deep influence in Miskitu society added to the urgency of these nationalist designs and provided a ready explanation for their failure: U.S. cultural imperialism engendered Miskitu people's "anti-Nicaraguan" sentiments, just as imperialism in general blocked the state's legitimate aspirations for sovereignty.

Accounts that take the Miskitu perspective expose the racism inherent in this nationalist hyperbole and focus on the Miskitu aspirations that the state denied at every turn. The Reincorporation was little more than a cruel hoax; the Sam Pitts episode and the mobilization for lands were heroic expressions of Miskitu national resistance. Amid contention between much stronger political-economic forces, the argument goes, Miskitu people always managed to maintain key elements of their traditional culture, their moral economy, which in turn guided their resistant, defensive posture toward threats from the outside. Although such accounts proliferated after 1979, when contemporary ethnic conflict began, they had their roots much earlier, in a vantage point infused with the premises of Anglo-American hegemony. Moravian missionaries, U.S. officials, and affiliated observers put forth these premises in a most blatant fashion. They also are more subtly present in scholarly analysis that followed: Helms on the Moravians, MacDonald on the U.S. companies, Brooks on Sandino.

I have sought to avoid the shortcomings of earlier accounts with analysis that assigns central importance both to Miskitu agency in response to state oppression and to the impact of Anglo hegemony in Miskitu consciousness. Miskitu people actively sought relations with the Moravian church as a means to meet concrete needs and to advance political interests. A sense of belonging to the church and an assertion of historic ties to the British bolstered Miskitu aspirations for autonomy and increased the resources available for their resistance to oppressive Nicaraguan government rule. The same holds for Miskitu responses to North American companies, which provided Miskitu with access to coveted consumer goods, new skills, and a series of highly valued improvements in their standard of living. In northeastern Nicaragua, Miskitu people developed compelling reasons to support Sandino's army, rooted in concrete experiences of the war. Sandino sought to meet townspeople's needs and worked through respected local leaders, while his adversaries, the marines, proved inept and abusive.

This careful attention to Miskitu consciousness and action must not preclude, however, parallel analysis of how hegemonic premises became embedded in the cultural forms they create. Mary Helm's account of the reciprocal relationship between Miskitu culture and the Moravian religion vastly understates the missionaries' considerable institutional power, as well as initial Miskitu resistance to conversion. It overlooks the dominant ideas that Miskitu people assimilated as they became Moravians and as collective memories of conflict and resistance to the church gradually faded. The same flaw can be found in MacDonald's assertion of the providential fit between the Miskitu moral economy and North American companies.

Miskitu people did not come to espouse Anglo affinity because it was coercively imposed upon them. It developed out of their efforts to secure subsistence, resist oppression, and assert or defend a separate identity while living under multiple spheres of inequity. By drawing nearer to the institutions and practices of the North American–dominated civil society, they strengthened their distinct identity and acquired tangible political resources to advance their struggle. Thus from early in the century, the premises of both ethnic militancy and Anglo affinity became deeply embedded in Miskitu people's consciousness, mutually reinforcing each other.

These premises grew stronger during the first three decades of the Somoza dictatorship (1934–60), becoming so pervasive that Helms could perceive them in the early 1960's as "traditional" components of Miskitu culture.[62] This was the era of Moravian ascendancy, when the church constituted virtually every facet of Coast civil society. If Miskitu people became educated or received health care, indeed if they improved their welfare or moved up the socioeconomic hierarchy in any way, the odds were that they had the Moravian church to thank (Wilson 1975). Although Coast people were far from uniformly content with Somoza, the major irritants of the past—exorbitant taxes, oppressive military presence, land usurpation, and government abuse—appear to have diminished. Demands for autonomy lost their urgency but did not disappear; they flared up episodically when the central government's neglect or heavy-handed presence became especially blatant. Until the 1960's, the Somoza state's presence in the coastal region consisted mainly of petty government officials and sleepy military outposts. From the perspective of Managua, the Coast became, as the title of a travelogue by the adventurer László Pataky (1956) had it, *Nicaragua desconocida* (unknown Nicaragua).

North America's neocolonial presence on the Coast became directly linked to the national political culture's intolerance of regional ethnic identities and demands. From the time of William Walker's infamous foray in the mid-nineteenth century, the United States had posed the principal barrier to Nicaraguans' achievement of an independent national identity and a sovereign state. The Sandinistas' renewed call for national liberation in the 1960's inherited an exclusionary stance toward Indians, especially difficult to eradicate because Miskitu people appeared to be aligned on the opposite side of the struggle against U.S. imperialism. The nationalists' disdain for ethnic or regional demands and the Indians' dismissal of Nicaraguans' claims to sovereignty developed as mirror images of each other, and each side's relationship to the United States deepened the emotional charge of the disparity. The logic of this triad makes it clear why Coast people feared what the revolution might hold in store and why Sandinistas could hardly avoid reinforcing those fears. The very fact that this part of Nicaragua had grown more "desconocida" since the 1930's meant that the Sandinistas had less impetus to challenge the exclusionary premises associated with that term. Although the Sandinistas would decry the Somozas' neglect and the North Americans' exploitation of the Coast, their images of Miskitu people as passive, co-opted, outside the flow of history—and therefore unknown—would live on well into the revolutionary era.

3 Miskitu Narratives of History, Politics, and Identity

Oral history testimonies do not form a simple record, more or less accurate, of past events; they are complex cultural products. They involve interrelations . . . between private memories and public representations, between past experiences and present situations.
—Popular Memory Group, 1982

WHAT WERE THINGS LIKE "first time" for the community, for Miskitu people? How did all the troubles get started? These questions guided and focused much of my energy during the initial months of field research in Sandy Bay. They arose not from an elaborate plan to make extensive use of oral history or to explore the theoretical complexities of the narrative form, but rather from a more elementary anthropological premise. The study had to be grounded in a systematic effort to understand this conflict from their perspective. Gradually, as I listened to people's answers to these questions, they came to inform a major conclusion of the resulting analysis. Sandy Bay people's collective memories of the past contain, and often eloquently express, central elements within their consciousness, which in turn help us make sense of their role in the conflict. Although inquiries on diverse aspects of the community—economics, kinship, internal politics, religious practices—all contributed to my understanding of the tumultuous years between 1979 and 1987, I learned most by listening to people's unstructured responses to those two simple questions.

The oral history accounts that resulted from these conversations form part of the historical record. They include valuable information about local conditions and sharp insights into Miskitu perceptions and actions at these times, and they help us to resolve problems of historical interpretation that are left obscure by other sources. At several points in the previous chapter and in analysis elsewhere (Hale 1991c), I have used the accounts in these ways. But my purpose here is not to present a systematic Miskitu oral history, parallel (even if in pale reflection) to, for example, Richard Price's magisterial account of four centuries of Saramaka history in Suriname (1990). I doubt such a project would have been possible in any case, since Miskitu collective memories were more uneven and acquired great vigor and salience fairly recently. This last point was confirmed in passing by Bernard Nietschmann, whose work among the Miskitu in the mid-1970's included efforts to elicit their views of the past. He concluded that people from Kuamwatla (a community just north of Sandy Bay Sirpi) had a "collective historical perspective [that] seemed to go back no further than the 1920s and 1930s when foreign missionaries and businesses began to expand into the area. [We] were seeking a point in their history which had long been erased by a new ideology and economics" (1979a: 53).

The transcribed collective memories presented below partly contradict Nietschmann's report, because they point strongly to a continuous oral tradition that must have existed in the 1970's as well. Mauro Salazar's vivid description of the Reincorporation and Manuel Rodriguez's narrative of the community's founding are good examples. Yet Nietschmann's comment probably does accurately reflect a facet of the profound change that took place in Miskitu communities throughout the Coast between 1978 and 1985. During the time of his research, Miskitu people probably assigned much less importance or urgency to knowing about their own past. History became deeply politicized later, as the post-1979 mobilization gathered strength. MISURASATA activists mined community-level memories but also drew on a wide range of other sources; grass-roots intellectuals such as Mauro Salazar strained to remember more but also probably filled in gaps with elements of the leaders' discourse or with creative extrapolations. As the conflict grew more intense, these memories, which explained what the struggle was all about, grew all the more urgent.

There is no way to confirm this assertion regarding the recent politicization of Miskitu people's history without a diachronic analysis of their collective memories, which would require data that almost surely do not exist. Nietschmann's comment and a few other scattered observations do not suffice. The claim that people's memories in 1985–87 provide a key analytical opportunity in relation to contemporary politics is on much firmer ground. Especially in light of the highly charged political atmosphere of the previous eight years, it is reasonable to assume that people's consciousness and actions during that time became deeply intertwined with their interpretations of the past. Precisely because Sandy Bay people extensively revised their narrative, it provides a window on the emotions, appraisals, commonsense notions, and refined analysis that guided them to embark on the antigovernment mobilization.[1]

Historical analysis in the previous chapter revolved around a central antinomy in Miskitu consciousness between what I call Anglo affinity and ethnic militancy. I explained this antinomy as an outcome of Miskitu people's responses to the combined forms of structural inequities in Coast society. Yet the crucial evidence to sustain that argument was admittedly scant. The historical sources do not provide many chances to hear Miskitu voices or any other sustained insights into their consciousness. That leaves us with consequences, which are a crucial part of the analysis but ambiguous when they stand alone. An image from Sandy Bay that has stayed with me helps to epitomize this ambiguity.

About one Sunday a month, the Moravian church in Sandy Bay Sirpi holds Holy Communion. After scrutiny by the parson to make sure that they have committed no "sins" during the preceding weeks, church members attend the main service, which starts at 11:00 A.M. sharp, to participate in the ritual. Although I usually attended as well, on this Sunday in April 1986 I decided not to because an unusual opportunity had arisen. A young Sandy Bay man who had recently returned from several years of fighting in the bush had come by to ask if I could take his picture on the beach. When we finished, we sat on the veranda talking about why he had gone to fight, his experiences as a MISURASATA combatant, what he thought about the revolution. A while later the church service ended and, according to custom, some 25 church elders formed a procession behind the parson to visit the members too old or sick to attend and deliver communion in their homes. As they walked from house to house they sang hymns with tunes that were vaguely familiar to me—Moravian Protestant standards, translated into Miskitu. We stopped talking to watch, and the young man nodded approvingly as the parson, white robe flowing in the Caribbean sea breeze, led the white-clad faithful past our veranda.

In this largely monolingual Miskitu community, people developed a militant ethnic consciousness that led them to take up arms against the state, while remaining deeply engaged with a conservative religious institution implanted by white North American missionaries. The meaning of this juxtaposition of practices remains ambiguous unless we know much more about how people think about and evaluate what they do. This is precisely what the collective memories presented here should help to achieve. With them I am able to provide empirical support and add ethnographic detail to the historical argument of Chapter 2: that Miskitu people's consciousness contained an antinomy rooted in their responses to unequal relations with Anglo-Americans on the one hand, and the Mestizo state on the other. This does not make Miskitu culture unusual or unique. Similar contradictions surely can be found in all human cultures, created as people respond to the multiple, often crosscutting, spheres of inequity within their societies. I do, however, assign special importance to that conclusion here, arguing that it holds a key to understanding Miskitu politics both before and after 1979. After examining Sandy Bay people's memories and doing the same for the Sandinista narrative in the next chapter, we can then analyze their contemporary relations with a more informed and critical eye.

The Narrative

The richest and most detailed historical account I collected in Sandy Bay came from Mauro Salazar, a man about 80 years of age. I taped an initial lengthy interview with Salazar in October 1985 because numerous townspeople, in lieu of answering my queries about "old people's times," referred me to him as an authority on the subject.[2] Although Salazar had an impressive grasp of distant history, he knew much less about recent events. Gradually, I found others—generally younger adults who had been active in the mobilization—to fill out this part of the account. Asking many people the same historical questions naturally brought to light disparities, which I have included in the narrative when they corresponded to broader patterns of community politics. The contributions of about ten people who provided the richest detail are included here, though I collected stories from many more.[3] The narrative stops around the end of 1981, before the war began in earnest. It will resume in Chapter 6, in a somewhat different form, for reasons explained there. This is not the only reading that could be made of these collective memories. They contain many other elements of analytical importance, regarding gender, kin- and age-based intracommunity divisions, and the role of religion in community life, to name a few. I leave them unattended here to bring the central question into sharper focus: What led Miskitu people to mobilize against the government after 1979?

How Things Were "First Time"—in the Old Days

The most important themes in collective memories of the distant past are Miskitu people's ascendancy over the whole Atlantic Coast, alliance with the British, and bitter resentment against the Spanish. Salazar explained:

"At first there was no king. When Columbia [sic] reached Cape Gracias [a Dios], only Miskitu and Sumu lived there, no Blacks, no Spaniards. Later on, when the Miskitu crowned a king, England found out. Then there were two: here the Miskitu king, there the English king. Our king ruled this whole area from Roman Bar to San Juan. He lived in Bluefields, had guns and everything. His suit and cap, gifts of the English, glowed like hot coals. All these things were kept on the Río Coco until recently, when the Spaniards stole them."

Simon Gonzales explained these origins even more pointedly:

"A group of Miskitu lived deep in the bush near Cape Gracias. They wore no clothes and were ignorant farmers. In those times there was gold everywhere. One day at sunrise a boat appeared. The Miskitu ran for their lances and prepared to fight. They were wild and had never seen a boat before. Spaniards came ashore, gave away some trinkets, then asked permission to carry the rocks back with them. (That was gold!) 'Take it,' said the Miskitu. The Spaniards loaded up, making trip after trip. Finally, an educated Miskitu caught on. He said: 'Let's name a king, someone to take care of our land.'"

Reflecting on these memories of "king times," Salazar's daughter-in-law added a crucial detail:

'I heard that Creoles didn't count (*kulkras*) back then. If a Miskitu walked into a bar and Creoles or Spaniards were there drinking, they all had to leave.'

Her image of the ethnic hierarchy "back then" was precisely the inverse of the current one.

The site where Sandy Bay Sirpi now stands was not settled in the 1820's, when a British trader named Orlando Roberts traveled extensively through the area and wrote an account with detailed descriptions (1965 [1827]). Salazar explained how his ancestors came to live in the community:

"My grandfather, a man named Thompson, came from Krukira; my grandmother from Dakura. They first settled in a place near Tasbapauni, named Karaslaya. But that place had too many sand flies, so they moved up here. At that time, the only man who lived in the community was Teodore. My grandparents built a house, where my father lived and I was born."

Through community genealogies, I identified Teodore as the great-grandfather of the present village headman, Manuel Rodriguez. Teodore's name, with the title of mayor (*alcalde*) appears as a signatory of the Mosquito convention of 1894.[4] For nearly a century the position of village leader has remained in a single family, passing from Teodore to his daughter's husband, Benito, to his three grandchildren, to Manuel Rodriguez (see Fig. 1). In an early interview Rodriguez provided his account of the community's founding, which he recounted frequently in community meetings and other settings:[5]

"[In] my grandfather's [time] Sandy Bay was not community like right now, you see? No place, no house at that time. And my grandfather him is from Cape Gracias [a Dios] and him travel come to Sandy Bay. When he reach Sandy Bay was pure bush. Nobody there. OK, well my grandfather make a house and start live. And then, next fellows come to Sandy Bay and join up with Benito. All

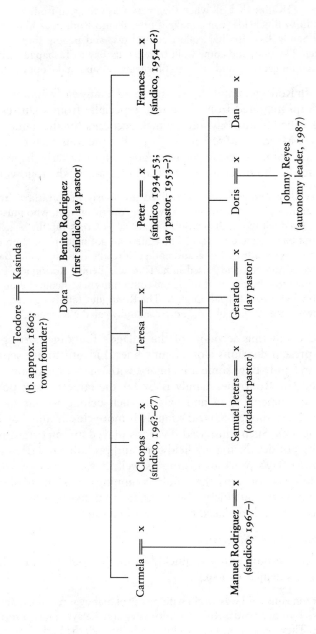

FIG. 1. Selected members of the Rodriguez family, Sandy Bay

Miskitu from up the coast. So the next people them go and live like that because Sandy Bay wide place, and big savanna, and good Río Grande river, and good seaport. OK, like that till when the treaty was calling in from all the community come in to Bluefields, come make a title. Benito Rodriguez him is the first man come Sandy Bay, [so he] collect some eggs, and people them give him some chicken, like that, and come walk from Sandy Bay to Tasbapauni, and then from Tasbapauni get dory and come to Bluefields . . . and make out that title."

As both Rodriguez and Salazar indicated, many early inhabitants of Sandy Bay Sirpi migrated from the north, especially from a cluster of communities called Sandy Bay Tara, which accounts for the name (*sirpi* means small in Miskitu and *tara* means big).[6] But the consensus ends here. Elders who are not members of the Rodriguez family bitterly disputed the effort to place Benito on center stage. David Lora gave the following account:

'Yu Twilkan and Amador, who lived previously in Karaslaya [to the south], founded this place. Meanwhile, a [white] American man, who must have been a pirate, lived with an Indian woman near Snook Creek [up the beach]. The woman's first baby came out black. The American got mad, packed up the baby in a box and sent it adrift. My grandmother [already living in Sandy Bay] found the box, saved the boy and raised him. That was Benito Rodriguez. Later, when it came time to take out land titles, the community sent Benito because he was the only one who could speak English. The Rodriguez family has ruled the community ever since . . . just like the Somoza family ruled Nicaragua.'

These conflicting accounts of the village's founding correspond closely with present divisions along family lines. I identified five separate family lines in Sandy Bay; some are aligned with one another, some overtly opposed. The Rodriguez family is by far the largest, most powerful, and most prominent. Lora and Salazar each belong to one of the smaller family lines, though Salazar's family is more closely allied by marriage to Rodriguez's. Such kin-based divisions played an important role in community politics during my fieldwork and probably did during the course of Sandy Bay's previous history as well. Because much of the narrative that follows concerns the whole community's (or all Miskitu people's) relations with "outsiders," however, internal divisions tend to recede into the background, replaced by a gloss of unanimity.

Coming of the "Spaniards"

Salazar's account skipped quickly from the origins of the Miskitu kingship to its demise in 1894:

"First time this land was virgin with plenty of mahogany, rubber, and many other riches. Two Spaniards, Ruben Darios [sic] and Zelaya, plotted to take over the Coast. They came from Leon to Bluefields through the bush. Upon arriving they called the king. He answered them: 'Why did you come here? You have no business here.' They replied, 'You Miskitu are too poor. We want to help you. You do not know how to read, you are ignorant; we'll give you schools, help your poor and widowed, give you all kinds of things. Just give us a chance [to rule] for 50 years, and then we'll return it to you.' The king said: 'I can't do that, England has not given permission.' They kept talking, the Spaniards kept telling lies, and took out two bottles of rum. The king drank a little with them. When he went to sleep, they stayed behind, writing a document. In the morning when the king awoke, they said: 'You see, you made the deal, you signed when you were drunk.' The king claimed he hadn't done it, they argued, and finally the king gave in: 'All right, I'll give you 50 years, but when the time is up, you have to keep your promise and give the land back.'"

Simon Gonzales later provided a similar though less elaborate account of the episode. I asked, "If the Miskitu felt so strongly about the land, how could the king have given it away?"

"Well you know, Nicaragua wanted to buy the land. But the king wouldn't do it because to sell the land would be to sell out his people. Instead of selling, he wanted education for his people. After some good schooling, then the Miskitu would be able to oversee their land again. That was the promise."

Any adult in Sandy Bay could recount the broad outlines of this "promise" and would hasten to point out how it has been broken. The Nicaraguan government provided none of the benefits stipulated in the agreement, and when the 50 years passed the Miskitu never got their land back. The names of Teodore and two others appear as signatories of the Mosquito Convention Decree, signed on November 20, 1894. Salazar's account elaborated on that decree, which stipulated that the central government "invest all the revenues that the littoral produces for its own benefit, thereby preserving its economic autonomy." The 50-year "promise," often repeated by both Miskitu and Creoles today, remains a mystery to me because no such clause appears in that document.[7] Finally, the idea that Rubén Darío (a prominent Nicaraguan modernist poet of the early twentieth century) teamed up with José Santos Zelaya (Nicaraguan president in 1894 and architect of the Reincorporation) to commit the act could have been someone's surmise after visiting the Bluefields city park. There stands a monument to the Reincorporation, with a bust of Zelaya on one side and one of Darío on the other.

Wars Between Liberals and Conservatives

During the decade preceding the Reincorporation, North Americans began to invest heavily in the Atlantic Coast. Salazar explained how this production took place:

"From the time the Nicaraguans took over, they told us nothing but a pack of lies. The American companies came and began to cut mahogany like crazy. Only the big ones—40 inch, 50 inch—35 inch on down they left behind to rot. They got plenty of good mahogany. The Nicaraguans made a killing from this. They gave permission to cut, and received payment for every log. The Miskitu got nothing. The poor things, they didn't even understand what was going on. President Zelaya got rich from the companies. . . . Enormous ships loaded to the brim with bananas left from here each week. The Americans paid a tax for each bunch, and the Nicaraguans got it all. The Miskitu received absolutely nothing."

By 1909, Zelaya's growing nationalism placed him at odds with the U.S. government, which threw its support behind the opposing Conservative party. Salazar described in remarkable detail the following years of political conflict, which subsided only with the establishment of the Somoza family dictatorship in 1934. He began with the downfall of former president Zelaya's proxy, José Madriz, in 1910:

"The Americans thought it through and decided that the Spaniards were oppressing them too much. They told Estrada: 'Fight, take out Zelaya, and we'll give you something good in return. When you win we'll go half and half.' He fought and fought and fought, but couldn't win, until finally, a man-o'-war appeared off Bluff, and suddenly there were marines all over. Up and down, pure marines. They won, Zelaya fled, and the Americans put Chamorro in his place. But Chamorro exploited the Coast just the same and kept all the benefits. The Miskitu got nothing."

For the next fourteen years various factions of Chamorro's Conservative party controlled the central government, although seriously outnumbered by the Liberals, who relentlessly sought a return to power. Only with massive U.S. aid and military intervention could the Conservatives stave off successive Liberal assaults, both electoral and military. In 1926, a full-fledged Liberal revolution broke out. Salazar:

"The Spaniards in Managua were getting filthy rich. Three of them got together, stole some of the money, bought some arms and escaped to the Río Grande. They were reds, Liberals, Moncada's crowd; Chamorro's people were blues. The Liberals came here looking for six men; I was just a boy but they grabbed me, and I had to go. They rounded up Miskitu like hogs (just like the Sandinistas are doing today). Miskitu died in this war and got nothing in return. They made me a *comandante*, in charge of 35 men at Río Grande Bar. . . . They fought and fought, then the Americans told Moncada: 'Stop fighting, that's an order. Go to Managua, and I'll give you four years as president of Nicaragua.' So they stopped. The Spaniards always fight among themselves, just for money. They charge taxes on all the products that leave the coast—lumber, bananas, gold. Whenever the Americans get fed up they take over the government and put in a new set of leaders."

Salazar made it clear that, although Coast people fought on the side of the Liberals, this was not a Miskitu struggle. He therefore could report on American intervention without disapproval. Americans supported the Conservatives only with the goal of ending "oppressive" taxation of their companies.

In May of 1927 the Liberal army, headed by General Moncada, signed a peace accord and agreed to participate in presidential elections the following year. Conceived and orchestrated by the United States, this Espino Negro Pact marked the beginning of a close partnership between the Americans and the Liberal party. One renegade general from the Liberal army, Augusto César Sandino, refused to submit to the pact and carried on the struggle against U.S. economic and military intervention in Nicaragua for five additional years. Efforts to crush Sandino's guerrilla army, led by U.S. Marines and the nascent National Guard, brought to the fore Guard General Anastasio Somoza, whose family would rule Nicaragua for the next 45 years. Salazar:

"Now Sandino (these same people!) was Sacasa's nephew, but out of greed he decided to overthrow Sacasa and name himself president. Sandino got help from Mexico and began to fight. He killed Miskitu, marines, people from all different nationalities. [CRH: Why?] Why do you think they are doing it today? Innocent people slaughtered. . . . On the Río Coco they buried alive a German man, Steadman [Fagoth's] father. Marines like Davis were in charge, but their foot soldiers were all Miskitu. Marines and Miskitu, unified. And those marines were tough! . . . At this time, Somoza was minister of arms. The Americans told him: 'Whenever Sandino comes around, catch him unaware and kill him.' Somoza responded, 'I can't, he's my comrade.' (The two of them were next-door neighbors, you know.) The Americans persisted, making a promise: 'We'll give the presidency for life, to you, your children, and grandchildren too. You'll have the good life, we'll give you everything. And forty years from now, you'll still be there.' Somoza agreed. He lured Sandino to a meeting and while Sandino was together with his family, Somoza killed them all at once. That same day the Americans told Somoza, 'Take over.' And he stayed for 45 years."

The Americans: Company Owners and Missionaries

In Salazar's account of the Liberal-Conservative rivalry, Americans play a central role. Powerful but upright, they intervene to defend their own legitimate interests and to keep the unruly, opportunistic "Spaniards" in line. David Lora provided a more specific, characteristically glowing appraisal of the Americans during "company times":

"Things were good in the company times. People had money, lumber, everything, and everyone had work, every day. We never ran short of food; the store shelves were full of rice, beans, lard . . . and we had money from all the work. Americans were good mannered, respectful. They would talk to us, just like you and I right now, never cussing or speaking sharply. And if you worked well, they paid you well. Previously people had been ignorant; with no companies, who were they supposed to learn from? But with the companies, we began to learn all kinds of things (to be mechanics, truck drivers, everything). . . . The Americans don't like the Spaniards, who they call 'greasers.' First time, they were enemies, back when the marines fought Pedrón and Sandino. But they are friends with the Miskitu and the Creoles. We all talk the same language, but the Americans don't speak Spanish."

Sandy Bay Miskitu often volunteered comments on the topic of the Americans. A woman of about 50 years pulled me aside specially to say:

'The Sandinistas want us to fight against the Americans, but we won't. They are our friends. They have helped us. There always were plenty of good things to buy when the Americans were here. I "had" an American right here in this house when I was young but no children came of it.'

From a conversation between two men, while we were walking together to their farm:

'We cannot [develop our communities] without the Americans—we have the riches but they are intelligent (*sinskira sa*). We just don't understand (*Yawan nani tanka briras*). God didn't give us as much intelligence (*Dawan bui yawan ra sinska laka yaras kan*). Some nations got intelligence, others did not.'

In the same historical period when the U.S. companies were still present, community members reportedly sustained more respectful and caring relations with one another. Salazar:

"In the old people's times, they grew cassava, *duswa*, *tawa* in abundance. You would visit, maybe someone else would come. If you didn't have any food, you'd say, 'Lend me a hand of bananas.' I'd give to you, to the other. Not for money—a present. After killing a cow, we'd sell the meat for ten cents a pound. But if you didn't have money, you'd get it on trust. Green turtle meat would be shared all around. That was old people's times, no one went hungry. We were unified (*kupia kumi*, lit. 'of one heart') and caring. Those times the community was well off. One or two people would drop by my house, and we'd eat together, with one heart. Now, if you don't have any money, you starve."

Salazar directly associated this way of the elders—*kupia kumi laka*—with the presence of a second group of Americans, the Moravian missionaries:

"The white Moravian parsons had a way about them, they were caring people. They would teach others to be this way. Anywhere you go with them, you go with unified hearts. . . . When the parsons had food, it was the same as we having it. They'd give it away. Now they've all left. We Miskitu were unified with them and they never did anything wrong. Those were good days."

The deep respect for the white parsons extends even to endorsing a Christian version of Miskitu history. When asked how the Miskitu lived before the Moravians arrived (in 1849), townspeople commonly begin with a self-deprecating joke, which underscores their chagrin at having been "heathens."[8]

Simon Gonzales even linked the missionaries' teachings to ethnic demands:

"The white parsons worked in the Moravian church. They taught us about our rights. If they had not, how would we know about them today? Miskitu rights was part of Christian education."

Gonzales is a man of 35 to 40 years who played an active role in the contemporary mobilization, alongside many committed Moravians. An interesting contrasting view of the Moravians' effects on ethnic militancy came from Peter Rodriguez, who was born around the turn of the century (see Fig. 1). When asked why, in the "old days," the Miskitu did not resist the "Spanish oppression" about which everyone complained, he responded:

"It was like this. When the parsons started preaching God's word, the Miskitu became timid. It was a sin to kill, they said; a sin to speak badly of others; a sin to be in arguments. So the Miskitu turned meek and helpless. Before, I heard, they were courageous. They'd grab a knife or a machete and fight their enemies to the death. Hearts of steel. But when God's word came, they minded its teachings. That's why they didn't resist the Spaniards."

Despite this critical insight, Peter Rodriguez followed his father Benito's example and served for years as village headman and Moravian lay parson. His nephew Samuel Peters is now the ordained minister, while two other nephews—Dan and Gerardo Peters—are central figures in the church (see Fig. 1). For at least three generations, the Rodriguez family has dominated both church and secular community leadership positions.

Although only elders can remember the heyday of company times, the younger generation has more recent memories of Americans. Like this woman, people spoke often of U.S.-funded and staffed health programs that directly affected Sandy Bay people's lives:

'[My husband] broke his leg in an accident while clearing the plantation. If it had not been for Alas de Socorro (an airborne ambulance service), he wouldn't be walking today. The American doctors were top-notch and they had good medicines. When people entered the hospital, they would be cured; they did not die in the hospital as they do today.'

Memories also include American bosses in the fishing industry and an American dredging company that received a contract in the mid-

1970's to construct an inland water route from Bluefields to Puerto Cabezas. As the dredge drew near to Sandy Bay, an enterprising young woman named Maria Stevens decided to take advantage of the newly arrived clientele:

"When I heard the dredge was coming I said [to my husband], 'Let's open a bar.' We bought cement and lumber. He went to Bluefields and brought back twenty cases of beer, fifteen cases of rum, juice, soft drinks, cigarettes, a whole lot of things. I had a record player and a Coleman lamp. I also placed a bed in a room apart that the Americans would use with women from right here. They'd drink rum day and night when the Americans weren't working. Creole and Cayman Islanders would come too. Anybody could use the room, as long as they paid. Sometimes they went in for a couple of minutes and left."

When asked if the parson didn't get angry, she replied:

"What could he say? I wasn't a Christian. The Americans gave the women money, which kept them very happy. One of the Americans carried Mauro Salazar's daughter with him when he left. Cristina was supposed to go too, but the man she was seeing had a wife. He was just having a good time with her. Eleven people in town sold liquor from their homes, but only I had a real bar, complete with the bedroom. I had four tables, chairs, and good dance music. People would party all night, and I made a pile of money. When the Sandinistas were about to win, the Americans left. At that time, I was pregnant. My husband continued to run the bar, and I sold goods from my house. But then I began to hear that he was using the bedroom with the women! When that happened I got mad, fought with him, and finally closed the bar. Done."

Stevens did not tell me the cantina story until I had gotten to know her well. The first week of my arrival in the community, however, I heard numerous accounts of Salazar's daughter (now living in Costa Rica with her American husband) and the (by everyone's account) less fortunate woman, who still lived in the community, with a five-year-old, blond-haired son.

Somoza and the Miskitu "Ethnic Awakening"

Because Salazar leaves no room for doubt that the Americans placed Somoza in power, it is striking that complaints about the ensuing 45 years of dictatorship do not include condemnation of the Americans as well. Manuel Rodriguez:

"In Somoza days he just promise, fool the people them, bring everyone here to Bluefields [for elections] and make whole pile of fiesta, and pay money like that. . . . Old Somoza, Luis Somoza used to come to the Bar, Karawala, Sandy Bay, he himself come there and promise we whole pile of thing. He say don't worry you all will get a nice school and nice clinic and all kind of thing. When he get Managua he forget us. . . . Somoza build the interior—Managua, Leon, them place—put all kind of school like that but our area . . . no do nothing."

When I pursued this anomaly further, people generally elaborated in one of two ways. First, they blamed Somoza for alleged exploitation by the Americans. David Lora:

"Somoza was to blame. He [told the Americans]: 'the wages you pay the Miskitu are too high.' So they started paying less. Somoza after all, was a Spaniard."

Second, though virtually no one praised Somoza, many expressed nostalgia for the economic conditions of Somoza days. Gerardo Peters was the community shopkeeper:

'In Somoza times, the Chinese men had shops in Bluefields. All you had to do was send a slip of paper, stating what you wanted. They would load the groceries on the next boat and collect the bill later. Back then, everything was cheaper.'

This latter sentiment led many to an ambivalent stance toward the past. Salazar:

"Somoza's crowd oppressed us, just the same, but it was a little better then, because things were cheaper. Chamorro time, cloth was a shilling a yard, flour six cents a pound, everything cheaper . . . Miskitu didn't have it so hard, you see?"

Another man summarized these recollections with the appropriately ambivalent phrase, "We were exploited back then, but we didn't feel it [*wan taiban kuna pil munras*]."

"Somoza times" also was when Miskitu began to develop a deepened awareness of their rights. People often associate the roots of this process with Miskitu efforts to secure rights to community lands. They all place special emphasis on a document (*wauhkataya*) or map (*mapka*), issued by the British to each Miskitu community, which guaranteed community land rights. The event to which Simon Gonzales referred occurred about 1915:

"The English king said to the Miskitu king: 'You know what? We'll take over your land. I'll give you money, or anything you want for it.' The Miskitu king said no. He wanted nothing other than the land and a formal title to back up his claim. This title, the king said, would be a source of strength for his people. When England heard this, she agreed, handing over the title with signature and all. Each community received one."

Sandy Bay Sirpi received a joint title, which included the neighboring communities of Insinkita (later abandoned), Walpa, and Río Grande Bar. The adjacent predominantly Sumu community of Karawala received a separate title.[9]

During the same period when land titles were granted, the Nicaraguan government established the position of *síndico*. Formally a government appointee, the síndico was a community member who acted as a liaison to the government for community affairs. The síndico rapidly became the highest political authority in the community, assuming grave responsibilities as guardian of the "document" and overseer of community lands. Manuel Rodriguez is the current síndico:

"Well the síndico is a man, no getting no salary from nobody. Síndico is he one that responsible for all the community riches. Any company come to the government and tell him, well we want to do some work in Sandy Bay, government can't accept it. Government have to tell them: 'You go to such and such a community and talk to the síndico there. There is private land and you have to see that man.' And the síndico will accept you and the síndico have to call everybody, and make them understand good, this company is coming for do this work, and síndico is the one to give the company a good understanding not to destroy the tree them, any time you cut a tree you have to plant it back and like that. Benito Rodriguez [the first síndico] was a tricky old man. No trust to no one and him hardly fool around with the government. Any time he have business to come [Bluefields], my old man no get money from the government. He collect eggs and fowl and come here and see the [British] consul and talk to them and go right back home."

Everyone assigns solemn importance to this mandate of protecting community lands. Rodriguez has a collection of tattered documents, including some with the British seal, which have passed through the hands of successive síndicos since 1915.[10] He laboriously rereads and brandishes them at crucial points in community meetings to give his message additional clout. Beyond their significance for present-day community land rights, these documents conjure up images of a time when the Miskitu king ruled the Coast and stood on equal footing with his British ally and counterpart.

Despite these continuities, people tend to emphasize a major turning point in their political consciousness, which occurred in the final years of the Somoza regime. Samuel Blandón, a schoolteacher, active church member, and up-and-coming Sandy Bay leader put it this way:

'In Somoza times, Miskitu were oppressed, on the bottom. If you were in a public place, you couldn't even speak Miskitu. You were ashamed. Creoles were definitely above us. Little by little Miskitu from the north, especially Waspam and Puerto Cabezas, began to get educated. They formed ALPROMISU, which studied and taught people about Miskitu rights.'[11]

Simon Gonzales elaborated:

"This is how ALPROMISU came about: they say a pregnant woman from the Río Coco was about to give birth, and she went to the city government [in Puerto

Cabezas] to ask for help. They refused her roughly: 'Go have your baby out on the street.' A Miskitu parson from the Río Coco grew upset when he heard what happened. 'We Indians are so poor,' he said, 'and those people won't help us. We need to start defending our own rights.' And the parson went to England, to the States, all the big places to seek help. Everyone agreed that the Miskitu demands were just. So they decided to create an organization that would teach people and get them to work together. Once unified, they would confront the government. Some of us might die fighting for our rights, they said, but some will survive and continue the struggle."

Sandy Bay people can remember the meetings to select delegates, who at least once made the three-day trip by foot to the north to attend an annual congress of the ALliance for PRogress of MIskitu and SUmu (ALPROMISU). The principal significance of ALPROMISU, however, is not the organization's tangible achievements in the community (none are mentioned). Rather, ALPROMISU represents the contemporary origins of Miskitu efforts to achieve their rights. The crucial catalyst for this movement, by all accounts, was education. Elements of oral history contributed by elders may offer important corroboration, but young, educated Miskitu are invariably credited with bringing the full scope of Miskitu rights to the attention of the rest.

This group, of which the most prominent members were Brooklyn Rivera and Steadman Fagoth, are said to have struck an early deal with the Sandinistas. According to Gonzales:

"Then Steadman and Brooklyn decided to join the Sandinistas, hoping to advance the struggle for Miskitu rights. The Sandinistas said: 'You support us and when we win, you'll have your territory.' We [Miskitu] agreed and gave the Sandinistas our backing. Many Miskitu combatants lent a hand."

The Revolution's First Eighteen Months

Manuel Rodriguez and many others claimed that they welcomed the Sandinista triumph enthusiastically:

"We all was hearing when Sandinista was fighting say Sandinista government is good government when take over going to be better than Somoza in everything. . . . And Manuel bring all me people them to Bluefields, women and man and young boys all the central here . . . happy because we all free from Somoza hand."

But there is no consensus regarding this early period. Rodriguez is among those who gave the Sandinista government ample credit for its initial performance:

"The [Sandinista] government first . . . walk and see all the place them and put in medicine, doctors, and help him in the food line. And everything was good.

And start . . . to tell the people them, OK who want the piknini [children] to come and get school in Bluefields, everything is open and no problem, and right away put bank in Karawala, the community them don't have to come here to Bluefields [to get loans]. So the people them happy."

For others such as David Lora, bitterness permeates even those first memories. Why was everyone happy when the Sandinistas won? Lora said they were:

"Damn fools. At first, I was jumping for joy. The Sandinistas said gold coins would circulate again. Somoza said, 'Communism's on the way.' In a couple of days, the lies began. 'We'll build you a new house, give you everything. . . .' Empty promises. Every day, every time you look up, a meeting. I say that's bad. Only Communists hold so many meetings."

Regardless of how people construed the government's early economic initiatives, experiences with political organization in their communities are much more prominent in their memories. The Sandinistas acted first. Soon after July 19, a Miskitu man in military garb arrived in Sandy Bay to organize a Sandinista Defense Committee (CDS). The community held an election and named about ten CDS leaders. Conspicuously absent from the group was Manuel Rodriguez, who had served as síndico for the last fifteen years. David Lora explained why:

"The townspeople didn't want Manuel because he lived too much like Somoza. He ate and drank the money that belonged to the community. When the revolution won, the Sandinistas didn't take him out, we did. We put in Fredie [Rodriguez], but he was the same. So we elected the CDS crowd. All this time, Manuel Rodriguez remained as síndico. Then, at the big Bluefields meeting, Steadman and Brooklyn named him as MISURASATA leader. We had nothing to do with it."

Rodriguez and his supporters had a more benign explanation: he needed a rest and stepped aside to let younger leaders gain experience. They hastened to add that, luckily, Rodriguez did not turn over the coveted community land documents.

The FSLN organized popular militias in communities throughout the region. Late in 1979 all militia volunteers were summoned to Bluefields for a two-week training course. About eighteen young men from Sandy Bay attended. Conrad Kelly, who served as *jefe de pelatón*, described the experience: [12]

'Our pelatón came out the best in everything . . . the training was hard—running, exercising, how to shoot gun, and they never feed us good. They only teach us who is Sandino mother, where he born, and that we must fight against the imperialist Yankee. We got ignorant and made a strike, our whole pelatón. The trainer, a man from Managua, took us to Bluefields for three days. Then a boat carried us home.'

No one spoke of lasting consequences of this conflict. Both the militia and the CDS continued to function in Sandy Bay; the latter promoted collective work for community benefit and acted as liaison to government representatives visiting from Bluefields. People's accounts indicated that neither organization generated much excitement or made noteworthy achievements.

The Indian organization MISURASATA, by contrast, took the Miskitu communities by storm. Under disputed circumstances, Manuel Rodriguez became the MISURASATA representative for Sandy Bay and attended the organization's founding congress in Puerto Cabezas in the last days of October 1979. His most salient memory of the event concerned the name:

"The first was not MISURASATA but MISURA. But the government called a big meeting to Puerto Cabezas. I was there in the meeting. The government want to put the SATA. That mean to say, Miskitu, Sumu, Rama, and Sandinistas. So when we have the meeting, plenty of them no want to put the SATA, but well the old parson them, Mullens, all of them was there and well say that the Indian them, when the Yankees them want to kill Sandino, looking all about, want to catch him, the Indians them help Sandino hiding out on the Coast. So we all have right, we all the same Indians, we all have right to be brothers with Sandino, so right there put the SATA."

Why did people not want the "SATA"?

"Because some people figuring well if the government and Indian—Miskitu, Sumu, Rama—and Sandino going be brother, maybe the government going humbug we up in our property, so no want to be too brother with the Sandinista government. [But] when we get to a *historia*, Indians them is the one saving Sandino so now this same Indians, we all have right to be brother. Then MISURASATA put me as leader for the Sandy Bay district."

Soon after this founding meeting, MISURASATA held a regional inauguration in Bluefields. About 30 people made the trip from Sandy Bay; the community selected a few as delegates, and the rest went along out of curiosity. According to one from the latter group, the high point of the visit was a march through the streets of Bluefields, during which participants raised the Miskitu *plakin* (emblem of the Mosquito Reserve government). Apart from some delegates' complaints that Manuel Rodriguez usurped their authority, memories of the inauguration were exuberant. This was the birth of their organization.

MISURASATA immediately carried out activities that made a great impact on community members. Manuel Rodriguez:

"Well MISURASATA come and put a law, we all from now on . . . we all going be brother. Not like first time, anybody have thing you all have to sell it, no. Suppose I bring my breadkind, maybe one dory load. Hand to everybody one, one; maybe you kill turtle, you don't have to sell, you have to give piece. Everybody eat well. No one beg. And MISURASATA put next law out tell me anybody building house, I must call a meeting and cut stick cut leaf and everything. All the community going to do that work and maybe that brother have house quick."

Samuel Blandón:

'MISURASATA leaders arrived to give seminars on autonomy. They explained that the economy line would be in Indian hands. The autonomous government would then pay 20 percent to Managua and keep 80 percent for the Coast.'

MISURASATA also promoted Miskitu cultural revival. To celebrate its first anniversary, regional leaders sponsored a *pulanka tara* (celebration) in Sandy Bay, ending with a dance in Manuel Rodriguez's newly completed house. A young man remembered:

'The old people, like Miss Doris and *kuka* [grandmother, title of respect for elder women] Melina, led a dance around the community. Everyone joined in and marched around the town. They wore clothing made out of leaves and bark and drank out of gourds. The elders showed everyone else the old-time Miskitu traditions. There was food and drink galore.'

A year of intense activity and organizing culminated with the persistent question of Miskitu land rights, which also figured prominently in all versions of the narrative, as, for example, that of Simon Gonzales:

"Steadman and the others were waiting for the government to fulfill its promise. The government told them: 'If you know where your land is, give us the measurements.' Since we have no professional surveyor, Steadman asked a Salvadorean named Mauricio Polanco to help. After much work, they established the boundaries: from Santo Tomás, to Yakal Pahani, near the mines. From San Juan to Cape Gracias, on the border with Honduras. Just as they finished, the surveyor drowned. We all contributed to his memorial fund. But his mother said she wanted no money. She only wanted the Indians to have their freedom."

In the course of the survey MISURASATA leaders asked the síndico of each community to part with the communal land title so as to present a more effective claim to the government. MISURASATA also collected money from each community to defray the expenses of the land survey. Esteban Blandón remembered that everyone in Sandy Bay contributed and that from communities throughout the coast they raised a total of 185,000 cordobas.[13] (For a depiction of territorial demands that emerged from this process, see Map 2.)

The flurry of activity regarding Indian land rights (August 1980–February 1981) coincided with a massive mobilization of Indian youth *brigadistas* (volunteer teachers) for the literacy campaign in the languages of Coast peoples. The Miskitu language campaign began in October, co-ordinated jointly by MISURASATA and the government. An adult community member who lived up the Río Grande at the time reported:

"MISURASATA sent teachers from the Río Coco; it was really wonderful. Our bri-gadista was named Pablo. He taught us about how things were first time; we had no idea before. He taught us that Indians have many rights, our own territory, the right to self-government and to live in harmony with one another. At the same time, they sent people to measure our land."

Another adult student of the literacy campaign understood that it oc-curred just before the "revolution" began:

'When the revolution was near, Miskitu youth came and held classes in each community for us older people. They taught in Miskitu, in a real Indian language. They also taught us Miskitu history, about the Miskitu king. Back then, we learned, people lived in harmony, shared everything with each other. We also learned about our land rights.'

Although most of the brigadistas were high school students (or gradu-ates) from the north, four women and eleven men from Sandy Bay also taught. The Sandy Bay brigadistas, who were assigned to small upriver settlements along the banks of the Río Grande, remembered the cam-paign as hard work under adverse conditions, but this only deepened their pride in its achievements.

I sensed the collective excitement of this period only through brief ex-cerpts in accounts burdened by all that followed. "Troubles began," people repeatedly explained, with the events of Prinzapolka (February 1981), a community located about 30 miles north of Sandy Bay. Thomas Bowman:

"When the teaching was about to end, people were gathered in the church at Prinzapolka. The Sandinistas arrived from Alamikangban, with Comandante 'Tigre' in charge. They surrounded the church, went inside, and began to shoot, killing three Miskitu. Then the crowd grabbed the arms and fought back. The women fought the hardest—Maralena, Anisela, Loina. They killed five Sandinis-tas, but a few got away."

Magarita Rodriguez, a brigadista, explained what happened when news of the Prinzapolka melee reached her and the other Sandy Bay brigadistas:

'At the end of the campaign, the *Express* [a transport boat] was to carry all of us to Bluefields for a big celebration. Then we heard about the problems, that the

Spaniards lied and tricked us [*kunin wan munan*]. We went to the bush, punishing, trying to move our people [*nisan*] ahead, and they responded by cutting us off. The [Miskitu] boys from Puerto Cabezas became furious, vowing to fight the Sandinistas to the death. Everyone from Sandy Bay just went home. No awards or prizes as [the government had] promised. Back in the community, people started getting scared. We burned or buried all papers written in Miskitu. There was a rumor that the Sandinistas were going to arrest everyone who was connected with the literacy campaign.'

In some versions of how the conflict began, the narrator attributed no rational motive to the Sandinistas' actions. A former MISURASATA combatant noted:

'At first we were overjoyed with the Sandinistas. Then everything changed: they started to catch guys and beat them up. They put all our leaders in jail, and wanted to kill us off, catch us and kill us. And we were civilians taking this abuse.'

When asked why the change occurred, he said:

'The Miskitu had made a map, and the Sandinistas had agreed to it. But when the time came they backed down. I don't know why they changed. They decided to kill off the Miskitu. If we hadn't fought back we'd all be dead today.'

Simon Gonzales offered more analysis:

"Then the Sandinistas came to sign the land document. But when they saw the measurements they were shocked: 'In the Pacific we don't have anything, just a little cotton and coffee.' All the riches are on the Coast, you know, gold, lobster, oil. The Sandinistas changed their minds because they didn't want to give up these riches."

A Final Commentary

Mauro Salazar had very little to say about the eighteen months after July 1979. In contrast to his remarkably detailed memories of the 1920's and 1930's, his commentary on the postrevolutionary period filled only a single transcribed paragraph. Although this contrast could be an artifact of my own questions, I attribute it primarily to Salazar's life stage. I never saw him anywhere but his house (usually sitting in a rocking chair on the front veranda) or at church, 50 yards away. He could not have followed MISURASATA's mobilization as closely as those who had played an active role. For that reason, perhaps, Salazar's commentary eschewed details and summed up with particular eloquence a unifying theme in descriptions of Miskitu decisions to fight: deep pride in their resolve to stand up to abuse by "Spaniards," against great odds:

"The Miskitu went into the bush empty-handed, armed only with kitchen knives. They said, 'We have no guns, but God is on our side in the struggle for our land.'

They went in and have not come out to this day. They could be hungry, thirsty, shoeless, and we wouldn't know. We send them help secretly, behind the government's back. When they went in the Spaniards said: 'Armed with kitchen knives, you Miskitu are idiots. You know nothing about fighting a war. Poor things. We'll catch you and kill you all.' The Miskitu responded, 'No problem.' Secretly, they trained in the bush. They learned. With a few old rifles they killed some of these people and recovered some guns. They kept fighting and kept winning. The Americans saw this. 'The Miskitu are doing pretty well,' they said, 'if we contribute, maybe we'll get something back.' So they began to work together."

Defining the Antinomy: Ethnic Militancy and Anglo Affinity

The first theme that stands out in this narrative is the consistent expression of what I call ethnic militancy. Complex and multifaceted, ethnic militancy cannot be defined as a discrete variable or attribute. It is a central part of people's political worldview, fed by memories of past oppression, present perceptions of inequality, and unrealized aspirations. Drawing on material from collective memories expressed in open-ended discussions and structured interviews with 27 community members,[14] I have identified four principal demands that stem from the ethnic militancy of Sandy Bay Miskitu. Each demand is militant, I contend, because it contradicts a basic element of central government authority. First, the Miskitu have rights to an immense portion of eastern Nicaragua, covering as much as one-third of the national territory. Second, natural resources inside this territory belong to the Miskitu, who would manage their use and turn over part of the proceeds from exploitation to the central government. Third, the territory would be governed principally by Miskitu leaders, with minimal involvement of the central government. Fourth, Miskitu cultural practices would prevail within the territory, defining the norms by which non-Miskitu inhabitants must abide.

Simon Gonzales expressed these four elements succinctly:

"In old times the Miskitu had a king, and much more. . . . The Miskitu are a nation with rights, a people that deserves respect. The government should grant us our lands, and inside that territory, Indians should rule. Spaniards can live here, but Miskitu must be the boss. We've become friends with Spaniards who have lived here for a long time. They have developed Miskitu ways. But if the Spaniards started to act badly, we'd run them off our land. . . . There are all kinds of riches on the Coast, you know. We have gold, lobster, oil, you name it. Most of [Nicaragua's] riches are here, and they belong to us. If people come from overseas and sign a contract for so many years, they can work here, no problem. Of the earnings from that work, part would go to the government and part to us. With our part, we would help the poor people, build schools and churches."

As Gonzales made clear, ethnic militancy expresses a deep defiance of Spanish-speaking Nicaraguans ("Spaniards") from the Pacific Coast or western side of the country. Interview respondents unanimously asserted that "Spaniards" were degrading (*wan kulkras*) and disrespectful (*rispit munras*)—in a word, racist—toward Miskitu during Somoza times: [15]

'In Somoza days, the Spaniards would cuss at us, call us *mosco* [fly in Spanish, taken as a great insult] or Waspuk [a river located deep inside what is considered the uncivilized jungle]. . . . Spaniards have always wanted to run us off our land, that's why they are belligerent [*praud*] toward us.'

When accounting for Miskitu poverty, narrators made "Spaniards" out as the chief culprits:

'The Spaniards got our ancestors drunk and tricked them into signing away all our land. From that time on, Spaniards have ruled (*bas munan*) the Miskitu and kept us poor.'

Analysts often cite such evidence to demonstrate that the Miskitu had acquired an intense ethnic consciousness to the exclusion of a class consciousness. This purportedly helps to explain the ensuing conflict with the revolution, which promoted a class-based program for political change (e.g., Vilas 1989: 82). For reasons laid out in the theoretical discussion of Chapter 1, I have tried to move away from this class/ethnic dichotomy. Implicit in the dichotomy is the idea that Miskitu are hapless victims of ideological domination, which keeps them from seeing the "real" nature of their oppression and the "correct" basis for political action. In contrast, without abandoning the notion of hegemony, I place fundamental importance on Miskitu people's active creation of a political worldview that embodies extensive knowledge of their life conditions. Consider this response to my question about the "Spaniards":

'Spaniards see us as blubbering idiots [*babusu nani*], and they want us to remain as wage laborers. They always give us the worst jobs. One time, I was working in the sugar mill [at Kukra Hill], and a better job became available. The boss man gave it to another Spaniard. I got angry. "We Miskitu are humans too [*yawan sin upla sa*]," I told him. He responded by firing me. Spaniards only want to help their countrymen.'

Although the response clearly highlights ethnic oppression, it is not accurate or analytically useful to claim that the speaker lacked an awareness of class oppression.

I contend that the ethnic militancy of the 1980's contained a perceptive critique of the dominant society, an eloquent series of insights into the structural and historical factors underlying Miskitu oppression. It entailed an understanding of the workings of the system and gave rise both to profound feelings of empowerment and an explosive inclination for collective action. Under Somoza, Sandy Bay Miskitu explained, "we were blind, like children," and ignorant of "our rights." Then, in the mid-1970's, a group of young Miskitu leaders acquired education, discovered Miskitu rights, and formed an organization. These leaders "opened our eyes, taught us about our history." Such claims, laced throughout the Miskitu narrative, are indications of a deep historical self-confidence that arose with the mobilization itself. The Miskitu exerted control over their destiny and struggled for rights they learned were theirs, guided by new-found knowledge of their history.

A second pervasive theme in their narrative, closely entwined with ethnic militancy, is a frankly approving stance toward the Anglo-American world. This stance is associated with a collection of values, which I refer to as Anglo affinity. The term requires careful definition. It is not a set of ideas—much less an ideology—that has been imposed on Miskitu people against their will or "better interests." Nor do I view it as an immutable part of Miskitu culture.[16] Anglo affinity is part of the cultural form that Miskitu people themselves created through a complex historical process of resistance and accommodation in response to multiple axes of inequity. It consists of ideas, values, and notions of common sense that entail understandings of past and present life conditions, which correspond closely to understandings immanent in the discourse of North American institutions that have surrounded them. This correspondence occurs because, through sustained contact, Miskitu people came to accept some of those institutions' self-justifying premises as their own. That Americans were benevolent allies, that North American companies brought unmitigated benefits, that the "Spaniards," not the Americans, are responsible for Miskitu people's poverty, that white people are superior in phenotype and intelligence, are all examples of such ideas expressed in the narrative.[17] The point is not to suggest that these ideas have no basis in history, that they are somehow "false"—to the contrary, they are grounded in Miskitu people's daily experiences and are undeniably real. They form part of the conventional wisdom, the unspoken and at times explicit premises, of the dominant institutions that Miskitu people accommodated and even embraced.

Although the persistence of Anglo affinity in 1985–87 does serve to corroborate my historical argument in Chapter 2, its primary significance lies in its relationship to the post-1979 mobilization. From the late nineteenth century until 1979, North American companies operated extensively, during successive "boom" periods, on Nicaragua's Atlantic Coast. They exploited natural wealth (rubber, minerals, lumber, marine resources), often until resource depletion rendered the operation unprofitable, and established enormous enclaves of banana plantations. Nearly all these activities took place inside the boundaries of what, according to people's current demands, are now considered ancestral Miskitu lands. Regardless of Miskitu perceptions at the time, one might expect the militant assertion of land and resource rights to include a critique of historic North American presence. When asked, "What did Americans think about Miskitu rights in Somoza times," 26 Sandy Bay Miskitu gave responses that I grouped into three categories. The list below contains one typical response from each category.

1. They knew about Indian rights, but they wanted to keep us down. The Americans were partners with Somoza, and that meant no benefits for us. Americans helped the Spaniards but didn't care about the Miskitu. They only told us lies. (N = 5; 19 percent)
2. The Americans cannot be blamed. Somoza ordered them not to pay us good wages. But still, the Americans treated us well, and back then, everyone had a payday. (N = 10; 37 percent)
3. There was lots of work. I worked a long time in mines with the Americans and I have no complaints. Pay was low but the goods we bought were cheap. The Miskitu are close [*baila*, often used in the context of kin relations] with the Americans. (N = 11; 41 percent)

Only a small minority indicted the companies directly, while the rest either blamed Somoza (or the "Spaniards") or simply denied American "exploitation" altogether.

My point is not to negate Miskitu perceptions of the substantial benefits they accrued from the presence of American companies. Their examples of such benefits included acquiring new skills (e.g., as a sawyer, mechanic, truck driver), a sense of economic security from a steady payday, and, most important, access to a range of highly valued consumer goods. One woman respondent, after answering this question, justified her positive appraisal:

'Americans did carry away our gold . . . but I want to be able to buy Levi's jeans and perfume, like we could when they were here. When I worked at the Bluff [as a barmaid], American ships would come in with goods to sell. [In those times] I had all kinds of nice things.'

Others referred to what might be considered more practical items—work implements, clothing, foodstuffs. These perceived benefits need not be derided as "false consciousness" for one to note that Miskitu tend not fully to confront (much less criticize) the broad impact and implications of U.S. presence on the Atlantic Coast.

This reluctance is equally evident in responses to a second question: "If the Miskitu gained control of their territory, should the American companies be invited back, just like before?" I grouped the 25 responses into three categories:

1. No, we could never invite them back. The Americans were allied with Somoza and with the FDN [Nicaraguan Democratic Forces, or contras]. The Americans are opposed to Miskitu rights. (N = 3; 11 percent)
2. We are like children and don't have the materials to work with. Only the Americans can do this. But they wouldn't be allowed in like before. In those days, the government in Managua made the agreement and they got all the benefits. [Now it would be according to Miskitu laws.] (N = 7; 26 percent)
3. Yes, we'll invite them back. . . . The Miskitu have all kinds of riches, but we are poor; Americans would help us exploit the riches and get their share of the benefits. [In Somoza times] it was American know-how that brought development (*pawanka*) to this land. (N = 15; 56 percent)

The data from these interviews and from the narrative lead to the conclusion that most Sandy Bay Miskitu have not critically examined the North American role in the system that (by their own account) oppressed them. Instead, they express Anglo affinity, which characterizes Americans as benevolent senior partners (at times even implying fictive kin ties)[18] with interests that unify the two against a common adversary, the "Spanish."

For most Sandy Bay Miskitu, these two facets of their political worldview—Anglo affinity and ethnic militancy—coexisted with no apparent tension. Consider, for example, responses to a third question, which focuses more directly on the link between these two: "What do Americans think about Miskitu rights today?"

1. The Americans are opportunists. They would never respect our rights, and we know it. The Americans are just after our riches. (N = 4; 15 percent)
2. They are helping us, but it's not charity. We are going into debt right now with the Americans. Later they are going to come in, work, and with the proceeds from that work we will pay back our debt. (N = 4; 15 percent)
3. Now they understand about Miskitu rights, and that's why they are helping us. The Americans are training our young men who left to fight, giving them intelligence [*sins laka*]. (N = 15; 56 percent)

Taking these three questions together, a clear pattern emerges: a small number of respondents were adamant dissenters from the dominant premises of Anglo affinity, a slightly larger group endorsed moderated versions of these premises, and the rest endorsed them strongly. Given that everyone also expressed a strong or moderate degree of ethnic militancy, we can conclude that the great majority espoused both elements.

Conclusions

There are limitations in presenting the data as a composite historical narrative and aggregated responses to structured interviews. In the inherently murky and imprecise task of interpreting the relationship between the consciousness of a group of people and their collective actions, knowing the context is paramount. What have emerged here as key elements of Sandy Bay people's worldview could take on diverse meanings and inflections depending on the context in which they were uttered and could conceivably motivate a variety of collective actions. Ideally, then, we would want ethnographic data to show how people were thinking while they were acting, thereby challenging rather than reinforcing the dichotomy between thought and action.

Political realities of the Atlantic Coast in the 1980's made the achievement of that ideal nearly impossible. I set out to examine a period in recent Miskitu history—around mid-1981 to mid-1984—when no one, community member or outsider, could safely have asked the questions that elicited the responses recorded above. In this respect, then, the narrative and interview data serve as a proxy, slightly removed but nevertheless useful, for people's reckoning as they joined the antigovernment mobilization.[19] Moreover, even if we did not face this problem of temporal lapse, the framework laid out in Chapter 1 would dictate methods roughly along the lines of those used here. That is, if the notion of contradictory consciousness has analytical value, it must refer to attributes that can be identified empirically. It must be possible, through conversations with members of a given group, to elicit the ideas and values that purportedly reflect the impact of hegemony. This step has limited value in isolation because it tells us nothing about how those ideas came to form part of a given culture or how they relate to people's ongoing daily practice. Combined with previous and subsequent steps that address those concerns, however, a textually rich window on people's consciousness at one point in time provides great analytical insight. This assertion will be borne out in Chapters 5 through 7, which draw on the data offered here to fashion comprehensive explanations for three distinct phases of Miskitu collective action.

4 Miskitu Indians in the Discourse of Revolutionary Nationalism

The myth of Sisyphus is incarnate in Nicaragua. This peculiar combination of geography, history, space and time makes up the stone out of which we seem to have been hewn. . . . Perhaps that's where our tenacity comes from, this almost innate obstinacy to follow the same path as many times as necessary, to come into our own as a people, as a nation, fully and authentically, without the chains of poverty, without foreign domination, and less vulnerable in the face of natural disasters
—Sofía Montenegro, *Barricada*, October 29, 1988, days after Hurricane Joan devastated the country

The ideological theme of national belonging may be malleable to some extent but . . . [there are limits on] the extent to which nationalism becomes socialist at the moment that its litany is repeated by socialists. The intention may be radical but the effects are unpredictable, particularly where culture is also conceived within discrete, separable, national units coterminous with the boundaries of the nation state.
—Paul Gilroy, *There Ain't No Black in the Union Jack*

FROM THE ASHES of Sandino's brutal assassination in 1934 came a legacy that would inspire an entire generation. The harsh inequities of Nicaraguan history guaranteed that their struggle would be cast in profoundly heroic and redemptive terms. Propelled by a surge of spontaneous popular protest against Somoza, Sandinista guerrilla leaders crystallized the insurrection in a series of stark dichotomies: brutal dictatorship versus popular democracy, bourgeois corruption and decadence versus moral regeneration, gross disparities between rich and poor versus economic justice, and, most important, humiliating subservience to U.S. imperialism versus national sovereignty and pride. The victory of the Sandinista Front for National Liberation would mean the dawning of a new era, the true birth of the Nicaraguan nation. A vast majority of Nicaraguans, from all walks of life, understood the revolution in these terms, and there was no question which side they were on. The triumph of July 19, 1979, brought euphoria and an outpouring of energy to imagine and build the new society.

Miskitu people of Sandy Bay felt very little of this euphoria, judging at least from how they later portrayed their reactions. They viewed the revolution as a distant battle, then allowed their skepticism to give way to cautious support, and soon felt their hopes turn to bitter disappointment. In the narrative of the previous chapter, people associated the revolution with an explosion of century-old smoldering resentments against the "Spaniards," violation of deeply held political demands and cultural values, and, later, experiences of repression that confirmed their worst fears. This jarring contrast provides the central motivation for the analysis that follows. Rather than dwell on the particulars of Miskitu people's critique, I address the broader questions that it raises. What did the Sandinista revolution, which captured the aspirations of so many, offer to the Indians of Nicaragua? Were there premises, embedded in the way leaders and cadres analyzed, talked about, imagined, and portrayed the revolution, both its history and future, that contributed to the conflict? If so, where did these premises come from and how integral were they to the revolutionary program?

Like the Miskitu narrative in the preceding chapter, the material presented here is not meant to constitute a full explanation of what Sandinista cadres, leaders, or institutions did. It is limited to what people said and wrote, what they thought they were doing (or wanted others to think), in an effort to examine the key premises that made up their consciousness. Although the rationale for this approach is the same as in the previous chapter, the presentations of Miskitu and Sandinista narratives are not completely parallel. Sandinista leaders have left numerous written sources, which permit analysis of their thinking at various points in time. I begin with a preautonomy composite account of Nicaraguan history, based on the work of four prominent Sandinista authors: Ernesto Cardenal, Jaime Wheelock, Humberto Ortega, and Omar Cabezas. For the period between 1979 and 1984 I examine published statements by Sandinista leaders as they observed, analyzed, and explained the failed alliance and deepening conflict with the Miskitu. To document the rise of autonomy, I draw on both official statements and the voices of local-level Sandinista cadres with whom I spoke in Sandy Bay. These latter voices help me to illustrate persisting disparities between base and leadership and to document how preautonomy premises retained currency at the local level long after official policy changed. Even at the national level, I conclude, the contradictions that plagued the original formulation of revolutionary nationalism proved too tenacious to be fully eliminated from the discourse of autonomy.

Subjugated but not Subjects: Formative Premises

Ernesto Cardenal, the priest and world-renowned poet, became a strong and active supporter of the FSLN in the late 1960's. Cardenal deeply admired pre-Columbian Indian civilizations for their religiosity, impressive achievements, and what he portrayed as their near-utopian forms of social organization. He published an anthology of poems by Native Americans and a collection of his own poetry, which passionately expresses this admiration. In addition, Cardenal's treatment of pre-Columbian civilizations is grounded in a strong belief that they offer a model for political change in the new Nicaragua:

> Their priests had no earthly power
> and their pyramids were built without forced labor
> The peak of their civilization did not lead to an empire
> And they had no colonies. They did not know the arrow.
> ("Lost Cities," Cardenal 1973 [1970]: 12)

Beginning in the mid-1970's, his efforts to promote the study, active recovery, and celebration of the Indian roots of Nicaraguan nationalism were readily incorporated into the FSLN leadership's cultural program. This Indian revivalism—present in Cardenal's poetry, in the "primitivist" art form that he helped to found, and in his more recent programmatic statements on the politics of culture—has the dual effect of evoking Nicaraguans' pride in their own history and encouraging the radical assertion of Nicaraguan sovereignty in the face of U.S. imperial domination.[1]

Although writing history rather than poetry, Jaime Wheelock's work is thematically similar to that of Cardenal. Wheelock begins his narrative with the Conquest in a study titled *Raices indígenas de la lucha anti-colonialista en Nicaragua* (Indigenous roots of anti-colonial struggle in Nicaragua). Trained as a political economist in Salvador Allende's Chile, Wheelock was already a leading Sandinista intellectual in 1974, when he completed the book. He later became a member of the FSLN National Directorate and served as minister of agriculture throughout the revolutionary era.

The stated objectives of his study are to challenge the racist portrayal of Indians in Nicaraguan historiography and to debunk the myth of harmonious *mestizaje*, whereby Mestizos emerged through peaceful "conciliation" between Indians and Spanish. He presents an impressive chronicle of continuous indigenous resistance and rebellion in response to Spanish domination, from the onset of colonialism through the struggle for independence. During this period, in Wheelock's account,

Indians clearly were agents of history: "They were many times defeated, even annihilated," he writes, "but they had a staggering capacity for recuperation. . . . They could not have fought with more heroism and sacrifice" (1974: 36). This generalization applies also to the Miskitu and other Atlantic Coast Indians, to whom he devotes a chapter of the book.

Wheelock then identifies a critical shift that occurred sometime in the mid-nineteenth century: "Now the Indians no longer fought simply for racial demands, nor did they assume the ideas of a colonized people or race. The independence [struggle] revealed their class enemies, and demonstrated the flaws of a consciousness based on the prejudices of tribalism, or of ethnic superiority. . . . Instead, it placed them side by side with other oppressed groups, and focused them squarely on the class struggle between exploiters and exploited" (p. 89). This transformation came about at times as a gradual process, "culminating in the Indians' complete conversion into smallholding peasants [*campesino de tipo minifundista*], with the consciousness of petty owners of property. From that point their struggle acquired a more forthright character, more economic and class-based, less ethnic and religious" (p. 89). In other cases the conversion was violent. In 1881, in a final desperate response to the loss of communal lands, 7,000 Matagalpan Indians rose up in rebellion against the coffee oligarchs. They were brutally defeated, Wheelock observes, "and this closed a cycle of contradictions in bitter synthesis. But as always occurs in history, a new process opened. The destruction of communal property separated Indians from their lands, and thrust them into the wage labor market as agricultural workers. This gave rise to a new historical subject, more capable of destroying the system of oligarchic exploitation at its foundations" (pp. 116–17). This shift from Indian to "popular class" as historical subject is the key to Wheelock's concluding assertion of continuity, from the first act of resistance to Spanish colonizers, to contemporary political struggles. Indians no longer exist as a distinct social group (except on the Atlantic Coast), but the legacy of their struggles forms part of an enriched Mestizo national identity.[2] Class, ethnic, and national consciousness become fused into one.

Two years after *Raíces indígenas* was published, Humberto Ortega Savedra completed *50 años de lucha sandinista* (50 years of Sandinista struggle), which begins where Wheelock left off. Minister of Defense and member of the FSLN National Directorate during the Sandinista era, Ortega was a principal strategist of the FSLN-led military victory against Somoza. His study begins with a detailed account of the guerrilla war led by Augusto César Sandino (1926–33) and then examines the subsequent 44 years of popular struggle (1933–76) against the Somoza dictatorship.

Three principal themes unify Ortega's analysis. First, he places great importance on Sandino's legacy for the contemporary revolutionary movement. This includes lessons from Sandino's sophisticated military strategy, his strong ties with the peasantry, and, most important, the dual commitment to nationalism and anti-imperialism in his political thought. Second, Ortega makes these last two principles inextricable from the process of class struggle: "Anti-imperialism . . . has become deeply rooted in the Nicaraguan popular consciousness. The oppressed classes' struggle for liberation is at the same time an anti-imperialist struggle, and a struggle to recover our national sovereignty, which the Somoza tyranny has dismembered and sold off" (1979 [1976]: 9). Finally, he emphasizes the FSLN's central role as the vanguard of the national liberation struggle. Although during the 1960's spontaneous popular protest outstripped the FSLN's leadership, by the 1970's the relationship had regained equilibrium: "With the advance in the FSLN's leadership capacity, spontaneous protest persists, but now is being channeled through political organizations that the vanguard clandestinely directs" (p. 114). "The people have integrated themselves with the political program and strategies of the FSLN, which is the only viable means to successfully overthrow the tyranny" (p. 10).

In addition to writings focused specifically on the Atlantic Coast, the FSLN confronted an aspect of the "Indian question" in relation to the small pockets of persisting Indian identity in western Nicaragua. Monimbó and Subtiava are widely known as "Indian barrios," with traditions and identities separate from the cities of Masaya and Leon, of which they respectively form part. Omar Cabezas, a prominent FSLN comandante, has published an autobiographical account of his participation in the FSLN, which includes descriptions of his work among the Subtiavan Indians. He writes:

Our work in Subtiava took off like wildfire, but very quietly and out of the light. . . . We started presenting the image of Sandino in Subtiava. The Indians had a leader, a historical figure, who more than any other was representative of their people: Adiac. We presented Sandino as an incarnation of Adiac, then Adiac as an incarnation of Sandino, but Sandino in the light of the Communist Manifesto, see? So from shack to shack, from Indian to Indian, ideas were circulating: Adiac . . . Sandino . . . class struggle . . . vanguard . . . FSLN. Gradually a whole movement was born in Subtiava. (1985: 37)

We had discovered the Indian origins of the Subtiavans and encouraged these as a strength; we tried to transpose the old ancestral struggles of Adiac, their ancient chief. And to remind them how they'd been dispossessed, humiliated. How both Liberals and Conservatives had bullied them and ripped off their lands. How Sandino had rebelled, just as Adiac had rebelled. And then there was the question of the bourgeois classes having all the power. (p. 40)

*   *   *

From the early 1960's, when the FSLN began to formulate its program and to devise a political strategy, until the introduction of autonomy, Indians occupied an ambiguous and marginal position in revolutionary theory. To an extent, this simply reflected demographic, political, and geographic realities. The vast majority of Nicaraguans were Mestizos with no distinct Indian identity, and the FSLN had little to gain by extending the revolutionary struggle to the Atlantic Coast region where most Indians resided. It therefore followed that the FSLN leadership would not conceive of the "revolutionary subject" as including Indians, organized to achieve specifically Indian demands. Because the FSLN did not work among the Miskitu, its analysis of the Miskitu question drew on information and images shaped under long-standing conditions of inequity between the Atlantic Coast region and Mestizo elites. It therefore is not surprising that the FSLN espoused assimilationist premises, even while seeking to advance revolutionary ends and condemning the "hateful discrimination" against Atlantic Coast ethnic groups. In this line of reasoning, Miskitu people's "passivity" resulted from their "cultural backwardness" and would be overcome when they joined the (revolutionary) Nicaraguan national community. These premises are present in all four of the works discussed here.

Consider first Cardenal's eulogies of pre-Columbian civilizations and the assertion that their values could form the basis for a new Nicaraguan nationalism.[3] This cultural revivalism cannot be equated with state-sponsored *indigenismo* in Latin America because it is designed in conjunction with a program of wide-reaching social and economic reforms in a country where over 90 percent of the population is Mestizo.[4] Yet Cardenal sent an ambiguous message to the Miskitu and other minority peoples. While recognizing the Miskitu contribution to Nicaragua's cultural diversity, he stopped decidedly short of fully recognizing "Miskituness" as a political identity distinct from that of Nicaraguan Mestizos. The thrust of his message, rather, was to erase this distinction altogether. To be Nicaraguan Mestizo now meant having Indian roots, celebrating survivals from this Indian past, and actively making use of them to construct a revolutionary future. For Mestizos it was a creative and liberating idea. For those who had shaped their identity in direct opposition to Mestizos, it entailed a call to assimilation and conformity.[5]

Wheelock's historical analysis of Indians' resistance to colonialism contains a more explicit version of this problem. In his view, Indians were subjects of history in Nicaragua only until the late nineteenth century, when the combined forces of capitalist economic development and cultural domination eliminated them as a distinct group. From this point on, Mestizo peasants and workers carried on the struggle; they were empowered by the legacy of their ancestors' resistance, but their newfound class consciousness made them more capable of achieving revolutionary goals. Wheelock's analysis therefore creates a compelling sense of historical continuity, from an Indian past to a popular-class Mestizo present and future. Contemporary Indians stand outside this narrative because, although suffering the same structural oppression as Mestizo peasants, they have lost their capacity to be historical subjects. Implicitly, Wheelock and Cardenal offer the same solution: Indianness is a cultural attribute, surviving from a more illustrious past, while political identity corresponds to class and nation. Miskitu could only become revolutionary subjects by sharing in Mestizo-defined nationalism and class-consciousness.

The significance of Ortega's study to my argument lies in the complete absence of reference to Miskitu Indians. Sandino operated extensively throughout the northern Atlantic Coast, where, as Ortega notes, three of Sandino's nine guerrilla columns were based. Yet reading the account one must conclude either that the Miskitu did not support Sandino or, more likely, that they supported Sandino for precisely the same reasons that Mestizo peasants did. By omitting the Miskitu, Ortega equated them with Mestizos, who have a strong Nicaraguan national identity, albeit with Indian roots. Implicitly, anyone who fell outside the bounds of this identity had no place in the coalition that would soon overwhelm the Somoza dictatorship and bring the FSLN to power.

Toward the end of the period about which Ortega wrote, the FSLN put forth the "Historic Program of the FSLN," which contained five articles referring specifically to the Atlantic Coast. One provision commits the FSLN to "stimulate the flowering of [the region's] traditional cultural values," and a second vows to end the "hateful discrimination" against Coast ethnic groups. The three remaining points refer to the goals of sovereign economic development of the region. This program is consistent with the position of revolutionary nationalism described thus far. In the new revolutionary order, Miskitu would have full rights to express their cultural values free from discrimination; the region where they lived would benefit from nationally planned egalitarian economic development. But because Indians were not a distinct political entity, guarantees of ethnic or regionally based political power had no place in the equation.

The exceptional case of the Subtiavan Indians helps further to specify how FSLN leaders had come to view the ethnic question. Although Subtiavans played a leading role in the insurrection, it is difficult to discern from Cabezas's account why they joined the FSLN or the role of Indian identity in that decision. Cabezas's description is most revealing as an indication of what FSLN cadres might have concluded from their resoundingly successful attempts to organize these Pacific Coast Indians. Subtia-vans responded heartily to simultaneous appeals to assert their Indian cultural heritage, engage in class-based revolutionary struggle, and con-tribute to the new Nicaraguan national identity. The viability of this three-pronged analysis had been proven in tangible political deeds.

During the insurrectionary period, the FSLN had every reason to believe that a similar analysis applied to Atlantic Coast Indians. The Miskitu, Wheelock wrote in 1974, "continue to be a segregated minority, with extraordinarily difficult life conditions, exploited by North American companies" (p. 66). The root causes of their oppression were the same, their material needs were the same, and their expression of Indian iden-tity could easily be accommodated within a reformulated Nicaraguan national identity. Consequently, in the FSLN leadership's notion of the revolutionary subject, the Miskitu were included, though often unnamed and always in the absence of a systematic examination of their distinct history and consciousness. This anonymous inclusion actually reinforced the perception of Miskitu passivity and backwardness; they had not yet awakened, but they eventually would. It created a well-defined political space, which the Miskitu were expected to fill in order to activate their potential as subjects of history.

Failed Alliance and Conflict, 1979–84

Soon after coming to power, FSLN leaders clearly stated their com-mitment to respect and promote Miskitu culture. In a speech to the ALPROMISU congress in November 1979, Comandante Daniel Ortega, coordinator of the three-member government junta, assured his audience, "We support the revival of your customs that are disappearing, your songs, your beliefs, your language, all these things that were on the verge of being lost." The newspaper article that describes the event then sum-marizes Ernesto Cardenal's statement: "He . . . promised to open a Coast University, so the Miskitu and Sumu can relearn the culture of their el-ders; these customs and practices [that] are on the verge of being lost. . . . Also, the Ministry of Culture will publish books in Miskitu and Sumu." Both these excerpts come from the November 27 issue of the Miskitu-language edition of *Barricada* (official organ of the FSLN), published weekly during the second half of 1979. The very existence of a Miskitu-language edition of the party newspaper, quite apart from its content, is another clear indication of this commitment.[6]

Certain aspects of Miskitu culture did give the FSLN leadership cause for concern. Comandante Luis Carrión, another member of the National Directorate, in a mid-1979 interview on the topic, stated: "We know that

Front page of *Barricada* in Miskitu (November 27, 1979). Photo by author, used with permission of *Barricada*.

work will be hard in [the Atlantic sector] above all on account of the people's wish for independence, strengthened by Somozists . . . we know that the spearhead of the counter-revolution could happen there."[7] The prospect of separatism and counterrevolution appeared even more threatening in light of the widely perceived pro-U.S. sentiments of Coast people. Yet the FSLN also put forth a countervailing analysis: "If one takes account of the fact that in the urban areas, indigenous peoples have always belonged to the most oppressed social groups, then many [Indians] sympathized objectively with the popular political stand of the FSLN. In addition they sympathized with the [revolutionary] process as it accorded with their own collective character."[8]

Ortega arrived at the ALPROMISU congress intending to disband the organization, while simultaneously exhorting Miskitu people to revive and promote their culture. In the face of stiff Miskitu opposition, however, Ortega abandoned his original proposal and granted full government support to MISURASATA. With official recognition, MISURASATA gained a place within the revolutionary alliance and thereby acquired the rights and responsibilities of other mass-based organizations. This new status heightened government responsiveness to MISURASATA demands. Over the next four months, MISURASATA achieved political representation in the national legislative body (May 1980), a commitment to carry out the literacy campaign in three Coast languages (July 1980), and a favorable preliminary agreement on forest resource rights for Indian communities (August 1980). MISURASATA demands in each case gave rise to conflict, and FSLN leaders portrayed the outcome as evidence of their flexibility and support for the Miskitu organization.

By February 1981, however, the alliance was in crisis. The Sandinistas' explanation for the rupture brought much more critical views of the Miskitu to the fore. Their description of the Prinzapolka melee, for example, could hardly have differed more from the Miskitu account recorded in the previous chapter.

A member of the State Security (who was unarmed) asked the minister of the Moravian Church that he hand over Elmer Prado. . . . Realising that the soldiers were coming to arrest him, [Prado] started to shout separatist political slogans. . . . Prado's followers surrounded the compañeros of the Armed Forces and started to beat them up and finally cut their throats. . . . Disregarding the voice of authority of the Armed Forces, [brigadista] Ariel Zuniga threw himself onto a compañero from the State Security and wrestled with him until he got his gun. . . . [Then] the rage of the aggressors turned from blows to atrocity. Anastasio Peralta, from Prado's gang, beheaded the compañero from the State Security in front of the [other] participants.[9]

A year later, war broke out on the northern border of the Atlantic Coast, and the Nicaraguan government decided to move the 30,000 Miskitu inhabitants of this area to resettlement camps in the interior. At the press conference held to announce the evacuation, the army spokesman described Miskitu life conditions: "The Miskitu were maintained in such absolute misery and lack of knowledge of their own existence that, even in this country of abundant corn production, many of them do not even know how to make tortillas." Speaking of the marginal and impoverished lives in which they were trapped, he continued: "The life of a Miskitu family can be summarized in the following manner: they build a house out of bamboo, with a palm roof, and no walls or floor. . . . At daybreak they get into the dugout canoe with their wife, child, and dog, and head upriver. They fish, or hunt a bird, eat, then in the afternoon they return home again." [10] The strong implication is that resettlement could only improve this wanton backwardness.

The FSLN attempted to recast its Coast policy in light of the failed effort to work with MISURASATA. Issued as a Declaration of Principles in August 1981, the new guidelines committed the FSLN to fight discrimination, promote cultural expression, and guarantee the Coast's economic development. Luis Carrión summarized the main thrust: "Integrate without destroying, integrate with respect, integrate conserving the positive and genuine contributions of these minorities. . . . In our Declaration of Principles, we bring together all that which should justly be returned to our Indians, to recompense them for the historical marginalization to which they were subjected, and to integrate them in a conscientious way into the development of our revolutionary process." [11] Comandante William Ramirez delineated the position more specifically in regard to MISURASATA, whose principal leaders had fled to Honduras:

[MISURASATA] has become practically leaderless, and even more divorced from the legitimate interests of the Indian communities. . . . At present in this country there is no organization that can be said without doubt to represent all the Atlantic Coast . . . therefore, at present we maintain a frank and dynamic communication directly with the Indian communities. . . . Yet we also recognize that the Indians should be represented by their own organization, if that is what the communities want. [12]

Another important theme in the FSLN's wartime stance toward the Miskitu was vindication. Sandinistas marshaled firm evidence that the former MISURASATA leaders—especially Steadman Fagoth—had joined Somocistas' and the U.S. Central Intelligence Agency's efforts to overthrow the government. [13] Military aggression against Nicaragua, in turn, imposed the logic of defense and national security on all facets of government decision-making. In December 1981 William Ramirez concluded: "Today, the forces of North American imperialism are manipulating the Miskitu leaders who are in Honduras, inciting them to carry out aggressions against the Nicaraguans, using Fagoth and his followers together with the remaining National Guards of Somoza to achieve this end. Imperialism has promoted separation among the Miskitu." [14] According to this logic, MISURASATA leaders' actions bore out the FSLN's worst fears and served to justify the arrests, the evacuation, and the other measures that had been taken to guarantee national security. As Luis Carrión explained in early 1982, the war forced the FSLN to suspend consideration of any Miskitu demands beyond those specified in the Declaration of Principles:

It has not always been possible to implement our principles in the way we would have wished. It has not always been possible to give the Miskitu all the autonomy that theoretically we would have wished to give them. This is because the struggle of the Miskitu minority for their demands is subordinate to another greater struggle: the efforts of imperialism to destroy the Sandinista Revolution and the duty and right of the Revolution to defend revolutionary power and the conquests of the Nicaraguan people as a whole.[15]

From about mid-1982 until mid-1984, the FSLN fought the war on the Atlantic Coast in earnest. Sandinistas portrayed their Miskitu adversaries as contras whose goals were undifferentiated from those of the principal contra organizations. In August 1983, at a "Face the People" (De Cara al Pueblo) with internacionalistas, Daniel Ortega answered a question about conflict with the Miskitu:[16]

The revolution has made important achievements on the Coast; we have "incorporated it into the process of Nicaragua's development." We have "invested many resources" there. The Coast was incommunicado, and we installed telephones. . . . In Somoza times, "exploitation did not distinguish between Mestizo, white, Indian. Everyone was exploited and marginalized in the same way. Marginalization was not unique to one ethnic minority." Now, Mestizos and Miskitu both have entered the counterrevolution, out of fear and manipulation. . . . Conflict with the Miskitu is the product of manipulation, by the United States, of problems that they caused in the first place.

Apart from general statements of this sort, Miskitu communities dropped out of public FSLN discourse, either because they had been evacuated or because they were engulfed in war.[17]

The resettlement communities, by contrast, received great public attention and an enormous portion of the government's scarce economic and human resources. Known by the Miskitu term Tasba Pri (Free Land), these five communities, housing some 9,000 refugees, became a crucial line of defense for the FSLN in a two-sided political battle. On the international front, the FSLN had come under intense scrutiny and criticism for its alleged mistreatment of the Miskitu.[18] To control the political damage, the government ferried hundreds of international observers into Tasba Pri to see for themselves. Locally, Tasba Pri presented the revolution with an opportunity to win over a group of Miskitu. FSLN cadres confronted the challenge with characteristic zeal and self-confidence, undaunted by residents' bitter resentment over the evacuation and relentless longing to return home. At first, public statements regarding Tasba Pri had a strongly developmentalist thrust, as in the following much-cited passage in a government publication: "The Tasba Pri program is not new nor improvised. It has as its immediate antecedent a feasibility study conducted by the Revolutionary Government through the Nicaraguan Institute for the Atlantic Coast (INNICA) in November 1980 for the purpose of improving and dignifying the living conditions of the Miskitos that inhabit the Nicaraguan shore of the Coco River."[19] Gradually the message changed as developmentalism met with patent failure. Through the experience of Tasba Pri, FSLN leaders now claimed, cadres had finally begun to understand the Miskitu and to find common ground between Miskitu demands and the revolution.

✳   ✳   ✳

A central element in many retrospective analyses of the FSLN's Atlantic Coast policy in the early years of the revolution is *desconocimiento* (lack of knowledge). FSLN cadres, the argument goes, knew nothing about the Coast or about the "idiosyncracies" of the people and consequently imported inappropriate political models from the Pacific. This argument, though valid, does not go far enough. FSLN leaders knew some things about the coastal region: that it formed part of the national territory, contained abundant natural resources, and had been exploited by North American companies. What they did not know was not merely a vacuum or a gap to be filled in but rather a direct outcome of Coast people's subordinate relations with the central government. These relations embodied key premises about Indians—their backwardness, and the inviability of Indian culture as a basis for modern economic and political development—that in turn assured the reproduction of desconocimiento. This helps to explain why the considerable knowledge of Coast people that the Sandinistas acquired in the years after 1979 brought about no fundamental shift in policy. The underlying premises had to change, which did not begin to occur until the sixth year of revolutionary government.

A closer look at two key moments in the initial period of alliance—the founding of MISURASATA in November 1979 and the arrest of its leaders fourteen months later—will help to substantiate this assertion. At the congress in Puerto Cabezas, Daniel Ortega began by urging the delegates to disband the organization, suggesting that they could be adequately represented by other mass-based organizations, especially the Association of Rural Workers (ATC). When Miskitu resistance to that idea became evident, he agreed to recognize MISURASATA; finally, he exhorted the organization to preserve and promote Indian culture.[20] This suggests that the FSLN originally assumed that MISURASATA would represent Indians' cultural and social needs, while other organizations such as the ATC would represent their political and economic (class) interests. Although the FSLN scheme had a well-established commitment to Indian identity as a complementary component of revolutionary nationalism, it had no place for a separate organization devoted to Indian empowerment. By the time it became clear that MISURASATA leaders intended to pursue ethnopolitical demands as well, the organization already was an acknowledged member of the revolutionary coalition. For a brief period FSLN leaders assumed that these demands would develop in relative harmony with the revolution, given the Indians' position in the national class structure. When this did not happen, the crisis and arrests of February 1981 inevitably followed.

Government officials arrested the MISURASATA leaders and cited a document called "Plan 1981" to support their claim that the organization had assumed a "separatist" course. Yet the document contained no explicitly separatist language.[21] Even MISURASATA's territorial demands, though extensive and profoundly challenging to central government prerogatives, were not necessarily separatist in conception. (For a depiction of these demands, see Map 2.) The significance of "Plan 1981" and accompanying demands, rather, was the clear message that MISURASATA had rejected the fundamental condition on which FSLN leaders interacted with all popular organizations. These organizations were expected to defer specific demands when the FSLN deemed it necessary in order to defend the strategic interests of the revolution. With Ronald Reagan's election pledge to "roll back" the Sandinista "takeover" and the Miskitu people's well-known anti-"Spanish" and pro-U.S. sentiments, MISURASATA leaders' new stance took on deadly serious implications. It placed them on the opposite side of what was already a highly threatening configuration of forces. The FSLN viewed MISURASATA's withdrawal from the revolutionary alliance, regardless of specific rhetoric and documentary evidence, as a de facto separatist declaration.

Over the subsequent months of deepening conflict, FSLN statements regarding the Miskitu expressed a sense of betrayal and, correspondingly, a retrenchment on the question of Miskitu people's status as subjects of history. To have rejected the revolution, the Miskitu were either wanton opportunists, objects of imperialist manipulation, or hopelessly backward, all of which stood in contradiction with a positive notion of Miskitu agency. During this period, therefore, the Miskitu slid back into their prerevolutionary status as "exploited other," while the FSLN sought—under the daunting conditions of escalating U.S.-backed aggression—to fit them within the existing discourse of revolutionary Mestizo nationalism.

The Rise of Autonomy, 1984–87

In November 1984 the central government announced that it would recognize Coast peoples' historic rights to autonomy. Although not without antecedents, this announcement was most noteworthy for its sharp break with the past. FSLN and government leaders profoundly changed the way they talked about Coast history, people, and politics. Previously the very term "autonomy" had been taboo, and its connotations of ethnic demands were associated solely with the Miskitu and (to a lesser extent) Creole contras. Suddenly, FSLN leaders could publicly express affinity with Coast people's perception of having always been "oppressed," "marginalized," "second-class citizens"; they could declare that the Nicaraguan nation "had never been unified"; they could actively encourage ethnic pride and condemn all forms of racism, including the internalized "depreciation of who we were, who we are." [22]

The new policy could not have emerged without lengthy internal discussion within the FSLN, which surely involved a critical evaluation of past failures, based on input from party cadres and others with intimate knowledge of the Coast. In addition, it cannot be a coincidence that the commitments to autonomy and to negotiations with MISURASATA arose nearly simultaneously. Both policies formed part of the same critical re-evaluation and of a new, unified analysis and strategy. On December 5, 1984, President Ortega announced the formation of a National Autonomy Commission (CNA) consisting of three leading Pacific Coast intellectuals and two prominent Coast leaders, under the leadership of Luis Carrión. [23] Within a few months the CNA had passed the initiative on to a southern and a northern Regional Autonomy Commission (CRA), which coordinated the specific activities that led to the formulation of an autonomy law. Despite the importance assigned to the two regional commissions, national FSLN leaders continued to exert a decisive influence over the legal definition of autonomy, while local-level cadres determined what autonomy would mean in daily practice in places like Sandy Bay.

A View from Local Cadres

The Nicaraguan armed forces first established an ongoing presence in Sandy Bay in about April 1983. They set up headquarters on the western edge of the community, in a house that had belonged to community members who had been early activists with MISURASATA and therefore were forced to leave when the Sandinista military arrived. That house, now known simply as the *comando*, became the center of activities for the leader (*jefe*), a few other officers, and the 30-odd soldiers of the detachment (or *tropa*). When I first visited Sandy Bay in May 1985, the tropa already had changed three times; four new detachments would be stationed there by mid-1988.

From 1983 through mid-1986 tropa officers acted as the principal representatives of Nicaraguan state authority in Sandy Bay. For the first two of these years they could hope to achieve little more than their immediate military objective: to maintain control of the comando under constant military threat from MISURASATA forces, which had extensive support in the community. After the Nicaraguan government and MISURASATA entered into negotiations in December 1984, the tropa began to play a more active political role. Through community meetings and discussions with community leaders, the soldiers promoted autonomy, the state-endorsed plan for meeting key demands of Coast peoples and bringing the region back to peace. They also participated actively in community works (e.g., building a cement schoolhouse) and even administered small amounts of economic aid (e.g., credit for production and harvest of cacao).

It was not possible for me to focus sustained ethnographic attention on the tropa. An incident that occurred in October 1985, during my first week in Sandy Bay, helps to explain why. It was dusk, and I was on my way back to the home where I had begun to live. I came across a group of teenaged Miskitu men who stood watching, from a distance of about 40 feet, some tropa members gathered around a bonfire. The tropa members began shouting slogans in unison: "Sandy Bay es nuestra trinchera, autonomía es nuestra lucha!" (Sandy Bay is our trench; autonomy is our struggle!); "Comandante Ché Guevara, Presente!" (Commander Che Guevara lives on!); "La soberanía de un pueblo no se discute, se defiende con las armas en la mano!" (The sovereignty of a people is not to be discussed but defended with arms in hand!). The Miskitu youths quietly exchanged comments and joked among themselves. With my still-rudimentary Miskitu, I tried to join in their discussion, asking "What are the Sandinistas doing?" One turned to me and grinned, "They're cooking Yankees." Everyone laughed, and the banter continued. "Does anyone know who Ché Guevara was?" I asked before leaving. They shrugged with indifference.

Throughout Nicaragua, on October 8, supporters of the revolution commemorated the death of Ernesto "Ché" Guevara. Tropa officers decided to hold a ceremony, which consisted of the bonfire, the slogans, and some readings that spoke of Guevara's legacy for Latin American revolutionaries. No townspeople participated, and I doubt that the officers expected them to. The tropa members held such activities to keep their own morale high and perhaps to impress onlookers with their political fervor. I did not recognize the Miskitu youths who watched. The stiffness of our brief exchanges led me to suspect that some of them were bush people who, leaving their guns and uniforms at the nearby base, had come into town for the evening.[24] I imagined them to be sizing up "the enemy," whom any day now they might be meeting in combat.

Experiences like this one convinced me early on that as long as politics in the community remained so polarized I could not possibly hope to conduct participant observation among both groups at once. I could either take part in the tropa's bonfire ceremony or participate with the Miskitu youth watching it, but not both. When this dilemma arose, I opted to be with the Miskitu. The choice was simple in one sense: I knew that an ethnography from the Miskitu perspective would be my most valuable and unique contribution to an understanding of Nicaraguan ethnic politics. As a result of this choice, the Miskitu narrative acquired a greater depth and richness of detail.

At the community level, I could counteract this imbalance to a limited degree through informal conversations and interviews with tropa officers during periodic visits to the comando.[25] Every four or five days I spent a couple of hours there, discussing a loose agenda of issues, some of which I prepared ahead of time and others of which came up by chance. The comando was a dilapidated, one-room wooden structure, with a leaky roof and rotten walls and floor. From the walls hung three hammocks, in which the officers could be found most of the time, receiving visitors, conducting business, eating, or sleeping. They invariably invited me to a meal, consisting of standard army rations—rice, beans, and coffee—cooked by a rotating team of tropa members. I accepted reluctantly, knowing that the food would be far inferior to what my Miskitu hosts would be serving. Despite such disparities in both diet and living conditions, the tropa rarely complained. Both soldiers and officers were highly spirited, disciplined, and resolutely proud to be serving the cause of the revolution.

The content of our discussions varied widely because each successive group of officers had their own interests, level of knowledge, and style. Officers of the first tropa, described at greater length in Chapter 7, were intensely analytical. They spent hours puzzling over what the townspeople thought of them and what they could do to improve communications. They were deeply reflective about the implications of ethnic conflict for the revolution and aware of the still uncertain outcome of autonomy as a solution. Others were more operational. They tended to answer my questions about the Coast with a combination of slogans and invocations of orders from above and to prefer conversation about lighter topics.[26] All of them, however, vaguely understood my work to be contributing to the autonomy process and welcomed my presence. I think my choice to spend most time with the Miskitu appeared logical to them; it posed no evident problems, except for their occasional complaints that my visits were too infrequent.

With a few exceptions, tropa members were Mestizos from Pacific

Coast cities who had not previously been to the Atlantic Coast.[27] Their own collective memories covered a flow of events—the legacy of Sandino's guerrilla war, the humiliating years of U.S. domination, the insurrection against Somoza, the construction of a revolutionary society—in which the Atlantic Coast appeared at the extreme periphery, if at all. When our conversations evoked these memories, tropa members became animated, eloquent, and expansive about their own personal experiences. Rather than making a systematic effort to record all this, however, I focused my questions on their analysis of the Atlantic Coast, about which they generally had sketchy, incomplete information. Their answers offer a window on how the revolution's cadres viewed the ethnic question between 1985 and 1987.

Gustavo Chow served in the Sandy Bay area from April to December 1985. The son of a Chinese shopkeeper from the mining town of Bonanza, Chow was one of the few tropa members with firsthand experience of the Coast. He had received a degree in economics in Managua and had not returned to the Coast for some years. Chow became involved with the FSLN during the final months of the insurrection, providing logistical support to FSLN combatants in Managua. He served as an officer in the Marco Arévalo Brigade, a contingent formed by the Ministry of Interior early in 1985 to carry out political and military work in the Sandy Bay area.

In October 1985, the tropa held a workshop on autonomy for primary school teachers, who also were community members. Chow introduced the session with a historical summary:

'There are many differences between the Atlantic and Pacific. . . . In 1504, Columbus discovered the Atlantic Coast. The Spaniards killed and enslaved thousands of Indians who inhabited the Pacific but did not penetrate into the Atlantic owing to its inhospitable conditions. On the Atlantic, the culture was extremely backward. The British arrived and through the exchange of trinkets conquered these Indians and then manipulated them. They used the Indians to fight against the Spaniards. From that point the differences between the two coasts began. The hatred between English and Spaniard passed to the Nicaraguan Indians.'

In a later interview, he elaborated on these differences:

"[In addition to] British colonization, there is the triumph of the revolution. In the Pacific people struggled. The people there understood much more of what the revolution was all about, owing to this struggle, to the triumph. They have suffered a series of problems of bourgeois oppression, more than on the Atlantic, where the bourgeoisie kept people oppressed by giving them rum. . . . The Miskitu were the only ones who worked in the depths of the mines. But they didn't really understand that they were not being paid fairly for all that risk. They just drank rum and felt happy with the bit of food, imported goods . . . clothing, shoes, things that the commissary brought."

Carlos Gonzales, a tropa officer who served in 1987, provided a similar account of the company period:

"When the North American companies arrived to exploit the mines, the lumber, these people didn't even notice that the resources were being taken out. They simply worked for the companies, without realizing what was taking place. I think that if the insurrectional struggle for the liberation of Nicaragua had extended to this region with the same force that it did on the Pacific, these people would have another completely different understanding of the reality that Nicaragua is passing through right now."

Gonzales's deep confidence about the effects of revolutionary struggle surely had to do with its profound impact in his own life:

"In Somoza times, my mother worked as a seamstress. My father died in 1972, when I was five years old. I didn't know much about him, except that he worked as a mason. My two older brothers worked in carpentry. They were helpers, and they earned a miserable salary. Ten pesos a week, and they gave eight to my mother to cover the cost of our studies. . . . Sometimes we didn't use shoes because our family fell short of funds. With great sacrifice, my mother worked day and night to provide us with what we needed. . . . During the popular insurrection of September 1978, I developed a fuller political vision of what was happening in the country, and I became involved in the demonstrations against the Somoza regime. I also was influenced by my older brothers, who were active participants. [CRH: How old were you then?] At that time I was eleven; now I am nineteen. My older brother died during the insurrection in Rosita, the 31st of May of 1979, just a few days before the triumph. . . . All our family is deeply involved with the revolution, and we defend it at any price, because we have a brother who died during the insurrection. His death is what most motivates us to participate in the revolution to our fullest."

Although I made no systematic inquiry, I suspect that most tropa members had had similar experiences. Most probably had lost at least one relative or close friend in the insurrection and another in the contra war, already in its third year. These tropa members would have been in their mid-teens when the FSLN triumphed, in an age group that supported the revolution with near unanimity.

I asked Gonzales what he knew about the Miskitu before coming to the Coast:

"I for one had never traveled here, not even to Juigalpa. I know the northern region like the palm of my hand, but here, my first time was 1985. In the Pacific, our idea was that people in the Coast lived in some kind of tribal form . . . and that the Miskitu were wicked and treacherous, things like that. Now I stop and laugh when I think about how ignorant we were."

How did these conceptions come about? Was it discrimination? Racism? Ignorance?

"This was the result of ignorance. Never in the course of our education, or studies, were we taught something about the cultures and peoples that inhabit the Atlantic Coast. As for racism, negative. Because people from the Coast frequently traveled to the Pacific, perhaps in search of a better way of life. . . . [these attitudes] were produced by the way Somoza had the Atlantic Coast marginalized. We, in different parts of the Pacific, lacked knowledge about the reality of the Coast. The exploitation that goes on here, we didn't think about it because the situation here did not enter our political analysis."

Have your conceptions changed now that you've lived here?

"I have new conceptions, logically, the fact that I have been here since August 1985, this has allowed me to radically change my conceptions regarding the ethnic groups that live on the Atlantic Coast. Now, my conceptions are the opposite from before. To start with, the Miskitu are not an agricultural race. In principle, the work that a people does determines its character . . . these people don't dedicate themselves to agriculture, but rather, they work only for the moment. That is, their work doesn't produce a surplus, to put away for times of scarcity, or to make a contribution to the country's economy. Here there are optimal conditions for the cultivation of different crops, but these people aren't accustomed to doing it. I imagine the progress that there could be in these communities, things would be very different, like in the Pacific."

A third officer with whom I conducted a taped interview, Gonzalo Martinez, had been stationed briefly in the northern Atlantic Coast soon after the Sandinistas came to power:

"As I explained to you, in a Miskitu community up in North Zelaya, people told me: 'Give my regards to the general [Somoza].' I realized that at first, the people did not see any difference between Somoza and us. They saw the same rifle, and they said to themselves, 'This is the same army,' understand? Then, when we began to work the people began to perceive the differences, little by little."

Martinez and all the other officers I interviewed admitted freely that the FSLN committed errors in those early years, which contributed to the conflicts:

"As I told you before, we committed some errors, which to a certain extent brought on the problems of the war that led the Indians to rise up in arms. The National Directorate of the FSLN has been self-critical and has acknowledged the fact that various cadres of the central government have committed errors. But they were unintentional; they were made with the idea that it was in the best interest of the people, and in the effort to do the right thing, they made mistakes."

I asked him to be more specific. He answered:

"The troops that were sent here committed abuses, and the people complain about that. One has to understand the difficult times, that the compañeros faced a very difficult situation and had to take measures, although in some cases they got a little carried away, understand?"

And this has stayed in the people's memory?

"Yes, this has influenced people deeply, and logically, it would do that to anyone, not only the people of the Coast. Because I always am going to feel what the National Guard did to my relatives, and what they still are doing. . . . But, for example, if a group of Guardsmen were sufficiently human, capable of recognizing their errors; if they would stop fighting and come back and be accountable for what they did, and let the people pardon them; if they would come back and work on behalf of the people, then I would understand. . . . Everyone on earth commits errors."

Martinez and the others stated emphatically, however, that these errors were not the principal cause of ethnic conflict:

"We need to be clear about one thing, that we are not the real cause of this problem. . . . We acknowledge some mistakes, which have affected Coast people, but the principal architects of this problem have been the North American imperialists, who took advantage of the errors we committed, manipulated the forms of organization, the culture, the historic traditions of the Coast people, placing them in confrontation with the revolution."

Carlos Gonzalez concurred:

"These people were used, manipulated. Those who today are in armed opposition to the revolution are there owing to imperialist intervention in the internal affairs of Nicaragua. Otherwise, if these people were not armed and fighting in the bush, the revolution would have brought about notable progress here. The people from here north to the Coco River all have been used by imperialism to broaden a little more this unjust war against Nicaragua."

To press this point further, I asked Gonzales how he would describe the Atlantic Coast Indians' aspirations, their concept of well-being. He said:

"I would say, regarding those things that you are asking me, that they have been developing gradually through means of the revolution. . . . Within the historic program of the Frente Sandinista, there is a commitment to attention, or a special project for the Atlantic Coast. From this time on the people's interest has been awakening, interest in communal development, in social welfare. . . . Based on the Frente's initiative, people's interest has been growing, because otherwise, these people would not attempt to improve their life conditions, their homes, owing to their ignorance, they don't worry about or don't perceive these problems."

Finally, I asked about autonomy. What was the most important task that lay ahead in the autonomy process? Carlos Gonzales answered:

"The principal task for autonomy is to increase people's understanding of autonomy, that is, education. . . . I cannot talk with a person about autonomy if I don't teach him or her first what autonomy is, the benefits that it will bring to the zone, all this . . . and in a very explicit way, with the simplest possible words so that they can understand. Owing to the educational level [*nivel cultural*] [28] that these ethnic groups of the Atlantic Coast have. . . . I would start there, that is, to work developing a clear understanding of the autonomy project."

Gonzalo Martinez responded to the same question:

"Look, autonomy will be able to resolve the problems of the Atlantic Coast, but some of these problems will be resolved in the short term, and others in the long term. If the people would understand this well, then things would go more smoothly. We are capable and sufficiently courageous to die defending this revolution, which gave the Indians liberty. [CRH: In what sense?] They are free to elect their own leaders, to work their own land, to educate themselves in their own language, to integrate themselves into the nation, as one single nation, to make the Atlantic Coast a single country, unified with the Pacific. The revolution is the only means by which they will have a chance to achieve economic development, cultural development, and only the revolutionary government has respected their customs, laws, traditions, their race . . . so you can see that since we have so much love for our people, since we came with so much love and willingness to work on behalf of the Atlantic Coast . . . and since the people here are among the most backward, it is our task to teach them, and to make it known to them what the revolution is."

*   *   *

Three premises emerge with striking uniformity from these excerpts of my conversations with the tropa officers. First, they placed great emphasis on the dual pattern of North American exploitation and the Somoza government's "abandonment" of the Atlantic Coast, but beyond that they knew little about the particulars of Coast history. They portrayed the Miskitu role in this history as passive and the people as backward objects of oppression. Second, fully consistent with the passivity of Miskitu people in the past is their present susceptibility to manipulation by North American imperialism and a few opportunist leaders. As Gustavo Chow explained:

'[The MISURASATA] bush people are fighting because a leader is telling them to, not because they know what they're fighting for. When I ask them why they are fighting they respond: "Go ask our leaders." They don't handle on a concrete level the reasons for their struggle.'

Third, these disparaging comments about the Miskitu generally come paired with contrasting observations about the Pacific, where the peasants are more industrious, where people fought to overthrow Somoza and thereby became subjects of history, guardians of their own destiny. One officer captured this contrast succinctly, while explaining to me why, with many fewer soldiers, they could successfully defend the comando: "Each one of us is worth ten of them, because we are fighting for an ideal." None of the three premises should come as a surprise. Although at times unelaborated or condensed, they are fully consistent with the images and analysis of the Coast promoted for years by the FSLN leadership. Tropa members were relying on conventional wisdom, deeply rooted in the preautonomy political culture of revolutionary Nicaragua.

It is more difficult to understand how these premises could have survived the radical shift in national-level policy toward the Coast. The advent of autonomy clearly did have an effect on tropa members' analysis. They struck a tone of humility and self-reflection and struggled to reconcile their deep historical confidence in the revolution with the unavoidable implication that previous government policy toward the Coast had been in error. They achieved a new equilibrium through a measure of self-criticism—remarkably frank for local military commanders operating under wartime conditions—combined with an incongruous return to the same three premises described above. For example, they described autonomy both as a political arrangement that will correct the "errors" of the past and as a means to help Miskitu overcome their "cultural backwardness" and, implicitly, to become more like Mestizos. In part, this outcome corresponds to the inevitable lag between a rapidly changing official policy and the resilient character of any grass-roots political culture. In part, however, the tropa's incongruous return to the original premises reflects a broader problem within the national-level conception of autonomy. Even in its most sophisticated formulation, autonomy still embodied an unresolved tension between the endorsement of Miskitu people's demands for ethnic-based political power and the FSLN's prerogative to determine which demands were compatible with their overall program and vision of revolutionary change.

The National-Level Discourse of Autonomy

Luis Carrión had "attended" the Atlantic Coast for the National Directorate since 1982. His analysis at the beginning of that period, as noted above, was predicated on the need to "integrate . . . conserving the

positive and genuine contributions of these minorities" and the need
to subordinate Miskitu demands to broader exigencies of the revolution.
In January 1985 Carrión delivered a speech in Puerto Cabezas to a gathering of activists from the FSLN. He called for both self-criticism and
comprehension:

"We have the responsibility to engage in energetic struggle against every form of
racism, within our ranks and outside them. Within our ranks, this racism can
manifest itself in the form of scornful comments. More than once I have heard
phrases like 'these damned Miskitu' [*estos miskitos jodidos*]. Maybe even some
of you have uttered them. Such comments have a fundamentally racist ideological
content. . . .

We know that if we start talking with people here in Puerto Cabezas, or in
Bluefields, or anywhere on the Coast, we'll hear all kinds of different ideas, and
some of them will be essentially separatist. But why should we be afraid of this,
if it is the reality? Our job is to initiate free discussion on these topics. This is the
only way to help the people achieve clarity and to formulate a just concept of
autonomy. Because if we do not talk, discuss, and offer alternative notions, we
inevitably will strengthen the counterrevolutionary positions."

In regard to the relationship between ethnic demands and national revolution, he stated:

"The conditions of this region present the revolution with an ethnic question,
which stands as the fundamental issue to resolve in a correct and revolutionary
way. . . . We have to forge a new national consciousness, not just here on the
Atlantic, but throughout the country. This consciousness must reflect the fact that
we the people of Nicaragua have distinct sociocultural characteristics; it must
include the Miskitu, the Sumu, the Creoles."[29]

Manuel Ortega Hegg, a top adviser to the government and member of
the National Autonomy Commission, explained this evolution of political analysis: "After the fiasco with MISURASATA, the government became
convinced that it was necessary to learn more, to the greatest depth possible, about the history and idiosyncracies of Coast people, in order to
achieve constructive communication with them. Beginning in 1982, efforts centered on determining which demands were legitimate and which
were not. The autonomy project emerged from this reflection."[30]

Around March 1985, the National Directorate replaced Carrión with
Tomás Borge as primary liaison to the Atlantic Coast. Borge's first major
speech in his new capacity, delivered in Bluefields on April 23, had a
distinctly preautonomy flavor, including the much-cited exhortation:
"The constitution of this republic should not speak of Blacks, nor of
Whites, nor of Miskitu. . . . Here there are no Blacks, Whites, or Miskitu,

here there are only Nicaraguans! The only thing that differentiates us is the attitude we assume toward the nation." [31]

After six months of direct experience with autonomy, Borge began to assume a different tone. In October 1985 he attended a Cara al Pueblo in Puerto Cabezas and responded to the litany of complaints and demands by the predominantly Miskitu audience. Borge's statements included a frank admission of past errors:

"If we do not have the honesty and the goodwill to admit our errors, then we will never be able to resolve these problems. There were cases in which Miskitu prisoners were tortured, physically abused, even killings, burning of homes, measures that were overly repressive even in the state of war in which we were living. . . . We are genuinely ashamed that our own *compañeros*, many of whom have been punished, would have committed these gross abuses against civilians. I think we should start there, confessing our errors in a humble manner, and why not? Because we are proud facing imperialism, facing the powerful, but we are humble facing our humble brothers and sisters of the Atlantic Coast. And let me make something very clear: the CIA agents, the FDN leaders, the National Guard, capitalizing on these problems, exaggerated what had happened, multiplied by one thousand times the errors we committed, making the international public believe that we had carried out a veritable genocide."

He followed with a call to unity with the Miskitu combatants in dialogue:

"To a great extent, the struggle of the Miskitu has been for just demands of the Atlantic Coast. . . . The majority of the men from here that rose up in arms did so to struggle for rights of the Atlantic Coast, rights with which we always have been in agreement. . . . They used methods that were mistaken, violence that only brings bloodshed, pain, death . . . and we, the FSLN, were not capable in that moment of understanding that these were just demands, even though they always had fallen within our vision and program for struggle." [32]

Finally, in a later speech, he gave these changes a theoretical explanation:

'We are demonstrating to the world that we are capable of overcoming our own mistakes . . . that we have the modesty to enrich our knowledge of reality. Practice has shown us that it is scientifically incorrect to reduce social reality exclusively to class distinctions. . . . We therefore recognize that . . . ethnic diversity is among the moving forces of the revolution.' [33]

A contrasting facet of the FSLN's political discourse on autonomy could be found in the autonomy law (for the full text, see Appendix C). Delegates to the Multi-Ethnic Assembly in Puerto Cabezas endorsed a proposed version of this law in April 1987, and it subsequently received national approval with minor alterations. From then on (and even previously) the autonomy law became a central reference point for FSLN leaders in their portrayal of government policy toward the Atlantic Coast.

The rights and responsibilities defined in the autonomy document include equality before the law, the right of ethnic minorities to preserve and develop all aspects of their cultures, and universal duties of obedience to the nation-state (e.g., regarding defense, judicial norms, and national laws). As for political structure, the law stipulates two regional councils, each constituted through the free and direct election of approximately 45 representatives, who in turn select a six-member board of directors and a regional coordinator. Each ethnic group living in the region is to have at least one member on the board of directors to ensure equal ethnic representation. Otherwise, delegates will be distributed throughout the region in a manner roughly proportional to population.

Any assessment of the law's impact hinges on the extent to which political power is turned over to the democratically elected autonomous governments. The attributes that fall within the exclusive competence of the autonomous regional governments include the authority to: resolve boundary disputes between communities; elect a regional coordinator and replace him or her when necessary; request reports from the representatives of the ministries and state institutions working within the region; elect its board of directors; appoint permanent and special commissions to analyze and decide upon matters related to the administration for the region; appoint executive officials to the regional administration;[34] and administer the Special Development and Social Promotion Fund. On most other points the law includes no clear delineation of authority. It generally provides for the autonomous government's "participation" in the decision-making process, together with the central government, on unspecified terms.[35] In at least one case the actual arrangement for cogovernance remains fundamentally ambiguous.[36]

*   *   *

The autonomy law was promulgated at the beginning of a transition to a new political arrangement for the Atlantic Coast. Its strictly legal content strikes a balance between, on the one hand, expressing a broad commitment to the principle of regional self-government and, on the other, requiring the central government to relinquish very little authority. The law allows the central government to define the conditions under which Miskitu (and Coast people in general) will participate in the revolution and to decide—paraphrasing Manuel Ortega Hegg's statement quoted above—which Miskitu demands are legitimate and which are not.

Yet other aspects of the FSLN's political discourse point to a different conclusion. Tomás Borge's statements in particular endorse a much more radical interpretation, which coincides in spirit and in principle with the demands that led Miskitu people to take up arms in the first place. Sandinista political discourse therefore embodied a tension between two tendencies: an expansive notion of autonomy, which fully defined the Miskitu as historical and revolutionary subjects, versus a more restrictive legal definition that allowed FSLN leaders to place limits on what Miskitu could demand and achieve through the exercise of their newly recognized rights.

This tension is expressed eloquently in the statement of a Miskitu former combatant, who entered into dialogue with the government sometime before October 1985:

They still underestimate us. They think we cannot see beyond our own noses, that we are not aware of what they call the fundamental contradiction between the revolution and imperialism, that we are confused, that we lack political development. It is they that need political development. If we are in dialogue with the government it is because we trust the revolution. Only with the revolution can our struggles achieve results. . . . It is not that the Sandinistas do not want to resolve our demands, but rather, that they still have not achieved a deep understanding of our situation [*la problemática costeña*]. . . .

Perhaps intellectuals can explain to other intellectuals the origins of the contradictions between the Miskitu and the revolution, what caused the Frente Sandinista to adopt the positions it did toward the Coast . . . [and they can probably even explain] why the deer flees when she smells the hunter's scent. . . . Everything, after all, has a cause. . . . But here is the crux of the matter. . . . [The Sandinistas] must have confidence that the people know what is best for themselves, and [the FSLN] must trust the leaders that the people select. They must let the Miskitu enter the revolution in our own way, not being forced by someone else. . . . It is possible that we will reach a satisfactory agreement with the government; but [they] must understand that the problems will always remain latent as long as they do not cede the power to us.

The statement's publication in *Barricada International* (*Archivo* edition, Oct. 1985)—the official organ of the FSLN—provides clear evidence that Borge's statements in the Cara al Pueblo were no aberration. The FSLN publicly endorsed the principle of ethnic-based political power—the radical innovation of autonomy—while at the same time leaving this principle largely absent from the law itself.

Conclusions

Mestizo revolutionary nationalism portrayed "Indianness" as a historical experience and a set of surviving cultural traits, both of which meld unproblematically with the broader political identity of Nicaraguan nationhood. As the excerpts from interviews with tropa members in Sandy Bay suggest, the popular expression of this discourse embodied a depreciation of Indian culture and the none-too-subtle premise that Indians lack the capacity to shape their own destinies. At the same time, this revolutionary nationalism cannot plausibly be equated with the highly assimilationist stance of Latin American Creole ruling elites. It urges Mestizo peasants to be proud of their Indian roots and even demarcates the Nicaraguan nation as Indian, in defiance of white cultural domination from the North. It merges with a vision of social transformation—for economic justice and an end to foreign domination—that forms part of a compelling discourse of resistance for Nicaragua's majority classes.

My point is, then, to affirm this liberating potential of Sandinista revolutionary nationalism and also to specify its constituent premises, which led the Sandinistas to neglect, actively preclude, or seriously minimize the particular demands of the Miskitu Indians. This, in turn, has substantiated my earlier allusion to Sandinista ideology as a contradictory consciousness. Sandinista nationalism largely excluded Miskitu Indians, or included them nominally, rather than considering them protagonists of political struggle and transformation. Barely beneath the surface of the call for national unity lay a dichotomy that associated civilization with the revolution and backwardness with Miskitu culture and people. Finally, although the Sandinistas called emphatically for the elimination of structural inequities, they paid least attention to the particular form that worried Miskitu people the most: unequal relations between cultural minorities and Spanish-speakers, between their region and the nation-state. These contradictions help to explain why the revolution could not be expected to achieve and maintain Miskitu people's support.

What, then, of the post-1984 transition to autonomy? Though ambiguous in many of its details, autonomy made a radical break with the past, most strikingly conveyed in the statements of Tomás Borge. The FSLN came to recognize the Miskitu as subjects of history. Miskitu combatants entered into negotiations with the government, having fought for ethnic demands that Borge described as congruent with those of the revolution. This statement signaled a newly opened space for Miskitu political participation, even if the organizational channels remained undefined and fluid. It signaled a reformulation of the revolutionary project, replacing the previous model with an emphasis on ethnic pride and political power within a multiethnic Nicaraguan national identity.

Yet other aspects of the discourse, most significantly the text of the autonomy law, point to more cautious conclusions. The law assigns rights to regions, not ethnic groups, and stipulates very little obligatory devolution of power from central to autonomous government. In most key clauses the phrasing is ambiguous, open to interpretations ranging from expansive to highly restrictive. The Miskitu Indians' new status as revolutionary subjects therefore remained provisional, affirmed by an expansive political discourse but left an open question in the legal statute. This analysis of the discourse of autonomy foreshadows conclusions that will emerge more sharply in Chapter 7, which provides a grass-roots account of the transition. Though impressive, even visionary in many respects, autonomy did not—and perhaps could not—fully overcome the contradictions from which it arose.

5 From Quiescence to Mobilization, 1960–81

In the Atlantic Coast work is proceeding according to a modern conception of development. . . . At last the Motherland will become a healthy, robust entity, because that could never have been possible with only half of its body alive; but the question remains, What will become of the Atlantic Coast natives? Will we let them disappear, through the inevitable process of absorption, as immigrants [from the west] continue to arrive? Will we keep pushing them toward the inhospitable northern plains, treating them like a national pariah? Or will we learn to take advantage of their potential, preparing them for the true reincorporation into the process of national development?
—Jorge Jureidini, president of the Commission for the Development of the Atlantic Coast, May 1966

PERIODIZATION OF THE PAST, though essential in any effort to understand historical change, also exerts a subtle influence on the analysis itself, allowing and encouraging certain insights, obscuring others. This is particularly evident in the scholarship and political discourse on postrevolutionary Nicaragua. According to conventional wisdom, July 19, 1979, is the great watershed. Writers from a range of perspectives almost invariably have divided their analyses into "before" and "after" sections, accepting and reinforcing the a priori premise of rupture, discontinuity, and contrast. There are many good reasons for adopting this approach; indeed, it would be foolhardy to address any facet of contemporary Nicaragua without assigning great importance to the revolutionary victory. Yet the narratives presented in the two preceding chapters should also have provided reasons for caution, for asking questions that are not predicated on the centrality of that watershed.

The triumph of July 19, 1979, does not play a decisive organizing role in the collective memories of Sandy Bay Miskitu. Their epochal events, rather, are the founding of ALPROMISU in 1974, its transformation into MISURASATA in November 1979, and the beginning of armed conflict some fourteen months later. The subversive effects of Miskitu memories on conventional periodization are crystallized by an elderly man from Prinzapolka: "Just before the revolution began," he recalled, the literacy campaign had taken place. In an offhand comment, he erased the first two years and equated the revolution with the beginning of the war in 1981. Although the "triumph" certainly does permeate and organize post-1979 Sandinista discourse, this does not preclude continuities in premises regarding the Miskitu Indians. Using those premises as a guide and taking the Reincorporation of 1894 as the starting point, we might want to mark 1984, not 1979, as the crucial moment of disjuncture. Such insights from the two narratives orient my effort in this chapter to move beyond standard accounts of Miskitu politics during the last two decades of the Somoza dictatorship and the initial months of revolutionary government.

The first imperative in any attempt to explain the Miskitu people's turn to militant collective action is to avoid the implicitly derogatory contrast between their alleged "passivity" before 1979 and their mobilization afterward. Judging from Jureidini's statement quoted in the epigraph to this chapter, Somoza government officials certainly held the view that Miskitu were passive and somehow unaware of their interests. In the first months after coming to power, some Sandinista cadres were apparently of a similar mind. Beginning with the observation that almost no one from the Coast fought in the insurrection, these cadres often went on to portray *costeños* as having been "asleep" (*adormecidos*) during the Somoza era and as having suffered from a "backward" (*atrasado*) political consciousness.[1] As the analysis in Chapter 4 suggests, these statements corresponded to premises deeply ingrained in Sandinista political culture, which contributed substantively to the conflict. Such portrayals of Miskitu passivity also are misleading because they minimize the real political change that was under way. Beginning in the 1960's there was a marked rise in Miskitu ethnic militancy and political organizing, propelled by state-promoted economic development, intracommunity economic and ethnic change, and external political factors.

Yet the question remains, because this surge in militancy did not develop into a potent challenge to the state. To the contrary, in the months prior to the Sandinista victory, the Miskitu organization ALPROMISU took a decidedly accommodationist stance toward the besieged Somoza dictatorship. By all accounts, the Miskitu did turn quiescent in 1978, reversing the trend of the previous five years. This stance contrasts sharply with the mobilization that followed. My analysis of this contrast begins by affirming the fundamental differences between the Somoza and revolutionary states. One was brutally repressive, subservient to the United States, and dominated by what Carlos Vilas (1989) calls a "predatory" drive for wealth and power that defied even the rationality of the capitalist profit motive. The other enjoyed widespread popular support and put forth a comprehensive program of social, economic, and political reform grounded in the "logic of the majority." Despite these differences, there also were important continuities in the pre- and immediately postrevolutionary periods, including structural conditions conducive to ethnic mobilization. In the eighteen months after July 1979, the existing trend toward state penetration and control accelerated, which brought the Miskitu into increasing contact with a Mestizo-dominated bureaucracy. Government programs accentuated people's economic aspirations, which had been rising steadily since the 1960's. Even the greatest difference—between the revolutionary state's promotion of popular organization and Somoza repression—must be qualified. Because Miskitu political organizing during the Somoza era was mildly oppositional at most, it confronted little state repression and at times had implicit government support.

These broad continuities make the contrast in pre- and post-1979 Miskitu collective action all the more puzzling. The argument that the Coast was abandoned by the state and therefore that the Miskitu had little impetus to mobilize, though more accurate before 1960, cannot be sustained for the post-1960 period. Yet given the crescendo of revolutionary struggle against Somoza throughout the Pacific Coast of Nicaragua, the level of Miskitu opposition to the state seems oddly moderate. Similarly, given the continuities in structural conditions favoring mobilization—even accepting that they became more decisive—Miskitu collective action after 1979 appears perplexingly militant. In this chapter I offer an explanation for the first part of this puzzle, drawing on insights gained from the Miskitu narrative presented in Chapter 3. Before 1979, I contend, the premises of Anglo affinity that Miskitu people espoused had the effect of defusing potential conflict and encouraging quiescence. Chapter 6 will then show how these same elements provide a key to understanding the antigovernment mobilization that followed.

The Emergence of Ethnic Militancy

By the early 1960's, the prosperity of "company times" had already been canonized in Miskitu people's collective memories. Mary W. Helms carried out fieldwork along the Río Coco in the mid-1960's and found townspeople from Asang in the throes of economic depression, deprived of access to consumer goods, and complaining bitterly about their forced return to the drudgery of subsistence production. Traumatized by their own poverty, Asang Miskitu "introduced every conversation" by complaining, "We are poor, we are miserable, we have no work, we have no food" (1971: 156). Helms portrays the Northeast as entering another downswing in the interminable boom-bust cycle that had characterized the Atlantic Coast economy since the late nineteenth century. Consistent with this portrayal, the Atlantic Coast during the final decade of *somocismo* has been characterized as an abandoned region, a backwater for corrupt low-level state officials (e.g., Bourgois 1982: 311). Subsequent research, especially by Carlos Vilas (1989), provides a more complex view, suggesting that this "bust" had very different consequences from previous ones.

State-Promoted National Integration and Development

By the early 1960's Nicaragua had entered a phase of rapid nationwide economic growth, reflected in sharp increases in both agroindustrial production (mainly cotton and cattle) and manufacturing. The Somocista state played an integral role in this economic expansion, as producer, creditor, and provider of productive infrastructure (roads, electricity, port facilities). But the state also faced the explosive consequences of an economic model that, despite spectacular rates of growth, left the majority of the population in desperate poverty.[2] This contradiction became particularly evident in the countryside, where the expansion of cotton and cattle production forced thousands of peasant producers off their lands, leaving them no alternative but to migrate eastward. Somoza state planners began to view the Atlantic Coast as a strategic "escape valve" for growing demographic pressure in the west and virgin territory for further economic expansion. Unlike the previous boom-bust patterns that Helms describes, this time, when the U.S. companies departed, the Nicaraguan state already had begun to take their place.

A primary thrust of this expansion into the Atlantic Coast involved colonization schemes. The Agrarian Reform Institute (IAN) was founded in 1963 with a mandate to resettle landless peasants in the Zelaya Department. Its largest colonization project, located in southwestern Zelaya, came to include 4,000 square kilometers and some 24,000 participants. Another colony was established near the northern mining town of Siuna. These planned efforts represented only a small portion of the eastward migration because most peasants moved "spontaneously," without any government support.[3] This eastward migration produced some direct conflict with Indian communities over land rights and a generally heightened Miskitu and Sumu Indian awareness of Mestizo presence. The IAN also initiated a colonization project that moved Miskitu inhabitants of the lower Río Coco to a group of interior settlements known as Tasba Raya (New Land). The project ended in conflict between the French agronomists who worked as advocates of the Miskitu settlers and state functionaries who feared that plans for collectivized production had become too politicized (Jenkins Molieri 1986: 179–80).

Foreign development aid allowed an expansion of social services and economic infrastructure. In 1955 the Ministry of Education initiated a UNESCO-supported pilot project for primary education in the Río Coco area; within a decade, rural education throughout the Coast had passed from the hands of Moravian missionaries to the government.[4] With funds from the United Nations and the Alliance for Progress, the state placed two grain silos along the Río Coco, built or improved the roads and bridges to connect the major population centers of the region, and began construction of a deep-water port. Technical and financial assistance also came from the Food and Agriculture Organization (FAO) of the United Nations to begin an ambitious reforestation and integral development program in the Northeast (FAO 1969). Miskitu community members protested restrictions that the project imposed upon them, burning down several reforested pine stands to make their point (Jenkins Molieri 1986: 148–49).

Finally, instead of unfettered foreign investment, the post-1960 Somoza state favored arrangements that allowed its own direct involvement in production. The Somoza family coterie followed a diversified investment strategy. Their agroindustrial concerns centered in the southern community of Kukra Hill. Aided by funds from the Alliance for Progress, President Luis Somoza initiated a banana export enterprise and then shifted to sugarcane. Until 1979 the Somoza family and associates operated the Tierra Dorada sugar mill and surrounding plantation. The Somoza portfolio also included sawmills—owned jointly with Cuban exiles in Bluefields and Spanish capital in the north—and cattle ranches in both the north and south.[5]

The new productive activity of greatest magnitude and economic importance was shrimp and lobster fishing. This began in the late 1950's, on the initiative of Creole fishermen and North American venture capitalists. Production remained relatively low until 1970 and then increased rapidly. Through the 1970's the value of marine exports grew at an average yearly rate of 28 percent, reaching a maximum value of $24 million in 1977, 4 percent of Nicaragua's foreign exchange earnings.[6] An operating fleet of nearly 200 industrial fishing boats delivered products to six packing plants in the southern region, four in the Bluefields area that processed mainly shrimp, and two in Corn Island that focused on lobster. Somoza family associates had a central role in this burgeoning industry, owning at least partial shares in four of the six companies. The remaining capital came from Cuban exiles and North Americans.

This expansionary thrust provided a crucial impetus for the development of Miskitu ethnic militancy in the 1970's. The state's economic involvement in fishing, agroindustry, reforestation, and colonization focused mainly on projects and activities designed to serve interests of Spanish-speakers from Managua. Coast people saw economic "progress" that did not benefit them and came into increasing contact with the Mestizo functionaries—project administrators, petty bureaucrats—who personified these inequalities. The nationalist rhetoric surrounding state expansion must have appeared blatantly hypocritical in its professed objective to "attend to a territory that for so many years has longed for its effective incorporation into the progress and cultural life of the nation" (Proyecto Piloto 1960: 16).

Community-Level Economic and Ethnic Change

Uneven development and increasing state penetration into the Coast also brought about community-level economic change, which further heightened interethnic tensions. When Helms worked in Asang, Río Coco (1964–65), her informants complained bitterly about the absence of opportunities for wage labor and the resulting lack of access to foods they considered necessary (flour, oil, coffee, sugar), clothing, and other items. Asang Miskitu were so desperate, Helms observes, that they sold or exchanged all their locally produced rice and beans on highly disadvantageous terms to acquire these consumer goods. Miskitu farmers' economic bind had no easy solution because they could not increase production of market goods (such as rice and beans) without cash to pay wage labor.[7] Moreover, even successful harvests brought frustrating results because the local market—still poorly integrated with the rest of the region—was easily glutted. In the early 1960's local merchants had sufficient leverage to refuse to pay cash for rice and beans, offering only to barter the goods they wanted to sell.[8] Gradually Miskitu farmers began to organize to gain relief from exploitative merchants. Because the merchants were predominantly Mestizo, organization took on an overtly ethnic dimension.[9] Helms (1971: 222) reports, for example, that in Asang, "the price differential between selling and buying rice and beans is blamed on the . . . underhanded cunning of the Spanish [i.e., Mestizos]."

During the 1970's, integration with the regional market deepened. Miskitu townspeople, who long had been participants in the capitalist economy as wage laborers and consumers, now obtained cash as small-scale producers of commodities. In river communities they grew rice and cacao and raised cattle; in coastal communities they fished shrimp, green turtles, and even a few lobsters. Bernard Nietschmann's extensive research in the community of Tasbapauni (1973, 1979b) provides additional insight into these emergent economic patterns. Located on the seacoast about 45 miles north of Bluefields, Tasbapauni was ideally situated to benefit from the fishing industry's post-1965 takeoff. When Nietschmann began his study in 1968, Tasbapauni residents were "at the bottom of a long economic depression" (1979b: 7), parallel to the one that Helms describes in Asang. The extensive fishing and sale of green sea turtles launched the first phase of their transition to commodity production. Although turtles had been sold intermittently for decades, opportunities heightened in 1968 when companies in Bluefields and Puerto Cabezas began to buy and export the animals. Tasbapauni turtle fishermen intensified production and sold increasing proportions of their catch for quick cash, which led Nietschmann to offer a gloomy prognosis for the community's future. The turtles could not last, he observed; residents were abandoning their well-adapted subsistence strategy and kin-based food distribution patterns for dependence on a regional market over which they had no control (1973: 231).

Yet a decade later Tasbapauni had survived this trauma remarkably well. Green turtle production had declined in relation to a range of other commodities that Tasbapauni residents sold on the regional market, from lobster and shrimp to rice and coconuts. In a follow-up article (1979b), Nietschmann reiterates his original argument that the community's economy had grown less stable and more vulnerable, but his own data suggest why some Tasbapauni residents might have seen it differently. The goods they were buying at local stores had increased in price an average of 82 percent between 1969 and 1975, a substantially lower rate than all but one of the products they regularly marketed (see Table 1). Rice, coconuts, chickens, and pigs were not subject to the "ecological cul-de-sac" that Nietschmann claimed would limit the growth of Tasbapauni's monetarized economy. Although the problem of local resource depletion did affect green and hawksbill turtle production, by the late 1970's many Tasbapauni fishermen had moved on to pursuit of a more lucrative product: lobster.[10] They started out small, driving or pulling traps from dories (dugout canoes) and selling the lobsters to company boats that worked in the area. Subsequently, the more successful fishermen acquired their own boats and developed direct relationships with companies in Bluefields and Corn Island. In 1979 Tasbapauni was a community on the rise. A prosperous group of townspeople operated at least ten lobster or transport boats, a rice mill, a small movie theater, and several cantinas and stores.[11]

One reason Nietschmann may have deemphasized this dynamism in Tasbapauni's local economy was the uneven distribution of its benefits. Throughout the Coast, commodity production gave rise to increased economic differentiation within Miskitu communities. In the Río Grande

TABLE I
Prices of Commodities Sold in Tasbapauni, 1969–75[a]

Commodity	1969 price	1975 price	Percent increase
Green turtle (whole)	60	80	33%
Hawksbill shell (lb.)	21	40	90%
Rice (hulled, 100 lbs.)	60	130	117%
Coconut (200)	25	60	140%
Shrimp (dried, lb.)	2	5	150%
Chicken (whole)	4	12	200%
Pig (whole)	75[b]	250	233%
Food purchases (avg./day)	7.9	14.3	82%

SOURCE: Nietschmann (1979b).
NOTE: All prices are in cordobas.
[a]The most important product in the Tasbapauni takeoff, lobster, is inexplicably absent from Nietschmann's analysis, except in one footnote.
[b]This figure comes from Nietschmann's earlier work (1973: 190). The 1979 article quotes 300, which must be a misprint.

area, for example, one Miskitu family owned a rice mill and planted ten to twenty hectares of rice yearly; another planted a similar-sized cassava plantation. These families hired other community members as wage laborers and produced many times more than the community average.[12] One family from San Esquipulas (Río Coco) had 30 hectares of cacao (MIDINRA 1985); at least a dozen Río Coco families had large herds of cattle.[13] Of the three wealthiest men in the coastal Miskitu community of Awastara in 1978, "two owned small stores . . . two had cattle herds of 50–100 head, and all of them had various enterprises including fishing boats."[14] Greater integration with the market was clearly more traumatic for the majority who failed to make the transition to the status of a middle-level producer. Although Nietschmann notes the increasingly "disproportionate family incomes in what was an egalitarian society" (1979: 10), his conclusions read as if everyone suffered equally from the loss of "subsistence security."[15]

The few Miskitu community members who achieved upward mobility faced a dilemma between making profits in a competitive market and staying in favor with fellow townspeople. Some remained at least partly committed to the norms of reciprocity that went along with community membership. But many, in response to this dilemma and as part of a strategy of upward mobility, gradually distanced themselves from their people and began to identify with one of the more privileged ethnic groups—Mestizos in the north and Creoles in the south. Along the Río Coco in the 1960's, Helms observed Miskitu-speaking schoolteachers "who claim to be ignorant [of the language] and prefer to speak Spanish" (1971: 176). A decade later Bourgois and Grunberg (1980) noted the same pattern among government employees and larger merchants who worked along the Río Coco. Although of Miskitu descent, they scorned Miskitu culture as backward and took every opportunity to emphasize their affinities with Spanish-speakers.

A similar pattern occurred in Tasbapauni, where two ethnic groups lived side by side in the early 1970's. According to Nietschmann, Creoles were "a minority," distinguished from Miskitu by the latter's preference for the Miskitu language and adherence to "Miskito customs and social responsibilities." He reports that Miskitu considered "the Creoles to be stingy, abrasive, and mean, [people] who sell rather than give, who hire people for agricultural work rather than exchange labor communally" (1973: 59). By presenting the categories as static, however, he misses the relationship between economic and ethnic change. As people "made it" economically in southern Zelaya, they often came increasingly to identify as Creole. Such ethnic change occurred at the level of individual families and in Tasbapauni's case—perhaps owing to its unusual prosperity—encompassed much of the community. By the early 1980's most Tasbapauni townspeople, especially those under the age of 30, considered themselves of mixed descent but with stronger affinities for Creole culture.[16]

In sum, socioeconomic changes beginning in the mid-1960's heightened ethnic tensions in three interconnected ways. First, as the Atlantic Coast entered a phase of state-driven political and economic development, Miskitu came into greater contact with the Mestizos who implemented and enforced various facets of this expanded state presence. Second, commodity production drew Miskitu communities into an increasingly integrated regional market, placing them at the mercy of a Mestizo-dominated merchant class. Third, economic development generally raised Coast people's aspirations but left a highly uneven distribution of benefits. Miskitu remained at the bottom of the socioeconomic hierarchy, while the beneficiaries, no longer limited to white North Americans, now included an increasing number of Mestizos (both Coast-born and from the Pacific). A small number of Miskitu managed to overcome these class/ethnic barriers through education, commerce, or commodity production. Upward mobility, in turn, often entailed a shift in ethnic identity toward one of the two more privileged ethnic groups; this tendency deprived Miskitu people of middle-class allies and accentuated their sense of political-economic deprivation.

The Rise of Ethnopolitical Organization

Miskitu efforts to ameliorate these inequities occurred in the context of two broad forces of change operating throughout Latin America. First, motivated by the perceived threat of the Cuban Revolution, U.S.-based development organizations—both private and governmental—took the need for reform much more seriously. Cooperatives, integrated rural development, leadership training, and even agrarian reform became standard rhetorical components of the Alliance for Progress, a massive U.S. government aid program initiated in 1963. Although political constraints generally impeded substantive change, the rhetoric sanctioned (and at times the program funded) grass-roots work with great transformative potential. Second, the Latin American Catholic bishops held their General Conference in Medellín, Colombia, in 1968. Stimulated by Vatican II, they redirected the mission of the church, exhorting religious workers to place themselves on the side of the poor and to view the work of spiritual redemption as including collective efforts to improve people's immediate life conditions. The Medellín edicts reflected the impact of a new body of theological thought and action known broadly as liberation theology and gave great impetus to its further development.

Both of these influences were present in the emergence of Miskitu activism on the Río Coco. In 1967, with guidance from North American Capuchin missionaries and funding from U.S.-based development organizations, Río Coco Miskitu farmers formed a network of producers' cooperatives called ACARIC (Association of Agricultural Clubs of the Río Coco). They received backing from the National Development Institute (INFONAC), a quasi-governmental Nicaraguan agency heavily funded by the United States, as well as from USAID, Catholic Relief Services (CRS), and the American Institute for Free Labor Development (AIFLD).[17] Although it promoted a mildly adversarial stance toward the government, ACARIC's economic goals fit squarely within the reformist vision of the Alliance for Progress: higher prices for agricultural goods, improved productive techniques, collective solutions to common problems.

The educational work of the Catholic church had a more radical thrust. Guided by the edicts of Medellín and his own "anthropological" approach to religious instruction, a North American Capuchin priest named Gregorio Smutko reoriented the mission's Río Coco work toward explicit "liberational" objectives. This involved training native "delegates of the word" and conducting educational programs that combined church teachings with more overtly political messages. The programs challenged all forms of paternalism and exhorted Miskitu people to organize themselves to improve the conditions of their lives.[18] Smutko's program also sought to promote Miskitu cultural pride and self-affirmation, using biblical references to draw parallels between the "Miskitu nation" and the tribes of Israel. The study guide for this course emphasized Miskitu political ascendancy ("the dominion of the Miskito kings was greater

than that of the Kings of Israel"), heroism ("The Miskito repeatedly confronted and defeated the Spanish invaders"), and invincibility ("The Miskito submitted peacefully to Nicaraguan sovereignty [in 1894] but *no
nation ever succeeded in conquering the Miskito*" (Smutko 1975: 56–
57). This message bears a striking resemblance to the discourse of
MISURASATA, which brought about a profound deepening of Miskitu ethnic militancy a decade later.

ACARIC ran into financial problems and fell apart in 1972. Efforts to
fill the gap began immediately and received funding from the U.S.-based
CRS. A provisional organization called the Miskito Alliance functioned
during 1973, and at a meeting in Bilwaskarma on March 29–31 of the
following year, it formally changed its name to ALPROMISU. Miskitu Moravian pastors Silvio Diaz, Samuel Downs, and Wycliffe Diego, in addition to a number of lay pastors, were prime movers in this meeting
(Richter 1986: 62). Though North American Moravian missionaries had
remained largely impervious to the post-1960 theological change, a
group of Coast people trained by the Moravians gained higher degrees
from the Theological Seminary of San José, Costa Rica, where they became exposed to liberation theology.[19] Upon returning to the Coast, these
"progressive" (their own term) clergy—mostly Creoles—pushed for
changes in the church's orientation: liberalization of strict rules regarding
baptism and Holy Communion, greater emphasis on meeting church
members' material needs, a more central role for native clergy. These
demands precipitated the North Americans' decision to grant the church
"national" status and abandon Nicaragua. Announced abruptly at a
meeting of the Moravian Synod in 1974, "nationalization" suddenly
placed the church under full control of these progressive Creole pastors.[20]

Oral histories provide contradictory evidence on the role of Miskitu
clergy and lay pastors in these reform efforts. Norman Bent (a pastor of
mixed Miskitu-Creole descent who identified with the Creole group) describes Miskitu participation as minimal, whereas Miskitu pastor Fer-
nando Colomer claims that he and other Miskitu were active protagonists in the initiative.[21] This disparity is indicative of long-standing ethnic
tensions within the church, which deepened after the North Americans'
departure. Miskitu Moravians resented what they viewed as favoritism
toward the Creoles, who had advanced higher in the church hierarchy,
even though Miskitu made up about two-thirds of the total membership.[22] While the group of Creole seminarians achieved advanced degrees
in Costa Rica, Miskitu received less prestigious training at the Bible Institute of Bilwaskarma, Río Coco.[23]

It cannot be a coincidence that within months of the 1974 Synod, Miskitu pastors with reformist inclinations channeled their political energies

toward the founding of ALPROMISU.[24] Although these Miskitu pastors surely sympathized with the "progressive" Creoles' demands, they could not have been pleased when it became clear that nationalization would put these same Creoles fully in charge of the church hierarchy. Moreover, within the incipient Miskitu middle class, pastors were the one group for whom assimilation was not a viable option. Because their daily activities required them to remain Miskitu, pastors had an added impetus to organize the people with whom they worked.

From the outset ALPROMISU promoted ethnic demands. With a mandate to represent all Miskitu, the organization attracted support from throughout the northern region and, later, from the south as well. About 500 Indian participants from 84 communities attended the first annual congress of ALPROMISU, held in May 1974 in the community of Sisin. Some regional Mestizo elite felt threatened, especially when large numbers of Miskitu congregated for the annual congresses. They harassed and attempted to intimidate ALPROMISU leaders.[25] By Pacific Coast standards, however, this repression was mild, and it never kept ALPROMISU from functioning. From 1975 through 1977 delegates from throughout the Coast attended ALPROMISU meetings and carried the organization's message back to their communities.

Lina Spark, elected president of ALPROMISU in 1974, summarizes the organization's philosophy:[26]

"Pawanka[27] was our goal. . . . We worked with Somoza, because he had agreed to help the Miskitu, to build schools, bring pawanka to our communities. . . . We pressured the government to provide scholarships for our children. With more education, they could become nurses, doctors. . . . We pushed for all kinds of projects (*proyecto nani*). . . . We wanted to build a market in Waspam. . . . The Miskitu exchanged a few pounds of beans for salt, clothing, etc. How could they progress in that way? The merchants profited and left the Miskitu empty-handed, impoverished. Those merchants were real exploiters. . . . Our living conditions were dismal . . . when you look at the coast, you see Spaniards and Creoles whose pawanka is much better. Why can't the Miskitu have that same pawanka? After all, the riches of the Coast belong to the Miskitu, but when you go to the Coast, there's nothing. Only the Pacific seems to benefit from our gold and all the rest. We want to get [some of those riches] back, so we can educate our kids. Education is the key to everything."

Given the conditions under which ALPROMISU arose, these demands sound remarkably conciliatory—working with the government to get a bigger piece of the pie. Spark voiced the militant idea that "the riches of the Coast belong to the Miskitu," only to reach the moderate conclusion that "education is the key." She and other ALPROMISU leaders were exposed to militant Indianist ideas when they attended meetings of the Pan-

American Indian movement in Canada (1975), Kiruna, Sweden (1977), and Geneva (1977). Yet when I asked Spark if they wanted autonomy or considered fighting for their rights, her response was emphatic:

"We didn't think about autonomy. We were looking for pawanka. The idea of fighting did not cross our minds. We were not interested in overthrowing the government. You see, all the ALPROMISU leaders came from Christian families . . . the Moravian parsons were all on our side. . . . I always sent [ALPROMISU] communications to the communities care of the parsons, and they read them in the church services. They agreed with our approach: to convince the government to give us pawanka."

In 1978 ALPROMISU went into decline. No annual congress was held that year, and the leaders faced serious challenges from a group of Miskitu university students who advocated more militant demands. In Awastara and neighboring communities, most townspeople had come to view ALPROMISU as a distant, urban group of Miskitu intellectuals. Moreover, the organization was about to receive a "large grant" from the Somoza government, an indication that the adversarial stance of previous years had been abandoned.[28] As the struggle against Somoza in western Nicaragua deepened and the state responded with acts of repression that betrayed its own weakness, the Miskitu organization turned quiescent. This outcome is more puzzling still in light of the events that followed. Soon after the Sandinista triumph, Miskitu people engaged in a mobilization of unprecedented breadth and intensity.

Continuities amid Revolutionary Change, 1979–81

During the first eighteen months of revolutionary government, state policy toward the Coast developed mainly as an expression of civilian politics. The incidents of February 1981 mark the turning point. By mid-1981, Miskitu opposition had assumed a decidedly military character, and actions of the state revolved largely around military exigencies.[29] It is therefore crucial to separate this initial period (July 1979–February 1981) from the subsequent one, when experiences of military conflict became the primary frame of reference both for state policy and for Miskitu political decisions. Once under way, the war created its own self-perpetuating rationale.

State-Promoted Economic Development

The Miskitu mobilization did not occur under conditions of economic desperation or even moderate economic decline. In spite of destruction caused by the war and myriad logistical problems associated with the transition to revolutionary government, Nicaragua's economy steadily gained strength during the first eighteen months. Shortages in consumer goods were temporary, not chronic; prices were stable; most sectors were well along toward recovering prewar levels of production. Moreover, the government immediately enacted a series of nationwide economic policies that favored workers and small-scale producers—curtailing exploitative intermediaries, guaranteeing high prices for agricultural products, vastly increasing the availability of short-term credit. Nevertheless, these policies had the effect of deepening tensions with the Miskitu, often in unintended and even unperceived ways.

The revolutionary state immediately gained control of most productive enterprises on the Coast, either because they had belonged to Somoza associates or because the foreign owners chose not to continue operations.[30] These enterprises struggled to overcome the problems associated with the transition—lack of spare parts, operating budget, reliable marketing channels, and qualified administrative personnel—and most managed briefly to regain pre-1979 production levels.[31] Concerned primarily with economic recovery, government-appointed administrators of these beleaguered companies initiated few substantive changes in their internal organization. FSLN cadres found themselves in the position of encouraging workers both to organize for their rights and to accommodate the administrators' plans. Challenging under the best of conditions, such mediation proved extremely difficult when workers were Coast people and managers were Pacific Coast Mestizos. This hierarchy prevailed throughout the southern region (Hale and Yih 1986) and was especially evident in the Camilo Ortega sugar mill, where Miskitu workers were uniformly at the bottom (see Table 2).[32]

Small-scale fishers and farmers had a more favorable initial encounter with the state.[33] Because these rural producers constituted the majority of the economically active population (and an even higher percentage among Miskitu), their experiences must carry more weight than those of wage laborers in the analysis of post-1979 economic change. Within months of coming to power, the revolutionary government initiated a massive agricultural assistance program. Makeshift bank offices, supplied by periodic visits of bank airplanes (known in Spanish as the Banco Aereo), sprang up in isolated communities. They offered loans to thousands of Miskitu farmers preparing for the 1980 agricultural cycle and credit to upgrade fishing equipment (e.g., nets, outboard motors) or to make improvements in community infrastructure.[34]

Miskitu farmers also suddenly found themselves freed from the grip of exploitative market conditions. The wealthiest merchants, who also tended to have the closest political ties with the Somoza government, fled

TABLE 2
*Labor Hierarchy by Ethnic Group in the
Camilo Ortega Sugar Mill, Kukra Hill, 1983*

	Miskitu		Creoles		Mestizos		Totals	
	N	%	N	%	N	%	N	%
Administration	0	0	12	11	26	14	38	6
Skilled labor	4	5	23	20	51	29	78	11
Unskilled labor	22	15	79	69	48	27	149	22
Field labor	360	80	0	0	53	30	413	61
Totals	386	100	114	100	178	100	678	100

SOURCE: Hale and Yih (1983).

the country in anticipation of the Sandinista victory. A few wealthy merchants remained, as Bourgois (n.d.) observed: "In San Carlos [Río Coco], there are three or four families of merchants who live in relatively lavish luxury. They have private electric plants, take trips to Miami and their profits come directly from buying rice, beans and corn at cheap prices . . . and selling basic necessities at inflated prices. . . . There is a great deal of hate for the two biggest merchants." This group that remained also found its power curtailed. The FSLN vowed to protect the subordinate classes, Bourgois reports, and created a climate of intolerance for exploitative practices: "When the FSLN came [to San Carlos] they asked the people in the community to denounce people who behaved badly during the former regime. The people were scared, but a couple denounced the merchants." The state also directly influenced market conditions in favor of small-scale producers. State-decreed price controls increased people's access to many consumer goods, and the state-run Basic Foods Enterprise (ENABAS) purchased rice and beans at five to eight times the previous price, forcing merchants to do the same (CIERA 1981: 117). These economic measures gave rise to what Bourgois (n.d.) described as euphoria among Río Coco farmers.

Yet the very expansion of the state and the actions taken to implement these new programs also contributed to tensions with the intended beneficiaries for two reasons. First, while the National Development Bank (BND) distributed credit, activists from the Agricultural Ministry (called INRA and later MIDINRA) and the Association of Rural Workers[35] worked to transform the organization of production. Following a nationwide mandate, they sought to form cooperatives, provide agricultural services, and stimulate increased production. The highest ideal of the cooperative movement was to convince peasants to band together in a Sandinista Agricultural Collective (CAS), which carried out production in a fully collectivized manner. Not only did Miskitu farmers resist this idea, but, according to Bourgois (n.d.), their inclination upon receiving credit was to hire wage labor.[36] When INRA and ATC activists used mildly coercive measures to encourage "cooperation" (e.g., making assistance contingent on such practices), Miskitu farmers reacted with resentment: "The [San Carlos?] villagers are not enthusiastic about organizing in a cooperative for planting rice. They do not see how they will benefit and INRA does not want to help them unless they are organized. . . . The only reason they are making this effort to cooperate is because they think [that otherwise] they will get no aid" (Bourgois n.d.). These activists who encouraged cooperativization often were local Mestizos, who had no particular aptitude or qualifications to work with the Miskitu communities and displayed disdainful attitudes toward Miskitu culture.[37]

Second, though the revolutionary government's programs were conceived to meet the needs of the predominantly poor Miskitu, a middle stratum of Mestizo elite often benefited as well. These Mestizos generally had closer ties to the government, if only because they spoke the same language and moved within an overlapping cultural milieu. This made it easier for them to work the system, to achieve credit and other forms of government assistance, and to promote their particular interests.[38] In addition, these Mestizos maintained leverage simply because the economic functions they performed were not easily replaced. On the Río Coco, for example, ENABAS (the state marketing entity) could not develop a fluid marketing system on its own. It offered advantageous prices but lacked river transport and the budget to purchase steadily in the communities. Mestizos merchants provided transportation in return for reciprocal agreements that allowed them to maintain their privileged economic and political status.

The profound differences between the Sandinista and Somoza states therefore did not eliminate all continuities in interethnic relations. Miskitu townspeople continued to face Mestizo government functionaries who were intent on implementing nationally conceived plans for socioeconomic development. Marketing conditions improved considerably but Mestizo merchants did not disappear, and perceptions of collusion between these merchants and the government had reason to persist. Most important, the Sandinista state's new standards of economic justice heightened Miskitu people's aspirations, which had been rising steadily since the mid-1960's. When implementation fell short of these aspirations—whether in state enterprises, agricultural credit, or market relations—Miskitu held the state directly responsible.

Hardly unique to the Atlantic Coast, revolutionary change established a similar set of tensions between people and state throughout Nicaragua. The crucial difference lay in the nature of organized political responses to these problems. The very methods that allowed mediation of conflicts in western Nicaragua—popular organization promoted by the party and endorsed by the state—brought contrary results on the Coast.

Political Conditions of Mobilization

Indians and Creoles of the Atlantic Coast were largely insulated from the armed struggle against Somoza. Although an important force of the FSLN guerrilla army—the Pablo Ubeda Brigade—operated in the jungle area north and east of the mines, it interacted mainly with Mestizo peasants (Calderon 1981: 150). Miskitu university students—a total of perhaps 30—assumed a generally oppositional stance toward the Somoza regime, but their contacts with the Coast were limited to sporadic visits during breaks in classes (Law 1982).[39] Groups of high school and university students from Bluefields—both Creoles and Mestizos—also opposed the government, and in the final months some joined the armed struggle. These pockets of activism around Bluefields were the closest Coast residents came to experiencing the political culture of insurrection that engulfed the rest of Nicaragua. Miskitu from Sandy Bay Sirpi monitored the FSLN combatants' advance through snatches of radio news reports from Costa Rica or the United States. To them, as to Miskitu throughout the Coast, the revolutionary struggle and victory of July 19, 1979, were distant events.

Long after Brooklyn Rivera became an avowed anti-Sandinista, he still emphasized the profound effects of the revolutionary victory on the Miskitu people: "I would say that the triumph, or more precisely, the fervor of the revolutionary triumph, filled people's spirits and hearts, creating an atmosphere of new things to come, new conditions in which we all could express ourselves, we all could participate. Previously, the atmosphere was dormant, with no incentive [to think about change]."[40] An FSLN cadre from the southern Creole community of Pearl Lagoon provides a similar description. Although no one had fought against Somoza, these people interpreted the victory and the accompanying FSLN slogans in a most favorable light. "Power to the people" meant "Now we're going to do our own thing, control our own communities." In their first "revolutionary" act, Pearl Lagoon townspeople traveled up the Wawashang River to a ranch owned by a former member of the National Guard, butchered some cattle, and organized a big feast in town. Everyone responded with jubilance: "This is what we've been waiting for, from long time."[41] The triumph opened the floodgates of Coast peoples' aspirations, despite confusion and anxieties about what the revolution actually meant. Indeed, such anxieties may even have added intensity to the surge of political sentiment.

A clear state policy on political organization in the Atlantic Coast did not emerge during the first few months. State entities (such as the BND, INRA, and ENABAS) and mass-based organizations (such as the ATC) began work, often at cross-purposes with one another. The problems inherent to the consolidation of a new state were particularly severe on the Coast, where revolutionary cadres had little preexisting organizational presence or experience. Although numerous incidents during these initial months—resulting from miscommunication, lack of coordination, and unauthorized low-level decisions—created tensions, at the time they must have seemed transitory and thoroughly surmountable.

The state's first chance to define its relationship to the Miskitu came at the end of October 1979, when ALPROMISU held its fifth annual congress.[42] Propelled by post-triumph ebullience, the group of radicalized Miskitu university students—Steadman Fagoth, Brooklyn Rivera, and Hazel Law, among others—worked to revitalize and assume leadership roles in ALPROMISU. They pushed to convene the congress, which brought together over 450 Indian delegates from 187 communities in Puerto Cabezas. The government position reflected ambivalence more than orthodoxy. The FSLN—represented by Daniel Ortega and Ernesto Cardenal—backed the formation of popular organizations on the Coast and the strengthening of Indian culture and identity but resisted Miskitu demands for an ethnic-based organization.[43] After an initial attempt to convince Miskitu delegates that an existing peasant syndicate (the ATC) would adequately represent them, Ortega acquiesced, and the new organization MISURASATA was born. Ortega's decision reflected adherence to the principle of popular organization and optimism grounded in the pro-revolutionary sympathies of the new Miskitu leaders. It did not embody a clear analysis of how MISURASATA's orientation toward ethnic empowerment would fit within the FSLN vision of revolutionary change.[44]

This problem became evident in subsequent months, as MISURASATA rapidly gained strength and became a formidable political force on the Coast. Throughout Nicaragua, state and party cadres viewed grass-roots political participation in mass-based organizations as fundamental to the revolutionary process. But they applied this principle to the Atlantic Coast with hesitancy and ambivalence. While formally assigning MISURASATA the status of other mass-based organizations—even to the point of awarding it a seat in the Council of State—they distrusted its leaders and goals. Deep-seated premises toward Indians underlay that distrust and made MISURASATA's increasing militancy and clout appear all the more threatening.

MISURASATA followed a political course that confirmed FSLN leaders' worst fears, appearing determined to achieve uncontested political authority on the Coast. Bolstered by widespread popular support, MISURASATA challenged and sought to displace all its FSLN-backed competitors, from the Sandinista youth organization (JS19J), to the ATC, to labor unions, to local elected officials. Confrontations with the state occurred on a wide range of issues: wages in state-owned enterprises, rights to export marine products, jurisdiction over a proposed national forest reserve, community land rights. Each confrontation sharpened the Miskitu protagonists' collective memories of past oppression and evoked more vivid, tangible goals to motivate subsequent action. With each struggle, victory, and prospect of further victories, Miskitu ethnic militancy deepened.

This mobilization encompassed religious as well as civil authority. Within the Moravian church Creoles represented at most 25 percent of the membership, yet they had controlled the upper echelons of the institution since the North Americans departed in 1974. In a surge of activism at the 1980 Synod, Miskitu pastors reversed the ethnic balance of the governing board and elected the first Miskitu superintendent.[45] Because many Miskitu pastors and lay workers also played key roles in MISURASATA, religious and secular activism became practically inextricable. MISURASATA organizers employed evocative religious imagery and (following ALPROMISU's precedent) made full use of Moravian church social networks and material infrastructure to promote their message. This civil-religious alliance rested on a fundamental convergence of interests: both sectors sought to empower the Miskitu people.

The climax of civilian Miskitu mobilization occurred during the literacy campaign. Typical of these initial months, the campaign began with a political struggle. The Ministry of Education planned Spanish literacy only but then acceded to MISURASATA's demand that classes be offered in the students' native tongue. Bolstered by yet another victory, MISURASATA gathered hundreds of Miskitu high school and university students, including many of its most committed activists, and sent them to work as brigadistas in remote Miskitu communities throughout the Coast. These were ideal conditions for the growth of ethnic militancy, especially since the brigadistas had a mandate for political education as well as literacy.[46] Rural dwellers learned about Miskitu rights, while brigadistas gained an emotionally charged sense of identity and solidarity with their people.

During this same period—October 1980 to February 1981—the negotiations over land rights reached a moment of decision. For most of the year MISURASATA leaders, under the direction of Steadman Fagoth, had been at work on a proposal for Indian territorial rights that would encompass most of the Atlantic Coast, about one-third of Nicaragua's total territory (see Map 2). The details of these demands are contested because they were never formally presented to the government. MISURASATA leaders had planned to unveil their proposal in Puerto Cabezas at the closing ceremony of the literacy campaign. Brigadistas from throughout the Coast would have been present, with collective aspirations of ethnic militancy at their height; the government would have been virtually forced to concede.[47]

Instead of allowing that plan to unfold, beginning on February 21 the government moved to thwart MISURASATA's ascendancy by summarily arresting about 50 of the organization's principal leaders. Most were detained only briefly, but a core of top leaders were accused of "separatist" intentions. The government also presented documents to prove that MISURASATA "general coordinator" Steadman Fagoth had worked as a covert intelligence agent for Somoza. Within two weeks the government had released all the leaders except Fagoth, who remained in jail until May, gained conditional freedom, and promptly fled to Honduras.

No definitive assessment of the covert U.S. role as provocateur in this initial period will be possible until crucial documents become available. At present, the most one can do is cite what I consider to be rather convincing circumstantial evidence. The CIA followed the escalating conflict closely and demonstrated full awareness of its anti-Sandinista potential.[48] USAID funded the Managua office of MISURASATA and offered the organization additional funds. Two important MISURASATA leaders— Steadman Fagoth and Norman Campbell—maintained extensive contacts with the National Democratic Movement (MDN) headed by Alfonso Robelo, which almost surely was receiving CIA funds.[49]

MISURASATA's positions also have a rationale in internal politics, however, regardless of whether any of its leaders had been "bought" by the CIA.[50] As I argue in the next chapter, the United States exerted greatest influence on Miskitu mobilization during the first eighteen months through the less tangible realm of political affinities. After November 1980, President-elect Reagan publicly called for the Nicaraguan government's demise, and most Miskitu viewed North Americans as historic allies. It required only a small additional logical step for Miskitu to conclude that the United States would surely back their bid for power.

In the wake of the February arrests, Miskitu communities exploded into widespread, spontaneous, and remarkably bellicose collective action. As mentioned earlier, when government soldiers arrived in the coastal community of Prinzapolka to arrest a MISURASATA leader, they found townspeople and brigadistas gathered in the Moravian church. The soldiers entered the church well armed, and a struggle ensued that left four soldiers and four Miskitu youths dead. As we have seen, the precise sequence of events that led up to this tragedy is told in starkly divergent ways in Sandinista and Miskitu accounts. Regardless of the details, for the incident to occur unarmed Miskitu brigadistas had to take on armed Sandinista soldiers, an indication of the deep animosity and inclination to mobilize that had been building. Although particularly violent, this response was by no means exceptional. Upon hearing of the arrests, 3,000 youths fled to Honduras—some out of fear but many out of a firm commitment to fight.[51] Thousands more of all ages traveled to the regional towns in protest and refused to move until their leaders were released. Most important, as the narrative in Chapter 3 suggests, rural Miskitu youths—many of whom had no prior involvement with MISURASATA—showed an outpouring of unconditional support for the armed mobilization that followed.

Explaining Miskitu Quiescence

The full extent of the contrast should now be apparent. Government policies and structural conditions within the Coast economy after 1979 heightened interethnic tensions, and the political ideals of the revolutionary government, emphasizing "popular power" and grass-roots organizing, certainly encouraged collective action. Yet conditions conducive to Miskitu mobilization were also present during the last two decades of Somoza's rule, when they gave rise to a widespread ethnopolitical awakening. Analysts have explained the Miskitu people's relative quiescence during the first period by pointing to two factors, neither of which I find completely satisfying.

First, Carlos Vilas has asserted that in broad structural terms, the "objective reality" was that "conditions for revolution ripened *outside of the Coast*" (1987: 64). To a certain extent he surely is right, and by extension we can argue that structural conditions before 1979 were not sufficiently conducive to Miskitu rebellion. Each of the factors that I examined—penetration of the state, increasing contact with dominant Mestizo political and economic actors, and a political atmosphere of rising expectations—though present in both periods, took on greater proportions after 1979. In a variation on this same argument, analysts often point out that because the Miskitu did not experience the severe repression of the Somoza state apparatus, they had less reason to mobilize. Dennis (1981b: 292) reports that the Miskitu were recruited to Somoza's National Guard in large numbers, which also might have helped to attenuate that organization's repressive image.

Although additional comparative research would certainly help us to make a definitive assessment, it is my contention that such structural explanations cannot stand alone. In the first place, they assume part of what needs to be explained. If the Miskitu had turned militantly oppositional, for example, Somoza's army surely would not have hesitated to employ repression. Such arguments neglect the formative impact of grassroots Miskitu initiative on what counts as "structure" and work with an obscure, deductive portrayal of Miskitu consciousness. The Miskitu stance during the final months of somocismo points to a less explosive path that postrevolutionary ethnic politics might have followed. Conversely, the tremendous force of collective sentiment unleashed in 1981 redirects our attention to 1978: despite broader conditions conducive to mobilization against a decadent "Spanish" regime, the Miskitu remained quiescent. This contrast challenges us to formulate a more explicit analysis of Miskitu consciousness and political motivation.

A second explanation comes closer to achieving this objective but ultimately proves inadequate as well. Both Miskitu oral histories (including those I collected) and academic analyses explain that Somoza "bought off" ALPROMISU leaders. Lina Spark, for example, described ALPROMISU leaders' relations with Somoza:

"A selection of four leaders [went to Managua in 1974] and talked directly with President Somoza. They said 'We are educated, and we have no one in the government. We want to work as intermediaries between you and the [Miskitu] people. We the educated Miskitu will be in the middle. You are here, doing good things, but you don't see the oppression that goes on in the Coast. There are *karas* [ruthless exploiters, lit. alligators] there . . . so we need to be in the middle, to bring the people's troubles to your attention, and to convey your word back to the people.' Somoza said, 'That sounds great. A new election is coming up, and I'll give you all positions. We will work together.' That is how Adolfo Bushy became *diputado* [representative to the national parliament] and Enrique Marley mayor of Waspam. Somoza really kept his word. . . . But then something happened: Enrique had been the ALPROMISU president—when he was made mayor he came under a new pressure. He could not attack the government any more because he was in a government job. Enrique could not say a thing, could not do a thing, so he said to me, 'Lina, why don't you try. . . .' The government job shut his mouth."

Later in the interview, Spark explained how the same strategy was used on her:

"Somoza respected me. He made me a member of the Municipal Board [of Puerto Cabezas]. I didn't do any work, but my name was there. . . . It happened in 1977, I was on a trip in Europe, and when I came back ten days later, I heard my name was included as a member of the board. (It's prohibited to use someone's name that way, you know.) I was not a Somocista. He did it without asking me. And whenever there was some task—like an election—[the government people] would come to me saying, 'Lina help us with this, Lina help us with that.' I did not want to, but I helped anyway. By refusing, I would have given the impression that I was against the government. I helped at election times to prove I wasn't against him. So our relations were good. When I traveled to Managua, they treated me really well. They respected me because I was a representative of the people."

In short, by making certain concessions and drawing Miskitu into the fold, Somoza undermined the potential militancy of Miskitu demands. Spark describes herself as an astute political actor: she had learned to work through the system, to compromise, to gain more in the long run by being accommodating. Miskitu collective memories that became dominant after 1979 contain a less flattering conclusion: Somoza had bought off their leaders.[52]

Although that explanation (whether with a "co-optation" or "tactical accommodation" emphasis) moves us closer to an understanding of Miskitu quiescence, it also begs the crucial question: why was the leadership, and by extension the base as well, so susceptible to Somoza's palliatives in the first place? And why did palliatives of much greater content offered by the Sandinistas just two years later not produce similar effects? The anthropologists who worked on the Atlantic Coast during this period provide additional information that helps us to approach this question through further scrutiny of Miskitu consciousness. Mary Helms reports that "Miskito [express] enthusiasm for Americans and their culture. [They] tend to view Americans . . . as high level relatives interested in the fate of their Miskito kinsmen" (1971: 221–24). She also observes that "Spanish-speaking Nicaraguans are distrusted because, unlike Americans, villagers claim, the 'Spanish' are interested only in taking advantage of them" (p. 222). She and Philip Dennis both note that, paradoxically, despite Miskitu resentment of the "Spaniards" in general, they respected and admired President Somoza. Both explain the paradox by arguing that Somoza passed himself off as non-Spanish. "He was educated in the U.S., spoke fluent English, and used English during periodic personal visits to the East Coast," Helms explains (1983b: 7). "In a situation of ethnic antagonism," Dennis notes, "Somoza could legitimately claim to be not entirely Spanish" (1981b: 281).

The analysis of Miskitu consciousness in Chapter 3 suggests a different—and, I contend, more convincing—interpretation of these data. No one in Sandy Bay referred to Somoza as anything but a "Spaniard." While their vehemence corresponds in large part to the deepening of ethnic militancy that occurred after 1979, it seems doubtful that they were misled about Somoza's ethnic identity. Somoza's flamboyant pro-

American posture, I contend, had political significance for a different reason. Listen, for example, to Manuel Rodriguez's response when presented with the puzzle:

'We all knew about our rights [in Somoza time], Zelaya's promises and all that. But Somoza and the Americans were partners (*wal kumi kan*). When Somoza would talk with them [the Americans], whatever he said was well done.'

Somoza's speeches on the Coast reinforced the already widespread perception that he and the Americans were close allies, which placed the Miskitu in a dilemma: to oppose Somoza would mean to oppose the Americans as well. Quite apart from the question of what people perceived Somoza's ethnic identity to be, the premises of Anglo affinity would have impeded the deepening of people's antigovernment militancy.

The comments of Lina Spark quoted above take on new importance if reinterpreted in this light. When asked whether ALPROMISU considered adopting the radical demands and tactics that MISURASATA later followed, she responded without hesitation. "The idea of fighting did not cross our minds. We were not interested in overthrowing the government. You see, all the ALPROMISU leaders came from Christian families." Yet the reasoning implicit in Spark's response (that Christian values exert a moderating, pacifist influence on their adherents) confronts an empirical problem. Christians played leading roles in the post-1979 mobilization, and many Miskitu saw themselves as fighting in the name of their Christian beliefs. Her comment contains a key insight, however, if we remember that the Moravian church had been a principal institutional site from which the values of Anglo affinity had emerged. Through the church, Coast people received a constant flow of American donations (clothing, food, and other items) and came into contact with innumerable North Americans who had come to the Coast with benevolent intentions.[53] The content of Moravian teachings subtly and overtly reinforced people's adherence to a most conservative version of North American political culture. Consider, for example, what values are apt to be reinforced in Miskitu Christians' minds each time they sing hymn number 216. As the hymnal indicates, and parsons often reiterate in prefatory remarks,[54] that hymn is dedicated to the Moravian church's only "martyr" in Nicaragua, the Minnesota farm boy turned missionary, Karl Bregenzer. As church legend has it, Bregenzer was stoically singing that very hymn when one of Sandino's generals chopped off his head with a machete. More overt political messages were also delivered. From Awastara in 1978, Dennis (1981b: 282) reports hearing "sermons (delivered by lay pastors, but obviously repeating the opinions of higher level missionaries) warning that if Somoza left, the Communists would gain control and religion would be outlawed. One dramatic warning was that the communists would 'take away a man's sailing dory or his animals, which he had worked so hard to acquire, and give them to his lazy neighbor across the village, who never worked at all.'

Such observations take on particular importance when combined with my argument regarding the continuities before and after 1979. If structural conditions conducive to mobilization were present in both periods, then the explanation for Miskitu quiescence must shift to focus more centrally on the content of their consciousness. At a time of growing militancy and resistance elsewhere in Nicaragua, Miskitu people submitted to Somoza's clumsy attempts at co-optation. A key unexamined factor in this response, I contend, was that the premises of Anglo affinity encouraged accommodation. How else are we to interpret Rodriguez's statement, quoted above, to the effect that Somoza and the Americans were "partners"? The partnership deterred militant opposition because Miskitu people were reluctant to oppose a government that was an ally of the Americans, and because Anglo affinity engendered an attitude of dependence on aid from the outside. Although this assertion would benefit from additional insight into Miskitu consciousness during the late 1970's, it makes effective use of the evidence available and has the added advantage of parsimony. In the following chapter I argue that after 1979 Anglo affinity again exerted a great influence on the course of Miskitu collective action, but with precisely the opposite effect.

6 Explaining Miskitu-Sandinista Conflict, 1981–85

> Somoza never wanted to give Indians schools, because he knew they would learn about their rights. The Sandinistas gave the Indians schools, and sure enough, they learned.
> —Manuel Rodriguez, Sandy Bay Sirpi, 1985

THE NARRATIVE ACCOUNT in Chapter 3 ends with the arrests of February 1981 and their immediate repercussions. In the collective memories of Sandy Bay townspeople, these events serve as a historical divide between "before," when, despite some complaints, relations with the government were tolerable, and "after," when the government backed down on its promises, arrested their leaders, and sent the military to repress them. A few months after the Prinzapolka affair, MISURASATA took up arms against the government and received an outpouring of support in Sandy Bay. By 1984 every household had someone—a sibling, son, daughter, or cousin—who had joined. Community members called these MISURASATA combatants *bui nani* (the boys) or *unta uplika nani* (bush people). To the Nicaraguan army detachments stationed in Sandy Bay, however, the bush people were contras. The two military forces clashed repeatedly; civilians who gave the contras food, information, or other forms of aid—and many did—risked arrest and punishment. To most people in Sandy Bay the army, and the Sandinistas in general, were the enemy.

How did such fierce political and military conflict come about? Existing answers to this question cover a range of political standpoints but have tended to rely on structural analysis with an implicitly deductive portrayal of grass-roots Miskitu consciousness. Whether emphasizing the Reagan administration's interventionist policies, the Sandinista state's oppressive presence, or the power and charisma of MISURASATA leaders, these explanations implicitly assume that Miskitu community members responded to forces originating elsewhere, acting with the same general rationale as that expressed publicly by their leaders. Here I present a different view that begins by recounting how community members experienced the tumultuous years between February 1981 and May 1985 and then attempts to understand the consciousness with which they engaged in the mobilization.

Sandy Bay people's collective memories of this period are passionate, deeply moving, and always highly convincing. Suddenly, by their account, they had an opportunity for the "good fight," and they responded with gusto, deep commitment, and great expectations. By presenting this community-level perspective I hope to demonstrate the extent to which the ethnic militancy of people in communities like Sandy Bay influenced the content, breadth, and intensity of the mobilization. In keeping with the argument developed thus far, however, I also contend that this conclusion alone is insufficient, even misleading. The qualification comes from the research methods I employed and is consistent with my emphasis on Miskitu people's contradictory consciousness. If one steps back from the community and views the conflict from the Sandinista perspective, a radically different picture comes into focus. The Sandinistas were involved in a good fight of their own against the imperial pretensions of the Reagan administration. Taking that perspective seriously encouraged me to develop a more critical assessment of the Miskitu response, especially the elements that shaped Miskitu perceptions of this broader struggle. The result is an argument that maintains an emphasis on grass-roots Miskitu initiative, combined with a structurally informed analysis of their consciousness, to achieve a fuller understanding of the force and emotion behind their mobilization.

The Experience of Ethnic Mobilization, 1981–85

It would have been possible to continue the narrative style of Chapter 3 to cover the period through May 1985, when I first visited Sandy Bay. I decided against this approach for methodological, logistical, and ethical reasons. I approached the topic of political involvement in the antigovernment mobilization with great caution. In an initial phase of fieldwork, I did not attempt to tape-record any such information; when observations came out on tape they were, like Mauro Salazar's quotation at the end of Chapter 3, unsolicited general statements, without specifications of time, place, or person. I learned details of the war years from discussions in the homes of people with whom I had developed a relationship of trust, letting information come out spontaneously rather than in response to specific questions. Gradually, I developed an extensive knowledge of the war years, recorded in my field notes as my summaries of what people told me. However valuable the resulting narrative, it reads very differently from one consisting largely of the participants' own words.

Moreover, because key events were temporally proximate, everyone remembered a wealth of details and had important contributions to make. Levels of knowledge, of course, varied. There were not, however, several people known throughout the community as the "experts," as was the case of Salazar for more distant history. This proximity also immersed me in all the micro-details of what happened—personal rivalries, kin-based divisions, love affairs, unusual motives for seemingly commonplace actions—details that played an important role in each individual's story. I began to cross-check accounts of the same event or time period to achieve a fuller picture and to reveal quirky interpretations. Interviews with noncommunity people—members of the FSLN, armed forces, or organizations that had a presence in Sandy Bay—also added bits and pieces to the account. In short, I achieved greater precision in detail at the price of a more processed narrative that relies much more on my own editorial decisions.

Finally, the proximity of the war years made the political content of the narrative extremely sensitive. When I first arrived in Sandy Bay, I was not sure that I would have access to this information, and I doubted that collecting it would be appropriate. My initial research goals involved data collection on the less sensitive topics of oral history, production, social organization, and participant observation in daily affairs of the community. I did ask questions like "How did all these troubles get started?" but I did not at first direct inquiries toward recent or present circumstances. As people became willing to go further, I began to record their own political orientations in greater detail. This included community members' thoughts about and relations with the bush people, as well as detailed accounts of what people who were still in the bush thought, said, did, and planned to do. Although I have relied extensively on this information to formulate my analysis, it seemed injudicious to present people's stories of war during the period of most active and intense conflict in a verbatim form. These stories would implicate townspeople (even if names were changed), the government, and me in very specific ways and, more important, could be used for purposes of which I do not approve.

For these reasons I have opted to present an account, entirely in my own words, that conveys my own understanding of events between 1981 and 1985. It draws on numerous discussions in Sandy Bay, interviews with Sandy Bay refugees in Costa Rica, and entries in the Moravian station diary in Karawala. Although I also conducted a few brief interviews with FSLN, government, or army cadres with experience in the community, these sources play a minor role. The account is fundamentally from Miskitu community members' perspective; it describes the events they directly experienced and occasionally attempts to summarize the conclusions to which they came. I hope this will help in achieving a better understanding of the mobilization, but if read as an account of what actually happened, the standpoint of the people who are its sources and my own explicit editorial interventions must be borne clearly in mind.

The Narrative

For twelve months beginning in February 1981, not a single shot was fired between Miskitu combatants and Nicaraguan army forces in the immediate vicinity of Sandy Bay. Townspeople were, however, deeply involved in clandestine organizing and military preparation, which created an atmosphere of anticipation, excitement, and fear. The Prinzapolka melee had a deep impact on the community. That day, a State Security unit had arrived in Sandy Bay in a speedboat to arrest three or four Miskitu brigadistas, who also were MISURASATA activists. Then the news came that a man from the neighboring community of Karawala had been killed at the Prinzapolka church. A few days later, some Miskitu brigadistas who had fled from the Prinzapolka incident turned up in Sandy Bay. Community members kept them hidden until, following mediation by the local FSLN representative, they turned themselves in to the government.

The FSLN representative was an unusual person. She had grown up on the Río Coco in a Mestizo family but spoke fluent Miskitu. Through these language skills and nearly a year's work in the Sandy Bay area, she had gained the trust and friendship of many residents. A few weeks after the arrests, she received instructions to confiscate a two-way radio that had been donated to Sandy Bay in the mid-1970's for reporting medical emergencies to the hospital in Puerto Cabezas. The government had determined that MISURASATA was using the radio for clandestine organizing. When she arrived in Sandy Bay unarmed and announced her intentions, community members surrounded and physically threatened her. She left badly shaken up, aware of the growing polarization and feeling that she could do little to stop it. Channels of political dialogue between government authorities and Sandy Bay people, never particularly effective, largely ceased to function.

The first Miskitu and Creole combatants reached Sandy Bay about mid-1981. They were members of a small group headed by Floyd "Can" Wilson and came from the nearby community of Tasbapauni. Armed with one automatic weapon and some old hunting rifles, they made occasional visits to talk politics and recruit followers. These combatants spoke mainly Creole English; Sandy Bay people called them the Tasba-pauni boys and distinguished them from the Miskitu organizers who came later. Although Sandy Bay people fed and housed the Tasbapauni boys, few if any heeded the call to arms.

By about August 1981, Sandy Bay townspeople began to hear about clandestine organizing in the north, and a few decided to join. Marco Pa-rrales left for the Waunta Haulover area to make contact with a group in military training near there. A few months later, Pedro Rodriguez and four other young men hijacked a fishing boat from Río Grande Bar and headed for Honduras. They had worked as lobster divers on the boat and had a reputation for being rowdy (*rukkira*), drinking heavily and getting into brawls. Rodriguez made it known that they were leaving to "join the fight for Indian rights."

Active recruitment of Sandy Bay youth by MISURASATA began in De-cember 1981. Marco Parrales had returned to the community with a man named Fisher and two others, all from the north. They spent Christmas in Sandy Bay, stayed at Parrales's house during the day, and held meetings at night, mostly with the young people. Fisher told them that it was time to unify, to struggle for land, and for Miskitu to become "their own bosses." He reported that Miskitu communities throughout the region were organizing and that victory would come quickly. He also warned of dire consequences if the Sandinistas were allowed to remain in control of the Coast.

In January military training began at a clandestine camp near the com-munity. About 70 youths went to the camp, both men and women, the latter in many cases without their parents' consent. They marched with sticks and went hungry because the arms and food that Fisher had prom-ised never materialized. One mother, whose sixteen-year-old daughter had joined Fisher, claims to have criticized him angrily: "You have our children there without guns—you're going to get them killed." After about twenty days they came back unharmed, and Fisher left for a camp near Walpa Siksa, to the north. Marco Parrales took charge of collecting food and money from townspeople and sending it to Fisher.

By February 1982, although sympathies in Sandy Bay lay clearly with MISURASATA, Nicaraguan government troops still had no presence in the community. Alarming rumors swept through the community that the Sandinistas "were killing people and burning churches on the Río Coco." But no local incident had occurred to increase the polarization of com-munity and government. A dozen young men went to the Walpa Siksa base to receive military training, but half returned to the community be-cause recruits were more numerous than arms. A small group, including one Sandy Bay man, operated in the area with a few old firearms, using the name of MISURASATA. They had a reputation as thieves and received little community support.

The head of State Security for the Río Grande zone, a Bluefields Mestizo named Aldo, still acquired "intelligence" from his contacts within the community. A timely report from one of these Sandy Bay informants led to the death of Wilson in March 1982. Government security forces had been after Wilson's group for some time and had charged Aldo with the mission. Tipped off by the informant, Aldo's men caught Wilson off guard on the beach a mile south of Sandy Bay. Wilson escaped seriously wounded and took refuge in a nearby farmhouse. Security forces killed him in another confrontation two days later. Although no Sandy Bay people were directly involved, they heard the machine-gun fire and all the stories that followed. It was their first direct experience with the war.

Almost a year passed before further combat occurred in the vicinity. During that time, government troops periodically passed through Sandy Bay, searching for MISURASATA combatants. State Security began to single out the families of known bush people for questioning and surveillance. But when government troops were absent—most of the time— bush people drifted back into Sandy Bay to talk politics, enlist recruits, and enjoy the hospitality of community members. When the army returned, these combatants vanished into the bush or blended in with civilian townspeople.

As the bush people established a more active presence and displayed a more convincing array of weaponry, additional youths decided to join. Most older men with families generally avoided direct involvement. The notable exception was Saul Duran, a man of about 50 years from another community, who had married a Sandy Bay woman. Duran was a highly respected lay preacher and the wealthiest man in Sandy Bay. He had a well-stocked store and a large farm a few miles away, both of which he put at the disposal of the bush people. By the beginning of 1983, Duran and his two adult sons, fearing arrest, lived mainly in the bush.[1]

At around this time the war entered a new phase. The bush people, well armed and growing in numbers, had established a base near the Sasing Laya Creek, an upriver tributary of the Río Grande. Under the leadership of Bruno Gabriel, an audacious and relentless combatant, MISURASATA forces took the offensive. They attacked militia posts in small upriver settlements and ambushed government speedboats heading up the Río Grande. Gabriel also infiltrated the small army unit stationed at Río Grande Bar and convinced one member of the unit to become a collaborator. One night in March the turncoat soldier riddled the bunkhouse with machine-gun fire while his six comrades slept, then fled to join the bush people.

By early 1983, the government faced a desperate set of conditions. It could no longer provide basic services in the Río Grande zone because the area had become too dangerous for any civilian political presence; there were few troops who knew the terrain or spoke the language; the adversary, MISURASATA, had widespread local support and a direct supply line from the CIA.[2] With little hope of stopping the war through political means, government leaders responded with a show of military force. They deployed a large detachment of voluntary militia recruited from the Pacific department of Masaya to the zone in April 1983, the first unit to be stationed in Sandy Bay. The Masaya militiamen were young, without much military or political experience, but enthusiastic about the revolution and itching for a fight.

Sandy Bay people remember the "Masaya boys" with a shudder and a litany of accusations. The soldiers confiscated the houses of Marco Parrales and Saul Duran—the two townsmen most overtly involved with MISURASATA—and turned them into command posts. They forced the wives of these two men to cook for them and decreed that anyone who had washed clothes for the contras would now wash clothes for them. They slaughtered and ate domestic animals without compensation, shot off their guns indiscriminately at night, and treated community members abusively. One of the most frequently recounted transgressions involved coconuts, a basic subsistence item grown by every family. The Masaya boys shot young nuts from the trees and collected them as they fell, to drink the sweet water inside. Community members watched with impotent rage, knowing that gunshots would kill the trees, cutting short their bearing years by decades.

Simultaneously with the deployment of Masaya militiamen, State Security took active steps to cut ties between community members and bush people. They replaced Aldo with a more aggressive official, Juan Bimbo, who enacted new security measures: curfew, restrictions on travel outside the community, and jail for anyone suspected of aiding the contras. Although a core group of Sandy Bay community members had gone to the bush long before the Masaya boys arrived, direct military presence and strict security measures greatly increased the number of recruits. Seeing friends and relatives arrested, mistreated, and sent to jail (at times locally, other times to Bluefields or even Managua), many more young men turned to the bush, whether out of conviction, unprocessed anger, or merely self-defense. A smaller number of young women took the same decision.

MISURASATA's impressive string of military victories became another impetus to join the bush people. In June 1983, in the community of Tasbapauni, Bruno Gabriel's forces surrounded and killed Juan Bimbo. A month later they destroyed the army command post in Río Grande Bar, freeing eight Miskitu prisoners from the adjacent jailhouse, and they overran an army post in the upriver settlement of Kiwa. From that time on, MISURASATA controlled the entire Río Grande waterway, between the river mouth (Río Grande Bar) and the town of La Cruz de Río Grande, about 100 miles upriver (see Map 3). This forced the government to supply La Cruz and other remaining upriver outposts by airlift. In September the beleaguered Masaya militiamen marched northward up the beach from Sandy Bay, straight into a bloody ambush at a place called Laul Siksa. Completely demoralized, the survivors were pulled out and replaced shortly thereafter.

Although most Sandy Bay townspeople supported MISURASATA voluntarily, bush people were not averse to using threats, coercion, and physical abuse. In April 1983, the bush people publicly accused one community member, Maria Stevens, of being an informant (*kiamka*, literally "ears"). Without hesitation, she gathered her family and fled to Bluefields. Her brother Billy and another man, Faustino, continued to serve on what remained of the Sandinista Defense Committee. When the bush people passed through the community in July 1983, they captured both men and beat them badly. Only the pleading interventions of Parson Peters and village headman Manuel Rodriguez kept the men from being killed. Faustino promptly left for Corn Island, and Billy became an avid supporter of MISURASATA.

Townspeople recounted these abusive acts of coercion only occasionally and in a matter-of-fact way. Their incessant accounts of abuse from the Nicaraguan army, by contrast, were deeply emotional. They told of being held inside the Moravian church for hours, while government troops searched their homes, and of arrests, which began with a knock on the door at midnight. And they described being forced to serve as scouts for army units on missions to ferret out contra camps. The most bitter and vociferous complaints came from those who lived on the Río Grande and were caught in the combined armed forces air and land offensive of April 1984. Before the war began, the 75 miles of fertile Río Grande bottomland (between Kara and Kusuluhpia; see Map 3) had been lined with farms of cacao, plantains, rice, beans, and livestock. Some of the inhabitants were permanent riverside dwellers; most divided their time to benefit both from river production and the amenities of larger communities like Sandy Bay. Since early 1983, the bush people had controlled this entire stretch of richly productive Río Grande settlements. The April offensive drove out both bush people and civilians, forcing as many as 500 river people to abandon their farms and take refuge in Sandy Bay and other nearby communities. The refugees bitterly denounced the bombing that occurred as part of the offensive and deeply resented the government order that prohibited their return upriver.

At the time of the April 1984 offensive, MISURASATA's military strength and political support in the zone was probably at its height. Despite incipient efforts at rapprochement, the government's relations with Sandy Bay people still revolved almost entirely around military affairs and state security. The community had lost all semblance of normality. At least 55 community members, mainly young men, had left to join the bush people from 1981 through 1984.[3] Others were in jail, and most of the remaining young men had left to work in safer places such as Corn Island. Both fear and periodic prohibitions by the army prevented travel to distant farms. Production activities had dwindled; people tended small plots near the community and did a little fishing. Families depended for their daily survival on donated or highly subsidized food sent by the church, the Red Cross, or the government.

Epilogue to the Conflict, Preface to Reconciliation

The FSLN faced tremendous odds in its efforts to achieve a rapprochement with Sandy Bay community members. The entire weight of the Miskitu narrative, both remote and contemporary history, worked to ensure maximum distrust and sinister interpretation of any government action. Nevertheless, early in 1985 profound improvements in Miskitu-government relations began, which are the subject of analysis in Chapter 7. Small indications of the coming reconciliation reached Sandy Bay sooner. The government declared an amnesty for Miskitu prisoners in December 1983, which benefited some Sandy Bay men. The troops who had replaced the Masaya militiamen were more disciplined and civic-minded; they built a sturdy cement wharf for the community. In January 1984, the FSLN assigned a representative to the zone, a young Garifuna man from a community to the south. He believed that economic projects could help mend relations, and by June he had achieved renewed government support for Sandy Bay's fishing cooperative.

Sandy Bay people acknowledge a watershed in November 1984, when the government opened negotiations with MISURASATA's leader, Brooklyn Rivera, and announced a commitment to autonomy. Both steps sent a clear message that the government had admitted errors and promised to begin anew. Initiatives that followed confirmed this view. In January 1985 the Ministry of Interior (MINT) in Bluefields recognized Manuel Rodriguez as the head of Río Grande peace commission, which would work toward dialogue and reconciliation between bush people and the government. Rodriguez's first demand was removal of the State Security official assigned to the zone, whom community members feared and hated. The MINT promptly acceded.

Government soldiers left Sandy Bay in mid-December 1984 and were not replaced until April 1985. The bush people spent Easter week there, relaxing, playing baseball, and attending church. News of formal negotiations between MISURASATA and the government raised hopes that peace would be possible. Manuel Rodriguez went to Bluefields to attend a ceremony at which the government released three captured MISURASATA bush people as a gesture of good faith.

Yet many in Sandy Bay must still have doubted that peace negotiations would prosper. In late December 1984 Rivera had held a meeting in Sandy Bay with his chief of staff. The meeting took place in Manuel Rodriguez's house, a source of great pride for community members. A few days earlier, MISURASATA forces had attacked the southern Creole community of Pearl Lagoon. The army moved to retaliate and clashed with MISURASATA on the savanna outside Sandy Bay a few days after the meeting. When I first visited in May 1985, community members bitterly recounted the details of this combined air and land attack. Their memories of the war were still fresh.

Explaining the Mobilization

The limited range of sources on which the preceding summary of the mobilization is based already has been noted. The account reads as if taking up arms was an absolutely justified and natural response to the course of events because it is intended to convey the perspective of people who, on the whole, believed exactly that. It also reads monolithically, which is a simplification. I intentionally created one voice by cross-checking evidence, choosing more plausible versions, and omitting unconfirmed or unreconcilable details. Could this mean that I have obscured a group of "dissenters," people who would reject outright the highly politicized premises of the account?

The interview data presented in Chapter 3 provide a basis from which to address this question. One set of questions in the survey concerned people's orientations toward the revolution, a reasonably good indication of whether they endorsed the premises of the narrative above (for details on the survey, see Appendix B). Of the 27 interviewed, only 4 consistently answered in ways that indicated a positive orientation toward the revolution. There was a great contrast between typical responses from these two groups when asked, "What would have happened if the bush people hadn't left the communities to fight the government?" This is the typical majority response:

'We would all have been slaves, just like in Cuba and Russia. There would have been Cubans in every community. The Cubans were already here once [in 1980], and we learned how they live. They don't have nice things to wear, no perfume. They don't even have money! No payday. The government gives them everything. If the boys hadn't gone into the bush, we'd be living that way today.'

Maria Stevens gave a dissenting opinion:

'The government would have been able to help us even more. I may be crazy but I like these Communists.[4] They help the poor people, giving away food and medicine. It's only the rich people who they come down hard on.'

Maria Stevens was by far the most "revolutionary" of the four dissenters. A mother of six in her mid-thirties, Stevens has a sharp wit, a remarkably precise memory, and an unusual capacity for synthetic analysis. She, it will be recalled, was the enterprising woman who built the cantina/brothel in Sandy Bay during the Somoza years. Her description of the war years coincided with much of what I presented above but with details and editorial comments that cast the events in a very different light. She claimed that Marco Parrales, the man who collected food and money for MISURASATA, was a thief. A large part of what Parrales collected on behalf of the bush people, she said, stayed in his own pocket. Saul Duran, she explained, went into the bush on the insistence of his wife, who wanted him away because she was having an affair with another man. Stevens also named people (not from Sandy Bay) whom the bush people had accused of being Sandinista informants and killed in cold blood. She emphasized the deceptive methods that MISURASATA activists had used to win the community over:

'They told us the Sandinistas are bad people, who want to bring in Communism. The Communists, they said, will kill the Miskitu alive and use our skin to make shoes [laughs]. They told us all kinds of terrible things about the Cubans too. People got scared and decided that they better fight. . . . I heard that business about the Communists making shoes out of our skin, and soap out of our children, and I believed them too.'

The claim that the Miskitu were tricked into joining the struggle implies a veiled broader interest at work, which Stevens had no trouble identifying. The Americans have always been "oppressors," she argued, and "they're helping the bush people now because they want to get their hands on our riches again." Her view also implies that the Miskitu are political naïfs. One of my interview questions asked whether the Miskitu are capable of running their own government. Stevens responded:

'I don't like that idea. The Miskitu people have a bad way of handling themselves politically [*uba la saura brisa*]. Way back, the Sandinistas offered us three-quarters of our rights. That would have been good. But the leaders wanted everything and decided to fight. The Miskitu are *simple* [this English loan word is used in Miskitu to mean "stupid"], and they have no sense of gratitude [*tinki apu*].'

In short, Stevens revealed the underside of the mobilization—ineptitude, base motives, treachery—and led the listener to her own conclusion: it was a bad idea.

To explain townspeople's actions after 1981, however, it is crucial to know when Stevens began to espouse her current views. By her own account, at first she believed the sensational warnings about Communism and became an active MISURASATA supporter. Then in mid-1983 she was accused of being a government informant and had to flee the community. Two years later a bush commander exonerated her, which supports her contention that the original accusation was groundless. Nevertheless, this incident probably served as a catalyst for the development of her highly critical stance. The other three dissenters were less flamboyant, representative of a somewhat larger category in Sandy Bay: people who tolerated or passively supported MISURASATA at the height of the mobilization without becoming actively involved. They probably had a more sympathetic view of the revolution from the outset, and by the time of my interview questions (1986–87), conditions allowed them to express it more assertively. The two CDS leaders who were victims of the bush people's abuse in mid-1983 may also have belonged to this category. Although it is difficult to know the size of this "ambivalent" group, the interview data suggest that even by 1986–87 it still was only a small minority of the community. Moreover, beginning in 1983, "dissenters" came under great pressure—both moral and physical—to adopt the majority view.[5] In sum, although the mobilization of Sandy Bay was not completely unanimous, it was not publicly contested either. The dissenters, a minority to begin with, either stayed very quiet or left the community.

U.S. Provocation, Funds, and Promises

Intervention by the U.S. government had a tremendous impact on the scope and initial success of the Miskitu mobilization. After November 1981, when President Reagan approved the first $19 million of direct covert aid to the nascent contra army, Miskitu bush people's main source of military supplies was the CIA. Well before the November authorization, the U.S. government supported the training of former National Guard .

members, using Argentinians as intermediaries. When 3,000 Miskitu youths fled to Honduras after the Prinzapolka affair in February 1981 and MISURASATA leader Steadman Fagoth joined them that May, they began immediately to receive training from Somocistas. These youths knew that the Somocistas were receiving U.S. funds.[6] Moreover, evidence presented in Chapter 5 suggests the strong likelihood that the CIA was involved in provoking a conflict between MISURASATA and the Nicaraguan government even before the February arrests.

By early 1983, Sandy Bay townspeople began to see massive evidence of U.S. support. High-powered speedboats carrying food and military supplies arrived periodically from Costa Rica and landed at a creek just north of the community or on the offshore cays. Bush commanders would then order people to bring their dugout canoes from Sandy Bay, help unload the goods, and ferry them up the creek to the camp. Community members described these trips with a combination of awe—especially of the advanced technology such as walkie-talkies—and deep pride that the United States was taking such a direct interest in supporting the struggle for Miskitu rights. I frequently heard derisive comparisons between the ragtag Nicaraguan army and the bush people, outfitted with up-to-date U.S. matériel.[7] Quite apart from political sympathies, it must have seemed foolish not to support the side that had such a powerful ally.

Finally, as one moves from the bush people camped near Sandy Bay up the chain of command, the U.S. government's role in promoting the mobilization becomes greater still. By 1982, U.S. funds had underwritten the formation of "high command" centers for both MISURASATA and MISURA in Costa Rica and Honduras respectively, complete with offices, budgets, salaries and homes for the leaders, and logistical equipment necessary to maintain contact with field commanders.[8] Using future funding as leverage, the CIA then attempted to control these leaders, to dictate how they would fight the war, the alliances they would form, and the content of their political program. These efforts eventually had unintended consequences, alienating Miskitu combatants, convincing many to lay down their arms, and further dividing the ranks of those who remained. Yet the combatants did not seem to object so much to their utter dependence on U.S. funds as to specific conditions that the CIA sought to impose.[9] Even the much-touted "independence" of Brooklyn Rivera's MISURASATA faction never kept him from lobbying the Congress and State Department for "his share" of the *contra* funds or from accepting additional covert contributions.[10] Especially when viewed from the top down, the determining role of U.S. intervention in the Miskitu mobilization can hardly be exaggerated.

Yet the evidence presented above and in Chapter 3 contains two reasons to resist explaining the mobilization as a product of U.S. manipulation. First, a substantial amount of clandestine organizing occurred in Sandy Bay, with explicit military objectives, well before there was any tangible evidence of U.S. material aid. There clearly were promises. But if Sandy Bay Miskitu had lacked their own well-developed rationale, it seems doubtful that promises alone would have been sufficient to motivate such intense political activity. Second, and more important, the narrative presented in Chapter 3 demonstrates that such a rationale existed in sufficient originality and detail to contradict any contention that it was a fabrication of U.S. operatives. Neither point mitigates the enormous influence of U.S. policy. Both, however, caution against the conclusion that the Miskitu acted in a way that furthered U.S. geopolitical interests solely because the United States desired and sought such an outcome. The narrative from Sandy Bay suggests the need to distinguish between U.S. policy and Miskitu political consciousness and to make a thorough analysis of both.

State Penetration and Army Abuse

In Chapter 5 I argued that the Miskitu ethnic awakening of the late 1960's arose in large part from macro political and economic changes, especially the penetration of the Somoza state. Moreover, I found an important continuity in the nature of state presence on the Atlantic Coast after July 1979, despite the fundamentally different program of the revolution. In both periods, the state took an active role in the economy and pursued policies that brought Miskitu community members into increasing contact with Spanish-speaking regional government bureaucrats. I concluded that this structural continuity, especially in the exuberant political atmosphere that encouraged the exercise of "popular power," was highly conducive to ethnic mobilization.

The account recorded above also suggests that direct government military presence was an important contributing cause of the mobilization. After the Masaya militiamen were stationed in the community and State Security began to take actions against contra supporters, many townspeople must have perceived going into the bush as the only alternative. Manuel Rodriguez described the utter frustration of this period from the perspective of a village headman:

"Really them days when militia them go to a community, you can't lift up your head. Doing plenty, plenty problem, sometime you go to a house they catch you carry you to jail, no give you no permit to go do your work all kind of thing. We all was prisoner. So through that the young boy them, going every day to the bush like that. . . . And first time, the government pressing too much with the food line. No give them no food say we all feeding contra and that's not right. . . . [A next] pressure, when you get up in the morning me people them crying: 'Tonight he come to my house and gone with my boy, the security them. . . .' In the night, them have a ears, him is the one carry security to such a house . . . the mother them cry, go to me, but what I must do? I come to Karawala and tell them, ahhh them no respect me . . . them no respect pueblo."

David Lora, who served on the CDS committee, offered a corroborating account:

'A militar came to me one day and said that I must go along with some others on a mission for eight days to look for contra. I said no and that he must respect my authority as CDS. He told me: "I don't give a shit about your CDS; who named you CDS?" [*me vale mierda* CDS, *quien puso* CDS *aquí?*] From that day, the CDS ceased to exist.'

My analysis, though confirming the importance of both state presence and army abuse, also emphasizes the limits of this explanation. Continuous military presence did not begin in Sandy Bay until April 1983; for more than a year community members responded to MISURASATA activists' call to organize with near impunity. Harsh government military measures—especially the evacuation of the Río Coco—occurred earlier in the north, but Miskitu armed actions began earlier there as well. In Sandy Bay, a core of ardent Miskitu combatants with reasonably well-organized community support came first. The government then responded with military measures, which gave rise to a second wave of active participation with the bush people. Throughout the southern region, until well into 1983 government military presence amounted to a handful of State Security operatives and voluntary militias. Indeed, one reason that subsequent measures were so severe was that bush people had worked with a relatively free hand for so long.

State penetration, as distinguished from military presence, preceded the mobilization, but this explanation has clear limitations as well.[11] As I pointed out in Chapter 5, under the Somoza regime, just when one would have expected explosive collective action, the Miskitu instead turned quiescent. I also argued that grass-roots Miskitu responses to the arrests of February 1981 had a quality of vindictive militancy that could not have been precipitated solely by state penetration. To understand Miskitu perceptions of the state and reactions to these state policies requires serious consideration of the particular content of their consciousness.

The Role of Organization and Leadership

A third approach to explaining the mobilization is to place great importance on the role of MISURASATA leaders, especially Steadman Fagoth, who had immense charismatic appeal among Miskitu townspeople. It is now widely accepted that Fagoth previously had worked as a secret informant for Somoza's National Security Office, reporting on his own Miskitu comrades.[12] He was an opportunist, fully capable of placing MISURASATA on a collision course with the government when political solutions were still available, merely because it served his own interests to do so. The evidence that Fagoth was a megalomaniac is extensive and convincing; skeptics need only be reminded that even the CIA operatives found Fagoth so extremist and erratic that they came to consider him a public relations liability.

The second contention implicit in this argument—that Fagoth controlled MISURASATA and was largely responsible for its deepening militancy—is more complex. Observations of MISURASATA during the civilian period (November 1979 to mid-1981) seem to confirm that Fagoth held undisputed authority within the organization. In a 1982 interview, Hazel Law, a member of the MISURASATA directive committee, explained: "No one ever talked back to him. When the committee met, Steadman would say this and that and everyone would say yes. If anyone dared to disagree, it was me. . . . I was the one who criticized him most. . . . Steadman would respond: 'That's a Marxist position. . . .' What Steadman said was law." Brooklyn Rivera, in a separate interview, confirmed Fagoth's overwhelming popularity with the Miskitu base, expressing bitterness and a hint of envy:

"The people did not want to hear about [the government's] accusations of Fagoth. They would not believe it, and Fagoth became the symbol of the people's struggle at that moment [February 1981]. The image of Fagoth strengthened and consolidated them; Fagoth became their heart and soul. When I was released from jail, the people embraced me, but then they said, 'That's nice, but we are not stopping here, we want Steadman Fagoth.' . . . In that moment, no one could contradict Fagoth without committing political suicide [*el pueblo le cortaba la cabeza*]."[13]

By Rivera's account, Fagoth retained this popular mandate even after fleeing to Honduras and joining the ex-Somocista armed organization. The people "lost their confidence in me," Rivera admits, and completely believed Fagoth's propaganda, broadcast over Somocista radio, that if "I am still in Nicaragua I am a traitor, working for the government." Weeks later, Rivera left for Honduras.[14]

There emerges from these descriptions a sense of the uncompromising militancy of both Fagoth and the "people," which contrasts sharply with the MISURASATA program approved only a year earlier. This radicalization was noted in Chapter 5 and elsewhere.[15] Drawing on the narrative and interview data presented in Chapter 3, however, we can now contrast key elements of MISURASATA's program with grass-roots Miskitu political consciousness. The MISURASATA "General Regulations," approved in April 1980, vehemently condemned "U.S. imperialism" (1980: 11) although Sandy Bay Miskitu believed that the U.S. company owners were their friends. The regulations spoke of "each community's rights to its communal property" (p. 7), whereas according to the narrative Miskitu have both community and territorial rights to a vast portion of the Atlantic Coast.[16] Finally, the regulations called for a campaign of cultural rejuvenation and pride (p. 8), while Sandy Bay Miskitu espoused a deeply rooted Anglo affinity, which, as I will demonstrate, included internalized racism.

It has always been asserted or implicitly assumed that MISURASATA leaders initiated this radicalization and that grass-roots political orientations followed dutifully. Elements within the Sandy Bay narrative support this interpretation. For example, people attribute their "awakening" to the influence of a group of educated leaders who taught them about Miskitu rights. These claims notwithstanding, there are sound empirical reasons to conclude that the influence between leadership and base was reciprocal rather than unidirectional. Consider again the three key issues: cultural pride, land rights, and orientations toward the United States.

In the case of MISURASATA's campaign to heighten Miskitu cultural pride, it appears that the leaders did challenge and transform attitudes at the base. A significant sector of Sandy Bay Miskitu espoused a set of ideas that I refer to as internalized racism, which forms part of the legacy of Anglo-American presence on the Coast. These ideas are the negation of cultural pride: self-denigration and a belief that others, especially white people, are superior. Three of my interview questions addressed this facet of the Miskitu political worldview. In contrast to their near unanimity on many other topics, the 25 respondents split fairly evenly on these questions. When the respondents are further subdivided into leaders and non-leaders,[17] a clear pattern emerges (see Table 3). Community leaders are much more likely to have rejected internalized racism.

By the time the questions were asked, community leaders had interacted extensively with government institutions and with MISURASATA. Although both contacts could have shaped their views, I suspect that MISURASATA's influence was decisive. Although FSLN cadres did defend the principle of strict racial equality, they assigned high priority to challenging internalized racism only when the outcome of such an effort would tend to generate support for the revolutionary project. This is, they consistently challenged prevailing Miskitu ideas about past and continuing North American presence on the Coast, but, as demonstrated in Chapter 4, they also tended to think of Miskitu people as backward or

TABLE 3
Internalized Racism and Community Leadership in Sandy Bay

| | Internalized Racism | | | | | |
| | High | | Low | | Totals | |
	N	%	N	%	N	%
Leader	3	27	8	73	11	100
Nonleader	12	86	2	14	14	100
Totals	15	60	10	40	25	100

uncultured. This assertion that Sandinistas generally left Miskitu people's internalized racism unchallenged is confirmed by the views of Belina Morales, whom I interviewed in Bluefields. A Miskitu and an active Sandinista cadre, Morales worked closely with Sandy Bay people between 1985 and 1987.[18]

Below I present the three questions focused on internalized racism, juxtaposing the responses of Morales to two contrasting responses from Sandy Bay. The first is typical of those who rejected the premises of internalized racism (labeled "low"); the second is typical of those who displayed adherence to those premises (labeled "high"). The numbers and percentages indicate how many responses (of the 25 total) were associated with each category.[19]

1. What ethnic group would you most like your children/relatives to marry?

    Morales: I'm not a racist, but I have my opinions. I've had all kinds of boyfriends. But I thought: "If I marry a Black, my child's hair would come out bad." My mother had beautiful, long, straight hair. I don't want my children to marry Blacks.[20]

    Low: It has to be a Miskitu. That way we can build up our nation. (N = 9; 33 percent)

    High: My first preference would be an American. The Spaniards are too violent and the Blacks don't respect their in-laws [no mention of Miskitu]. (N = 8; 30 percent)

2. When a baby is born, how do you like that baby to look?

    Morales: I like straight hair, not dry. The skin can be dark, that's OK. The nose, we straighten it on the baby so it won't be flat.

    Low: I don't agree with all that looks business. If they have schooling they will come out the same, no matter how they look. (N = 5; 19 percent)

    High: I like light skin, straight brown or blond hair, fair eyes, and straight pointed noses. (N = 8; 30 percent)

3. Why are some nations or ethnic groups poorer than others? Did God have a hand in making it that way?

Morales: It has to do with education. Miskitu have a low level, but I don't agree with the idea that this is God-given. It comes from the people, and that's where culture [used as a synonym for education] becomes important.

Low: God gave everyone common sense. But schooling is something else. If we had the same amount of school, we all would be the same. (N = 11; 41 percent)

High: Miskitu are less intelligent, that's why we're poor. The Americans can help us. God made the Americans that way. Of all the nations, Americans are the best. The Americans help other people; that's why God looks kindly on them. (N = 8; 30 percent)

Morales's views fall somewhere in between the two responses but in general correspond more closely with the high ones. While I cannot prove that this reflects the broader orientations of FSLN cadres, it does suggest that challenging Miskitu people's internalized racism was not among the Sandinistas' top priorities. The reverse was true for MISURASATA leaders. These self-deprecatory ideas would have acted as a direct impediment to the mobilization by undermining Miskitu people's confidence in their ability to take political action. One community member's memory of the thrust of a speech by Brooklyn Rivera in the community of Set Net exemplifies this point:

'The coast is rich, the Miskitu have many rights. Now you have been left with nothing. You are dirt poor. You have no way to help your elders. The Spaniards have benefited from all these riches [leaving you] like animals. But it does not have to be that way. Act like human beings!'

The call to mobilize against the "Spanish" and the challenge to internalized racism are intertwined and interdependent. Sandy Bay community leaders would have been the first to assimilate this political message, which explains the split portrayed in Table 3.

On the other two points of the MISURASATA program—demands for land and orientations toward the United States—the influence between leadership and base is reciprocal. The specific territorial boundaries that Simon Gonzales cited in the narrative in Chapter 3 are taken directly from the land rights study carried out by MISURASATA leaders in 1980 (see Map 2). Yet the Sandy Bay narrative also expresses another idea: that Miskitu people once had a king and a government on the Atlantic Coast and then lost them owing to Spanish trickery. This idea clearly preceded not only the mobilization but also the formation of both MISURASATA and ALPROMISU. In other words, when Steadman Fagoth made the radical leap from individual community land rights to territorial rights for Indian peoples, the more militant position resonated with existing elements in Miskitu collective memories.[21]

The argument becomes even more persuasive in the case of Miskitu orientations toward the United States. Although MISURASATA's General Regulations harshly condemn both U.S. "imperialism" and the Somoza legacy, there is no evidence that leaders attempted to propagate this anti-imperialist message. To the contrary, testimonies from Sandy Bay suggest that MISURASATA activists played repeatedly on people's deep fear of Communism and unwavering confidence in the Americans' historic friendship. Maria Stevens made this point in a more analytical way; most people merely reported what they remembered. Gaspar Blandon, for example, said:

'When the MISURASATA boys first came to town, preparing to fight, they said that the Sandinistas are bringing in "Communist laws." I wasn't sure what that meant. They explained, religion will be eliminated, any man could have your woman, food will be scarce and sold only in small amounts [*kulki mai atki kabia*].'

A former combatant explained:

'The [MISURASATA] organizers told us that the Sandinistas would take away our dories and cattle . . . but from the time we began training, we knew the Americans would help us to drive out the Russians [*Rusia nani kangbi sakaia*].'

Top MISURASATA leaders received university education in Managua during the height of the revolutionary insurrection. Most of them were sophisticated enough to doubt the sincerity of U.S. government "friendship" for the Miskitu, to know that the Sandinistas did not as a practice make soap from live babies, and that the Russians were not about to colonize the Atlantic Coast. Yet they also had to be aware of the power of such discourse at the community level.[22] The only plausible explanation is that MISURASATA leaders abandoned the critique of these aspects of Anglo affinity, perhaps sensing that it would be politically costly and that the mobilization would be stronger without it.[23]

These analyses of land rights and Anglo affinity point to a new interpretation of Fagoth's great appeal. He quickly developed an acute sense for the discourse that worked with Miskitu townspeople and pursued it regardless of contradictions with the formal MISURASATA program. The other leaders, more moderate by conviction, used the inflammatory discourse less and acquired correspondingly less grass-roots Miskitu support. Fagoth's charisma, in this interpretation, was in part a reflection of preexisting Miskitu political orientations, on which he consciously capitalized. This conclusion, again, shifts attention toward the causal importance of community-level initiative and consciousness.

Toward a Unified Explanation

Although structural and macro factors certainly contributed to the mobilization, efforts to impute this causality cannot rely on a deductive treatment of community-level Miskitu initiative and consciousness. Much of the material presented thus far has been intended to address this empirical problem through both historical and field research. It should now be possible to reinterpret the mobilization, drawing on this evidence and using the framework introduced in Chapter 1.

In Chapter 2 I reviewed key episodes in the past century of Atlantic Coast history to document the evolving relations between Miskitu people and the state and to trace the impact of these relations on Miskitu consciousness. Oral history and interview data in Chapter 3 broadened our understanding of this legacy. I then drew on this analysis to help explain the puzzle of Miskitu quiescence during the period of the Somoza dictatorship. Before the Sandinistas came to power in 1979, I argued, Anglo affinity helped to engender Miskitu people's quiescence. They deeply resented petty (Spanish-speaking) government officials but did not broaden their critique to encompass a direct confrontation with Somoza's political power. Rather, they organized to pursue moderate demands, which stopped short of a broader systemic challenge. Greater militancy could not prosper as long as the premises of Anglo affinity remained unquestioned: Somoza was known to be the North Americans' "partner," and the enclave economy (even if it allowed "Spanish" foremen to mistreat Indians) was evidently a North American creation.

How, then, did this inherited consciousness influence Miskitu people's interpretation of and response to the revolution? Consider again the prevailing conditions of 1981. There were no troops around, but rumors of government atrocities had begun to circulate. Young men were especially restless, angry about the premature and violent conclusion of the literacy campaign, and imbued with rising expectations. The organizers arrived, talking in the same breath about the struggle for Indian rights and against Communism. The Americans were rumored to be sending arms and support; the struggle would be easy and victory sweet. Even the Moravian church was supportive. Many admired white people from the North— godly missionaries, powerful company owners. For elders, the association was much more concrete: their historic ties with Britain and their rights to autonomy were fused into one. The organizers called clandestine meetings at night; sons of prominent families began to enlist; young women joined them in the bush. The community was buzzing with excitement. Sandinista patrols arrived and everyone feigned innocence and then laughed afterward about how the Sandinistas had been "fooled up." Soon war stories began to circulate, with more proof that the Americans were helping. Speedboats faster than anything seen before arrived, and training camps were set up in Honduras. More youths joined. Elders remained skeptical, but only because they had more to lose. Ultimately their youth were the ones out front, seizing the chance to fight for "Indian rights," something that for elders had been little more than the subject of nostalgic memories. But when push came to shove, the elders' support was unanimous.

Consciousness is far too complex to dissect, attributing actions to discrete facets of the whole. Nevertheless, knowing about these dual, contradictory elements in Miskitu consciousness does help us to make sense of this scene in 1981. The revolution simultaneously fostered Miskitu ethnic militancy and eliminated the constraining effects of Anglo affinity. Because the Sandinistas were "Spaniards" and yet decidedly *not* partners with the U.S. government, Miskitu could criticize "Spanish oppression" without implicating North Americans. Similarly, Miskitu could develop a deep critique of the economic inequality from which they continued to suffer, attributing it now to "Communism" or to other systemic ills that clearly had nothing to do with North American capitalism. Anglo affinity persisted after 1979, but it no longer defused Miskitu people's analysis of systemic oppression or inhibited their inclinations for collective action against the state. On the contrary, by eliminating these constraining effects of Anglo affinity, the revolution paradoxically engendered an ethnic militancy of unprecedented depth and intensity.[24]

Moreover, the persistence of Anglo affinity provided additional impetus for the mobilization. Despite a brief relatively harmonious period after the Sandinista victory in 1979, Miskitu distrust lay just below the surface, highly susceptible to provocation. Through the lens created by the premises of Anglo affinity, the revolution personified hostility to a series of values central to the Miskitu way of life: North American company presence on the Coast, the Moravian church, and the perceived "partnership" (at times even expressed as fictive kin ties) between Miskitu and Americans. When the Reagan administration began to fund MISURASATA, Sandy Bay Miskitu interpreted the aid as yet another affirmation of this historic partnership with Americans. The interview data in Chapter 3 confirm that Sandy Bay Miskitu believed that Americans genuinely supported Miskitu rights. As one respondent explained: "They're training our boys, making them intelligent."[25]

MISURASATA combatants in the community of Kara (May 1985). Photo by author.

Announcement of the results of the autonomy delegates' elections (October 1986). The winner (center) is about to make an acceptance speech while two members of the tropa (in uniform) look on. Photo by author.

Four generations of Sandy Bay women and girls, all of whom live in a single cluster of homes, in accordance with the Miskitu practice of matrilocality. Photo by author.

Young men on the beach near Sandy Bay (1986). Photo by author.

Sandy Bay women on the way to Karáwala, passing a mature rice field on the bank (1987). Photo credit: Claudia Gordillo.

Sandy Bay people observing as a traveling *sukia* (healer) presents a jar of buried poison that purportedly had been the cause of sickness and death in the community (1987). Photo credit: Claudia Gordillo.

Inside a Miskitu family's house (1987). Photo credit: Claudia Gordillo.

Volunteer church workers gathered during a Sunday service (1990) as a white Jesus looks on from above. Photo by author.

Three ex-combatants from YATAMA, visiting Sandy Bay to oversee the turning in of arms after the 1990 elections (July 1990). Photo by author.

This argument moves us beyond the sterile dichotomy between structural and actor-centered approaches to ethnic mobilization. U.S. intervention played such a decisive role in the mobilization in part because Miskitu actively sought the alliance and reveled in the attention from their benevolent "partners." Similarly, Sandy Bay Miskitu had an elaborate foundation of collective memories to guide their understanding of recent encounters with the state and military. These were "Spaniards," who had been flouting Miskitu people's rights for centuries. Finally, MISURASATA's impressive organizational achievements and rapid radicalization acquire an additional explanation. Both Fagoth's influence and the deep resonance of MISURASATA's demands were in part a product of the particular way that ordinary Miskitu men and women made sense of the revolution. The mobilization occurred with such militancy and passion not only owing to Fagoth's maniacal charisma but also because Sandy Bay Miskitu—and others like them throughout the Coast—took the initiative to make it that way.

This interpretation also offers a framework with which to make sense of the acrimonious debate in the literature on the "Miskitu question." In much of this literature, the central antinomy that I have identified within Miskitu consciousness is not fully acknowledged, nor is its analytical significance explored. The political reasons for this neglect are apparent. The notion of Anglo affinity tends to conjure up images of Miskitu as duped coconspirators of the CIA, while ethnic militancy has been interpreted to mean that Miskitu people mobilized solely in response to oppressive conditions created by the revolutionary government. There also have been theoretical barriers. First, the axiom of cultural relativism, deeply ingrained in the anthropological tradition, offers no systematic means to understand the pervasive effects of power inequality and structural domination on subordinated cultures; it precludes arguments that use the hegemony idea to explain the persistence of Miskitu Anglo affinity. Second, the class/ethnicity dichotomy and the base/superstructure metaphor from which it derives also prevent a complete analysis of Miskitu consciousness. This dichotomy tends to deny the material basis of ethnic militancy and to equate Anglo affinity with false consciousness. This in turn yields an analysis that assigns limited causal importance to Miskitu perceptions and to their own reasons for what they do. Miskitu agency is lost amid structural determination.

The argument I have put forth here presents a challenge to most existing literature on the Miskitu question. Explanations that emphasize U.S. intervention tend to include a highly developed appreciation of one facet of grass-roots Miskitu consciousness—Anglo affinity—and a relative neglect of ethnic militancy. When the emphasis is on the oppressive presence of the Sandinista state, the converse problem applies. After 1984 there was more room for complex treatments of both contradictory facets, but the pervasive influence of this preautonomy analytical divide remained.

Carlos Vilas's perceptive study of Nicaraguan state presence on the Atlantic Coast during the Somoza and revolutionary eras has remnants of the preautonomy theoretical divide when addressing the question of Miskitu consciousness. He draws a broad distinction between the "material side of costeño identity . . . similar to that of [oppressed] classes and groups throughout the country" and the "symbolic dimension," consisting of what I call Anglo affinity, which "separated on an ideological level what economic exploitation and political oppression otherwise would have united" (1989: 53). During the Somoza era, he continues, Coast people tended to give "priority to the ethnic and cultural dimensions of [conflict with the state]," which "made it very difficult [for them] to see [its] underlying class nature" (p. 82). Finally, he describes what I have called Miskitu ethnic militancy as an "ethnic chauvinism" that "appears in the first stages of political development of any subordinated social group (women, youth, workers)," characterized by an "oversimplified view of reality" (p. 126). Although other aspects of Vilas's analysis are complex and nuanced, this portrayal of Miskitu people's consciousness tends to reinforce the notion that they had it all wrong until the autonomy process began in 1985.

Another group of analysts continued to focus exclusively on the deepening of ethnic militancy. The Miskitu were responding to oppression at the hands of Spanish-speakers and the Nicaraguan state, the argument goes, which continued unchanged (or worsened) after the Sandinistas came to power. These analysts simply do not make use of all the available evidence: that Sandy Bay Miskitu actively espouse Anglo affinity, that its premises helped to motivate their mobilization (e.g., unreflective anti-Communism) and to express their political aspirations (e.g., the return of U.S. companies). Consequently, this analytical position falls into the same pattern that characterized the Miskitu political response itself: allowing emphasis on one sphere of oppression to obviate the need for a parallel critical analysis of another, namely, past and present North American domination.[26]

Finally, my analysis here, combined with that provided in Chapter 4, should help to clarify how Sandinista ideology and policy contributed to the conflict. Sandinista leaders proceeded according to premises inherited from the past century of unequal relations between Miskitu people and the state and adapted them to the framework of Mestizo revolutionary nationalism. They tended to exclude Miskitu people from the category of "historical subjects" and to constitute a national identity nourished by an Indian past but headed resolutely toward a unified Mestizo future. In so doing, these leaders downplayed or negated the demands of Miskitu ethnic militancy as a matter of principle, quite apart from the potentially antigovernment thrust of those demands. Sandinista leaders focused political struggle and defiance on what had been, from the national perspective, the fundamental axis of inequality and domination: relations with the United States. Especially on the Atlantic Coast, these relations formed the cornerstone in their definition of exploitation and in their redemptive prescriptions for raising Coast people out of the miserable conditions in which U.S. imperialism had left them. Not only did this analysis contradict Miskitu Anglo affinity, but, equally important, it obscured and promised to perpetuate the axis of inequity that Miskitu people viewed as most exploitative: their relations with the state. Not surprisingly, to most Sandy Bay Miskitu, this Sandinista discourse was little more than deceptive, self-interested propaganda.

Miskitu people and Sandinista cadres locked themselves into cultural forms that were mutually antagonistic. Although rooted in state-society relations in the coastal region during the past century, this outcome can in no sense be derived or deduced from those structural conditions. Miskitu people came to embrace the premises of Anglo affinity in the course of resistance to the Nicaraguan state through a series of maneuvers in response to multiple spheres of inequity. Similarly, the Sandinistas embraced a cultural form that placed them in conflict with the Miskitu in the course of their efforts to promote resistance against the Somoza dictatorship and against the legacy of U.S. domination. Premises inherited from existing state relations with Indians survived the rise of Sandinismo and melded unproblematically with what became, for the majority of Nicaraguans, a compelling discourse of liberation. Both cultural forms, then, resulted from active resistance to inequities, from an interplay of previous moments of conscious, reflective human action and inherited structural conditions. This same interplay underlies my explanation for the contemporary conflict. Rather than deduce the logic of collective actions from structural factors, I have emphasized grass-roots initiative and shown how structural conditions reverberated in community-level Miskitu consciousness. Without this analytical step, the causal link to the explosive Miskitu response remains an unexplored assertion.

7 Community Politics in Transition to Autonomy, 1985–87

IT WAS AFTER MIDNIGHT and everyone in the high school auditorium looked exhausted. Since 8:00 A.M. some 250 delegates, representing all six ethnic groups from communities throughout the Coast, had been meeting in plenary to discuss and approve the proposed statute that would legally guarantee their rights to autonomy. This Multi-Ethnic Assembly, held in the northern coastal town of Puerto Cabezas in April 1987, marked the culmination of a participatory process of meetings, workshops, educational sessions with comic book–style materials, and opinion polls, known as the *consulta popular*. The decisions taken during the assembly resulted in a fully elaborated legal statute, which would be submitted to the National Assembly for approval.

Yet when the plenary finally ended and a Creole minister said a prayer to consecrate the outcome, instead of exhilaration, I felt a wave of frustration and perplexity. Over the previous two years in Sandy Bay, I had spent hundreds of hours listening to townspeople recount collective memories of age-old and recent struggles, describing in great detail the rights for which they had fought and died. Now, when they were finally offered the chance to codify those rights, Miskitu delegates had agreed to the Sandinista-backed proposal, which was cautious and ambiguous and stopped explicitly short of their own demands. Perplexity, combined with concern that the disparity might provoke a return to conflict, is the only way to explain my somewhat imprudent decision the next morning to talk on the record with a journalist who attended the assembly. He filed a story for the *Christian Science Monitor*, which included a quotation from Charlie Hale, North American resident of the Coast, to the effect that the Miskitu had been "cowed" into submission. Next came the contrary opinion of Comandante Tomás Borge, who had observed the plenary briefly during the afternoon and then announced: "One would have to be blind or perverse not to recognize that this Assembly is profoundly democratic."[1]

Quite apart from political imprudence, I later came to believe that my assessment was wrong, or at least seriously incomplete. Miskitu delegates' voting in the assembly, I now contend, was consistent with a multifaceted, ambiguous stance they had fashioned toward the entire autonomy process over the previous two years. They backed the transition to peace and autonomy, while retaining strong ties and affinities with Miskitu combatants in the bush; they expressed a newfound resolve to accommodate Sandinista rule, while continuing to espouse deep commitment to militant ethnic demands that the Sandinistas categorically rejected.

Sandinista delegates to the Multi-Ethnic Assembly—all of whom were costeños, many well-respected community leaders—worked hard to achieve Miskitu accommodation. Well-organized, talented, and forceful, they exerted a definitive influence on the direction of plenary deliberations by outmaneuvering opponents and advancing persuasive arguments at each critical juncture. They portrayed their position as the only sensible alternative, grounded in implicit or explicit "realpolitik" appeals: "The central government surely will not accept that," or "Trust us to secure from them the most possible benefits for the Coast." Miskitu delegates seemed to accede, without believing for a moment that they were getting all that they had been struggling for. Soon after the assembly, I asked Manuel Rodriguez what he thought of the newly approved law. His response was typical of those of most Sandy Bay townspeople, if slightly more elaborate:

'From first time, [we] have been fighting for Miskitu rights. The [bush people] had their document ready from long time. It was made overseas, together with the Americans. When the Frente heard this, they made their own document. . . . The two are different. According to the Frente document, you have to ask the government for everything . . . but we don't have any business doing that. . . . The government is just offering us pickings—like food, a motosaw to split our lumber. But we can't enter the mines. The riches of the sea are off-limits. Our territorial boundaries are not respected.'

Yet Rodriguez, like most other Sandy Bay townspeople of a similar mind, played a crucial role in sealing the return to peace. My purpose here is to examine in greater detail this dual, ambiguous, at times contradictory response of Sandy Bay townspeople to autonomy.

*   *   *

The new year of 1985 brought more of the same for Sandy Bay. Although one round of talks between MISURASATA and the government had taken place the previous December, no firm agreements were reached. MISURASATA combatants attacked the southern Creole community of Pearl Lagoon in late December, then retreated northward. The govern-

ment sent ground and air forces in pursuit, and the two sides clashed in
an intense combat on the savanna just outside Sandy Bay. At that moment
prospects for the talks or for positive results from the government's
promises of autonomy must have seemed bleak.

Shortly after the savanna clash, however, the tropa left the community
and no soldiers were sent to replace them. Bush people from MISURASATA
moved in and out freely; a large group spent Easter there, relaxing, playing baseball, flirting with young women. When a new tropa finally arrived in early April 1985, they sent word ahead, which gave the bush
people ample time to move peaceably to Kara, the nearby community up
the Río Grande (see Map 3). These new tropa members were much different from the previous detachments of Sandinista soldiers that had occupied Sandy Bay since 1983. On the average older and better educated,
they were trusted civilian cadres, mobilized by the Ministry of Interior
especially for this assignment. Perhaps most impressive to Sandy Bay
townspeople, they included both men and women.

The tropa officers[2] quickly grasped the political complexity of their
mission and set out with indomitable zeal, in the name of the Frente
Sandinista and the autonomy project, to bridge the gulf of misunder-
standing and to heal the wounds left by the war. Over the next nine
months, they built a schoolhouse and repaired the health clinic, carried
out immunization campaigns, helped to teach school, promoted various
community development efforts, and organized fiestas. They attended
church and engaged the Moravian pastor, Samuel Peters, in discussion.
They sought out townspeople, listened to the Miskitu perspective on all
that had happened in recent years, and talked incessantly with community leaders about issues of the day. They learned of, and openly criticized, excesses and mistakes of their predecessors and worked fervently
to repair the army's negative image. To promote mutual trust, they even
allowed unarmed bush people to enter and leave the community freely.

Major changes in high-level relations between MISURASATA and the
government did of course help to make this "new start" possible. The
two sides had signed a tentative cease-fire agreement on April 22, 1985;
peace talks and autonomy were at the top of the government's agenda. In
addition, shortly after the previous January's savanna combat, the regional government had promoted the formation of community peace
commissions to give the townspeople an active role in the process of reconciliation. Dan Peters and Manuel Rodriguez (see Fig. 1), both respected
community leaders, formed the core of Sandy Bay's peace commission.
They made frequent trips to Kara, reported to the bush people on the
tropa's recent words and deeds, and briefed the tropa officers upon returning. During periods of tension these trips took on an air of shuttle

diplomacy, with both military forces clearly dependent on the commission's services as intermediary.[3]

Yet by October 1985 it had grown clear that these efforts would have limited results. Negotiations broke down in late May. Shortly thereafter, Kara became the MISURASATA headquarters for that area, headed by a high-ranking commander named Felipe Nolan. Nolan continued to respect the truce but refused the tropa's repeated requests for a meeting. Loyal to his leader Brooklyn Rivera's edict, Nolan maintained that peace could be achieved only through direct high-level talks between MISURASATA and the government. During the tense interlude between the negotiation breakdown and a probable return to war, Nolan pursued political goals that mirrored those of the tropa. He sought to consolidate MISURASATA's already substantial support from community members and to keep the wedge of mistrust between tropa and community firmly in place. Within a few months, therefore, townspeople had become the focus of political and ideological struggle between tropa and bush people, which revolved around both everyday community affairs and Miskitu rights to autonomy.[4]

Explaining Community-Level Accommodation

In November 1985 I completed my first month of fieldwork and returned to Bluefields with much reason to believe that the tenuous peace in the Río Grande communities would not hold. Nolan's patience was wearing thin. He made it known that if the tropa did not leave the community by Christmas, he would move to expel them. The ultimatum both expressed his strength and betrayed his vulnerability. On the one hand, though community members wanted peace, there was little doubt which side they would be on if armed conflict resumed. During the long boat ride back to Bluefields I discussed the scenario with a young Sandy Bay man, asking how fighting might be avoided. It was simple, he replied: "If the Sandinistas were true to their promises, they would have pulled the tropa out of our community long ago. Then who would be left there to fight?" On the other hand, Nolan's escalating rhetoric signaled his concern about the probable effect of the tropa's presence. The tropa, after all, did not seek townspeople's unqualified support; they merely wanted recognition as legitimate interlocutors in the peace process. Nolan feared that such recognition would undermine support for MISURASATA.

The townspeople, therefore, found themselves in the middle of a tense dialogue between two military forces that remained at odds. A tropa officer who visited Bluefields in mid-November 1985 clearly identified the limits to such an endeavor. "We can negotiate almost anything," he explained, "but they [MISURASATA] must be clear about one thing: we are the ones who will stay with the arms." He admitted, "[right now] Sandy Bay is solidly MISURASATA," but "[the Miskitu] must be made to understand that they could never win militarily. When they die, there is no one to replace them. But we have thousands—a whole revolution—behind us." In contrast, MISURASATA refused even to consider laying down arms until Miskitu rights were fully guaranteed. If Nolan kept his promise to attack by Christmas, the two sides would fight over these first principles without exploring the common ground that community members like Manuel Rodriguez had begun to forge.

The expected attack never came. It is not known precisely why Nolan decided to desist, but a crucial factor in this case and throughout the three years in question was that townspeople wanted to avoid armed conflict. Church and community leaders made repeated pleas to the bush commanders to keep the peace, or at least to avoid fighting in or near the communities. Townspeople's increasingly cordial relations with the tropa and cooperation with the government sent the bush commanders a similar, less explicit, but probably more persuasive message. With actions such as these, I will argue, civilians in communities like Sandy Bay played an important role in bringing about the return to peace. Yet this conclusion raises another set of questions. Only a few years earlier, townspeople had fully supported the mobilization with a militancy that exceeded their leaders' expectations. What explains their sudden conversion to peacemakers?

Accounts of this period generally have avoided this question, assuming that Miskitu townspeople reacted to changing structural conditions with few real choices or room to maneuver. Such explanations appear especially persuasive when one retrospectively places the details of community-level politics in a regional perspective. The return to peace then fits neatly within the broad trend toward negotiated settlement of the contra-Sandinista conflict, which began in 1987 and culminated with the elections of 1990. The explanations have come in two main variants corresponding to the polarized views of the conflict itself. Analysts aligned with the Sandinistas have contended that the introduction of autonomy resolved the bulk of Miskitu demands, thereby eliminating the impetus to mobilize. Proponents of an opposing perspective have argued that military conditions favoring the struggle changed, making continued frontal resistance hopeless or prohibitively costly.[5]

The reflections of Sandinista and MISURASATA cadres during the process point to an alternative argument. Although the Sandinistas seem to have espoused a straightforward version of the "demands met" explanation, internal documents and informal discussions provide a more complex view. These cadres tended to associate transition with the achievement of "hegemony" through "political-ideological struggle."[6] This meant, first and foremost, Miskitu people's acceptance of the revolution's "unnegotiable principles" and, secondarily, their acceptance of autonomy as a legitimate forum for resolving any tensions or differences that might remain. Tropa members in Sandy Bay spoke frequently about their "political work" in precisely these terms, often with glowing assessments of progress and proud examples of townspeople whose sympathies had turned "Sandinista," interspersed with occasional frank admissions that MISURASATA "hegemony" remained largely intact.

MISURASATA cadres and leaders, in contrast, portrayed such political work as carefully calculated Sandinista maneuvers to undermine the Miskitu struggle, to erode the power they needed to negotiate a just solution to the conflict. Especially during the nearly three-year lapse in high-level negotiations (May 1985 to early 1988), MISURASATA leaders denounced autonomy as a "pseudo-project of administrative reorganization," consisting of "nothing but appearances and deceit" (MISURASATA 1985:13). By extension, those Miskitu who actively participated in the autonomy process were either opportunists, confused souls, or victims of Sandinista deception.[7] In the Sandy Bay area, such analysis led MISURASATA bush commanders to proclaim strict prohibitions and harsh threats of reprisal against those who participated in autonomy and always to regard the process with the utmost suspicion.[8] Felipe Nolan clearly believed that the return to peace both reflected and had the potential further to engender an increase in community acquiescence to Sandinista rule; in response, he engaged in political work of his own to maintain townspeople's support.

Thus cadres on both sides, though defending diametrically opposed positions, affirmed two key elements in their analysis of the return to peace. They concurred in assigning considerable importance to people's thoughts and actions at the community level; in the politics of the moment, achieving and maintaining legitimacy in the eyes of community members mattered deeply. Both also understood the return to peace as resulting in part from the deeply formative effects of more powerful forces on grass-roots Miskitu consciousness. The varying descriptive content and normative value attached to the outcome of this persuasion (from *toma de conciencia* [becoming politically conscious] to opportunist capitulation) is less relevant for the moment than the common assertion that a change in consciousness took place. Townspeople who ceased to confront the state and opted instead to participate in autonomy had (or quickly developed) an altered set of ideas and values that informed their political judgments.

My explanation for the return to peace builds on the insights implicit in these cadres' reflections. First, I challenge both variants of the argument that structural change alone can explain the transition—either because townspeople were forced to turn quiescent or because autonomy granted all or most of their demands. Next I demonstrate that community-level initiative played a central role in bringing about the return to peace, though I avoid a celebratory overstatement of Miskitu people's "everyday resistance" by also examining how the emerging Sandinista discourse and practice of autonomy shaped their consciousness. This dual emphasis on grass-roots initiative and on the constitutive impact of hegemony also informs my concluding analysis of what the transition to autonomy achieved, and of the serious problems that remained.

The Power and Limits of Structural Explanation

Especially after January 1986, when MISURASATA went back on a war footing and the three-sided dialogue with the tropa and bush people lost its viability, Sandy Bay townspeople turned despondent. "We are civilians caught between two military forces," went a common refrain; "we cannot do anything until the two sides with the guns get together and work things out." The meaning of such comments, one could plausibly assert, is that accommodation resulted from a sharp decline in the possibilities for continued military struggle, determined at levels well beyond Miskitu townspeople's influence or control. There is some evidence to support this assertion, but it does not survive close scrutiny.

Geopolitical and Military Conditions

Around October 1985, the Nicaraguan armed forces announced what they called the "strategic defeat" of the Nicaraguan Democratic Forces (FDN, or contras).[9] From that point on, despite massive, continuous infusions of U.S. aid (both covert and congressionally approved) and repeated efforts at reorganization and revitalization, the contras never recovered the initiative as an offensive military force. Their ability to inflict damage and threaten minor military targets could have lasted indefinitely, as long as funds continued to flow. Yet by the time of the Esquipulas II Accords (August 6–7, 1987), which set the stage for contra-government negotiations, no serious observer thought that the contras could win the war.[10]

A growing sense of the dim chances for military victory reverberated among antigovernment combatants on the Atlantic Coast as well, though in complex ways. Miskitu combatants knew the terrain, had de facto control of large portions of Coast territory, enjoyed a strong base of civilian support, and operated as small, mobile, and flexible military units—which together yielded them all the classic advantages of a guerrilla army. As a result, they probably felt the direct military impact of the FDN's "strategic defeat" much less than its indirect financial and organizational effects. For example, CIA efforts to make the FDN a more effective force included measures to unify the diverse anti-Sandinista organizations under a single chain of command.[11] Miskitu leaders and field commanders who refused to comply risked the loss of funds, supply lines, and logistical support, which rapidly limited their ability to sustain troops in the field.

These pressures yielded an array of responses by Miskitu combatants to the FDN: from joining outright, to aligning loosely while keeping a separate internal structure, to steadfastly refusing any contact at all. Field commanders in the last category, who also generally chose to negotiate with the Sandinistas—Nolan Escobar, Uriel Vanegas, Reynaldo Reyes, and others—all indicate that a lack of financial and logistical support figured prominently in their decisions.[12] As local negotiations proliferated, both the CIA and the non-negotiating Miskitu leaders sought repeatedly to regroup, overcome internal factionalism, prevent further defections, and reestablish the unity that had been destroyed in 1981 when Rivera and Fagoth parted ways. These efforts resulted in a steady flow of new organizational names (e.g., ASLA, FAUCAN, KISAN, YATAMA; for details, see Appendix D), yet unity remained elusive owing to personal ambitions and political differences among the leaders and, most important, to their utter dependence on U.S. aid. It became increasingly difficult to reconcile the contradiction between the main condition placed on that aid (alliance with the FDN) and most Miskitu combatants' reasons for fighting. Each effort at reorganization brought a new wave of defections by Miskitu combatants. In this sense, ironically, the Reagan administration's drive for a military solution in Nicaragua may actually have hastened reconciliation on the Atlantic Coast.

This geopolitical explanation for the return to peace, though persuasive, is limited by two further considerations. First, paired with complaints of inadequate funds and logistical support, field commanders' accounts of their decisions to negotiate always refer to pressure from Miskitu community members, who wanted the war to end. Although it is difficult to assess the timing, extent, and impact of this pressure, evidence from Sandy Bay indicates that it played a role largely independent of both the FDN's "strategic defeat" and the derivative financial-organizational problems for Miskitu combatants.[13] Second, at least two separate cases of negotiations between Miskitu combatants and Sandinistas preceded the broader shift in the military balance of power by months. In May 1985, in the northern community of Yulu, Sandinista officials signed the first local cease-fire with a Miskitu unit headed by Eduardo Pantin (Diskin et al. 1986). More directly relevant to Sandy Bay, President Daniel Ortega agreed to hold national-level talks with MISURASATA in October 1984, just when the FDN stood at the apex of its military ascendance. These early negotiations, as distinguished from military exigencies, deserve separate attention as catalysts for the peace process.

Negotiating Political Space

In late November 1984 government leaders declared their intention to respect Coast people's "historic rights to autonomy," a phrase they previously had dismissed as a counterrevolutionary slogan. A month earlier, the government and MISURASATA agreed to begin high-level negotiations, and local dialogue between field commanders of the opposing sides soon followed. Although we do not know precisely what gave rise to this dramatic reversal in Sandinista policy toward the Atlantic Coast, three distinct factors were clearly at play. First, the pragmatic idea that negotiations would enhance the perceived legitimacy of the upcoming elections surely had a place in the equation. The change also reflected an acknowledgment of Miskitu people's tenaciousness, which left little doubt that a continued effort to win the war by purely military means would be prohibitively costly and doomed to failure. Finally, the decision arose from a genuinely self-critical evaluation, provoked by the incongruence between the revolution's stated principles and the persistence of such overt and widespread conflict with a subordinate ethnic group.

Whatever the reason for the government's "new start" in 1985, no one could deny its significance: political flexibility, multilevel negotiations, and material concessions suddenly proliferated. This, in turn, suggests an understanding of the Miskitu communities' newfound quiescence as a response to an offer that granted them most of what they had been fighting for. Such a portrayal, though partly correct, obscures another facet of the process: the Sandinistas carefully managed the space they had opened, attempting to set rigid limits on the scope of legitimate political expression. This complex, and at times contradictory, fusion of opening and demarcation became the prominent feature of the autonomy process.

The first round of negotiations between MISURASATA and the Sandinistas was held in December 1984, and three subsequent rounds followed in January, April, and May of 1985. Although in April they agreed to a "cessation of offensive activities," the May meetings erupted into a stormy exchange of mutual accusations and ended in an indefinite suspension of diplomatic contact. Talks did not resume until early 1988, under much-changed military conditions and after an autonomy law had been approved by the National Assembly. The numerous accounts of the May session vary in details and interpretation but yield a fairly clear picture of the overarching problem.[14] The two sides began with conflicting visions of how the talks should proceed, which ultimately prevented them from broaching substantive issues. MISURASATA sought unconditional government recognition of the principles of Indian self-determination before the military question could be resolved. The Sandinistas wanted the order reversed: a cease-fire before discussion of Indian rights, which would have secured explicit recognition of their nonnegotiable principles—national sovereignty and the integrity of the armed forces.

The failure of the negotiations exerted a crucial—though rarely acknowledged—formative influence on what became known as autonomy. The unresolved question of principle—must Miskitu Indian self-determination be negotiated within the parameters of Nicaraguan national sovereignty?—followed directly from the two sides' very different conceptions of what autonomy entailed. Once the talks failed, the Sandinistas concluded that Rivera was unwilling to break definitively with the counterrevolution and viewed MISURASATA's position on autonomy as an extension of that intransigence. From that time on, the FSLN-backed autonomy proposal evolved in constant, though rarely explicit, antagonism with that of MISURASATA. That is, after May 1985 FSLN leaders demarcated the political space they had opened, making sure the militant ethnic demands championed by MISURASATA remained unambiguously outside the boundaries of their version of autonomy.

This demarcation became even more evident with the events of January 1986. Seeking to shore up his combatants' morale, enforce his strict prohibitions against unauthorized dialogue, and generate international support, Brooklyn Rivera organized a foray into the Atlantic Coast accompanied by North American journalists and Native American activists.[15] The government denounced his presence as illegal, portrayed it as a renewed declaration of war, and mounted a vigorous military search-and-destroy campaign. Although government forces were unable to apprehend Rivera, they did force the entourage to retreat hastily to Costa Rica and left everyone convinced that, as Sandy Bay people gloomily reported a few months later, now it would be *"bulit baman"* (only bullets). In addition, State Security continued to make political arrests—albeit many fewer and with more lenient consequences—and applied more subtle means to the same end, such as surveillance, stern warnings, and veiled threats.

The case of the newly formed Miskitu organization MISATAN provides another illustration of this demarcation of political space. The FSLN pro- moted the formation of MISATAN as a means to open a channel of com- munication with Miskitu people at the grass roots. A group of leaders among the few Miskitu openly supportive of the FSLN founded the orga- nization in July 1984 and emitted initial documents that left little doubt about their vehemently prorevolutionary stance.[16] As the leaders began to confront Miskitu militancy and to take positions as representatives of the Miskitu people, however, their discourse changed rapidly. By late 1985, MISATAN leaders had presented the central government with a pe- tition that put forth a series of militant demands, including an end to military service for Miskitu, removal of the local FSLN representative, and de facto recognition of the antigovernment Miskitu organizations.[17] Over the next months relations between MISATAN and the FSLN deteriorated into overt conflict, each placing blame on the other side.[18]

When it became clear to the Sandinistas that MISATAN had gone be- yond the demarcated political space of autonomy, their response was swift and effective. There was no repression, no arrests, and only a few scattered and minor incidents of violence. The government merely cut off the organization's funds and eliminated MISATAN's privileged access to high levels of regional political power. Office doors closed. MISATAN leaders were left without a strong position either as representatives of the Miskitu people—who were still largely mistrustful of their Sandinista ties—or as power brokers who had an inside line to the government. By mid-1986 what was left of MISATAN collapsed under the weight of its own unfulfilled promises and quietly became defunct.

As part of this same process, however, the Sandinistas worked intensely to promote Miskitu support for autonomy through what can only be described as a profound transformation of state presence on the Coast. By the end of 1985, the government had liberalized or completely aban- doned most of the measures, enacted in the heat of war, that Miskitu found most onerous.[19] Local dialogue with numerous groups of Miskitu combatants reinforced the impression that the Sandinistas were flexible, interested in peace, and willing to negotiate. By 1986 it was not uncom- mon to see former Miskitu commanders, who months earlier had been in fierce combat with the government, strolling through the streets of Bluefields and staying in hotels at government expense. These remarkable changes (at times bordering on the bizarre) were most evident in the north, where negotiations in the community of Yulu yielded an agree- ment with a large detachment of Miskitu combatants from the organi- zation KISAN (formerly MISURA).[20] Anyone who was in Puerto Cabezas on September 21, 1985, watching the scores of "KISAN por la paz" com- batants, fully armed, marching through the streets in parade formation,

Former Miskitu antigovernment combatants marching through the streets of Puerto Cabezas (October
1985). Photo courtesy of *Barricada.*

could hardly have doubted that serious changes were under way.[21] These
conditions of political opening, in turn, allowed the government to
resume an array of services to outlying communities left destitute by three
years of war. Although intentions and promises outstripped accomplishments, renewed government presence in the areas of health, education,
food distribution, and funds for community development made a significant impact that did not go unnoticed.

✳   ✳   ✳

Neither variant of the structural explanation for the return to peace
can suffice. The idea that political-military conditions essentially forced
Miskitu townspeople into compliance breaks down in the face of careful

scrutiny. During the critical period, both armed struggle and a path of nonviolent radical opposition to autonomy remained as viable courses of action that some community members followed. That the majority opted for peace, in Sandy Bay and throughout the Coast, well before nation-wide negotiated settlement was a foregone conclusion defies the logic of this "forced compliance" argument. The contention that changes in San-dinista policy granted all or even most of Miskitu townspeople's demands is equally suspect. Both the failed negotiations with MISURASATA and the conflict with MISATAN exemplify the Sandinistas' vigorous efforts to de-marcate the new political space they had opened. People in Sandy Bay were acutely aware of these limitations in the Sandinista offer; in Rodriguez's words, quoted above, "They are just offering us pickings." Yet when faced with the choice between participation in the limited political opening of autonomy and continued militancy to pursue the full range of their de-mands, Rodriguez and most other townspeople opted firmly to participate.

From Grass-Roots Resistance to Realignment, 1985–87

I cannot provide here a full account of community politics in Sandy Bay during these three years. Thick folders full of detailed notes on the complex, fascinating, and at times tragic events of everyday life in the community will have to remain filed away for another occasion. The nar-rative that follows illuminates a few key moments, selected for their value in helping to convey how townspeople thought about, participated in, and contributed to the transition to autonomy. Throughout this period they lived under the purview of two political-military forces, each with strong interests and expectations that could not be ignored. To a large extent, townspeople's actions were shaped by the exigencies of this dual subordination. Though at times severe, these exigencies always left room to maneuver, which townspeople used to exert influence on both Sandi-nistas and bush people, actually bringing them closer to reconciliation. Once this three-sided dialogue began, townspeople gradually came to ac-cept certain premises of Sandinista ideology that they previously had con-tested. As they were drawn into a process of negotiation over the meaning of autonomy, their political alignment shifted away from the bush people, and their inclination for struggle in the name of militant ethnic demands gradually faded.

Between Two Rulers: The Chicha Incident

Early one morning in late October 1985 a gunshot, apparently fired in the air, came from the direction of the lagoon. A member of the tropa soon approached, marching a young Miskitu man with long, unkempt hair toward the command post. The young man, Carlos Wong, had recently come back from the bush. Later that day Dan Peters explained:

'Carlos had been drinking [chicha][22] for two days. He woke up hung over, took some soap, and went to the lagoon to bathe. Three young girls were there, and he chased them away. Petrona, the mother of one of the girls, came back while Carlos was bathing and shouted insults at him. Carlos got angry, chased Petrona back [toward the community], and flogged her with the flat side of a machete.'

That evening, tropa officers called Peters to the command post to help adjudicate.[23] Petrona was there, crying, black and blue, but asked that Carlos not be sent to jail in Bluefields. Instead, she wanted him to pay her a 5,000 cordoba punitive fine. The tropa officers, Peters, and Carlos promptly agreed and closed the case. When Petrona's husband arrived home and heard the story, he demanded harsher punishment. Before the tropa could schedule a reconsideration, the husband went to Kara and presented his complaint to Felipe Nolan.

The flogging incident formed part of a larger problem that plagued the community. Especially since the tropa's new policy, which allowed unarmed bush people to enter and leave Sandy Bay freely, disruptive incidents involving chicha, rum, and marijuana had proliferated.[24] Reverend Samuel Peters led the outcry against drugs and alcohol, and all respected community leaders agreed (in public at least) that something had to be done. The question was, Who would handle the problem?

Felipe Nolan responded first with a programmatic statement. An effective military authority must be capable of making laws and enforcing them. There used to be problems with rum and marijuana in Kara, he explained to Dan Peters, but then Nolan decreed a strict prohibition. Now the situation was under control. If the tropa could not do the same in Sandy Bay, Nolan promised, he would send for the offenders and punish them himself. Anticipating the damaging political consequences of inaction, tropa officer Esteban Mora soon announced a new set of community rules, which he had discussed previously with the peace commission: curfew at 10:00 P.M. and a commitment to dump any chicha or rum found during periodic searches of people's homes. But no search-and-dump operations ensued.

A few days later, Nolan pressed the issue. He called all Sandy Bay's young men to Kara for a meeting, stated his views on drugs and alcohol, and meted out bodily punishment to some known offenders, including Carlos Wong. If offenses didn't stop, he warned, the bush people would

enter Sandy Bay themselves to take further measures. Nolan also summoned leaders from each of the surrounding communities to hear his
own final judgment on the flogging case. Peters, who attended on behalf of Sandy Bay, returned elated and fully content that justice had
been done:

'Five commanders and two officials heard the case. One commander named
"Tapu" presided. He read out of the Bible in Spanish, then translated into Miskitu. He has a high school degree [Peters added with admiration]. Tapu's message
was that God's law and the law of this court are one and the same. I was so
pleased to hear that. The court announced the judgment: Carlos would pay Petrona 5,000 cordobas when his cacao comes in. The comandantes then told me
that as a community leader I have the bush people's full respect. They told me
that anyone in the community who didn't follow the leaders' laws would have to
answer to the bush people.'

The tropa soon heard every detail of the Kara proceedings and expressed
bitter frustration with the outcome. Mario Contrera, whose legal training perhaps had led him to be more engaged in the flogging case than the
other tropa officers, was particularly forthcoming:

'We pass judgment, then the couple goes to Kara, where the same exact judgment is passed. But only with the endorsement of the bush people is the conclusion accepted. The bush people prescribe harsh punishments—shaved heads,
beatings, tying someone to a post for the night. If the tropa did that there would
be outrage, but the people make no comment. . . . So what are we doing here?
Painting a little schoolhouse, building a clinic, being industrious fools [*tontos
útiles*].'

But he made these remarks in only a momentary lapse, followed by
a typically self-confident and energetic response. The officers assigned
especially deep significance to Nolan's threat to come into the community and punish offenders himself. Every time they had offered to
negotiate with Nolan, his refusal had come with a simple demand:
take the army out of Sandy Bay. Since most community members sympathized with this demand, Nolan's threat struck at the heart of the
tropa's efforts to legitimate their political and military presence. In the
next community meeting Mora spoke at length and launched the tropa's
counterargument:

'Autonomy is not the caprice of the revolution, it arises from a recognition of
contradictions between the revolution and the Miskitu, and from a belief that
they can be resolved. Autonomy is going forward, and we want you to participate. It doesn't matter if you're not in agreement with the revolution. We want
you to express an opinion. . . . One day we will leave, and all these things—the

clinic, the schoolhouse, the bridges, an autonomy law—will remain in your hands.'

Then he engaged directly in ideological struggle:

'The tropa is for peace. Those who threaten to come into this community with arms are against peace. They are enemies of the community. . . . We also are committed to dumping the chicha. The bush people say we are doing nothing about the problem, but that is not true. We did resolve the flogging case, but the man went to Kara and told the bush people we did nothing. We won't dump the chicha alone, without the community leaders. That's what the bush people want us to do. Then the community would run to Kara and say we are mistreating them. But we won't fall into that trap. We Sandinistas are very intelligent and very careful. If you want the chicha dumped, tell your leaders to come to the comando and we'll do it together, immediately.'

Mora's response helped the tropa avoid an impending conflict with community members, and it contrasted the tropa's willingness to resolve community problems collectively with Nolan's refusal to negotiate. Not everyone accepted Mora's argument. But his speech, duly transmitted back to Kara, applied new pressure on Nolan to respond or risk losing civilian support.

Room to Maneuver: Community Leadership in Transition

After Rivera's foray into the Coast in January 1986, Manuel Rodriguez and his "second," Dan Peters, continued to promote dialogue but confronted growing problems. With the bush people farther away and on a war footing, there was less to negotiate. Although the bush people's contacts with the community did not cease, they turned largely covert and involved very little communication with the government. This left Rodriguez with the more limited role of mediating between town and tropa. Meanwhile, the regional government had begun to reestablish aid and services to Sandy Bay, giving Rodriguez endless matters of community business to attend to in Bluefields. He relished such tasks and found that skills honed during his many years as síndico under the Somoza regime served well in this new setting. During long stays in Bluefields (often prolonged by the difficulty of finding transportation back to Sandy Bay), Rodriguez developed close working relations with key regional government officials, spoke persuasively with them of his community's needs, and generally acquired more than Sandy Bay's share of the scarce resources—food, clothing, paint, agricultural tools—available to be meted out.

What transpired in such meetings and what exactly happened to the resources obtained, however, became subjects of great controversy back home. A growing number of townspeople grumbled openly that Rodriguez had moved too far toward the Sandinistas, that he and his kin benefited inordinately from what had been gained in the community's name.[25] Another group, composed mainly of extended family members, defended him, citing the need for a strong leader who "speaks all three languages" and "knows all the [government] offices in Bluefields." Echoing an attitude that would later come to predominate, one such supporter added: "The problem with Sandy Bay people is that they don't understand politics. This government is strong. We have to work with them." Far from new, such divisions reflected long-standing resentments over Rodriguez family dominance in community politics (see Chapter 3).[26] In contrast to past times, these divisions now took on geopolitical implications.

For the most part Manuel Rodriguez ignored the accusations and continued to assert his leadership as a broker with the Sandinistas and guarantor of the community's interests. But the tensions inherent in this role, combined with allegations of misconduct, made him increasingly vulnerable. In March 1986, for example, a delegation of the Regional Autonomy Commission (CRA) visited Sandy Bay from Bluefields in one of many efforts to involve Miskitu townspeople in the consulta. A mere 50 people attended the meeting held that afternoon in the Moravian church, and in a further gesture of reticence, they took seats mainly toward the back. Rodriguez was obliged to sit in the front pew and to welcome the commission. "The days of fear are over; the government doesn't want to make any more mistakes; we're here to talk about our rights to autonomy," he stated, in a terse welcome that betrayed his discomfort. The Autonomy Commission representative's stock speech, meant as a prelude to discussion, generated comments as sparse as the attendance. Afterward townspeople complained bitterly about the meeting, citing both their disapproval of autonomy and Rodriguez's acquiescent stance toward the government.

In the next community meeting a few weeks later, conducted in Miskitu, in which I was the only outside observer, I fully expected a showdown between Manuel Rodriguez and the disgruntled townspeople. It never happened. Rodriguez began with a solemn prayer and then launched into a long monologue, laced with biblical allusions and references to townspeople as "my children." The immediate item of business was a request from the CRA to send four community delegates to an autonomy workshop in Bluefields, scheduled for the following month. 'Others in the community go about their daily routines, while we leaders work day and night to achieve freedom for our people,' he began. 'The government is inviting us to a meeting in Bluefields to defend our community, and asking our pardon in return for giving us autonomy [*klauna iwanka*].' Next he reviewed the entire history of MISURASATA's conflict with the government and ended by affirming, 'We are deeply grateful that autonomy is now to be granted, and that the whole world—especially the democratic countries—knows about our problems.' As for the workshop, 'even the invitation contains a lie. I am not the *responsable* [person in charge] for this autonomy. Blood has spilled, our boys [in the bush] are still suffering. Two times they have tried to kill our esteemed leader [Rivera]. MISURASATA has sent me a document that explains our true rights to autonomy.' He then directed a teacher to read the entire clandestine MISURASATA document.[27] They stopped after each of the thirteen points to explain its meaning in laborious detail. Finally, to conclude this tour de force, Rodriguez brandished the original, tattered, 80-year-old community land documents, which served as a potent symbol of community rights, of the broader Miskitu struggle, and of his incontestable authority as síndico. Without a vote, or even direct discussion, Rodriguez had deftly silenced his opponents by linking the reassertion of his leadership to the moral authority of MISURASATA and to the widely supported refusal of the government's request for cooperation. The meeting came to a firm decision that expressed this defiance: Sandy Bay would not participate in autonomy until the government had reached an agreement with MISURASATA.

This collective decision, forged in mid-April 1986, lasted barely two weeks. In a subsequent meeting the community reversed its stance and selected four delegates to attend the Bluefields meeting, all inexperienced young men who became known as the "autonomy gang" (*autonomía gimka*). Rodriguez was conspicuously absent from the group. The explanation for the reversal was straightforward. Community members reported that Brian Smith, the FSLN representative, had delivered a stern warning that no additional government aid would come to the community if the delegates were not selected. The warning achieved the intended effect. Townspeople had no desire to jeopardize their access to material aid from the government or the other benefits that had begun to flow in the name of autonomy.

The explanation for Manuel Rodriguez's abrupt withdrawal from community politics came out only gradually as I gained his and other people's trust. The bush boys had given him an order: "Don't put your hand in this autonomy business," he reported. "This is a false autonomy, because it is dealing only with the civilians and ignoring the boys in the bush. People who get involved will have to watch themselves." Others elaborated on his account: sometime earlier in the year, the bush people had determined that Rodriguez had grown too close to the Sandinistas and ordered him to step down. As I learned more about these clandestine political edicts of the bush people, other aspects of community politics that had perplexed me began to make sense. For example, Maria Stevens, formerly a leader and clearly one of the most capable and astute members of the community, never said a word in meetings because the bush people had prohibited her from speaking.[28] The outcome of the zonal autonomy elections the following October also became more intelligible. The bush people reportedly had sent emissaries house to house to instruct people to vote for Johnny Reyes, which helps to explain why, despite his reputation as an irresponsible neophyte, he received nearly unanimous support.

Both military forces clearly influenced the scope and content of townspeople's actions during this period. When community resistance jeopardized smooth progress toward the consummation of autonomy, the Sandinistas intervened with a heavy hand. Likewise, the bush people had reduced Manuel Rodriguez, a crucial and powerful actor during the previous year, to grumbling from the sidelines. He turned deeply pessimistic and withdrawn, critical of the "autonomy business," yet cut off from his previous role as intermediary:

'We're living between two rulers, and the only way to survive is to stay strictly neutral. . . . No peace commission is possible any more. The boys have been punishing in the bush too long, and the government lost its chance to bring them back. Now they will fight to the end.'

It was March, the time of year when people prepare their fields. Rodriguez devoted his energies to planting rice.

Yet neither political-military force completely deprived the townspeople of room to maneuver. Although the bush people's coercive threats edged Rodriguez out of politics, they could not possibly hope to enforce a general prohibition against community involvement in the autonomy process because it offered too much that townspeople desperately wanted. The most the bush people could do was to make sure that the autonomy leaders remained sympathetic to their cause and responsive to their orders. Similarly, the Sandinistas became convinced early on that it was unrealistic to expect townspeople to support the revolution. The revised objectives, evident as early as the chicha incident of 1985, were merely to convince them to participate in the autonomy process and to accept the tropa leaders as legitimate interlocutors. Miskitu townspeople therefore asserted their demands and won partial concessions from both sides. They actively participated in autonomy, thereby allowing the process to move forward, and yet regularly challenged—in private or clandestine and occasionally public ways—the very premises on which these advances were based.

Contested Meanings: From Miskitu Rights to Autonomía

After their election in May 1986, Sandy Bay's four autonomy leaders attended a series of meetings in Bluefields, Pearl Lagoon, and other locations, where they learned of the latest version of the autonomy proposal and registered community input, which was to shape the proposal's final content. Each of these preliminary meetings ended with a general statement of endorsement of the proposal as it currently stood, foreshadowing the outcome of the culminating meeting in April 1987. The Bluefields workshop took place during the last days of May 1986. Delegates from every community in the southern region spent the first day in small-group discussions and the second in plenary.

Before discussion of the proposal began, Sumu and Miskitu delegates engaged workshop organizers in what turned out to be the most heated exchange of the entire two days. They had been given no *viático* (per diem), not even money to buy cigarettes, and they were crowded into hotel rooms with leaky roofs and uncomfortable mattresses. Indians always got the worst of everything, they complained bitterly. Such logistical matters were the responsibility of Felipe Salazar, an impatient and imperious Mestizo member of the Regional Autonomy Commission with ties to the FSLN. The hotel owner did not leave "good things" in the rooms for fear they would be stolen, he explained, which sounded to the angry delegates like an insinuation that they all were thieves. They calmed down only after Salazar offered a favorable resolution of the viático problem.

Workshop discussion finally began under the leadership of Belina Morales, an FSLN-aligned teacher originally from Tasbapauni who often served as liaison between the CRA and the Río Grande. The autonomy proposal had been translated into Miskitu, copied, and distributed to the approximately fifteen delegates who took part. They read each point, puzzled over its meaning, sought to clarify it by reading the Spanish version, and puzzled more over the comparison of the two, frequently concluding that the translation was faulty. Once a Creole delegate from Río Grande Bar tried to clarify the discussion by reading the English version, which only augmented the already substantial confusion. They grappled with the points' content in only a few cases, and even then only superficially. As discussion on each point was exhausted, someone (usually Morales) offered a summary and asked, "*Tanka briram?*" (Understood?). To which everyone answered, "Yes."

That afternoon each group identified concerns that delegates wanted to raise in the plenary, which provoked a string of substantive demands. When would the tropa leave the community and allow "our boys" to come back? When would the Atlantic Coast be "free" again? Would autonomy ensure better access to food, medicine, and consumer goods? Resolve intercommunity land conflicts? Provide bilingual education? Most of these demands arose in the plenary, and in one case—the "military question"—led to a heated exchange between delegates and a member of the CRA. But for the most part delegates stated these points as general demands, rather than specific modifications of the proposal, and nobody pursued the disjuncture.

When the plenary concluded, Salazar hastily circulated a statement that expressed overall approval of the proposal. Delegates had not even begun to sort out what it meant in relation to the previous two days of discussion when Salazar began to press them to sign it. As they lined up without further deliberation to sign, a Sandy Bay man made a statement that I heard repeatedly during the course of the autonomy consulta: "If the government really keeps all these promises, it will be great." Persisting ambiguities in the precise content of "these promises" did not seem to matter. The Sandinistas gained approval of the statement, proclaimed the workshop a great success, and thereby moved one step closer to the promulgation of an autonomy law.[29]

These advances occurred despite considerable political-military tensions in the community. Negotiations with MISURASATA had broken down in May 1985, and in January 1986 the armed organization had gone back on a war footing. In April 1986 the U.S. Congress renewed aid to the contras, which gave rise to general expectations that direct conflict soon would resume. They soon were borne out. In July 1986, a group of MISURASATA combatants attacked the neighboring community of Karawala. A few months later, State Security ordered the arrest of four Sandy Bay civilians accused of aiding the contras. The event sent shock waves of angry rebuke and bitter resentment through the community. Townspeople appealed to their newly elected autonomy representatives, who in turn confronted the security officer "in the name of autonomy," only to be told to get lost or they would be arrested too. "Autonomy is *bahki* [worthless, garbage]," went the refrain that morning. Many began to refer to government "promises" with a different inflection; rather than inducing optimistic anticipation, they became *pramis baman* (empty promises).[30]

Yet the Sandinista leaders' public commitment to autonomy and their high stakes in its success ensured that these tensions would reverberate differently than before. Whether acting on orders from higher authorities or in anticipation of them, State Security gave the detainees a warning and promptly released them. Although still angry, townspeople could not help but comment on the contrast with "first time," when harsh treatment and jail had been the norm. More concretely, regional government and party leaders devised a plan tailored especially for the Río Grande communities. Internal discussion of the "pilot project in zonal autonomy" began as early as May 1986, and around September the CRA formally introduced the idea. The introductory document announced: "Now it is time for audacious steps because the townspeople are claiming that we have talked too much about autonomy and the circumstances demand concrete deeds, tangible actions, to demonstrate to the communities and to the world that the Autonomy Project . . . is not a false promise and is irreversible."[31]

The oblique references to popular discontent and the call for "concrete deeds" are the document's key points. Alongside militant political demands, the decline of armed conflict in 1985 had generated renewed expectations related to community welfare. Townspeople wanted better health care and education, more reliable food distribution, and aid to resume productive activities. The "pilot project" marked the beginning of a fundamental shift in the meaning of autonomy, away from conflictive demands that pitted Miskitu townspeople against the Sandinistas, toward these pressing needs, which the government agreed were legitimate. It proposed that each community elect autonomy leaders, who would draw a salary and work closely with the regional government to achieve the goals of peace, reconstruction, and development, which now would all be encompassed by the term autonomía.

An advance team of Sandinista cadres and CRA members arrived in Karawala by speedboat on a Saturday morning in mid-October 1986 to supervise the zonal autonomy election. Voting took place in the schoolhouse after numerous delays created by various community members' critical statements. As one man put it, "We will vote only if we can be guaranteed that this time the government will fulfill its promises. Too often in the past, government people have spoken what turned out to be nothing but lies." Felipe Salazar, again in charge of the activity, at first attempted to dialogue, then grew irritated, cut off discussion, and demanded that the voting begin. Rather than resist further, most people complied. As Salazar called names from a prepared list, they filed forward and voted by secret ballot for one of the four "autonomy gang" delegates. By that afternoon 188 votes had been cast, giving a solid victory to Johnny Reyes, who made a brief, low-key acceptance speech.

Although voting did not proceed as smoothly in the other four communities,[32] Sandinista cadres could legitimately proclaim that the experiment in "zonal autonomy" had successfully begun. Before leaving, they announced their commitment to an impressive package of "projects," compiled from wish lists generated in previous community meetings. In townspeople's minds, autonomy soon became associated with these projects—the construction of schools, health clinics, boats, and wharves and assistance programs for farmers and fishermen—which the government expected to fund through international donations. Reyes and his counterparts from the other four communities, in conjunction with the local FSLN representative, would be responsible for the projects' implementation.[33]

Soon after the elections of October 1986, townspeople began to use the Spanish term autonomía, even when speaking in Miskitu, and seemed comfortable with its connotation, as defined by Sandinista cadres and the CRA. Autonomía referred to the work of Johnny Reyes and the other elected leaders and to the many "projects" that had been promised. This acquiescence did not spare autonomía from criticism. Despite his electoral victory, Reyes was a controversial leader from the start, owing to his inexperience, alleged extramarital liaisons, and reputation as an excessive drinker. Within a few months these criticisms intensified. Many townspeople viewed Reyes as a shabby administrator who had done very little to earn the salary he collected on monthly trips to Bluefields. They reserved equally vociferous complaints for "the government," which they held responsible for numerous unrealized promises and the generally disastrous state of the economy.[34] Community meetings held to discuss autonomía often erupted into boisterous debates, mutual accusations, and prescriptions as to how Reyes ought to act or how a given project should proceed. Yet this grass-roots ferment helped to deflect criticism of the Sandinistas by assigning partial responsibility for the problem to Reyes and the newly formed government of zonal autonomy.

At the same time, most people drew a sharp distinction between autonomía and another set of demands, elicited by questions focused on *Miskitu ai raitka nani* (Miskitu rights). The bush people were fighting for Miskitu rights, and most community members assumed that these rights were not included in the Sandinista version of the law. The evidence for this persisting convergence between the community and bush people was overwhelming, though not always in public view. In early 1987, when I presented Maria Stevens with my impression that people were moving toward the Sandinista side, she laughed. 'That's what it looks like on the surface,' she explained,

'but underneath something completely different is going on. Everyone still supports the bush people 100 percent. A commander named Tapu was just here for two weeks. He passed from house to house like a bat, staying inside during the day, holding meetings at night. A "committee" of townspeople carries out [the bush people's] every order, collects food, medicine, and money for them from the community, sends them information. The bush commanders have a different strategy now, no more threats of violence. They are telling people to play along with the government until further orders. The tropa, poor things, don't have a clue.'

As if to confirm her portrayal, in May 1987, twenty Sandy Bay youths suddenly fled from the community to join the bush people. The conflict was by no means over.

Yet astute tropa officers managed to prevent this ongoing militancy from erupting into renewed military conflict. At the time of the youths' flight the officer in charge of the tropa was a man named Guillermo, who worked especially hard to create a conciliatory atmosphere. Guillermo seemed to have fairly accurate sources of information about the "clandestine" goings on. He commiserated with the distraught parents of the absent youths and encouraged them to visit the bush camps to coax their children back. Many tried to no avail, which led them to contrast Guillermo's permissiveness and sympathy with the bush commander's refusal to release their children. Guillermo also knew that food sent for the community's use ended up in the bush people's hands. He even joked sardonically in community members' presence: "700 sacks of food just arrived from Bluefields, that means 350 for the contras." He made pointed comments about this "leakage" in meetings when people complained about the community's chronic food shortage. But he reprimanded no one.

For the festivities of July 19, 1987, Guillermo made an extra effort to deepen ties with townspeople. The festivities began inauspiciously, under a drizzle that had not let up for days. Tropa members gathered on the muddy baseball field around a 50-foot pole, outnumbering the children and schoolteachers who had been invited to participate. They shouted some slogans about Sandino and guerrilla struggle in Latin America, which the onlookers patiently ignored. The turning point came when the *gigantona*—a tropa member on stilts dressed as a giant woman—approached, dancing to a tin-can drumbeat, dispersing the crowd as children screamed with delight. The commotion attracted more participants for the rest of the games—greased pole, pin the tail on the donkey, horse races—each of which concluded with a prize for the winner. To the crowd's great satisfaction, a tropa member competed in the horse race and was beaten soundly by local boys.

In the afternoon the tropa hosted a sit-down meal and ceremony in the schoolhouse, with selected community members as invited guests. The tropa again began with slogans, which echoed on the cement walls and brought the same passive response from the guests. Next came the *politico*'s speech, for the most part a standard rendition of Sandinista orthodoxy.[35] It culminated with praise of autonomía as one of the revolution's most recent "conquests" and urged people to "devote themselves to autonomía, leaving all else for later." Then a group of five got up, stood arm in arm, and launched into an off-tune and unpracticed rendition of "Comandante Carlos," a popular Pacific Coast song about the revolutionary hero Carlos Fonseca. Townspeople responded with mild amusement, seeming to share neither my admiration of the tropa's commitment and fervor nor my disappointment at their choice of song. Last came the dinner, cooked and served by tropa waiters, while the community members sat with the officers at the banquet table. The político talked amiably with a young man who recently had returned from six years of combat in the bush; Dan Peters praised the abundant servings. Everyone left satisfied, especially Guillermo, who said that what he had most wanted to demonstrate was "the revolution's generosity." I marveled at the contrast with past years, when the Sandinista tropa members celebrated July 19 drinking rum in jittery seclusion, surrounded by an anonymous mass of townspeople with whom relations amounted to little more than visceral mutual distrust.

By October 1987, the regional government finally had achieved a commitment of outside funds for projects to improve transportation and strengthen the artisanal fishing program. When autonomy leaders traveled to Bluefields, they found a responsive, albeit nearly bankrupt, government, in stark contrast to the past. Interspersed with the standard complaints about autonomía's unmet promises came acknowledgment of this change and a greater willingness to adopt an incremental approach toward their unmet demands. As one man put it, with autonomía, "now we can speak directly to the government's face." Samuel Blandón, an influential Sandy Bay teacher, spoke at a community meeting and urged people to participate in autonomía: "Maybe someday God will take this government out, but until then, we have to work with them. IDSIM [the development arm of the Moravian church] is not going to support us forever." The autonomía leader from neighboring Karawala gave the position a more logical gloss, which captured the views of many:

'We can't achieve the whole thing all at once. It will happen gradually, piece by piece. The government made some big mistakes, but that won't happen again. They are sincere in what they offer. . . . [They have not conceded on every point.] For example, they haven't yet taken the tropa out of our community. But that's OK. We'll start with one piece, make sure that's working well [*wapni wapisa*], and then we'll go back for another.'

Although few Sandy Bay people had renounced their unmet militant demands, the days of frontal resistance and struggle were over.

Between Geopolitics and Everyday Resistance

The view from Sandy Bay leaves little doubt that political-military conditions did not force Miskitu people to comply with autonomy. As late as May 1987, when MISURASATA was still at war with the government, more than twenty youths left the community to join the armed struggle. Others expressed dissent in more peaceful but equally unequivocal ways, such as the community's initial decision to send no delegates to the Bluefields autonomy workshop unless the government negotiated with MISURASATA. Options for militant opposition to autonomía and to the Sandinista government in general were clearly available, yet most people chose to act otherwise. They rejected militancy in large part because autonomía offered much that looked very good to them. The zonal autonomy project brought government support for community welfare and development, a return to peace and economic normalcy, and an unprecedented voice for community leaders in regional government affairs.

One did not have to listen long to people in informal discussions, and at times even in public meetings, however, to perceive the disparities between what autonomía offered and what they understood to be the full extent of Miskitu rights. Table 4 summarizes the key elements of this divergence. Dissatisfaction did not stop with passive dissent but motivated constant semiclandestine political action as well, such as sending food to the bush people and secretly housing field commanders who visited the community. The same people who engaged in this "resistance" often participated fully in autonomía and thereby contributed directly to its success.

How then should this grass-roots Miskitu response to the state be interpreted? There is no doubt that Sandy Bay townspeople had what James C. Scott (1990) calls a "private transcript"—a critique of Sandinista power and authority that they did not always express in public. My questions often brought forth abundant and venomous anti-Sandinista sentiments, and many backed up such responses with action. For the same reason, the idea that townspeople were subject to Sandinista "ideological domination" is completely implausible. Yet these affirmations still allow room for the conclusion that Miskitu people's ongoing resistance to the state became fused with an incipient Sandinista hegemony, which helped bring about the return to peace.

Townspeople were virtually guaranteed to be confused and perplexed about many facets of the autonomy process. They were not equivocal in the least about what they wanted; as I have emphasized throughout this book, they expressed a cogent, passionate, well-elaborated notion of Mis-

TABLE 4

Miskitu Ethnic Militancy and the Autonomy Law Compared[a]

Demand	Explanation of demand	Rights granted by autonomy law
Territory	The Miskitu have rights to self-government in an immense territory of the Atlantic Coast.	All ethnic groups are guaranteed rights to the communal lands "that have traditionally belonged to their communities."
Economic control	All natural resources in the territory belong to the Miskitu, who then would turn over part of the proceeds to the central government.	Apart from those on communal lands, all resources are administered jointly by the autonomous and central governments.
Political exclusivity	The territory would be governed by Miskitu leaders with a minimal role for the central government.	State powers are shared between the central government and an autonomous council comprised of delegates from all six ethnic groups.
Cultural exclusivity	Miskitu cultural practices should prevail, defining the norms by which non-Miskitu inhabitants must abide.	Strict equality of rights and participation are provided for the six ethnic groups that live within the autonomous region.

[a]These points inevitably involve simplifications, one of which is to gloss over the relationship between the Miskitu and the other Coast ethnic groups. Although some Miskitu would claim these rights for all three Indian peoples (thereby including Sumu and Rama), this usually conceals a lack of serious commitment to redress past Miskitu domination of the other two. For precisely this reason, Sumu people express nearly unanimous opposition to being subsumed in the category "Indians." Another less common variation is for Miskitu to assign these rights to all Coast people, excluding only Mestizos from the Pacific. Though more easily reconciled with the autonomy law, this version still raises contradictions.

kitu rights. Nevertheless, they often were deeply uncertain about how to proceed in seeking these ends. Autonomy workshops like the one described in this chapter, for example, contained little evidence that Miskitu people acted according to a carefully elaborated strategy. They often seemed to be overwhelmed by the written text and to lack the patience to carry out a systematic analysis comparing its contents to their own notion of rights. Instead, they responded that "if the government really follows through with all this, it will be great," which reflected part confusion, and part cautious optimism, and eventually grew in an unintended way into the dual consciousness I have described.

Autonomía included many things that people very much wanted. Consequently, they felt virtually compelled to test the waters, find out more about what the Sandinistas offered, and engage in the political process that would fix the meaning and content of the rights they had been fighting for. Yet once this struggle over material goods and cultural meanings began, the Sandinistas, with far superior resources—both material and discursive—could almost single-handedly demarcate the boundaries of the dialogue. Townspeople were not fooled by these maneuvers; they maintained a critical and subversive stance toward the whole process. I often asked Sandy Bay people, "Will you achieve Miskitu rights through autonomía?" Most answered with a definitive "No," expressing gut-level distrust of the Sandinistas. Yet they tended not to devise a strategy that allowed them *both* to participate and directly to contest the rules of the game. Rather, their participation led them gradually to imbue the rules of autonomía with a certain legitimacy. It became more reasonable to adopt the attitude of the community leader who said, "We'll get this much secured and then go back for more." Here the notion of hegemony helps to specify not mindless adoption of a "dominant ideology" but, rather, the structured perplexity that defused militant opposition.

The coexistence of different possible understandings of autonomy contributed directly to this same outcome. Were they working on the details of a previously demarcated project, or on the prior step of defining the project's fundamental premises? Sandinista cadres vigorously promoted the former understanding, thereby differentiating autonomía from the more militant MISURASATA position. The FSLN *secretario* of the Río Grande zone portrayed this as a conscious effort to wean Miskitu people from their *"etnicista"* ideas and to reshape their conception of autonomy.[36] Townspeople gradually came to accept the dichotomy between autonomía and Indian rights, without abandoning their commitment to the latter. Yet the very displacement of militant ethnic demands, from the motivating force behind their collective action to the realm of a "private transcript," constituted a crucial victory for the Sandinistas. Indeed, it became the linchpin in Sandinista efforts to end the war and achieve consensual public endorsement of autonomía. The tropa officer Guillermo's permissive stance toward the parents of youths who had left to join the bush people is an example. As long as townspeople did not directly challenge autonomía, their ethnic militancy caused the tropa little concern. Indeed, astute officers like Guillermo seemed even to encourage this dual response, realizing that it would broaden the basis for dialogue and reduce the propensity for conflict.

Skeptics may still want to characterize the townspeople's dual response as rational, adaptive, even ingenious, and to question the need for recourse to the idea of hegemony to explain Miskitu actions. In one sense they would be right. Once Miskitu townspeople endorsed the distinction between autonomía and Miskitu rights, it made perfect sense to participate fully in the former, while viewing the latter as a desirable but presently unattainable ideal. Yet the very assumption that such a distinction was valid and sensible formed part of the ideology that the Sandinistas promoted as a means to bolster their legitimacy and achieve their political objectives.

Consider, for example, the divergence between autonomía and Miskitu rights in relation to Sandinista military presence in Miskitu communities. Although "get the tropa out" was at first a firm community demand, as tropa members had a chance to prove their goodwill it gradually lost urgency, overshadowed by a view of the tropa as relatively benign and even as a legitimate interlocutor in community affairs. Without such a shift in consciousness, autonomía would have appeared as a flagrant violation of Miskitu sensibilities, as MISURASATA exile leaders continually sought to portray it. I returned to visit Sandy Bay in July 1988, at the time of the revolution's ninth anniversary, and found a group of young men, all former combatants of MISURASATA, engaged in casual conversation about the "war years." The tone of their remarks expressed neither the flush of victory nor the demoralization of defeat. They saw no point in continuing the struggle and yet had nothing sanguine to say about what had been achieved. "It's too late now," one said wistfully. "When a tree has been growing for nine years, it gets strong and very hard to knock down." Once they assumed that the Sandinista state was invincible militarily—an idea that tropa members promoted as incontrovertible—the dual response acquired full-fledged rationality. But that does not explain how the idea emerged in the first place. I suspect that it had less to do with the hard facts of military force than with advances in the autonomy process, which made fighting the government much more difficult to justify.

Finally, we must assess the impact of Anglo affinity on this transition. If in previous years these premises motivated Miskitu people's mobilization against the state, did they not exert an influence in this third phase of collective action as well? This is not an easy question to answer because rapidly changing conditions gave Anglo affinity a multiple, at times contradictory, political valence. Although Anglo affinity did continue to engender skepticism of and militant opposition to the government, by 1987 the emotional charge behind these reactions had begun to fade. On the one hand, daily interactions with the tropa made it impossible to maintain the harrowing associations that Anglo affinity prescribed. Communists were supposed to prohibit religion and send parishioners to concentration camps; yet these tropa members talked pleasantly with the Moravian parsons, helped to underwrite church functions, and even attended services. Communists were supposed to ban the use of money, yet the tropa distributed credit and promoted community development. On the other hand, vicissitudes in U.S. funding for MISURASATA and other armed organizations began to shake some people's confidence in their old allies the Americans. Accounts of the cynical motives of CIA operatives working in Honduras began to seep back into the community.[37] Most townspeople continued to believe that the Americans supported Miskitu rights and to scoff at Sandinista anti-imperialist litanies as self-serving lies. But a minority view emerged, which portrayed Americans as opportunists capable of using the Miskitu and leaving them in the lurch. When mixed messages came from Washington, this dissenting position gained currency.

There is another, more complex facet of the relationship between Anglo affinity and the post-1985 transition. A prominent, deeply entrenched element of Anglo affinity can be summarized by the Miskitu notion of *ilp laka*: aid and economic development that originates with powerful, benevolent actors from outside the community. In Miskitu collective memories, the term ilp laka brings to mind company times, when opportunities for work suddenly appeared thanks to enterprising North American venture capitalists, and Moravian church social programs, which were heavily subsidized by donations from the North. Early Sandinista political discourse tended to challenge the paternalist underpinnings of this notion, attempting to substitute principles of self-esteem, popular organization, and empowerment. The deepening of ethnic militancy had a similar effect, inspiring townspeople's confidence in their own ability to stand up, demand respect, and fight for what was rightfully theirs.[38] In later years, however, in their efforts to ensure the success of autonomy, the Sandinistas developed a discourse that had the opposite effect of drawing a stark distinction between autonomía and ethnic militancy and defining the former in terms of projects that would come to the community with international funding. This shift tended to leave autonomía shorn of the language of empowerment and strangely resonant with the notion of ilp laka. Paradoxically, as the dichotomy between Miskitu rights and autonomía became more firmly implanted, the legacy of Anglo affinity engendered an attitude in Miskitu townspeople of quiescence, compromise, and willingness to make claims on the government's promises of ilp laka, saving empowerment for another day.

The townspeople's response to autonomía therefore combined everyday resistance with a newfound inclination to accommodate state rule. Sandinista cadres ignored the resistance and actively promoted accommodation by drawing Miskitu people into a political process, the parameters of which they retained the power to define. Gradually, as Miskitu people opted to participate in autonomía, and yet to desist in the struggle over its meaning, they moved in a tentative and preliminary way toward alignment with the Sandinista state. This conclusion affirms both the great advance that autonomy achieved and the persisting inequities built into the terms of accommodation, which Sandinista hegemony tended to obscure. The Sandinistas still proceeded through a form of political triage, whereby they defined "legitimate" Miskitu demands and sought to preclude the rest. Although Miskitu people publicly submitted to this demarcation, it was bound to make the new alliance fragile and the solution far from complete.

Might there have been an alternative of opening a wider political space that would allow the definition of autonomy to emerge from greater internal democratic struggle within the revolution? Put to Sandinista leaders repeatedly in a variety of contexts, this question always met with the same compelling reply: the conditions of U.S.-backed aggression made it too dangerous. In light of the outcome of the 1990 elections, however, the case for critique of the inequities built into autonomía and serious consideration of that radical democratic alternative may be more compelling still.

Epilogue

With hindsight it is clear that the Sandinista strategy was far from a complete success, even in its own terms. In the elections of 1990, which served to constitute the autonomous governments of the Coast, Miskitu people voted overwhelmingly in favor of candidates from YATAMA, the successor organization of MISURASATA. In the Sandy Bay area and throughout the northeastern region, YATAMA came to power.

These election results brought about two sets of unintended consequences. The measure of Sandinista success in the autonomy process was Miskitu people's acquiescence, which displaced militant demands into a realm of private discussion and semiclandestine everyday resistance. This had the effect of cordoning off a vital facet of Miskitu consciousness, making it impossible for Sandinistas to understand, much less respond to, what the Miskitu wanted and believed was rightfully theirs. The resulting mutual isolation helps to explain why the Miskitu voted overwhelmingly anti-Sandinista in the 1990 elections, even though the Sandinista government had just conceded autonomy, the Miskitu people's fundamental demand.

There were unintended consequences for the Miskitu as well. Through the autonomy process, most Miskitu people agreed to de facto accommodation, thereby desisting from civic political struggle within the revolution for the full range of their demands. Although we do not know what results such a struggle might have achieved, its absence resulted in an autonomy law that, for all its strengths, lacks the language necessary to guarantee what Miskitu now, as in the Sandinista era, claim as Indian rights. The inadequacy of this compromise, shaped in part by incipient Sandinista hegemony, has come back to haunt the Miskitu people. They now face a central government opposed in principle to autonomy, intent on turning the clock back to pre-Sandinista times, when political and economic elites viewed the Coast as little more than a reserve for exploitable natural resources. By 1990 Miskitu people gained a codified law and an elected regional autonomous government, but their struggle to exercise full rights of autonomy had barely begun.

8 Engaging Contradictions

> "Liberation" is a value worthy of science, and that should be the perspective
> from which the minority scientist seeks to advance knowledge, always in the
> spirit of respect for logical canons and methodological rigor, but for the pur-
> pose of emancipating (liberating) the bodies, minds and spirits of human kind.
> —E. W. Gordon, 1985

THROUGH THE 1980's, rapid political change on Nicaragua's
Atlantic Coast did not permit sustained research on a stable set of questions. When I began working there in 1981, the revolution appeared to
have great liberating potential for poor and middle-class Nicaraguans,
offering a model for Latin American states' relations with Indian peoples.
Within months incipient tensions between the Miskitu and the Sandinistas
had erupted into widespread conflict, fully enmeshed with the broader
geopolitical struggle under way. My research questions changed, their
scope narrowed, and their urgency deepened. What had gone wrong, and
how could the conflict be overcome? In early 1985, just as I embarked
on field research to study that question, the negotiated return to peace
began. My topic changed again, framed at least in part by the emergence of "autonomy": How would this new political arrangement be defined? Would it achieve a lasting peace? Would the contradictions be
resolved?

There was, however, a thread of continuity amid this rapid change.
While the Sandinistas remained in control of the state, each phase of their
evolving relations with the Atlantic Coast took on epochal importance as
evidence of the Left's ability (or inability) to improve its remarkably deficient record in confronting the challenges of multicultural Latin America.[1]
Correspondingly, in each phase my research proceeded with the assumption that it was possible simultaneously to analyze, critically assess, and
have some influence on this record and its legacy. The Sandinistas' electoral defeat in February 1990 severed that continuity. We do not know, for
example, the reach and impact of autonomy as originally conceived (i.e.,
an effort of internal reform by a revolutionary state), because it had not
begun to be implemented when the Sandinistas turned over state power.

Many of the questions raised by the preparatory phase, which I analyzed in Chapter 7, must for now remain unanswered; their practical implications have grown less pressing and immediate.

This political change and realignment after 1990 has begun to generate new information and analysis regarding the revolutionary era, which I have taken into account whenever possible. For the most part, however, this book must be situated squarely within that era, when the Sandinista revolution was locked in conflict with the U.S. government's imperial pretensions, and when Sandinista relations with the Miskitu Indians were in gradual transition from armed conflict to peace and autonomy. To study this process I sought to move back and forth between Miskitu townspeople and Sandinista cadres, to develop an analysis of the conflict from the standpoint of each, while subjecting each to critical questions that took shape and sharpened as I stood with, and listened to, those on the opposite side.

This chapter offers an overview of what the method has yielded and draws out some implications of its achievements. I begin with two parallel summary analyses of Miskitu and Sandinista roles in the conflict, with special attention to how my conclusions advance the theoretical propositions put forth in Chapter 1. A third section seeks to unify these parallel strands in a single framework and suggests some comparative insights that result from such an endeavor. In a final section I return to the book's central theme—the study of ethnic conflict—to assess the applicability of my conclusions for similar problems elsewhere and for Miskitu and Mestizo Nicaraguans as they confront the difficult times that lie ahead.

Miskitu History, Consciousness, and Collective Action

Since early colonial times, Miskitu people have occupied a geographic and political space deeply contested by larger and more powerful forces. This book has followed that history since the 1890's, when the earlier phase of the three-part relationship—involving an Anglo-Hispanic colonial rivalry—gave way to its contemporary expression: U.S. hegemony versus Nicaraguan state authority. These two modifiers, "hegemony" and "authority," signal the thrust of my argument. Miskitu people felt oppressed by and strongly resisted the manifestations of Nicaraguan state rule, while drawing near to and becoming integrated with the institutions and practices associated with U.S. presence in the region. Indeed, both tendencies formed part of a single process: adoption of premises associated with the Anglo-American world became a resource in Miskitu people's resistance to the state, while Anglo affinity deepened the militancy with which they asserted their right to be different. For example, when Miskitu leaders protested state oppression, they commonly asserted that the Nicaraguans were "more uncivilized than ourselves." [2]

Paradoxically, Anglo affinity—a complex of commonsense ideas and values that emanate from the dominant Anglo-American people, institutions, and cultural practices—helped to constitute Miskitu people's ethnic militancy. It bolstered their inclination and capacity to resist the Nicaraguan state, while reinforcing their adherence to loaded Anglo-defined premises, such as the distinction between being "heathen" and "civilized," and later between Communism and democracy.

In my efforts to understand three successive phases of Miskitu collective action, I have placed central emphasis on these dual elements within their consciousness—Anglo affinity and ethnic militancy. The argument came with certain qualifications and complexities. To some extent, Miskitu people did accommodate Nicaraguan state rule, following a pattern common to Indian-state relations throughout Latin America, which Steve Stern (1987) has called "resistant adaptation." Conversely, integration with and affinity toward Anglo institutions—the Moravian church, North American companies, the U.S. Marines—was not conflict-free, a point that often has been neglected. [3] Like their counterparts throughout Latin America, Miskitu people resisted and acted to transform the institutions to which they were subordinated. They pressed the government-appointed síndico to represent community interests, for example, and in certain ways they made the Moravian church into a Miskitu institution. Yet in my reading of the evidence, they accommodated the state relatively little and resisted Anglo-American institutions even less. Although transformation of the latter did occur, to emphasize this outcome is to miss the more important ways in which power relations acted to constitute Miskitu people's ideas and values, to shape fundamental elements of their consciousness.

This argument often has been confused with the loaded assertion that the Miskitu suffered from elite-induced delusions, which led them mechanically to reproduce, in thought and action, the conditions of their oppression. Quite apart from its politically unsavory and theoretically reductionist tone, that assertion runs aground on the single most impressive facet of Miskitu history. Miskitu people are preeminent survivors. Their population increased when other nearby Indian peoples were decimated. They fashioned masterful responses to precarious conditions; devised strategies to seek advantage from extraregional rivalries; found ways to benefit from opportunities for wage labor while retaining a base of subsistence security. I have argued that Miskitu people could make these achievements while also actively embracing hegemonic ideas and values, which in turn brought about unintended consequences.

Two examples figure prominently in the preceding chapters. In the first years of the twentieth century, the Miskitu leader Sam Pitts, with a significant following, organized an armed rebellion against the state aimed at reinstating the Mosquito Kingdom. Moravian missionaries vigorously opposed the rebellion and used their substantial power and influence to discourage Miskitu participation. The Nicaraguan army ultimately killed Pitts and quashed the movement, but the Moravians also contributed directly to that outcome. Shackled by the contradiction between loyalty as Moravians and militancy as Miskitu, the resistance movement was doomed from the start. In Chapter 5 I advanced a parallel argument to explain Miskitu people's relative quiescence during the final years of the Somoza dictatorship (1978–79). Somoza's widely perceived alliance with the Americans placed the nascent Miskitu rights organization in an untenable position. To pursue militant ethnic demands (already articulated by some Miskitu leaders) would have entailed not only opposition to Somoza but a frontal challenge to Anglo-American institutions and premises of Anglo affinity.[4] Somoza exploited this dilemma, delivering speeches on the Coast in idiomatic Standard English, emphasizing his deep and enduring ties with "the Americans."

A version of this hegemony argument also yielded a crucial part of my explanation for the explosive ethnic conflict in the revolutionary era. After the Sandinistas came to power Miskitu people's ethnic demands grew more extensive and militant, while their adherence to the premises of Anglo affinity remained strong as well. The consciousness that propelled their anti-government mobilization was constituted by a fusion of these two seemingly contradictory elements.

Several factors contributed to the deepening of Miskitu ethnic militancy after 1979. The new generation of Miskitu leaders had great energy, organizational skills, and political ambition. They created a dynamic movement with a compelling program, incorporating key elements in townspeople's daily experiences of oppression into the militant discourse of inalienable Indian rights. The revolutionary state also played a role, both provocative, as in the Sandinistas' top-down and at times repressive first months on the Coast, and permissive, as in their emphasis on grass-roots organization (epitomized by the slogan *poder popular*—popular power) and economic justice. Finally, although much of the key evidence is still unavailable, it can be strongly suspected that early on, before the first known United States support for the contras in mid-1981, covert intervention helped to ensure that ethnic tensions would not be peaceably resolved.

Yet any assessment of the impact of U.S. intervention, and indeed of all these factors, must also take seriously the mandate to understand how Miskitu townspeople perceived the revolution. In so doing, the emphasis I have placed on their inherited premises of Anglo affinity—and the resulting contradictory consciousness—returns to the fore. Not only was the new Sandinista government decidedly *not* a friend of the Americans, but Miskitu people soon came to perceive it as the antithesis of nearly every important premise that Anglo affinity entailed: Communist, atheist, against "economic freedom," hostile to the material aid that outsiders, especially Americans, always had provided. Everything fell into place when, early on, it also became clear that their old allies the Americans were willing to underwrite the antigovernment struggle for Miskitu rights.

The theoretical importance of this analysis lies in a basic proposition regarding the collective action of subordinated ethnic groups. Despite the many ways in which the Miskitu and the social formation of Nicaragua's Atlantic Coast may seem quirky or even unique,[5] I contend that the dual emergence of Anglo affinity and ethnic militancy in Miskitu people's consciousness follows from a broadly occurring process. Ethnic mobilization and conflict cannot be understood as a contest in the realm of brute political economic power. Rarely do people fully submit to, or fully resist, the material and ideological edifice that oppresses them. Rather, both resistance and accommodation proceed as a renegotiation of cultural symbols shared between dominant and oppressed, a contestation of some facets of that edifice, combined with an assimilation of others. This is not to say that resistance always fails to meet its objectives, or that victories are never achieved, but rather, that even successful resistance movements are apt to have incorporated certain premises of the preexisting dominant order they oppose. Miskitu people's relations with the Nicaraguan state before autonomy approach a limiting case to this assertion because they assimilated so few of the state's hegemonic premises. When civil society is added to the equation, however, an especially vivid illustration of this pattern emerges. Miskitu people's resistance yielded a complex, fused, contradictory consciousness, which then became central to their identity and to the logic of their collective action.

This conclusion—that ethnic group members' resistance to subordination generally involves the assimilation of hegemonic ideas—is not pleasant to assert, but there is no use in wishing it away. I contend that these hegemonic ideas deserve greater consideration as causal factors in explanations for ethnic-based collective action, whether it tends toward frontal resistance or toward accommodation. This proposition has varying specific implications, of course, depending on which facets of the dominant culture a group resists and which it accommodates. Such variation is best left to be puzzled out through empirical study, though one can certainly notice broad patterns that lend themselves to generalization. Miskitu history contains a clear pattern of accommodation of inequality within civil society, combined with vigorous resistance to state authority. This raises intriguing comparative questions: Have other peoples subject both to state rule and to the neocolonial presence of an external power responded in similar ways? To what extent does this constitute a recurring pattern in Indian people's relations with the nation-state, and with lower-class Mestizos in Latin America?

A principal reason for past neglect of these insights, and the questions they generate, is the image of bounded, discrete units of cultural production, which until recently has been a surprisingly common starting point for the study of ethnicity. Since the pioneering work of Fredrik Barth (1969), most research on the reproduction of ethnic identity has acknowledged "ethnic boundaries" as a privileged site of analysis. Yet the full value of Barth's contribution has rarely been realized, for reasons developed in Chapter 1: Most of that work has stopped short of bringing the reproduction of ethnic identity into analytical balance with the constitutive impact of structural inequities. Instead, once relations between the group and "the outside" have been recognized as unequal and the external constraints of subordination have been taken into account, the premise of bounded cultural production has given license for a return to community-level particularism, albeit in a transformed and more sophisticated guise.[6] The resilience of that premise, as Richard Handler (1985) and others have pointed out, arises from a deeper conceptual problem: people tend to project their identities and other facets of their cultures as unique, essential, bounded units. In our efforts accurately to describe, interpret, or analyze these "cultural products," we tend to replicate their assertions.[7] The hegemony idea, in contrast, forces us to explore how power relations render these seemingly bounded products "impure," combined, contradictory.

Let me further situate this insight by considering two objections that merit particular scrutiny. Proponents of a first critique affirm the validity of identifying structural inequities but doubt that subordinate people actually embrace the associated dominant values and ideas. How can I be sure that what I consider hegemony is not a subtle form of dissimulation? That question crystallizes the point of engagement between my conclusions here and the theories of everyday resistance pioneered in the work of James C. Scott (1985, 1990). Analysts of Scott's perspective might argue that Sandy Bay people have a "nonhegemonic, contrapuntal, dissident, subversive discourse" expressed when they are relatively free from the constraints of power (Scott 1990:25). In effect, they would reinterpret what I have called Anglo affinity as a strategic guise, a skin-deep adjustment to power-laden relations with Anglo institutions.

This objection has two distinct points of reference. The first is empirical. Was there a hidden Miskitu transcript deeply critical of Anglo affinity, which I did not perceive? This is of course possible, though I have much reason for doubt, explained fully in Appendix A. Paradoxically, the image that provides most reason to suspect such a transcript—people telling an Anglo researcher what they thought he wanted to hear—also contains persuasive evidence that one does not exist. Under conditions of political tension and insecurity, Miskitu people took me into their confidence to an astounding degree. Not only was it inconceivable that they improvised the premises of Anglo affinity for my benefit, but without those premises, it is doubtful that they would have accepted me at all.

At a certain point, this empirical challenge merges with the epistemological. If the analysis of subordinate people's consciousness takes the existence of a "hidden transcript" as an axiom, then there always is a ready explanation when it fails to appear: it was more strategic or beneficial to display the "public" transcript instead.[8] This is a more sophisticated version of the well-known argument regarding subordinate people's capacity for adaptation, which has been applied extensively in the case of the Miskitu. As long as "adaptation" is gauged by the ideas and values that a people hold in the present, then nearly any action they pursue or cultural change they undergo will by definition have adaptive value. The hidden transcript argument avoids this tautology, but only by introducing a dubious, though incontestable, axiom. Any empirical finding that might challenge the argument, like my own observation of Miskitu people's Anglo affinity, can be explained by the simple assertion that, in my presence, they chose to keep their *true* ideas, values, and interests hidden.

To remain productive, consideration of this challenge must broaden the scope of analysis to include consequences as well as consciousness. Whether or not the premises of Anglo affinity were in part dissimulation, they not only expressed ideas but guided actions as well. The same process that resulted in Miskitu people's discursive embrace of Moravian religious beliefs (whether feigned or otherwise), for example, entailed active involvement in church affairs. The same people who stated, "The Americans are supporting our rights, training our boys, making them intelligent" (whether they fully believed it or not), actively pursued an alliance with the United States. Whatever the motivation, in their practice they opted to accommodate a structurally inequitable relationship. One can always counter, as Scott does, that the "realities of power" make such accommodation necessary. At times that surely is the case. But the very definition of "necessity" at a given moment is the product of prior struggles, which help to determine what protagonists in a resistance movement perceive as their own limitations. When subordinated ethnic group members conclude that a negotiated accommodation of structural inequity is the only alternative (i.e., "necessary"), we must at least consider the possibility that such a conclusion reflects the prior impact of hegemony on their reasoning.

A second objection to the approach advocated here takes a different tack, questioning the very term "dominant ideas." Throughout this book, I go to some length to distance my analysis from notions of "ideological domination" and the associated Marxist tendency to reduce social processes to their class essences. Miskitu people's ethnic militancy corresponded to no one's "dominant ideology"; their resistance encompassed class demands but was unintelligible as a class movement. Yet my approach is predicated on the Gramscian premise that capitalist social formations are composed of a dominant bloc: a heterogeneous alliance that includes the society's political-economic elites, that is loosely unified by a common ideology, and that acts to maintain the class-based privilege and power of its leading members. This in turn allows one to situate sectors or groups in relation to that bloc, to identify dominant ideas, and to examine how these ideas reverberate in the consciousness of subordinated peoples. That is a simplifying assumption, to be sure, but as long as it is considered a starting point and not a finished statement, it clarifies much more than it obscures. Most important, it obliges us to keep a society's structural inequities centrally in mind, while exploring the multifaceted ways these inequities are culturally constituted.

The most vigorous challenge to this starting point comes from "post-Marxist" theorists, who associate it with class reductionism and vanguardist politics.[9] They prefer to portray these same societies as consisting of multiple axes of oppression, which create blurred, shifting, contextual boundaries between dominant and subordinate. The only way to come to terms with these conditions, they argue, is to view power as diffuse and subordination as multivalent and to understand people's identities ("subjectivities") as emerging from these multiple axes of inequity. Dismissed as a unifying framework, class analysis remains useful, if at all, as a means to specify one of these many axes of inequity and emergent identities. Dorinne Kondo (1990, esp. chap. 6), in this line of reasoning, considers the very term "resistance" too heavily laden with class reductionist overtones to do justice to people with whom she worked in a Japanese factory. Their acts of "resistance" were also capitulations, their adversaries in one context were allies in another, and the idea of class struggle resonated less than the image of a family, which simultaneously legitimated and undermined workers' demands. Kondo's argument for a "culturally mediated" notion of resistance is persuasive; her text is an eloquent celebration of irony and ambiguity that reveals terms like "structural inequities" as the clumsy approximations they are. Moreover, there is much overlap between this stance and my own, emblematic of which is how Gramsci's ideas have encouraged many to probe the analytical limits of Marxism and served as a bridge to various formulations of post-Marxist social theory.[10] To assess the status of that bridge and to trace the points of engagement and departure between the two sides is a task of great complexity that I make no pretension of undertaking here.

There is, however, a divergence that must be specified, if only in a crude and preliminary way. One is tempted to begin on empirical grounds: surely Kondo's conclusions, drawn from a postindustrial Japanese company, cannot apply to the shantytowns of Central America. Yet this tack—though not completely without merit—is ultimately evasive, both of serious attempts at such analysis of Central American politics and of the sharply widening incidence of class inequities in many postindustrial societies.[11] Nor does the divergence lie in the understanding of power as constitutive, in the affirmation of nonclass forms of political struggle, or in the critique of excesses committed in the name of socialism. All these are standard in Gramscian revisions of Marxist theory, and all can be found prominently featured in this book. My main objection, rather, is that this rejection of resistance as an analytical category tends to diminish and relativize subordinate people's experiences of oppression. By retaining a notion of power linked to structural inequity, in contrast, we gain some assurance that these experiences will be anchored in an analysis of society, that the daunting "weight of history" on their lives will be centrally acknowledged.[12]

This point might be illustrated further with a personal note. For a tragically brief moment in the early 1980's, the Nicaraguan revolution seemed to be changing the course of history in favor of the poor and powerless. Those conditions, in turn, presented politically engaged analysts with a fundamental choice: did we begin with a structural analysis, which brought to the foreground the revolution's great potential, and then seek complexity? Or did we take that irreducible complexity as a starting point? To choose the latter might well have been to conclude that there was no good reason to study Miskitu Indians by working in alignment with a revolutionary process that directly oppressed them. Put differently, there was plenty of irony and ambiguity to celebrate in those early years. To take that course, however, might well have been to conclude that it was safer, even more intellectually honest, to remain on the sidelines, expressing seasoned skepticism of the Sandinistas' revolutionary "heroics." In the meantime, the moment would have been lost.[13]

*   *   *

Whatever the value of the approach to ethnicity theory advanced here, it would be limited if it proceeded as if the object of resistance and accommodation were stable and transparent. Rather, one would expect the same insights to illuminate the other side: the state's particular cultural construction and historical evolution. I have attempted to achieve that analytical balance by placing both the development of Miskitu consciousness and Nicaraguan state formation in historical perspective, documenting the legacy of change in both sides, as well as the reciprocal influence of one upon the other. Chapters 2 and 5 traced successive phases of state presence in the coastal region, from the time of definitive annexation in 1894 through the first years of revolutionary government. In Chapter 4 I examined Sandinista ideology, with a particular focus on the changing role of the Indian within the newly forged expressions of Nicaraguan nationalism. A unified theoretical framework must incorporate that analysis as well.

Sandinista Nationalism and the Challenge of Cultural Plurality

A fundamental objective of the Sandinista leadership, and arguably one of the revolution's most resilient legacies, was the profound transformation of Nicaraguan national identity. Augusto C. Sandino, the man of humble background who from 1926 to 1933 led a ragtag army of peasants against U.S. occupation forces, became the ubiquitous "national signifier" (Palmer 1986).[14] History was rewritten, well-known events reinterpreted, and the texts of existing national icons culled to highlight the dual themes of imperial domination and popular resistance. Civic ceremonies, school textbooks, museums, and public monuments all came to reflect the content of this new national sentiment; thousands of place names were changed to honor the fallen "heroes and martyrs" in the anti-Somoza insurrection, often referred to as the "rebirth" of the nation.[15] These efforts of national transformation did not go uncontested, to be sure, and after a decade they were far from complete. But there can be no doubt that "Sandinista nationalism" had a radically different class content than the preceding versions. Indeed, the differences between the old and new versions of nationalism became the ideological terrain for struggle between the state and the counterrevolution.

Even if we focus exclusively on the place of Indians within the new national identity, the disjuncture remains evident. Drawing on the writings of Sandinista intellectuals such as Jaime Wheelock, Omar Cabezas, and Ernesto Cardenal, in Chapter 4 I identified a major two-pronged challenge to the prevailing orthodoxy. The first is illustrated most clearly in Wheelock's (1974) blistering historical critique of the "myth" of harmonious mestizaje, associated with the prominent Nicaraguan educator, poet, and newspaper editor Pablo Antonio Cuadra.[16] Wheelock chronicles the unspeakable brutality toward and subjugation of the Indian population during the colonial period and the continuous history of Indian resistance. The predominance of Mestizos in Nicaraguan society and of Mestizo culture in the national identity, he concludes, was the outcome of a "bitter synthesis" that rested on the broken backs of Indians. The second challenge, best exemplified by the work of Cardenal, flows directly from the first. Cardenal sought to recover and celebrate the lost, suppressed, or marginalized elements of Nicaragua's Indian past. The primitivist painting genre he helped to found, his poetry eulogizing Indian civilizations, the programs he promoted as minister of culture (e.g., a national campaign for self-sufficiency marked by the slogan "Maiz es nuestra raiz" [Corn is our roots]), all had the effect of assigning great value to Indian culture, even giving it the pride of place in the new Nicaraguan nation.

Despite these substantive changes, the Sandinista revolution's impact on Indians was still strongly assimilationist. In part this can be attributed to the centralist tendencies of revolutionary politics: the state was controlled by the Sandinista party, which had a strictly disciplined and hierarchical internal structure. Local cadres in Bluefields often spoke of political instructions that "came down" (*se bajaban*) from the national leadership in Managua. Although input was supposed to flow upward as well, FSLN leaders admitted that internal democracy within the party was incipient and deficient (e.g., Arce 1988). The problem was particularly acute for the Miskitu because the party included so few Miskitu members. Sandinista leaders did not understand what Miskitu people wanted, and when the Miskitu tried to tell them, it generated deep-seated Sandinista fears of separatism. None of the factors that mitigated the damaging effects of revolutionary centralism with other sectors of Nicaraguan society were operable for the Miskitu.[17]

Sandinista skepticism arose not only from a lack of understanding of Miskitu history and culture, however, but also from the premise of Miskitu "cultural backwardness." An early government slogan, prominently displayed on billboards in Managua, stated: "The Atlantic Coast: An Awakening Giant." Implicit was the idea that Coast people, heretofore asleep, would now assume their designated place within the nation and thereby become "awakened" agents of their own destiny (Adams 1981a). Mestizo soldiers stationed in the Miskitu communities, whose words I recorded in Chapter 4, often contrasted the Indians' lazy, torpid character to Mestizo peasants' alert, industrious, forward-looking ways. These folk notions and ethnic stereotypes, at the grass-roots and leadership levels, were well in place in 1979, inherited from the national political culture that had been shaped over the last century. They gained prominence as the conflict deepened. If Miskitu people opposed the revolution, they must be backward, unaware of their own interests (as members of the *clases populares* and as Nicaraguans), and therefore deeply susceptible to manipulation by external forces such as the U.S. government. "Cultural backwardness" made the job of explaining Miskitu opposition and prescribing solutions immensely easier.

The picture grows more complex still when we remember that Sandinista nationalism emerged principally as the antithesis not of Miskitu identity but of U.S. imperialism. Given the legacy of U.S. influence, it is difficult to conceive of a revolutionary movement in Nicaragua—indeed, throughout Latin America—that would not be intensely nationalist, regardless of internal conditions. A fusion of revolution and nation was probably essential to the successful overthrow of the Somoza dictatorship, and it formed a crucial part of the ideological cement that held the revolutionary alliance together after 1979. Yet that very conflation sent the Miskitu an ominous message: they had to embrace national culture or remain marginal to the revolution and lose out on what it had to offer. Those Miskitu who submitted and chose to identify with the "nation" abandoned important elements of a separate identity from which their militancy had arisen. As a Miskitu FSLN cadre eloquently put it in a post-election self-critical statement, "We forced them to make a choice between being Miskitu and being Sandinista." The premises underlying this predicament can be found in the work of Cardenal and Wheelock. They celebrated Nicaragua's Indian past but envisioned and promoted a Mestizo future. While genuinely affirming Indians' rights to be culturally different and free from racist deprecation, neither these intellectuals nor most other Sandinista leaders could fathom the notion that ethnic-based political power might be integral to these rights.[18] Thus Sandinismo embodied a debilitating contradiction: a promise of equality, fused with the premise of Indians' cultural backwardness; a discourse of radical inclusiveness, in which the nation continued to be defined and controlled by Mestizos.

Most analyses of Sandinistas' "mistakes" in the early years—including their own self-criticisms—do not confront this contradiction at its roots. Rather, they focus on the Sandinistas' overly economistic approach to society and politics, which led to intolerance of cultural diversity and a misplaced emphasis on class rather than ethnic affinities. Though certainly relevant, such a critique cannot be sufficient, either for the Sandinistas or for other movements of the Mestizo Left in Latin America.[19] The

Sandinista case provides an unprecedented opportunity to see what happens when a revolutionary movement takes power and converts rhetoric into full-fledged state policy. Suddenly, the interminable efforts of leftist intellectuals to refine their analysis of the ethnic question—from class reductionism, to class in the last instance, to the relative autonomy of culture, and so on—lose importance in relation to a deceptively straightforward question: Have Mestizos maintained the prerogative to control the state and define the content of national identity? If so, they most likely have come to justify this appropriation with a dual premise of Mestizo cultural superiority and Indian backwardness, which directly contradicts the egalitarian ideology of their movement.

The central theoretical thrust of this analysis is to call into question the idea that the nation-state confronts subordinated ethnic groups with relations of power that are solely coercive, constraining, or "negative." I draw support from recent revisionist approaches to state and nation building, such as Philip Corrigan and Derek Sayer's *Great Arch* (1985). By portraying the process of state formation in England as a "cultural revolution," they are contesting the conventional (liberal and Marxist) notion of the state as solely a coercive apparatus. Expanding on the word "legitimate" in Max Weber's famous definition,[20] they examine the state's power to reshape society, to govern by constituting "subjects," who then become amenable to its rule. In his effort to liberate the study of nationalism from limitations in both the Marxist and liberal traditions, Benedict Anderson (1983) makes a similar point. Following Anderson's lead, I have come to understand Sandinista nation building as a process whereby elites not only "imagined" their own community but also represented that political identity as universal, as a means to achieve broad-based legitimation of their rule.

Yet, at least for Latin America, Anderson does not carry the argument to its logical conclusion. In his enthusiasm to portray nationalism as profoundly creative, as an infinitely "imitable" cultural form through which people forge a unified sense of belonging, he leaves the implications for cultural diversity undertheorized. The word "imagined" in his celebrated definition receives most of the emphasis, while the tendentious premises underlying the notion of "community" go relatively unaddressed. He writes that "*regardless of the actual inequality and exploitation that may prevail* . . . the nation is always conceived as a deep, horizontal comradeship" (1983:16, emphasis added). But he does not theorize how elites manage to construct this basis for comradeship with a heterogeneous mass of people from whom they are profoundly divided by gender, race/ethnicity, and class.

*   *   *

This conclusion highlights a need to discern the systematic relationship between nation building, on the one hand, and class/ethnic identity formation, on the other. If the course of Miskitu-Sandinista relations can serve as a guide, each process tends to generate contradictions internal to the movement, which in turn help to explain the dynamics of their conflict with one another. That proposition can be further specified by taking a comparative perspective on nation, class, and ethnicity in Latin America. Specifically, I frame the comparison by examining two manifestations of conflict, which, though generally separate, became compressed into one in the Nicaraguan case: Indians' conflict with the state and the persistent tensions between Indians and lower-class Mestizos.

Toward a Unified Analysis

Latin American countries underwent a phase of liberal, capitalist "modernization" in the mid- to late nineteenth century, which had profound implications for Indian peoples who lived within their boundaries. In some cases Indians were effectively exterminated during this period, giving rise to an expression of national identity with a distinctly European inflection (e.g., in Uruguay), which I am not concerned with here. In cases where Indians resisted and retained some demographic stability, liberal nation building profoundly deepened the division between them, on the one hand, and Creoles and Mestizos, on the other. However predominant and powerful a role Creoles played in that process, the "national culture" that emerged always took on an important Mestizo—as opposed to exclusively Creole—content.

This claim stands in contrast with the position put forth by Anderson. His case for the origins of Latin American nationalism in the shared experiences of Creole fellow travelers is persuasive enough. And he does note that Creoles soon had to reconcile their status as a tiny minority of European elites, on the one hand, and their purported status as spokespeople for the "nation," on the other. For Anderson the statement of nationalist hero San Martín in 1821—"In the future the aborigines . . . are children *and citizens* of Peru, and they shall be known as Peruvians"—is emblematic of the Creoles' solution: inclusion by fiat (Anderson 1983: 52). But how long could that solution last? One infers from his book what he later makes explicit: "The southern American nation-states were, *and are*, creole nation-states, where the dominant groups have always been descendants of white immigrants, and speaking the languages of Europe, no matter what indigenous ancestries they have come, over time, to claim" (1988: 403–4, emphasis added). This leads him, in a comment on the Sandinista-Miskitu conflict, to the rather incredible conclusion that "the Miskitos, whether they speak English or Miskito, block the [Sandinistas'] Hispanic, *criollo project* . . . Daniel Ortega and his colleagues simply have no idea of what to do with the Miskito aborigines, except to Hispanicize, museumize, socialize and patronize them" (1988: 406, emphasis added).[21]

The problem with this assertion is not the harsh condemnation of the Sandinistas but, rather, the portrayal of the conflict as the outcome of a continuous legacy of "criollo" nationalism in Nicaragua. Consistent with this assertion of continuity, Anderson discounts indigenismo—the form of nationalism that emphasizes Indian roots, though in combination with European influences—as a cruel sham: "[When indigenismo emerged], the real aborigines of the Americas had been, if they were not exterminated, radically crushed and marginalized . . . the ascendancy of creoles and mestizos was based on this historic obliteration" (1988:404). This claim would come as a surprise to the some 40 million self-identified Indians in Latin America today and to the Sandinistas during their conflict with the Miskitu, who for an "obliterated" people put up a very good fight.

At stake here is a substantive divergence in both historical analysis and theoretical premises. Indigenista nationalism is not predicated on the prior obliteration of Indian peoples but on a systematic effort to overcome the contradictions created by their persistence; it was born of a profound reformulation of the exclusively Creole national identity. Whether or not indigenismo achieved its objective—the disappearance of Indians as distinct groups through assimilation, not obliteration—it represented a different solution to the predicament of cultural diversity than the Creole variety (indeed, various solutions because indigenismo has been far from monolithic). Anderson's overstated claim for the continuity of Creole nationalism leads him to miss this diversity and signals a broader theoretical problem. By focusing attention on those who do the imagining, he obscures how deeply contested nation building is and how this contestation helps to shape the content of national identity. He lacks a systematic account of the varied, changing, but always crucial relationship between representations of "national unity," on the one hand, and the profoundly conflictive forms of class and ethnic inequities among purported members of that nation, on the other. How can there be, to repeat the question, a plausible assertion of "community" under such divisive conditions?

Brackette Williams (1989) offers a different and—at least for Latin America—much more convincing response. In less prosaic but more penetrating terms, Williams argues that nationalism is a "race/class/nation conflation" (p. 435). It is a cultural form, constructed by the leaders of a dominant political bloc (who control the state or aspire to do so), which projects their particular race and class standpoint as universal to all who live under their rule. The privileged idiom for the diffusion of this conflation is race: the nation takes on a specific, homogeneous racial identity against which all potential members are pegged as either "inside" or marginal.[22] Neither the content of the racial standard nor the inside/outside boundary is fixed; both undergo change, resulting from political struggle, as elites fend off challenges from below or attempt further to consolidate their power. But at any given historical moment the prevailing standard of homogeneity and the corresponding inside/outside dichotomy give rise to systematic patterns of political interaction among all the distinct class/ethnic groups.

Applied to Latin American societies with Indian populations, these ideas call for a carefully differentiated analysis of four class/ethnic groups whose boundaries and relations are constituted by the political interactions that nation building entails: a dominant or elite political-economic bloc, subordinate members of the national culture, ethnics, and proto-nationalists.

The political-economic elites, drawing on state power and economic resources, construct a "national culture," predicated on the conflation of their own class and culture with those of the "nation." In nineteenth-century Latin America, when "national" and "Creole" cultures were initially coterminous, the inviability of this formulation soon gave rise to a shift from the Creole to the more inclusionary Mestizo racial standard. This inviability, I suggest, had to do primarily with its impact on Mestizos, not Indians. As long as the nation was defined in strictly "Creole" terms (those of white, European descent), *both* Mestizos and Indians were effectively excluded from the "imagined community," and the potential for opposition was tremendous. The more numerous and powerful the Indians, the stronger the pressure on elites to "Mestizoize" the nation as a means to mobilize Mestizo support and thereby lessen their own vulnerability. It follows, for example, that historian Steven Palmer (1990) would find in the nationalist discourse of late nineteenth-century Guatemala a general disapproval of biological racism in favor of the notion that Indians can be "redeemed" and "civilized" by conforming to the dictates of national culture. Though Maya Indians resisted these assimilationist pressures with great tenacity, the message was not lost on *ladinos* (Mestizos), who during that period assumed the role of political-economic intermediaries and the most visible representatives of "civilization." This coincides with the effect that Carol A. Smith (1990a:89) refers to as the Creole elite's increasing "invisibility" during precisely the period when its economic power and privilege were expanding.

The second group, subordinate Mestizos, share in the national culture but are largely excluded from power. Being "inside" nevertheless means that they too—through hard work, paying dues "for the nation," good luck, or even political struggle—could one day become national elites. Aspirations toward this future prize and the material benefits that accompany inclusion mean that nonelite Mestizos might well contest the elite class bias of the nation while endorsing the "race" component of the conflation. If they are successful in taking power, the language of national culture might shift toward a more indigenista discourse—as in the case of Nicaragua—while the basic inside/outside boundary remains intact. To challenge that boundary, to ally with those defined as "outside," would involve an additional, seemingly irrational risk to their own already precarious status as next in line to rule.

Those defined as outside the nation—Indians (and in some cases Blacks, though I will not discuss them here)—confront a complex dilemma. Elite constructions of the nation generally entail, as Williams puts it, some provision for "inviting them in." If they accept, they relinquish the power of identity rooted in difference and submit to the conditions of the race/class/nation conflation in return for a piece of the same promise to which subordinate Mestizos cling. These conditions do not necessarily include complete assimilation (ethnic diversity may well be defined as a valuable part of the "national heritage"), but they do involve domestication of oppositional potential. In Williams's words, people trade the "brick and mortar" of radical cultural difference for mere "feathers and flourishes" (1989:435). Members of this third group, for which she reserves the term "ethnics," are in an inherently unstable position: they tend either to assimilate to the national culture or to languish in the middle ground of being "inside," yet "different" and powerless. MISURASATA leader Brooklyn Rivera, while in negotiations with the Sandinistas about what the Miskitu should be called, summarized this point succinctly: "Ethnic groups run restaurants. . . . We are a people. We want self-determination."[23]

Rivera's insistence that Miskitu are a "people" encapsulates the fourth category: those who either actively reject national culture or are unable to accept it. In Latin America, these are the strongly self-identified Indians. They may occupy a variety of positions within the national economy (from isolated subsistence producer to proletariat) and take a variety of political stances (from quiescence to frontal resistance), but they do so from a space culturally defined as outside and in opposition to the nation. I call this fourth group the protonationalists.[24] Although the viability of protonationalist resistance depends on a host of factors, it can be expected to provoke both the ire and the energetic opposition of all those within the national culture, elites and subordinate Mestizos alike.

This last point is the crux. If the nation building process is even moderately successful, subordinate Mestizos will develop a stake in the national culture. They are drawn in through the diversity of means—education, civic ritual, religious conversion, distribution of rewards and promises— typically entailed in what Gramsci called the efforts of an "ethical state" to achieve hegemony. Only through a radical rejection of the cultural underpinnings of the nation do subordinate Mestizos come to view Indians as both equals and allies. Yet paradoxically, as subordinate Mestizos come closer to gaining the power that would allow them to pose such a challenge (either through revolution or middle-class reform), their inclination to follow this radical path diminishes accordingly, replaced by heady plans to remake the nation in their own image. Indian protonationalists, while vigorously resisting the dominant culture, also tend to embrace one of its key premises. Elites portray the nation as representing all Mestizo members of society equally and fully—a "horizontal comradeship" that knows no class divisions. When protonationalists experience this purportedly undifferentiated "Mestizo" cultural oppression, they assimilate its portrayal of class divisions in Mestizo society as insignificant. Their resistance therefore tends to reproduce the rationale, within their own consciousness, for the divide between themselves and subordinate Mestizos.

It is misleading to distinguish protonationalist and subordinate Mestizo resistance by arguing that only the latter involves class.[25] Both groups are engaged in struggle against an elite-controlled dominant bloc, but from completely distinct standpoints; both have created resistance movements that embrace distinct elements of the hegemonic common sense. Subordinate Mestizos resist the class bias of the conflation but leave the "racial" underpinnings of national culture unquestioned; Indians contest the legitimacy of a national culture from which they are excluded but use the commonsense image of the class homogeneity of national culture (i.e., all Mestizos are the same) to make their case. Miskitu-Sandinista relations in Nicaragua embodied this dual contradiction. Subordinate Mestizo resistance succeeded to the point of taking state power, but the fatal threat of U.S. imperialism made it even less likely that the racial underpinnings of Sandinismo would be challenged. Similarly, Anglo affinity conditioned Miskitu consciousness, such that they would downplay the many differences between Somoza and the Sandinista state and, most important, view the Sandinistas' challenge to U.S. dominance as futile and morally wrong.

In this sense, ethnic conflict in Nicaragua was a specific manifestation of a broader process. Sandinista ideology galvanized a nationalist insurrection with great liberating potential for subordinate Mestizos yet incorporated ideas and values that were anathema to non-Mestizo costeños. Miskitu Indians successfully resisted absorption and domination by the Nicaraguan nation-state yet came to view Mestizo culture in general as oppressive and subordinate Mestizos as their enemies. Admittedly, the Nicaraguan case is unusual in important ways: Anglo affinity is not widespread among indigenous peoples of the Americas; subordinate Mestizos are generally powerless, often as destitute as Indians themselves. Yet it is such differences that make the comparison so striking: ethnic politics in Nicaragua followed a pattern of conflict between Indians and subordinate Mestizos that has occurred in nearly every Latin American country with significant Indian populations.[26] The scheme presented here links this pattern with the role of indigenista nation building in societies divided by both class and ethnicity. Although the group to be "civilized" is always Indian, the political impact of nationalist discourse depends on its ability to draw subordinate Mestizos into the fold. Both groups resist the dominant race/class conflation but in the process adopt hegemonic ideas that act to reinforce the divisions between them. Nation and state building contribute to this outcome, not as a negative, constraining influence, but as a force that shapes the content of the groups' identities and political demands and the terms of their interaction. The Miskitu-Sandinista conflict helps to illustrate the logical conclusion of this process. By taking state power, subordinate Mestizos finally won the opportunity to realize their vision for a new society, but the vision's egalitarian promise remained shackled by premises that made it appear to Miskitu Indians as an ominous assertion of Mestizo dominance.

Activist Research and Ethnic Conflict

In this book I have reported on research guided by a simple methodological principle: to devote sustained ethnographic attention to both sides of a conflict, creating an account that encompassed the standpoint of each. This method informed the study's substantive findings in two distinctive but interconnected ways. First, immersion with the people of each side engendered analysis that portrayed them as fully constituted, complex, knowledgeable actors, whereas being obliged to step back and view them from a distance tended to highlight the structural determinants of their consciousness. In this sense, the method helped advance my broader theoretical concern to bring actor-centered and structural analysis of ethnic conflict into balance. Second, the method confronted me with contradictions that might otherwise have receded into relative analytical insignificance. Miskitu people's everyday consciousness revealed the shortcomings of the Sandinista ideology and program with an acute eloquence that would make the most enterprising right-wing critic from the United States appear tepid by comparison. Similarly, I never would have persisted in exploring the contradictions of Miskitu consciousness if I had not viewed the conflict from the standpoint of the Sandinistas' finest cadres on the Coast. Their deep commitment to the oppressed and powerless and their anguished incredulity that Miskitu people would ally with the Reagan administration against the revolution kept sending me back to delve more deeply for a complete explanation.

To make the case for the broader applicability of this method, however, I must begin with three brief caveats. First, advances toward reconciliation made it possible to embark on this project. Both sides became committed to conflict resolution, which in turn opened a political space, a mutually endorsed rationale for them to allow a researcher who had been talking with the "other side" into their midst. Second, the method must not be equated with the radical cultural relativist notion that each worldview is an insular system unto itself, unintelligible except in its own terms. Although I have emphasized the importance of a view from within, the relativism implicit in that emphasis is tempered by another countervailing premise. I intend for the method to be used in cases of conflict between subjugated peoples who, despite considerable inequities between them, have a broader experience of structural oppression in common; in this case, for example, both had been subject to long-standing relations of dependence upon and inequity with the United States.[27]

Third, it should be clear that the method is neither easy to implement nor conflict-free. Despite prior advances in the peace process, I was vulnerable to suspicion and criticism from both sides. There were Sandinistas who considered me a threat to state security and never became convinced otherwise. There were (admittedly fewer) Miskitu who mistrusted my "Sandinista sympathies." On innumerable occasions, I felt confused, disloyal, schizophrenic, torn by dual affinities. Moreover, the way I positioned myself as a fieldworker tended to attenuate that much-prized anthropological sense of belonging, of "being there," with the people one studies. While in Nicaragua, I felt this effect most strongly in the contrast with other internacionalistas who, unambivalently aligned with the Sandinistas, fit in and were accepted to a much greater degree than I was. When I returned to the United States, it became a point of divergence from other politically engaged anthropologists, who tend to express unambivalent alignment with the people they write about, to celebrate implicitly or explicitly those people's resistance. This research, in contrast, and the results it produced, left me with a complex dual alignment. Toward those uncritical of U.S. government policies I tended to stress my Sandinista affinities; in response to those who celebrated the Sandinistas' resistance to U.S. dominance, I tended to emphasize Miskitu people's radical critique.

Despite these difficulties, and in part because of them, the method has great potential for politically engaged study of ethnic conflict. The most convincing evidence in support of this contention is that progress toward conflict resolution required precisely the sort of dialogue and mutual understanding that my research was intended to promote.[28] The Sandinistas learned an enormous amount from daily interactions with the Miskitu and even more as the autonomy process moved the conditions of dialogue toward greater equality. The discourse of Sandinista leaders presented in Chapter 4 and the political practice of Sandinista cadres described in Chapter 7 provide a sense of these changes. Similarly, the onset of autonomy allowed Miskitu townspeople, for the first time, to take seriously the revolution's claims to liberating potential. Although many continued to dismiss them as false promises, a dialogue did begin. Indeed, the three years during which I worked in Sandy Bay make for an impressive chronicle of convergence between Miskitu people and the Sandinista state. Community members in general moved from a stance of resentment, hostility, and inveterate opposition to one of cautious political accommodation; the community's productive activities, which stopped almost completely during the war, revived and approached prewar levels; a steady flow of townspeople (mostly young men) who had fought as antigovernment combatants returned and reintegrated themselves into community life. Such achievements (and these are only a few) flowed directly from the Sandinistas' shift toward recognition of Miskitu people's rights to autonomy, which in turn allowed Miskitu people to acquire a broader, more balanced appreciation of the revolution.

Yet there were also clear limits to this convergence, serious tensions that the transition to autonomy proved unable to overcome. Community members participated in each phase of deliberations to determine the form that autonomy would take and threw their support behind the final version of the law, while harboring a subversive attitude toward the entire process. Militant ethnic demands, largely excluded from the evolving definition of autonomy, motivated their persisting doubts. They arrived at the judgment less by studying draft proposals of the law than through a practical assessment that the Sandinistas seemed still to be in charge, in a position to determine what autonomy could and could not be. No one seriously expected that by 1988 the structural inequities that gave rise to the struggle for autonomy would be eliminated. But Miskitu townspeople's assessment suggested—accurately I believe—that these inequities had not yet been fully acknowledged.

This sobering conclusion should serve as a final caveat against an overly voluntaristic notion of what the method proposed here can be expected to achieve. In the study of ethnic conflict, to neglect how the two worldviews in question are culturally and historically constituted is to miss the great creative potential for reconciliation. Indeed, the Sandinistas' transition to autonomy stands as testimony to that potential, to their flexibility and impressive ability to avoid many of the traps that led to the demise of "actually existing socialism." Yet it would be easy to take this line of reasoning too far, risking an understatement of the historically derived limits on the potential for change. In Nicaragua those limits were formidable indeed.

From the nineteenth century Miskitu people resisted the authority of the Nicaraguan state, and the price of that resistance was their assimilation of the premises of Anglo affinity. Although there is little point in attempting to determine the relative weight of ethnic militancy and Anglo affinity in Miskitu actions, the latter clearly helped to motivate their protonationalist reaction against the Sandinista revolution. Thus the unintended consequences of Miskitu resistance in the preceding era of nation building helped to ensure that they would remain outside, and opposed to, the revolutionary process. After 1979, the Sandinistas presented the Miskitu with a no-win choice—become "ethnics" or be excluded—which had a rationale in the inherited premises of their own political culture. Rather than submit to that dilemma, the Miskitu opted to fight. By the time the Sandinistas realized that these premises were profoundly flawed, the no-win choice had become theirs: continue to deny Miskitu people's militant demands, through rule by coercion, or concede and run the very real risk that rights to autonomy would yield demands for separatism in direct alignment with the Reagan administration.[29] To avoid submitting to that dilemma, the Sandinistas sought a middle ground: an autonomy limited enough to safeguard state prerogatives but expansive enough to engender participation, a measure of legitimacy, a chance to rule by hegemony rather than coercion.

As constituted in 1987, then, the autonomy law may have approached the outer limits of what could be achieved under conditions created by the interplay of U.S. dominance, Mestizo nationalist resistance, and Miskitu ethnic militancy. While the Sandinistas remained in power I sought constantly to interrogate those limits, while remaining ultimately within their bounds. This decision to conduct politically engaged research from within the revolution—whether judged prescient or myopic—was the initial defining premise of my research.

With the Sandinista electoral defeat of 1990 the field of analysis changed dramatically. The Sandinistas became a powerful but embattled opposition party. Miskitu people achieved a measure of autonomy, but central government officials soon began doing everything possible to undermine that achievement. Autonomy was necessary only as a response to Sandinista oppression, they argue. Economic destitution, combined with the neoliberal onslaught, they seem to believe, will soon cause the political clamor of the 1980's to fade. They may well be right.[30]

Yet these new conditions also have given rise to a striking paradox. Now that the Sandinistas are out of power, there is an unprecedented potential for them to ally with the Miskitu based on mutual interests. Both have strong reasons to be disaffected from central government rule; both need the banner of autonomy to motivate opposition and specify rights denied. In this sense, relations between Indians and subordinate Mestizos in Nicaragua have resumed a pattern common throughout Latin America—great potential for alliance and common cause, formidable barriers of distrust and cultural difference that must still be overcome.

Though focused on the revolutionary era in Nicaragua, this book is intended to speak to these broader conditions of ethnic conflict. I have drawn particular attention to the divisive consequences of ideologies of national belonging, whether voiced by Indians or subordinate Mestizos, and to the constitutive role of hegemony in subordinate people's consciousness, even when they are actively engaged in resistance. These insights, in turn, derive from my use of Gramscian culture theory as a bridge between structural and actor-centered approaches to ethnicity, and as a guide toward a unified analysis of relations between ethnic groups and the state. Most important, I have argued that the best way to understand such conflicts is simultaneously to work toward their resolution, and in so doing, to engage their contradictions. This implies a transformation in the social scientist's code of ethics and accountability, toward activist research aligned with movements of social change, yet capable of contributing to critique, even struggle, from within. Although the difficulties of this method are considerable, I hope this book has demonstrated that its rewards are greater still.

Appendixes

Methodological Implications
of Anglo Affinity

MY PRESENCE IN Sandy Bay Sirpi evoked a flood of people's memories and images of North Americans, which I explored systematically as part of my efforts to understand their consciousness and collective action. Gradually, I came to identify a complex of values, commonsense premises, and political judgments, which together constitute what I call Anglo affinity. As the term suggests, a sense of allegiance to and alignment with white North Americans is central to this complex; but many other elements—from a deeply ingrained and emotional anti-Communism, to a dependence on outside aid (ilp laka), to phenotypic preferences influenced by North American racism—were equally salient. In my explanations for successive moments of Miskitu collective action, both quiescence and mobilization, Anglo affinity played a crucial role. However convincing this analysis is judged to be, it rests in the first instance on the validity of my assertion that Anglo affinity forms an integral part of Miskitu people's consciousness. Doubts about this assertion come in the form of four queries, which I state briefly and then respond to in succession. The reader should bear in mind that here I address only the methodological complexities of writing with confidence about the salience of Anglo affinity. To evaluate my analytical arguments in their entirety, one must turn back to Chapters 5 through 7.

The image of a white North American researcher collecting data that confirm the legacy of white North American hegemony is problematic, to say the least. Especially in light of recent critiques of anthropological representation and ethnographic authority, one wonders immediately about the impact of power inequities on what I recorded as Miskitu people's consciousness. The first, most obvious (and simplest) version of this query would be to ask whether people concocted what I call Anglo affinity in anticipation of some real or perceived benefit from their interactions with me. Perhaps they expected to gain something from stating what they thought I wanted to hear; or, more generally, perhaps it seemed to be the safest, most pragmatic way to handle this "Anglo" outsider in their midst. A second, more sophisticated version of this query suggests that Anglo affinity long predated my presence but always has been a skin-deep, strategic response to interactions with an array of powerful North American institutions and actors. In this line of reasoning, I would have been incapable of grasping its superficial character because townspeople would logically have included me as part of the object of their dissimulation. Proponents of a third objection might concede that the premises of Anglo affinity formed a deep and integral part of Miskitu townspeople's consciousness but suggest that I have exaggerated their weight and significance. Surely fond memories of North Americans and deep adherence to Anglo ideology would have been more apt to surface in discussions with an amicable white American. Those same premises—to extend this reasoning further—could have remained largely submerged during the crucial moments of Miskitu collective action that this study is meant to help us understand. Fourth, and finally, one might wonder whether the people I interviewed most intensively and spent most time with were self-selected in favor of those most inclined to Anglo affinity. I simply did not hear the dissenting voices because they chose to avoid the Anglo researcher, of whom they were critical and suspicious.

I can respond to the first query with great surety. I find it wholly implausible that townspeople concocted the premises of Anglo affinity in response to my presence. The forms were too various—from phenotypic preferences, to fond memories of U.S. Marines, to a deep confidence in the benevolence of the U.S. government—and the content of each too consistent for that conclusion to be viable. In addition, people expressed Anglo affinity in contexts in which I was marginal or largely unperceived—conversations among various people, church services, remarks I overheard made by people unaware of my presence. The responses elicited through interview questions are entirely consistent with the gist of these chance encounters. Finally, Anglo affinity is an often-discussed phenomenon on the Coast, perceived by many nonwhite people who would not be subject to the effect under discussion here. Educated Miskitu leaders talked about Anglo affinity—using a different term—as a problem that merited urgent attention among their people. For example, I heard a leader of the Miskitu organization MISATAN lament that Miskitu elders believe that "Jesus Christ was a gringo" and that many young Miskitu women would "give up their virginity in order to have a white child."

The second query raises more complex issues. I did find evidence to support the idea that people developed Anglo affinity as an unintended consequence of their pursuit of other interests or ends. Indeed, to some extent this pattern is consistent with my broader explanation for the way Anglo affinity came to form part of Miskitu people's consciousness in the first place. For example, in Chapter 2 I argued that people embraced the Moravian church at least in part because of the tangible benefits they accrued, and, once consummated, this religious affiliation acted to reinforce their Anglo affinity. Yet I cannot accept the assertion of a fundamental or predominant dichotomy between the "superficial" premises of Anglo affinity and people's deeper interests or goals, purportedly unaffected by the former. In the first place, the ubiquity of these premises in realms where there is no plausible link to "strategic" advantages casts doubt on that dichotomy. The case of phenotypic preferences is an especially persuasive example. A high school graduate from Sandy Bay who had recently become pregnant came to me as I was about to make a trip to the United States. She asked if I could bring back some of the "pink pills," which she had heard would help make her baby "come out whiter." Structured interviews (see Chapter 4 and Appendix B) confirm how widespread such values were. In addition, I interviewed townspeople who previously had espoused the premises of Anglo affinity and then developed a critical stance toward them (e.g., the case of Maria Stevens, Chapter 6). Such people gave no indication that their previous beliefs had been feigned or superficial; to the contrary, they insisted both that they deeply subscribed to these ideas and that their fellow townspeople still do. At some point, of course, this question boils down to philosophical presuppositions. In response to my assertion that these Miskitu townspeople had no strategic "hidden transcript," one could always counter that I was among the powerful actors from whom they were intentionally hiding it. (The term "hidden transcript" comes from James C. Scott [1985, 1990]. For further discussion of this matter, see Chapter 7.) This response rests less on empirical data than on an article of faith: that all subordinate people have a deep core of true interests, immune from the exercise of power, unaffected by the power-laden processes of cultural elaboration. I am inclined to leave the matter as an empirical challenge. I have shown that the premises of Anglo affinity figure prominently in townspeople's memories, everyday discourse, and political analysis. Especially when they go on to cite these premises as part of their stated rationale for action, I submit, skeptics who interpret such statements as merely a guise, facade, or strategic "public discourse" take on the burden of empirical proof.

The third query concedes that Anglo affinity is a deeply ingrained component of Miskitu people's consciousness but questions its relevance to the moments of collective action that I seek to explain. For example, perhaps people's emphasis on American promises of aid—affirmations such as "the Americans are our partners," "the Americans are training our boys, making them intelligent"—are after-the-fact reflections, whereas during the mobilization itself ethnic militancy predominated. This challenge requires some plausible explanation for people's increased adherence to or expression of the premises of Anglo affinity in the post-mobilization period of my fieldwork (1985–87). For example, it could be that my presence brought these deeply seated premises to the fore with uncharacteristic prominence or intensity. Although this is possible to a degree, I doubt the effect was significant for reasons stated in connection with the first query. It also could be that, for reasons quite apart from my own presence, Anglo affinity acquired greater importance in the years after 1984. The problem with this suggestion is that one would logically have expected precisely the opposite to occur. U.S. government support for the Miskitu bush people began to wane in 1985; the Moravian church's ability to reinforce Anglo ideology had reached an all-time low. Consistent with these changes, a small group of townspeople—whom I refer to as the "dissenters"—had begun to rethink their previous adherence to Anglo affinity. In short, although there are inherent risks to explaining the mobilization (and the previous moment of quiescence) with data that are largely retrospective, there is much reason to believe that Anglo affinity was even stronger in 1981 than in 1985–87 at the time of my interviews.

Finally, in regard to potential problems of the representativeness in my selection of interviewees, I can offer three points of clarification. First, as explained in Appendix B, the 27 people with whom I conducted structured interviews were not a "representative" sample. The group was weighted toward community leaders because I was especially interested in knowing the views and orientations of these local opinion makers. If anything, these people were less inclined to endorse the premises of Anglo affinity than the nonleaders I interviewed. Second, among the townspeople who provided me with the most information and analysis were the few who had dissented from their previous adherence to the premises of Anglo affinity. Third, at one point or another I spoke with someone from all the community's 130-odd households. Some did respond to my presence with reserve or reticence, but to the best of my knowledge this resulted, without exception, from distrust of my possible connections to the Sandinista government. In the last analysis, townspeople's warm response to my presence, despite the polarized political conditions at that time, stands as the most persuasive evidence. They would not have so quickly taken me in, overcome their suspicions, and told me their stories if Anglo affinity had not been a deeply rooted component of their consciousness.

Interview Methodology

I CARRIED OUT this survey by means of extensive discussions with 27 community members of Sandy Bay Sirpi between October 1986 and November 1987. The sample was not random. I began by identifying community leaders, people whom I observed to be opinion makers in the community. A total of 10 of the 27 fit that description (including teachers, pastors, lay pastors, and elected or widely recognized community leaders). Later, I made a specific effort to extend my group of respondents to include nonleaders. This second group was biased toward those with whom I had established a relationship of particularly open and relaxed communication. But there were many other community members who would have fit that category who were not included. In general, the level of evident rejection of my presence or the questions that I asked was remarkably low. Finally, both the first and second groups were biased toward men, who represented 22 of the total of 27.

Given the delicate nature of some of the questions and the politically sensitive conditions, I took precautions, some of which directly affected the survey methodology. First, I carried out all discussions in Miskitu and made a special effort to limit the interaction to myself and the respondent. Although the atmosphere was always free and unrestricted, I felt that group discussions could introduce too many potential complications. Rather than taping or recording verbatim these discussions, I only jotted down the gist of responses in a notebook and transcribed them later. I approached the questions through lengthy informal discussions; it sometimes took several hours or more than one session to get through all the questions. I was very careful (probably overly so) not to persist if I sensed the least bit of resistance or evasion in response to my queries. As a result, I had a fairly high number of no response / not codifiable (nr/nc) questions.

The questions and main categories of responses appear below. Not all of the questions are included. Some were eliminated from the effort of quantification either because the question was understood in too variable a manner or because the percentage of no response / not codifiable was too high. This material then merely became part of my corpus of qualitative and ethnographic data.

Each of the four groups of questions constitutes what I consider to be a principal aspect of the Miskitu political worldview in Sandy Bay. After examining the full range of responses, I organized them in three categories for the purposes of further analysis. I created these categories such that in each case there would be "high," "medium" or "neutral," and "low" responses. The information below provides a summary of the content of each category, followed by the correspond-ing number of responses. Percentages were calculated using a base number of 27, which includes the fourth category of "no response / not codifiable."

Political Worldview Interviews: Aggregated Results

I. Adherence to Values of Anglo Affinity

   1A. *What did the Americans think about Miskitu rights during Somoza times?*

   19%   1. The Americans exploited us, treated us badly (Somoza did too). [5]

   37%   2. The Americans paid us badly, but that was because Somoza forced them to. They wanted to pay more; it was mainly Somoza's fault. [10]

   41%   3. Somoza, the Spaniards, did all the exploitation. Americans did no harm. They respected us, they paid for what they took. No criti-cism for the Americans. [11]

   4%   4. No response / not codifiable [1]

   1B. *What do Americans think about Miskitu rights today?*

   15%   1. They are working only out of self-interest, to line their own pock-ets, oppressing us, etc. (sense of inequality) [4]

   15%   2. They are helping us, but it's not charity. They made a deal to get something afterward (sense of equality). [4]

   56%   3. They support us, recognize our rights, no criticisms for the Ameri-cans. [15]

   15%   4. No response / not codifiable [4]

   1C. *If the Miskitu gained complete control of the Coast, would you want to invite the Americans back?*

   11%   1. Never, they would only exploit us. Only if the government agrees. [3]

   26%   2. Yes, but only on the conditions that we set; according to Miskitu laws. [7]

   56%   3. Yes, just like first time, to pay back our debt to them. [15]

   7%   4. No response / not codifiable [2]

II. Identification with Miskitu Ethnic Militancy

   2B. *Do all ethnic groups have equal rights?*

   15%   1. All have the same. [4]

   15%   2. Costeños have more. [4]

   70%   3. Miskitu have more; Miskitu, Sumu, Rama have more. [19]

   2C. *Will the Miskitu gain their full rights through this autonomy process?*

   74%   1. No, there are big differences between our version of autonomy and that of FSLN; Sandinistas are lying. [20]

11%   2. Resignation. [3]
15%   3. No response / not codifiable [4]

2D. *Are the "Spaniards" racist toward Miskitu?*

37%   1. In Somoza times that used to be a problem, but the Sandinistas have eliminated those practices. [10]
0%   2. Neutrality.
59%   3. Yes, strong resentment, us vs. them attitude. [16]
4%   4. No response / not codifiable [1]

2E. *Are the Miskitu capable of running their own affairs within an autonomous government?*

4%   1. Miskitu can't do it alone, power sharing necessary, with Spanish-speaking Nicaraguans. [1]
33%   2. Once they get educated, yes; Coast people must run the government together. Miskitu can do it, together with the foreigners. [9]
19%   3. Yes, Miskitu will run the show. [5]
44%   4. No response / not codifiable [12]

III. Orientations Toward the Revolution

3B. *Who is to blame for all these economic problems we are having?*

44%   1. The Sandinista government is to blame. [12]
30%   2. Logistics, etc., no blame implied; townspeople; the war (with implied neutrality). [8]
4%   3. The Americans, the contras, etc. [1]
22%   4. No response / not codifiable [6]

3C. *How is autonomy progressing?*

48%   1. Criticisms, mainly for the government. [13]
44%   2. Criticisms, mainly for the local leaders; badly, but no blame applied. [12]
4%   3. Indications of progress, hopefulness. [1]
4%   4. No response / not codifiable [1]

3F. *What if boys had not gone to the bush to fight?*

52%   1. Things would have been worse. [14]
15%   2. Neutral response. [4]
7%   3. Things would have been better. [2]
26%   4. No response / not codifiable [7]

IV. Internalized Racism Against Miskitu

4A. *With whom would you like your children/relatives to marry?*

33%   1. Only Miskitu; all are the same (no preference). [9]
22%   2. Equivocation, tending not to prefer Miskitu. [6]
30%   3. Prefer a foreigner (i.e., Americans); anyone but Blacks; anyone but Miskitu. [8]
15%   4. No response / not codifiable [4]

4B. *When a baby is born, how do you like that baby to look?*

19%   1. Anything is OK. [5]

19%   2. Miskitu characteristics, with explicit denigration of the African. [5]

30%   3. Standard Anglo characteristics. [8]

32%   4. No response / not codifiable [9]

4C. *Why are some nations or ethnic groups poorer than others? Did God have a hand in making it this way?*

41%   1. It all relates to school, opportunity. [11]

19%   2. God made us unequal, but with school, we can overcome our disadvantage. [5]

30%   3. God intended for some people/nations to be poor. [8]

11%   4. No response / not codifiable [3]

The Autonomy Law

WHEREAS
Imperialism, the oligarchy and the Somoza dictatorship brought about a divided nation whose people were strangers among themselves and mutually mistrusted one another; while the ruling class kept for itself the right to the enjoyment, use and benefit of the resources of both the Atlantic and Pacific coasts of Nicaragua.

WHEREAS
Only through the war of liberation and the victory of the Sandinista Popular Revolution has Nicaragua been able to dignify the laws of its history, to develop an awareness of its identity and to recognize that it is a multi-ethnic and multi-cultural nation.

WHEREAS
As a consequence of its interpretation of Nicaraguan history and the recognition of a resulting social dichotomy, as well as its awareness of political, economic, and cultural injustice, the Sandinista Popular Revolution has always set the unification of the nation as one of its main goals.

WHEREAS
The Communities of the Atlantic Coast have demanded autonomy as a historical right, in order to achieve genuine national integration based on their cultural characteristics and the use of their national resources, for their own benefit and that of the nation.

WHEREAS
Our Political Constitution holds that Nicaragua is a multi-ethnic nation (Art. 8) and recognizes the right of the Atlantic Coast communities to preserve their cultural identity, their languages, art and culture, as well as the right to use and enjoy the waters, forests and communal lands for their own benefit. It also recognizes their rights to the creation of special programmes designed to contribute to their development (Art. 89 and 90), while respecting their right to live and organize themselves according to their legitimate cultural and historical traditions (Art. 180).

The government of Nicaragua proclaims the following law concerning the
Autonomous Regions of the Atlantic Coast

Title I
Fundamental Principles

CHAPTER I
About the Autonomous Regions

Art. 1   This law establishes an autonomous regime for the Regions where the
communities of the Atlantic Coast live, in accordance with the Constitution of the Republic (Art 89, 90, 180 and 181) and establishes specific rights and duties for their inhabitants.

Art. 2   Nicaragua is a Unitary State, of which the communities of the Atlantic
Coast are an integral part, being entitled and subject to all the rights
and duties of Nicaraguans.

Art. 3   The Communities of the Atlantic Coast have a common history, and
it is a principle of Autonomy to promote unity, fraternity and solidarity among their inhabitants.

Art. 4   The regions where the Communities of the Atlantic Coast live will
benefit from a regime of Autonomy which, within the framework of
national unity and faithful to the principles, policies, and judicial system established in the Constitution of the Republic, will guarantee its
inhabitants and the real use of their legitimate historical rights.

Art. 5   In order to ensure full use of the autonomy rights of the Atlantic Coast
Communities, two Autonomous Regions will be established in what is
currently known as the Department of Zelaya.
1.   Autonomous Region "North Atlantic" will exercise jurisdiction
over the territory of Special Zone I and the adjacent islands.
2.   Autonomous Region "South Atlantic" will exercise jurisdiction
over the territory of Special Zone II and the adjacent islands.
3.   Other zones that have traditionally been considered part of the
Atlantic Coast, while remaining at this time under the jurisdiction
of other authorities, will be incorporated into their respective Autonomous Regions as soon as the circumstances allow for this
incorporation. These circumstances will be defined and determined by the respective Region.

Art. 6   The administrative seat for Autonomous Region "North Atlantic" will
be Puerto Cabezas, while Bluefields will be the seat for Autonomous
Region "South Atlantic." Under very special circumstances the admin-

istrative seat of the Autonomous Regions may be transferred to other locations in their respective territories.

Art. 7   Spanish is the official language of the Nicaraguan state. The languages of the Communities of the Atlantic Coast of Nicaragua will be official within the Autonomous Regions.

Art. 8   The Autonomous Regions established by the present law are legal entities and as such, in accordance with national policies, plans and guidelines, will have the following general functions:
1.   To participate effectively in the planning process and programmes of national development within the Region.
2.   To administer in coordination with the corresponding ministries, the programmes related to health, education, culture, basic goods distribution and communal services, as well as the establishment of economic, social, and cultural projects in the Region.
3.   To promote the rational use of the waters, forests, and communal lands for the benefit and enjoyment of their peoples, and the overall preservation of the ecological system.
4.   To promote national culture, as well as the study, preservation, promotion, development, and dissemination of the different cultures and traditions of the Atlantic Coast's Communities, including their historical, artistic, linguistic, and cultural heritage.
5.   To promote the traditional exchange with the Caribbean countries in accordance with the national laws and established procedures regulated to this matter.
6.   To establish regional taxes in accordance with the established laws related to this matter.

Art. 9   The rational exploitation of the mining, forestry, and fishing resources as well as other natural resources in the Autonomous Regions of the Atlantic Coast, must benefit its inhabitants in just proportions, in accordance with agreement between the Regional Government and the Central Government.

CHAPTER TWO
About the internal territorial divisions of the Autonomous Regions

Art. 10   For administrative purposes, the territory of the Autonomous Regions will be divided into municipalities. These municipalities will be ruled according to established laws concerning this matter. Such administrative subdivisions will be organized and established by the corresponding Regional Councils, in accordance with the traditions of each Autonomous Region.

CHAPTER THREE
About the rights and duties of the inhabitants
of the Communities in the Autonomous Regions

Art. 11 Within the territory of the Autonomous Region, all Nicaraguan citizens will benefit from the rights and guarantees granted by the Constitution and those stated in the present law.

Art. 12 The inhabitants of the Atlantic Coast Communities are entitled by law:

1. To full equality of rights.
2. To promote and develop their languages, religions and cultures.
3. To use and benefit from their waters, forests, and communal lands, in accordance with national development plans.
4. To organize their social and productive activities according to their own values.
5. To be educated in their own languages, through programmes that take into account their historical heritage, their traditions and the characteristics of their environment, all within the framework of the national education system.
6. To their own forms of communal, collective, or individual ownership and transfer of land.

Art. 13 The members of the Atlantic Coast communities have the right to define and to determine their own ethnic identity.

Art. 14 The defence of life, homeland, justice, and peace for the integral development of the nation is an essential duty of the inhabitants of the Communities of the Autonomous Region.

Art. 15 In Nicaragua, the defence of the Nation is based on the organized power of the people. In the Autonomous Regions, the Atlantic Coast Communities will hold the main responsibility for the defence of the nation within the framework of the Sandinista Popular Army, the Security Forces, and the Ministry of the Interior.

Title II
About regional administration

CHAPTER I
About the different regional administrative bodies

Art. 16 In each one of the Autonomous Regions of the Atlantic Coast, subject to the Political Constitution of the Republic and to this law, the following regional authorities will function:

1. Regional Council.
2. A Regional Coordinator
3. Municipal authorities.
4. Other authorities pertaining to the administrative subdivision of the municipalities.

Art. 17   The Council and the Regional Coordinator in their respective areas of work, will be the highest authorities within their corresponding Region.

Art. 18   The municipal administration will govern according to the law related to this matter. The remaining authorities will govern according to the resolutions enacted by the corresponding Regional Council.

CHAPTER II
About the Regional Council

Art. 19   Each Regional Council will be composed of a minimum of 30 representatives and a maximum of 50, elected by universal franchise: direct, free, and secret elections in constituencies determined by the Supreme Electoral Council according to the laws of the Republic. All the ethnic communities of the Region must be represented.

Art. 20   The representatives of the Autonomous Regions in the National Assembly will also be full members of the Regional Council.

Art. 21   The representative to the Regional Council must be:
1. A Nicaraguan citizen, 21 years of age or older, who has lived in the country for at least one year prior to the elections.
2. In full possession of civil and political rights.
3. Someone born on the Atlantic Coast, the son or daughter of a father or mother born in the Region, or someone who has lived there for at least five years.

Art. 22   The right to vote for electing members of the Regional Council will be given to those persons who having fulfilled the requirements of the electoral law, classify under one of the following requisites:
1. To reside in the Region three months prior to the elections, when the voter is a native of the Region or the son or a daughter of a father or mother born in the region.
2. To reside for a minimum of one year in the Region prior to elections.

Art. 23   The Regional Council will have the following functions:
1. To regulate regional matters pertaining to its domain through res-

olutions and by laws pertaining to its domain, according to Art. 7 of the present law.

2. To formulate the plan for tax collection in the Region.
3. To participate in the formulation, planning and implementation of social, economic and cultural programmes and policies affecting or pertaining to the Region.
4. To resolve boundary disputes between the different Communities.
5. To prepare the preliminary draft of the regional budget.
6. To ensure that the Region's Development and Social Promotion Fund, established by national and foreign donations, is correctly used.
7. To work out a preliminary draft for the division and organization of municipalities in the Region, taking into account their social, economic, and cultural characteristics.
8. To elect a Regional Coordinator from the Council's members and to replace him/her when necessary.
9. To establish the administrative subdivision to the municipalities in the Region by means of resources.
10. To draw up a preliminary draft of a law pertaining to the regional use and conservation of the Region's natural resources.
11. To request reports from the representatives of the ministries and state institutions working in the Region, as well as regional officials, and to summon such officials to appear before it, when necessary.
12. To elect its Board of Directors.
13. To accept or reject resignations submitted to it by any of its members or members of the Board of Directors.
14. To formulate and approve its internal regulations.
15. To promote the integration, development and participation of women in all aspects of political, social, cultural and economic life of the Region.
16. To deal with other functions conferred to it by the present law.

Art. 24   The resolutions and bylaws of the Regional Councils must be in accordance with the laws of the Republic.

Art. 25   The term of office for the members of each Regional Council will be in accordance with the laws of the Republic.

Art. 26   Quorum for sessions of the Regional Council is half the number of its members plus one, and resolutions must be approved by more than fifty per cent of the members present. Exceptions to this rule may be established by the internal regulations of the Council.

CHAPTER III
About the Council's Board of Directors

Art. 27   Each Council's Board of Directors will be formed by a President, two Vice-Presidents, two Secretaries, and two Alternates, ensuring that each of the ethnic Communities of the respective Autonomous Regions is represented; Their term of office will be for two years, and their functions will be determined by the present law and by the internal regulations of the respective Council.

Art. 28   The functions of the Board of Directors of the Regional Council are as follows:
1. To coordinate its activities and those of the Council with those of the Regional Coordinator and, through him/her, with other officials of the Executive Branch.
2. To convene ordinary and extraordinary meetings of the Regional Council, and to prepare the agenda.
3. To appoint permanent and special commissions to analyze and decide upon matters related to the administration of the Region.
4. To do everything necessary to safeguard the interests, welfare and development of the region.
5. To perform any other function conferred by the present law or by the internal regulations of the Council.

CHAPTER IV
About the Regional Coordinator

Art. 29   The executive functions of the region will be the responsibility of the Regional Coordinator.

Art. 30   The functions of the Regional Coordinator are as follows:
1. To represent the Region.
2. To appoint executive officials to the regional administration.
3. To organize and direct the executive activities of the Region.
4. To discuss matters pertaining to his/her office with the national authorities.
5. To comply with, and oversee the fulfillment of the policies, guidelines and decrees of the national Executive Branch, in accordance with the law.
6. To administer to the Special Development and Social Promotion Fund according to the policies established by the Regional Council.
7. To perform any other function conferred by the present law or by the internal regulations of the Council.

Art. 31   The office of Regional Coordinator is compatible with that of representative for the Presidency in the Region.

Title III
Consolidated Chapter
About the budget of the Autonomous Regions

Art. 32   In conjunction with the Ministry of Finance the Regional Council will prepare a draft for the administration of regional programmes for the Autonomous Regions, which will be comprised of:
  1. Regional taxes in accordance with the regional tax collection plan, which must include tax levied on profits of enterprises operating in the region.
  2. An earmarked fund from the general budget of the Republic.

Art. 33   A Special Development Fund will be established and will be composed of national and foreign donations, as well as other extraordinary monies not included in the regular budget. This Fund will be earmarked for productive, social, and cultural investments in the Region and will be administered by the Regional Councils in accordance with the law.

Title IV
Consolidated Chapter
About the patrimony of the Autonomous Regions and communal property

Art. 34   The patrimony of the Autonomous Regions will be constituted by its possessions, rights and obligations acquired through any legal means as a public legal entity.

Art. 35   The Autonomous Regions have the full and legal capacity to obtain, administer, and own the possessions comprising their patrimony, in accordance with the law.

Art. 36   Communal property is constituted by the communal lands, waters and forests that have traditionally belonged to the Communities.
Communal property is subject to the following provisions:
  1. Communal lands cannot be sold, seized, or taxed; their communal status cannot expire.
  2. The inhabitants of the Communities will have the right to work on communal plots of land and are entitled to the benefits generated therefrom.

Art. 37   The remaining form of property in the region are those recognized by the Constitution and the laws of the Republic.

Title V
Consolidated Chapter
About Law Reform

Art. 38 Two thirds or more members of both Regional Councils may request that the National Assembly reform the present law through the established constitutional channels.

Title VI
Consolidated Chapter
Final and tentative provisions

Art. 39 Once the present law has been passed, the National Assembly will call for the elections of the Regional Council in each Autonomous Region. The Supreme Electoral Council will then proceed to organize and direct the elections, to announce and publicize their results, and to give credentials to the elected Regional representatives.

Art. 40 The National Assembly will set the date of investiture for each Regional Council. The President of the Supreme Electoral Council will take the oath of office and invest the regional representatives. He will also preside over the meeting where the President of the Council and the Board of Directors are elected.

Art. 41 An especially appointed commission of each Regional Council will organize a solemn inaugural ceremony in the presence of the President of the Republic, or his representatives from the National Assembly and the Supreme Court of Justice.

Art. 42 The present law will be widely publicized throughout Nicaragua, both in Spanish and in the languages spoken in Nicaragua's Atlantic Coast Communities.

Art. 43 Those officials who are engaged in their duties at the time this law comes into force will continue in their positions until the newly elected authorities take office, in accordance with the new provisions.

Art. 44 The present law will take effect, from the date of its publication in the official newspaper, "La Gaceta."

Unofficial translation by the Southern Regional Autonomy Council, from Gaceta, *no. 238 (Oct. 30, 1987), pp. 2833–36.*

Evolution of Miskitu Armed Organizations

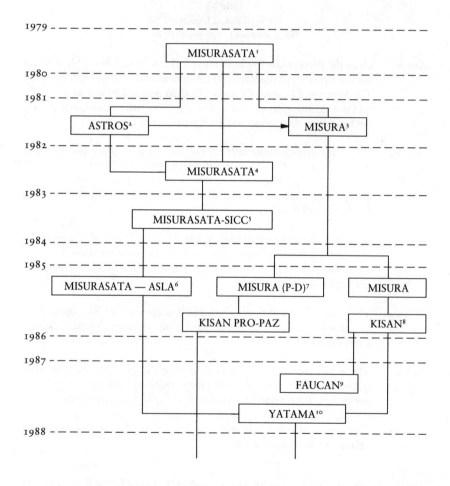

1. Miskitu, Sumu, Rama, and Sandinista, Working Together (Asla Takanka), founded in November 1979 following the dissolution of ALPROMISU.

2. Short-lived armed Miskitu group, formed in 1981 in the months after the Prinzapolka affair. ASTROS consisted of about 60 young men who had become alienated from Steadman Fagoth's authoritarian practices. It was purported to be responsible for the attacks on the Río Coco in December 1981 and January 1982, later known as "Red Christmas."

3. The largest and best-funded armed Miskitu organization, headed by Steadman Fagoth (although his leadership would later be contested), MISURA maintained close ties with the FDN and CIA.

4. Beginning in mid- to late 1982, MISURASATA established a formal presence in Costa Rica and became affiliated with the Revolutionary Democratic Alliance (ARDE) headed by Eden Pastora. MISURASATA combatants received U.S. funds through the structures of ARDE but remained disgruntled by what they perceived as unfair treatment by the ARDE directorate. Sometime in 1984 they formally severed these ties.

5. Beginning sometime in 1983, MISURASATA joined forces with the Southern Indigenous Creole Communities (SICC), an organization consisting mainly of Creole people from the southern Atlantic Coast, in exile since 1980. The recognized leader of SICC was Jenelle Hodgson.

6. ASLA ("unity" in Miskitu) was formed on June 18, 1985, in Miami, by an assembly of leaders from MISURASATA, SICC, and MISURA. The unity effort never prospered. By the end of 1985 leaders were signing their communiques as MISURASATA (or KISAN; see note 8).

7. On May 17, 1985, in the northern Atlantic Coast community of Yulu, Sandinista army officers and other government representatives met with MISURA commander Eduardo Pantin and signed a preliminary cease-fire. This faction became known as MISURA Pro-Dialogo (pro-dialogue). When MISURA reorganized four months later under the name KISAN (see note 8), the troops associated with Pantin took on the name KISAN Pro-Paz (pro-peace).

8. On September 3, 1985, MISURA was reorganized under the name KISAN (Indians of Nicaragua's Atlantic Coast). The delegates to the convening assembly replaced Steadman Fagoth with Wycliffe Diego.

9. Armed Forces of the Atlantic Coast (FAUCAN) was the product of a shortlived effort on the part of the CIA to unify Miskitu fighters into a single fighting force under the command of the FDN. Formed during an assembly in Honduras in March 1987, the organization collapsed almost immediately (Anaya 1987: 24–26).

10. YATAMA stands for YApti TAsba MAsrika nani (Descendants of Mother Earth). Formed in mid-1987, YATAMA was intended to achieve the unification of the diverse factions of Miskitu opposition organizations. Although the signatures of the principal leaders (Fagoth, Rivera, Diego) did appear on YATAMA communiques for a brief period, the unity was short-lived and soon gave way to renewed internal divisions. Despite these conflicts, YATAMA continued as the major organization representing Miskitu and—to a lesser extent—Sumu and Rama Indian people.

Reference Matter

Notes

Introduction

1. MISURASATA was an organization representing Indian peoples of the Coast, formed in 1979 with Sandinista backing.

2. All proper names in this study are pseudonyms, except those of people who are widely acknowledged public figures or who are deceased.

3. The word *officer* is a rough translation of the Spanish term *oficial*. I use the term to refer to Sandinista military leaders as well, though the Sandinista "officers" often were civilians recruited for temporary military service, not professional soldiers.

4. One of the five non-Mestizo ethnic groups that inhabit the Atlantic Coast, Creoles are a people of African descent who speak a creolized English. Their relations with the revolutionary government also were characterized by tension and conflict, though less so than those of the Miskitu.

5. The FDN was the largest contra organization and received most of the U.S. funding. During negotiations between MISURASATA and the government, the FDN offered MISURASATA field commanders enticements of equipment and funding and convinced some of them to switch loyalties.

6. The ARDE was a force commanded by Eden Pastora that operated mainly in the southern Atlantic Coast, at times in coordination with MISURASATA.

7. Community members spoke fondly of the three white North American social scientists who had worked in the area in the 1970's, "Mr. Barney" (Bernard Nietschmann), "Mr. Brian" (Brian Weiss), and "Miss Kate" (Dorothy Cattle). Their past experiences with these three made my own activities more comprehensible. For example, Cattle, a nutritional anthropologist, had studied people's diets, recording in minute detail their daily food intake. During one of the many periods of acute community food shortages, I visited a sharp-tongued woman who greeted me at the door saying, "Don't even think about asking me what I ate today. I haven't had a decent meal for a week."

8. If I had persisted, I probably would not have changed the people's understanding of the category Miriki. Rather, they would have simply banished me from it and considered me a "converted Sandinista" instead. I rejected that path because I valued my close relations with the townspeople and genuinely supported much of what they were fighting for.

9. "Redefinición del trabajo político-ideológico en Zelaya Sur," June 4, 1985. Although this document criticized previous approaches that merely imposed the party line and encouraged greater interaction, it stopped well short of questioning

the idea that the party defined unilaterally what the revolution's premises and priority tasks would be.

10. One indication of CIDCA's analysis just before the onset of autonomy comes from the lead article in the inaugural issue of its publication, *Wani*. The author, Edmund T. Gordon, emphasizes the relative autonomy of class from conditions of oppression that afflict ethnic or racial minorities and argues that this in turn necessitates "simultaneous struggle" against both class and ethnic oppression (1984). Gordon's analysis had a great influence on my own thinking.

Chapter 1

1. The term comes from P. Marchetti, "Nicaragua and the Disenchanted Liberals," in Vandermeer and Rosset (1986: 32–39).

2. Marcus and Fisher (1986), for example, call it a "crisis of representation." There is no monolithic analytical or political position on this crisis, and I make no pretense here of summarizing or distinguishing between the various perspectives.

3. Examples of structural analysis that emphasize U.S. intervention include Diaz-Polanco (1985), Dunbar-Ortiz (1986), Jenkins Molieri (1986), and Ramirez (1981). A somewhat propagandistic but otherwise typical example of the analysis emphasizing Nicaraguan state oppression is USDS (1987). Examples of the second perspective include MacDonald (1988), Mohawk and Davis (1982), and Nietschmann (1984, 1985, 1989). For an annotated bibliography of these sources, see Bourgois and Hale (1989).

4. In a review of the "debate," Bentley (1987: 25) argues that "most people in the field still locate their own work conceptually with reference to this dichotomy." I suspect that the authors to whom he refers are "instrumentalists" attempting to defend their position against an alleged "primordialist" critique (e.g., Rothschild 1981). It is much rarer to find scholars who consider themselves "primordialists" in the original sense of the term.

5. According to Rothschild, this second group (the "traditionals") are convinced by leaders to "perceive their fate in ethnic, rather than individual or class terms" (1981: 27), leading to political action that does not always reflect the traditionals' "true interests" (pp. 139–49).

6. In their strongest forms Geertzian hermeneutics and rational choice theory face an irresolvable difference in analytical goals. Do we interpret the meaning of social action or advance falsifiable hypotheses that explain its past and predict its future course?

7. This is the problem to which Sherry Ortner (a self-proclaimed Geertzian) refers when she admits that the approach lacks a "systematic sociology" and has an "underdeveloped sense of the politics of culture" (1984: 132).

8. Hechter does argue that the theory is advancing rapidly and soon will be capable of demonstrating that structures themselves are actually the product of previous rational choices. The widely acclaimed leader in these theoretical developments is Jon Elster. For a useful summary see Giddens (1984: 199–213).

9. Although Geertz soon abandoned these Parsonian premises, his original

article continues to inform the primordial-instrumental debate. For example, this explains why Laitin could associate Geertz with the un-Geertzian-sounding notion that societies tend toward "homeostasis" according to a "congruence hypothesis," whereby component subsystems conform to one another and bring society into equilibrium (1986: 17).

10. See Olzak (1983) for a review of the developmental theories.

11. See Ragin (1977) and Sloan (1979) for persuasive empirical and theoretical critiques, respectively, along these lines.

12. As often has been pointed out (e.g., Ortner 1984, following Giddens 1979), despite the title of Parsons's principal work (*The Structure of Social Action*), he locates causality fully in the properties of society.

13. Bonacich does repeatedly emphasize the need for historical analysis to answer both these questions and firmly resists explanations that resort to functionalism (i.e., racism persists because it serves the needs of the capitalist system). But simply adding a historical perspective, instead of resolving these theoretical problems, is apt to perpetuate them.

14. In more recent unpublished work, Bourgois has moved toward an approach that emphasizes "cultural reproduction," using a framework similar in many ways to the one developed here.

15. See, for example, Austin (1983), Fordham (1988), Fordham and Ogbu (1986), Gilroy (1987), and, especially, Edmund T. Gordon (1984, 1991).

16. I do not summarize his entire argument, because this has been done by others, e.g., Marcus and Fischer (1986) and Giddens (1984). The latter is particularly relevant, given my reliance on his ideas to develop a critique of existing approaches to ethnic politics. Rather than putting his own (abstractly stated) theory of "structuration" to the empirical test, Giddens chooses to summarize other studies that purportedly exemplify his approach. He features Willis's *Learning to Labor* prominently.

17. Jeffrey Gould (1990) has advanced a similar argument using the term "dual consciousness." In a later article that proposes an explanation for the 1990 elections in Nicaragua, he uses the term "contradictory consciousness" with a similar meaning to that developed here (Gould 1991).

18. See, for example, Scott (1990), following Abercrombie, Hill, and Turner (1980).

19. In contrast, Scott implies that "everyday resistance" generally represents the maximum response that a given set of structural conditions will allow and that such resistance has great potential efficacy. "Thousands upon thousands of such 'petty' acts of resistance," he writes, "have dramatic economic and political effects" (1990: 193). Without belittling everyday resistance, it surely can be noted that, to paraphrase Michael Hanchard (personal communication), when people resort to "weapons of the weak," this often is a victory for the strong. Moreover, although everyday resistance surely does have some effect, whether it brings about substantive change in the conditions of structural inequity is an entirely different question, which Scott leaves as an unsubstantiated assertion.

20. Paul Willis's study (1981a) is of little help here because he devotes little attention to the dominant class and state apparatuses and portrays them as rela-

tively stable. Marcus and Fischer (1986), though generally approving of Willis, make this criticism as well.

21. An exhaustive analysis would of course consider internal institutional workings at the apex of state power in Managua as well: the lengthy discussions and changing political configurations within the Sandinista National Direction (DN); the influence of various experts on the Coast who held the DN's attention; the broader policy concerns of state elites that may have made them more amenable to the autonomy experiment. Such analysis, however, will have to await historical research, drawing on data that to my knowledge are still unavailable.

22. Corrigan and Sayer (1985) have made an equally categorical plea for analysts to take seriously how states constitute themselves and legitimate their rule by incorporating people into a uniform cultural system.

23. See also Chatterjee (1985), Gilroy (1987), and Williams (1991).

24. See especially Orlando Nuñez Soto (1986). Socialist economic relations cannot be implemented if the economy is not even fully capitalist, Nuñez argues, and a "proletarian" consciousness is not likely to have developed where the proletariat itself has barely begun to form. See also Marchetti (1986) and Fagen (1986).

25. These conclusions follow from the tautological premise that "genuine" political expression could occur only outside and in opposition to the party. They generally are based on scant firsthand observation and offer no recognition of or explanation for the indisputable achievements of participatory democracy in Nicaragua. From them we learn little more than the authors' own (frequently passionate) political convictions. See, for example, Valenta and Valenta, who claim that the "new mass organizations . . . were conceived along the model of Lenin's 'transmission belts,' that is, as ancillary institutions used by the party to supplement other, more direct means of social control" (1987: 17). See also Nolan (1984).

26. For example, Ruchwarger cites three cases of conflict between the FSLN and the mass organizations to demonstrate the autonomy of the latter. The women's organization (AMNLAE) wanted women to be included in the draft, the rural workers' organization (ATC) wanted a more rapid pace of expropriation of large private landholdings, and the neighborhood organizations (CDS) were reprimanded by the FSLN for harassing opposition politicians (1987: 140–46). Fascinating and important as these cases are, they give the misleading impression that conflicts between the FSLN and the popular sectors generally fell within the thoroughly manageable category of specific demands for change, against a backdrop of militant general support for the revolution.

27. For an example of this analysis focused on women, see Molyneux (1986); for one on smallholding peasants, see Ortega (1986).

28. To encapsulate the theory of participatory democracy I have drawn heavily on the work of Orlando Nuñez Soto (1981, 1986, and, with Burbach, 1987), a leading Nicaraguan social scientist, member of the National Autonomy Commission, and high-ranking militant of the FSLN. See also Arce (1988), Borge (1984), and Marchetti (1986).

29. Nuñez goes on to specify the groups that constitute this "majority" and

makes reference to the ultimate goal: "transforming all salaried workers into freely associated workers" (1986: 245).

30. Ruchwarger's instances of conflict (see note 26) take place completely within this political space, as does what Carlos Vilas calls the "dynamic dialectic relationship" between party and base (1986: 207).

31. Speech at the celebration of the seventh anniversary of the revolution, Estelí, Nicaragua, reprinted in *Barricada,* July 20, 1986.

32. Doug Brown (1990) identifies the same problem in slightly different terms, drawing a distinction between "authoritarian" and "democratic" hegemony, and concludes (rather equivocally) that as of 1989 it was premature to determine which corresponded more closely to the FSLN's political practice.

33. Their best effort is to suggest that unity could emerge from an "equivalence principle," whereby diverse oppressed groups join in a shared commitment to liberty of expression and equality between themselves and others (see especially their fourth chapter). In addition to being just as "essentialist" as the class reductionism they reject, this principle flattens the social terrain of politics to an intolerable degree. In my view, we must move toward theory that validates the struggles of all these "subject positions," without resorting to the untenable assertion that class is but one of many equivalent axes of subordination.

Chapter 2

1. For additional information on this period, see Floyd (1967), Hale (1987), Helms (1971, 1983a), and Olien (1983).

2. I develop this argument at greater length in Hale (1987). For accounts of the military operations, see Gamez (1939: 159–60) and Sorsby (1972: 152).

3. The mission station of Sandy Bay Sirpi, where I conducted fieldwork, was founded in 1884.

4. Statistics reported in the Moravian mission publication *Periodical Accounts* confirm this dramatic increase. In the fifteen years between 1864 and 1879, the total number of Christians (baptized adults, candidates, and baptized children) increased from 600 to 980, an average of 25 per year. Between 1879 and 1894, in contrast, Christians increased to a total of 5,516, with an average yearly growth of 296. Zealots of the utmost conviction and piety, missionaries were not apt to fudge their data and were quick to exclude converts who failed to comply with their strict standards of Christian behavior. For an analysis of the connection between the "Great Awakening" and the penetration of North American capital in the region, see Rossbach (1986).

5. The best available account of the rise of the Creole elite can be found in Edmund T. Gordon (1987, n.d.).

6. Creoles spoke and continue to speak their own language, a creolized English known as Mosquito Coast Creole (Holm 1978). Through formal education and extensive contact with foreigners, they also developed the ability to speak Standard English, though continuing to communicate among themselves in Mosquito Coast Creole.

7. Evidence to support this point can be found in Hale (1987: 41–42). Among

other reasons for the king's lack of authority was his age. During 35 of the last 52 years of the Mosquito Kingdom (or chiefdom), either there was no designated king or the king was under the age of 21 (Olien 1983). Under these conditions, a member of the King's (later Chief's) Council presided.

8. Rather, they bickered constantly with the Reserve government over details until 1881, when both parties turned the matter over to the king of Austria, who served as an outside arbitrator. The case was decided in favor of the status quo, firmly rejecting Nicaragua's claims to absolute sovereignty.

9. William Sorsby, historian of the Atlantic Coast (personal communication).

10. Quoted in Cuadra Chamorro (1944: 11–13) from a statement by Carlos Alberto Lacayo, an official of the Zelaya government, made shortly after the occupation of Bluefields.

11. It appears that Britain's principal concern was to make a graceful exit from existing treaty obligations to the Mosquito government. The U.S. consul in London reported at the end of 1894 that "Her Majesty's Government is well pleased with the prospect of having [Mosquito Chief] 'Clarence' and his fortunes eliminated from their political responsibility" (Bayard to Gresham, December 22, 1894), Papers Relating to the Affairs of Bluefields, published as part of the *Congressional Record*, 53d Cong., 3d sess., Jan. 5, 1895, cited hereafter as "Papers").

12. Baker to Gresham (U.S. Department of State), April 2, 1894, Papers.

13. O'Neil to Herbert (U.S. Navy, Washington, D.C.), July 25, 1894, ibid.

14. Statement of American citizens, March 29, 1894, ibid.

15. Gresham to Baker, May 12, June 13, 1894, ibid.

16. Bluefields residents later justified the preemptive attack on Bluff, claiming that Cabezas, in response to the violence in Bluefields, had announced his intention to call in soldiers from Bluff "to lay the niggers low." Whether or not these were Cabezas's words (one wonders what the Spanish for "niggers" might have been), the statement is indicative of the racial antagonism—principally between Creoles and Nicaraguans—that prevailed throughout the episode. See Citizens of Bluefields to O'Neil, July 13, 1894, ibid.

17. Reprinted in the *Diario Nacional*, no. 62, January 12, 1895, Biblioteca Nacional (Managua).

18. There are discrepancies in different reports on the composition of the new council. I have relied on the observations of Captain O'Neil (U.S. Navy), whose warship occupied Bluefields at the time (O'Neil to Herbert, July 13, 1894, Papers). The Nicaraguan *Diario Nacional* (November 12, 1894) provides a different list, in which Creoles and British subjects are prominent and North Americans are absent.

19. The Moravian mission had previously stated its firm opposition to the annexation in a letter to U.S. Consul Baker: "If Great Britain, under whose protection our work was inaugurated, does not uphold the Treaty of Managua, we should feel very unsafe indeed" (Sifborger [Superintendent] and Berkenhangen [Warden] to Baker, April 30, 1894, Papers).

20. Despite efforts to make the Bluefields government representative, only one Creole, Davis Ingram, agreed to serve. Foreign residents, who had more to lose

from passive resistance, proved more willing to accommodate the new regime. Prominent U.S. businessmen served in the positions of mayor and alderman on the new municipal council (Wunderich and Rossbach 1985: 41).

21. Article four of the 1860 Treaty of Managua states that Miskitu people may take this course and thereby place themselves under Nicaraguan state sovereignty. The text of the treaty can be found in Wunderich, von Oertzen, and Rossbach (1990: 315–17).

22. *Gaceta del Norte*, January 1, 1895 (the editor was Rigoberto Cabezas). Quoted in Wunderich, von Oertzen, and Rossbach (1990: 400–401).

23. Indians and Creoles of the Mosquito Reserve to U.S. Secretary of State Charles Evans Hughes (March 7, 1924), *Records of the Department of State Relating to the Internal Affairs of Nicaragua, 1910–29*, microfilm roll 94, cited hereafter as *Records*. For an account by a "pro-British" observer with a similar thrust, see Wunderich and Rossbach (1985: 43).

24. Moravian missionaries, known to be highly sympathetic to Miskitu autonomy, would surely have found out about and reported this protest if it had occurred. For an example of their remarkably bland description of the convention, see *Periodical Accounts* 2 (March 1895): 465. An initial report from Moravian missionaries describes Indians in "the country districts" as "exceedingly angry that their land and their independence had been taken from them" (*Periodical Accounts* 2 [June 1894]: 322). Yet the only incident cited is a case of petty theft, and a subsequent update reports "less disturbance" than in the Creole areas. In September 1894, the Moravian superintendent visited all ten mission stations and found "that in comparison with Bluefields and Magdala (Pearl Lagoon), [the Miskitu Indians] had scarcely felt the effects of the Nicaraguan occupation of their territory" (*Periodical Accounts* 2 [March 1895]: 468).

25. DeKalb (1893: 275). Evidence demonstrating Miskitu disaffection is problematic, of course, because the principal observers had such strong prejudicial interests in the matter. Nicaraguan authorities' attempts to convince the Miskitu that they were "slaves" at the hands of the Creoles contained blatant self-interested hyperbole with racist overtones. Observations by laypeople such as DeKalb, well before the annexation began, can be assumed to be less guided by the need to justify a particular political outcome.

26. The description is by the Moravian superintendent, after a trip to the "country stations." Although he considered the promises "nonsense," he surely was biased by the Nicaraguans' qualification of church offerings paid by the Indians and the pious Moravian code of moral conduct as "oppression" (*Periodical Accounts* 2 [March 1895]: 468).

27. A petition to the British commander of the *Cleopatra* on March 17, 1894, for example, states: "[Mr. Lacayo's (a Zelaya appointee)] officials are endeavoring to force many of the Indians to sign their names as being adherents of Nicaragua against our own country, Mosquito" (Headmen of Mosquito Indians to Captain Curzon-Howe, March 17, 1894, Confidential Print 6547, Further Correspondence respecting the Mosquito Reserve Part V, January–June 1894, Public Records Office, London [copy in the CIDCA-Bluefields Archives]).

28. The term comes from O'Laughlin (n.d.).

29. Additional support for this idea comes from the memories of Salazar, as recorded in Chapter 3.

30. Village headmen to British Vice-Consul Belanger, September 20, 1898, Confidential Print 7146, p. 12, Public Records Office, London (copy in CIDCA-Bluefields Archives). The reference is to a massive increase in tariffs decreed by Zelaya in 1898, which put the more marginal economic enterprises out of business (Wunderich and Rossbach 1985: 48).

31. *Periodical Accounts* 7, no. 73 (March 1908): 39–53. For example, they reported that "one former [Moravian] helper has become entangled in Sam Pitts' intrigues, had to be spoken to about it, took that amiss, and has severed his connection with the Church!" (p. 52).

32. For a detailed account of the Pitts episode, see Rossbach (1985).

33. H. O. Chalkley (Bluefields) to C. Alban Young (Guatemala), November 17, 1915, Crowdell Papers, CIDCA-Bluefields Archives.

34. The cases of mining and especially banana production, however, are different. The need for plantation land to grow bananas brought companies into direct conflict with the Indians. The Sumu Indians who still lived along the Río Escondido near Bluefields in the 1870's, for example, were pushed aside by the banana boom of the 1880's (Wickham 1894).

35. Acting British Vice-Consul (Bluefields) to H. F. Bingham (San Juan del Norte), August 17, 1909, Crowdell Papers.

36. Creoles from Bluefields and Pearl Lagoon did present claims, mainly for urban lots, during this period. For purposes of brevity, this discussion of the land question refers exclusively to Indians.

37. H. O. Chalkley (Bluefields) to Lionel Cardens (Guatemala), May 27, 1911, Crowdell Papers.

38. C. Alban Young (Guatemala) to Sir Edward Grey (Foreign Office), March 17, 1915, ibid. See also Oliver Thomas (Bluefields Creole) to H. O. Chalkley, October 22, 1915, ibid.

39. In at least one case—the communities of the Río Grande area—the sequence of correspondence indicates that the Miskitu headman first made a claim for individual family plots and later, on Chalkley's request, changed it to a single claim for a large piece of communal land (H. O. Chalkley to A. W. Hooker, October 25, 1915; Benito Garcia et al. to Chalkley, November 8, 1915, ibid.).

40. *Periodical Accounts* 9 (March 1916): 421.

41. Station diaries of Yulu (1896) and of Karawala (1926), in Moravian Archives, Bethlehem, Pennsylvania.

42. For a detailed critique of MacDonald's argument, see Hale (1991c).

43. It is ironic that the Miskitu perceived the British in such a favorable light, given the disadvantageous legal terms of the agreement. The land allotments stipulated in the treaty amounted to about twelve *manzanas* of agricultural land per family—an inadequate amount for slash-and-burn agriculture in the tropical rain forest—with no provision for population growth or broader control of forest resources. All the land outside these demarcated community boundaries fell under the exclusive jurisdiction of the state. In the context of contemporary conflicts

over land rights, the Indian organization MISURASATA bitterly denounced this arrangement (Hale 1991c). One manzana is equivalent to 0.7 hectares and 1.7 acres. The exact provision of the treaty is for eight manzanas of land per family of four, with an additional two manzanas for each family member in excess of four. In addition, communities acquired rights to an amount of common pasture land roughly equivalent to the agricultural land grant.

44. Ferris (Managua) to U.S. Department of State, October 3, 1916, *Records*, roll 15.

45. Adams (1987: 55). Indicative of this support, in the elections of 1928 in the Miskitu community of Sandy Bay Tara, Liberals received 165 votes and Conservatives 28 (Station diary, Sandy Bay Tara, Moravian Archives, Bethlehem, Pennsylvania).

46. *Proceedings of the Society for the Propagation of the Gospel* (*Nicaragua Annual Report*), 1927: 63. Further substantiation comes from the Moravian church station diary in Karawala. The writer reports that during the height of warfare in the Río Grande area, nearly all the men from Karawala were "sleeping in the bush" to avoid forced recruitment.

47. Adams (1987: 55) suggests that the missionaries took this position out of solidarity with their parishioners, who were Liberal supporters. Given the power relations involved and the missionaries' intolerance of "deviant" Miskitu behavior, it is much more likely that influence flowed in the other direction. The Moravian hierarchy opposed the Conservatives for its own reasons, considering them "bigoted Catholics."

48. For example, the *Memorial* that Senator Horacio Hodgson presented to the Nicaraguan Congress in 1934 suggests that relations between the Coast and Managua did not improve markedly after 1928 (pamphlet, CIDCA-Bluefields Archives).

49. E.g., Ana Crowdell to Clayton McCoy (Staten Island), April 13, 1931, Crowdell Papers. A full examination of Creole consciousness is beyond the scope of this chapter, but Creole reactions are suggestive of developments in Miskitu consciousness during the same period.

50. Hatfield to Sandino, July 14, 1927, ibid.

51. For a detailed account of Edson's exploits, see Brooks (1989). Brooks reports that Miskitu reluctance to join Edson resulted from Sandinista "psychological warfare" and reprisals. This assertion, however, is based on little more than Edson's own diagnosis. The evidence Brooks presents suggests that only local elites (called bamboo whites) actively supported the marines, while the Miskitu response ranged from neutral to pro-Sandino. His conclusion that Edson "succeeded in winning the cooperation of the local population" (p. 338) is therefore perplexing.

52. See, for example, MacCaulay (1967: 189–223) and Wunderich (1989).

53. José Román (1983), who traveled with Sandino during the first months of 1933, describes these accomplishments and provides insight into the Sandinistas' relations with the Indians.

54. Rivera organized the fleet of dugout canoes and Miskitu oarsmen that

transported Sandinista columns up and down the Coco River (Román 1983: 118); in April 1932 Miskitu from the downriver communities of Kisalaya and Saklin overran a local National Guard post in vengeance for the murder of Cockburn. For an extensive discussion of the Cockburn case, see Wunderich (1989).

55. Sandinista forces staged a major attack against the Standard Fruit Company near Puerto Cabezas in April 1931. Karnes reports that in the weeks preceding the attack, "business had been slack . . . and many of the workers had been laid off. Some of these had joined in the looting and burning" (1978: 133). Sandinista attacks themselves also contributed to the economic deterioration. For a general description of the dire economic conditions, see *Proceedings of the Society for the Propagation of the Gospel (Nicaragua-Honduras Annual Report)*, 1931: 75.

56. The best evidence of this long-term commitment is that after signing the truce, Sandino returned to the remote Río Coco region to continue his work (Román 1983: 105).

57. Station diaries from Sangsangta and Andris, 1928, Moravian Archives, Bethlehem, Pennsylvania.

58. Wunderich (1989) seems to avoid this dichotomy and to achieve the theoretical balance that I advocate. The paragraphs that follow rely heavily on his work.

59. Quoted in Jenkins Molieri (1986: 165). Perhaps more striking than the statement itself is the fact that a Sandinista intellectual would cite it approvingly 50 years later, at the height of the conflict with Miskitu Indians.

60. Wunderich (1989) makes this argument as well, though he backs it with only circumstantial evidence. In 1929, the Moravian church had no presence in the Bocay District or in the downriver communities of Saklin and Kisalaya, all of which became centers of Sandinista support. See *Periodical Accounts* (June 1930): 402.

61. An eloquent example of such an account comes from Mauro Salazar, recorded in Chapter 3. For similar memories from the Río Coco, see Helms (1971: 113).

62. She uses this terminology most explicitly in a recent article (1989), but it is consistent with the content of her earlier monograph (1971) and is almost surely drawn from field research conducted during the 1960's.

Chapter 3

1. This claim faces a possible challenge, related to the fact that I recorded the oral histories not at the height of the mobilization but during the peace process. Had people's views of the past not already begun to undergo another set of important revisions as they participated in the return to peace? I do think that Miskitu people's consciousness changed in important ways over the course of those three years, as my analysis in Chapter 7 indicates. Yet these changes occurred gradually, were still incipient by 1987, and did not affect most of the fundamental premises that led Miskitu people to mobilize. Thus I assume that how people

answered these particular questions at the height of the war in 1983–84 would not have differed enormously from the way they answered when I posed them in 1985 through 1987.

2. Salazar spoke for 90 minutes in an almost uninterrupted monologue, prompted by my initial questions about the distant past. I interrupted infrequently because my command of Miskitu was not sufficient to catch all the subtleties of his story. This had the disadvantage of leaving certain ambiguities (difficult to clarify after the fact) and the advantage of yielding an account less encumbered by my own research agenda.

3. I conducted the interviews either in Bluefields, taking advantage of community members' occasional trips to town, or in Sandy Bay. With one exception (explained in note 5) we spoke solely in Miskitu, but for a variety of reasons, I did not always record the interviews on tape. People's reflections on history at times arose from informal discussions, and other times I sensed that a tape recorder might be inhibiting. Thus there are two distinct sources for these quotations: verbatim renditions of taped interviews, which I then translated into English, and reconstructions based on my notes, which generally combined English (for efficiency) and Miskitu (to capture key phrases verbatim). Occasionally I present excerpts in Miskitu to add something that I fear may have been lost in my translation.

4. The two other Sandy Bay signatories are referred to simply as "delegates," which suggests that Teodore had a position of greater authority.

5. This interview was taped in Bluefields in July 1985. Rodriguez spoke in fluent Creole English, of which he has a much better command than most Sandy Bay inhabitants.

6. All place names appear on either Map 2 or Map 3.

7. Memories of this "promise" could be a reformulated interpretation of clause IIIa of the Harrison-Altamirano Treaty of 1905. It states: "The government will propose to the National Assembly a law that will exempt, for a period of fifty years . . . all the Mosquito Indians . . . born before 1894, from military service and direct taxes on their person, goods, properties, animals and means of subsistence."

8. The term commonly used in discussions of the topic is borrowed from the English and transliterated into Miskitu as *idan*.

9. In most accounts I found people to be ambiguous about the chronological relationship between the Reincorporation and the granting of community land titles. I suspect that the Reincorporation has always been a pivotal event in Miskitu collective memories but that the notion of an expansive territory that belongs to a "Miskitu nation" emerged from the contemporary mobilization (see Chapter 5 and Hale 1991c).

10. The Rodriguez family's exclusive control of the síndico position has not gone uncontested. According to David Lora, a major dispute broke out in the community each time the title of síndico changed hands.

11. For more on ALPROMISU, see Chapter 5.

12. The speaker is from the nearby community of Río Grande Bar. He spoke in Creole English, though he is of Miskitu descendence. Militia members from all the Río Grande communities were part of the same pelatón.

13. There is a striking historical parallel here with the process in 1915 by which Indian and Creole communities acquired land titles. The British consul collected funds from each adult community member to cover the costs incurred in the surveying of lands (see Chapter 2). No one from Sandy Bay noted the parallel.

14. These interviews are the primary source of data on which this section is based. A full explanation of interview methods can be found in Appendix B.

15. Of 26 who responded, all made some reference to racism against Miskitu in Somoza times. Ten (37 percent) indicated that the problem diminished after 1979, and the remainder claimed that it persisted unchanged.

16. A common response to my analysis among Sandinista intellectuals was to argue that Anglo affinity was so deeply embedded in Miskitu identity that it was analytically and historically inextricable from their ethnic demands. Mary Helms (1989: 8) has made a similar argument, stating that Anglo affinity forms part of Miskitu people's "traditional cosmographical structure." Paradoxically, though Helms is sharply critical of the Sandinistas, both arguments informed the same rather pessimistic conclusion. If Anglo affinity were inherent to Miskitu people's worldview, then the idea of granting them autonomy while a war with the United States was under way would have been dangerous indeed.

17. Their "affinity" is with important elements of the ideology that dominant North American institutions espouse. It includes, but is by no means limited to, feelings of closeness with North Americans.

18. One response cited above contains this implication. For another pre-1979 example, see Helms (1971: 224). The dissenters will receive consideration in Chapter 6.

19. I also use insights from these data to explain the previous moment in Miskitu collective action—their relative quiescence during the Somoza regime— though with greater caution. Although the same basic antinomy did exist during that time, it clearly had a very different content and political meaning. Using scattered evidence from anthropological studies carried out during the 1970's and other sources, I attempt to situate the antinomy in its proper historical context before embarking on the analysis. See Chapter 5.

Chapter 4

1. The latter idea was captured nicely by a Ministry of Culture campaign in response to the U.S. government wheat embargo of early 1981. "Maíz es nuestra raíz" was the campaign's slogan—"Corn is our roots." By promoting the traditional Indian food, the ministry sought to heighten Nicaraguans' awareness of the Indian roots of national identity and their defiance of the United States. A more detailed summary of the development of Cardenal's ideas can be found in Field (1987). See also a collection of Cardenal's writings and speeches published by the Ministry of Culture (1982).

2. The Miskitu, who in previous centuries were what Wheelock calls "something akin to a nation" (1974: 46), drop out of the narrative later on, apart from one reference to their exploitation by North American companies (p. 66).

3. For a detailed analysis of how this political message is entwined within the poems of *Homage*, see Borgeson (1984: esp. 65, 173).

4. For a comparative analysis of indigenista programs in Latin America, see Barre (1983). The premises of Mexican indigenismo in its initial stage are spelled out nicely in Brading (1988) and Hewitt de Alcantara (1984).

5. It is indicative of this problem that Cardenal's eulogies of American Indian civilization in general contrast sharply with his specific treatment of the Miskitu. His poem "Mosquito Kingdom," for example, is a scathing satire of the Miskitu monarch, portraying him as a drunk, simpleton, and puppet of the British. Whether or not these characterizations have any historical basis, it is interesting that the notion of a separate, surviving Miskitu identity did not capture Cardenal's imagination. This poem appears in a collection titled *Zero Hour* (New York: New Directions Books, 1980).

6. I have not discovered why the edition was discontinued early in 1980. One FSLN member told me that the reasons included financial constraints and the recognition that its impact on Miskitu people was minimal.

7. Quoted in *Barricada*, September 2, 1979, reprinted in Ohland and Schneider (1983: 360).

8. *Poder Sandinista*, December 1979, reprinted in Ohland and Schneider (1983: 46).

9. All this information, the article indicates, came from the "eyewitness" account of a Miskitu man named Mauricio Martínez Cornejo. From the FSLN periodical *Patria Libre*, reprinted in Ohland and Schneider 1983: 95–105.

10. *Nuevo Diario*, February 9, 1982.

11. From an interview with Mario Espinoza, published in *Barricada*, September 2, 1981, under the heading "The Coast in the National Unity."

12. *Barricada*, September 4, 1981. The Declaration of Principles addresses the crucial question of organization with a statement that must have been intentionally ambiguous: "The Sandinista Popular Revolution will support the forms of organization that emerge in the [Coast] communities, through which they will achieve their necessary representation in the social, economic, and political entities of the Atlantic Coast."

13. For example, Fagoth spoke over the contra radio station "15 de septiembre" during this period, calling the Miskitu to arms against the Nicaraguan government.

14. Paper prepared for the U.N. Conference on Racial Discrimination, Managua, Nicaragua, December 14–22, 1981.

15. From a speech to Latin American intellectuals, given in Managua, March 7, 1982, reprinted in Ohland and Schneider (1983: 268).

16. De Cara al Pueblo, a political practice initiated by the revolutionary government, was an open meeting at which government authorities fielded questions from an assembled group of listeners. Internacionalistas is a term applied to foreigners who live and work in Nicaragua and generally support the revolutionary

government. The passage is a reconstruction from my notes, verbatim only where indicated by quotation marks.

17. When I visited Bluefields in August–September 1983, Kukra Hill was the northern periphery of what could be considered relatively safe terrain (see Map 2). Beyond there were a few well-armed communities of Sandinista supporters (e.g., Orinoco) amid a vast, undifferentiated war zone. To gain information about these outer reaches one chose between terse, sketchy government reports and personal accounts, often indirect and heavily embellished with hearsay.

18. Much of this criticism, of course, was blatantly hypocritical. The crowning acts of hypocrisy came in 1982, when Jeanne Kirkpatrick, then U.S. representative to the United Nations, accused the government of placing 250,000 Miskitu (three times the total population) into "concentration camps," and when Alexander Haig brandished a photograph depicting what he claimed were charred bodies of Miskitu, massacred by the Sandinistas. It was later determined that the photograph dated back to Somoza times. For a brief period in 1982, "Miskitu Indians" became a household word in the United States, conjuring up harrowing images of repression by a totalitarian state.

19. This assertion appeared in *Tasba Pri*, a publication of INNICA (1982: 12), the government entity charged with administration of Coast policy. It later became known that this statement was erroneous and that the evacuation had been an entirely military decision. Nevertheless, the assertion of prior planning is a telling indication of the developmentalist premises that reigned in the initial months of the effort.

20. This analysis draws on the evidence presented by Richard Adams, who was present at the congress and concludes that the government was confused and "far from clear about the issue of ethnic identity" (1981a: 55). Although there surely was a good measure of confusion, there is also a sense in which Ortega's actions followed logically from the premises of his (and the FSLN's) standpoint at the time.

21. See reprinted copy of the "Plan" (which I am convinced is authentic) in Ohland and Schneider (1983: 89).

22. From a speech by Ray Hooker, FSLN representative to the National Assembly from the southern region, Bluefields, May 1985. Although these ideas were not specifically proscribed prior to autonomy, such a speech could not have occurred between 1982 and 1984 except in the context of strong opposition to the government.

23. The three intellectuals were Manuel Ortega, Orlando Nuñez Soto, and Galio Gurdian López. The two Coast leaders were Ray Hooker and Hazel Law.

24. The tropa had recently announced a new policy that permitted bush people to enter the community as civilians. Many times during that first month, townspeople would tell me, "They were here last night," to collect food, see family, or just pass time.

25. Early in 1986, an FSLN-designated zonal representative (called a *secretario político*, or political secretary) formally assumed state authority throughout the five communities. But the secretarios made only sporadic visits to Sandy Bay, staying a few hours, long enough for a meeting with community members and a

brief discussion with the tropa. In the interim periods, which varied in length from a few days to months, tropa officials continued to exert state authority on a daily basis in Sandy Bay. For more details, see Chapter 7.

26. For example, they asked repeatedly about the relations they assumed I was having with Miskitu women, joked about unfaithful wives and girlfriends back home, and drilled me on details of U.S. society, for which they expressed a combination of disdain and fascination.

27. During the second half of 1987 the tropa consisted of a contingent made up entirely of volunteers from the Coast, primarily Bluefields. This experiment—unique in the entire period of military presence—lasted only a few months and evoked conflicting retrospective assessments from Sandy Bay community members. I was not in the community during that period and cannot offer my own observations.

28. A common way of explaining why Miskitu people didn't understand or support the revolution was to attribute to them a *bajo nivel cultural* (low cultural level). Although in this context (and I believe more broadly in Latin America) "cultural" is essentially synonymous with "educational," I assign deeper significance to the merging of these two terms. It evokes a single standard to which all members of the society must conform in order to progress, become more civilized, and so on.

29. Transcription of tape-recorded speech, CIDCA-Managua Archives.

30. From an interview with *Barricada Internacional*, special *Archivo* section, printed in October 1985.

31. I was present at the speech and took notes to this effect. The passage was later quoted in the *New York Times*, April 26, 1985.

32. Transcription of tape-recorded speech, CIDCA-Managua Archives.

33. Speech delivered at the closing ceremony of the Multi-Ethnic Assembly, Puerto Cabezas, April 1987, CIDCA-Managua Archives.

34. This point is ambiguous. Although it does not specify which entities constitute the regional administration, it is likely that major ministries (e.g., agriculture) and economic concerns (e.g., the Institute for Fishing, INPECSA) are excluded.

35. For example, decisions regarding the exploitation of natural resources were to be made "by agreement" between the regional and central government (Art. 9); the autonomous Regional Council was to have a series of functions, including "to participate in the formulating, planning and implementation of social, economic and cultural programs and policies affecting or pertaining to the Region" (Art. 23, sec. 3).

36. Article 31 establishes that the president of the republic could appoint a representative who is different from the coordinator of the regional autonomous government; there is no indication of how these two persons would share power in what would have to be overlapping spheres of authority.

Chapter 5

1. For example, on October 6, 1979, the FSLN newspaper *Barricada* published a statement by Miskitu leaders, which included complaints about the FSLN com-

mander assigned to the Northeast. The commander allegedly had publicly declared: "The coast people shed no blood [in the revolutionary struggle] so what right do they have to demand solutions to their problems now?" See also the words of FSLN cadres recorded in Chapter 4.

2. Between 1960 and 1965, Nicaraguan Gross Domestic Production grew at an average annual rate of 10 percent, almost twice that of the other Central American economies. It maintained a rate of 4 percent growth through the mid-1970's. Nevertheless, at the end of this period one-half the population earned a monthly income of less than U.S. $25 (Vilas 1986: 93–95). See also Booth (1982: 71–95).

3. In the Rigoberto Cabezas project of Nueva Guinea, for example, before project participants were transported to the zone, spontaneous migrants already occupied much of the land where colonization was to take place (Taylor 1968: 3).

4. The Moravians report the closing of most of their day schools to avoid competition with government schools established in the same locations (*Periodical Accounts*, no. 173 [1965]: 21).

5. Vilas (1989: 79) reports that 47 (72 percent) of the 65 concessions related to exploitation of Coast resources between 1950 and 1979 went to "the Somoza family, close family friends, and high officials of the National Guard."

6. Banco Central de Nicaragua, *Indicadores Económicos* 4 (June 1978): 78–79. These statistics are not broken down to distinguish between Atlantic Coast and Pacific Coast production. At the beginning of the 1970's, roughly two-thirds of this production was on the Atlantic, and the proportion increased thereafter as lobster (an exclusively Atlantic Coast product) gained importance.

7. The Miskitu have a strong tradition of organizing collective work parties, known as *pana pana*, to get through periods of peak labor demand (such as the rice harvest). In my observation, however, pana pana functions well only when plot sizes of participants are roughly equal. The individual farmer who expands production with the intention of selling the surplus is expected to pay for the labor he or she receives. Helms confirms this point for the prerevolutionary period (1971: 130–31).

8. Moravian missionaries expressed particular concern over this practice. The *Periodical Accounts* of the mission report in 1963: "In many places there was no market for the rice crop. . . . And in some villages the merchants agreed to take rice in exchange for goods, but would give no money. Thus the people had nothing to give to the church" (no. 171: 16).

9. The ethnic identity of merchants was complex and at times ambivalent. In addition to Mestizos from the Pacific, some merchants were of Chinese ancestry. The Chinese could be considered a separate ethnic group, though close to and gradually assimilating toward Mestizo. Finally, a still smaller number of merchants were Creoles and Miskitu.

10. In a footnote, Nietschmann refers to the rise of lobster production in the past tense, stating that "by the early 1970s the local [Corn Island] lobster grounds were fished out" (1979b: 16, n. 14). Yet during the 1970's, lobster exports increased at a staggering rate: from 310,000 pounds in 1971, to 3,069,000 pounds in 1977 (Banco Central de Nicaragua *Indicadores Económicos* 4 (June 1978):

78. Although the bulk of this fishing was done by industrial boats owned by Somoza and the North Americans, native fishermen from Bluefields, Pearl Lagoon, Tasbapauni, Río Grande, and especially Corn Island also participated in the lobster boom.

11. This information is from interviews with informants who knew the community well in 1979 and 1980. The most successful Tasbapauni lobster fisherman owned two boats. He and at least one other Tasbapauni family used money earned in the community to buy a second home in Bluefields.

12. Dorothy Cattle (1977) reports that in Sandy Bay Sirpi in 1972–73, one household had 20 head of cattle, while the other 29 households had a total of 32. Coconut tree holdings were distributed in a similarly disproportionate manner.

13. Bourgois and Grunberg (1980) counted eighteen cattle fincas, a term they use to indicate large (but unspecified) holdings; another source (MIDINRA 1985) reports five fincas with over 300 head.

14. These observations come from Philip Dennis's field notes, excerpts from which he generously made available to me.

15. In light of this analytical blind spot, Nietschmann's data on migration from Tasbapauni also call for reinterpretation. Between 1972 and 1975, fully one-quarter of the community's residents were absent for some period, a response he attributes to the "decline of security livelihood" (1979b: 21). This assertion presents a striking contrast to Mary Helms's (1971) analysis of Asang, where people felt poor because they had to stay home. Nietschmann's data show that these migrants were "mostly single" and that two-thirds of them found jobs within the coastal region, a day's trip from home. This leads me to interpret the migration pattern as an indication of regional economic dynamism to which people would have responded regardless of the status of their subsistence security. Many of the migrants are likely to have been unmarried youths seeking adventure and quick cash before settling down to raise families. They wanted and needed cash.

16. Because ethnic identity in Tasbapauni is transitional and ambiguous, any assertion along these lines is bound to be debatable. The numerous Tasbapauni residents I interviewed on this question offered varying characterizations of the community members' current ethnic identity, but they all concurred in the general direction of ethnic change from Miskitu to Creole. If we accept the veracity of Nietschmann's observations in the 1970's, Creole identity has increased remarkably since then. The great majority of Tasbapauni youth today cannot speak Miskitu, and they actively assert boundaries between themselves and Indians in surrounding communities like Sandy Bay.

17. See Smutko (1975: 78). AIFLD funds were channeled through INFONAC, according to a report by ACARIC's president, Rafael Dixon, called "The History of ACARIC" (CIDCA-Managua Archives).

18. Smutko lays out the details of this program in an edited collection called *Pastoral indígena* (1975: 21–30). Between 1967 and 1970, he reports, the team of missionaries trained 120 Miskitu delegates of the word who gathered for bimonthly meetings.

19. One could become an ordained Moravian minister with a sixth grade edu-

cation. Wilson (1975: 341) estimated that by the mid-1970's almost 90 percent of "pastors" (which I assume means lay and ordained) had no more than this minimal level.

20. This information comes from an interview with Reverend Norman Bent, a leading member of the "progressive" group, which I conducted in July 1988 with Edmund T. Gordon. There has been no published explanation for the North Americans' precipitous departure. Bent speculates that two factors were involved: rumors of an imminent Sandinista victory and the distasteful prospect of working as subordinates to native church leaders.

21. Colomer made this claim during an 1987 interview in Managua.

22. Wilson (1975: 321) estimates from 1974 data that church members were 79 percent indigenous (including 9 percent Sumu and Rama) and 21 percent Creole.

23. Dennis (1981b: 278) notes this resentment, as did many Miskitu leaders whom I interviewed. Bishop John Wilson expresses concern about the problem in his 1975 thesis: "There is a great discrepancy between the educational level of Creoles and Indians . . . this is largely a result of the fact that the missionaries assigned much greater importance to the preparation of Creoles" (1975: 321).

24. Because the synod elects its leaders democratically and Miskitu were in the majority, Miskitu delegates could have voted the Creoles out as they did in 1980. Perhaps Miskitu delegates felt restrained in 1974 and 1977 because Creoles were better educated and were the North Americans' handpicked successors.

25. Hazel Law, interview with the author, June 1982. Such acts and the general ire of regional Mestizo elite are also documented in Keegan to CRS, August 1974, CIDCA-Managua Archives.

26. Transcription from a taped interview in Miskitu by the author with Spark, conducted in Limon, Costa Rica, December 1987. I consider her account especially valuable because she left Nicaragua soon after the Sandinistas came to power and was not active in politics in the intervening years. Her views of ALPROMISU are therefore likely to reflect more of what she thought at the time, less influenced by the tumultuous events that followed.

27. Pawanka (noun) or *pawaia* (verb) translates roughly as to grow or develop. I retain the Miskitu term to avoid the connotations associated with the English term, meaning linear progress toward externally defined norms. Whether or not the speaker adopts these norms is debatable (I believe she does in some contexts, not in others). Retaining the Miskitu conveys this ambiguity. Pawanka can be contrasted with the more militant "Indianist" term of *Miskitu ai raitka nani* (Miskitu rights) commonly heard among Miskitu who stayed in Nicaragua and became involved with MISURASATA.

28. Philip Dennis (personal communication). His observations were made in 1978.

29. This is not to assert that national security played an insignificant role previously. Reagan had been elected in November 1980 with an aggressively anti-Sandinista platform, and Carter administration policy had become increasingly hostile. From the outset, FSLN leaders expressed concern about a possible alliance of Coast people with the U.S. or Somocista forces.

30. For example, the state nationalized the mines in November 1979 in response to flagrant decapitalization by the North American owners (CIERA 1981). The Nicaraguan government appears not to have objected to U.S. investment in general, given that the Standard Fruit Company continued to produce bananas in western Nicaragua until 1984. But no such arrangements persisted on the Coast.

31. According to Edmund T. Gordon (personal communication), the fishing companies' resurgence was due mainly to increases in artisanal fishing, rather than industrial production. This conclusion coincides with my data from the Río Grande, where a boom in artisanal lobster fishing occurred in the post-1979 period, allowing one family (whose members owned four boats) to make a small fortune.

32. A similar division between Mestizo and Creole managers and Miskitu workers probably prevailed in northern state-owned enterprises, but our data were collected only in the south.

33. Throughout this section I rely heavily on the observations of Philippe Bourgois, who conducted fieldwork in the Northeast from December 1979 to August 1980. I am indebted to Bourgois for providing me access to his extensive unpublished field notes from this period. They are cited hereafter as Bourgois (n.d.).

34. On a national level, the number of credit recipients increased from 28,000 to 101,000 between 1977 and 1980. In the same period, the number of manzanas (1 manzana = 0.7 hectares) financed rose from 88,000 to 427,000. The recuperation rate for the first round of credit under the revolutionary government was 26 percent (Enriquez and Spalding 1987: 117). Although specific data for the Atlantic Coast are unavailable, experiences there appear to have been similar. Given the dismal recuperation rate, the National Development Bank was forced to write off this first round of loans and subsequently to insist on more stringent criteria.

35. The ATC was not a state entity but, rather, a mass-based organization strongly supportive of the revolution. Especially in these early days, the distinction between state, party, and mass organization on the Coast was hazy to nonexistent.

36. This is not a postrevolutionary phenomenon; Helms observed the same pattern in Asang in 1964–65 (1971: 130–31).

37. Bourgois (n.d.) provides several examples. Although MISURASATA leaders bitterly denounced these Mestizos as "Somocistas turned Sandinistas overnight" (e.g., in their interview with Richard Adams in 1979, CIDCA-Managua Archives), it seems unlikely that many high-level Somoza associates remained politically active long after July 1979. Most middle-class families living on the Coast during the Somoza era (MISURASATA leaders included) probably had some connection with the government, which could be conjured up if necessary. I interpret such denunciations as tactics in a power struggle rather than merely as righteous attempts to ferret out Somocistas. The government used the same tactics on occasion.

38. Bourgois observed, for example, that "government functionaries are completely dependent on the privileged classes in the area for food, lodging and transport . . . dependent bonds are created that ingratiate the government functionary

with the local exploiting elite" (n.d.). This same problem led to denunciations by the Miskitu organization MISURASATA (see, e.g., MacDonald 1988: 123).

39. A group of Miskitu and Creoles did take active part in the insurrection, the most prominent among them being guerrilla commander Lumberto Campbell. These cadres generally had lived in western Nicaragua before joining the FSLN and remained fighting in the west until the victory. For biographies of Coast people who died in the revolutionary struggle, see Smutko (1980).

40. Unpublished interview with Brooklyn Rivera, by Philippe Bourgois, in San José, Costa Rica, 1984.

41. Interview with Peter Martinez, by Edmund T. Gordon and the author, Bluefields, 1986.

42. I give an extremely cursory review of key events during this period because they have been described so many times before. I doubt that new insights regarding high-level political machinations will be possible until additional evidence comes to light. For chronologies and descriptive analyses of the first eighteen months, from varying perspectives, see CIDCA (1986), Hale (1987), MacDonald (1988), Jenkins (1986), Vilas (1989), Adams (1981a), Bourgois (1985), and Dunbar Ortiz (1986).

43. Adams (1981a) notes the presence of these two seemingly contradictory messages. Analysis of this dual position, focusing on the underlying premises of the FSLN view of the ethnic question, can be found in Chapter 4.

44. Internal government documents written at the time noted this ambiguity, as did the report of one outside observer (Adams 1981a). It also has become a common retrospective self-criticism of Sandinista cadres.

45. Creoles were horrified by this Miskitu "takeover," for reasons that combined a general sense of their own superiority and specific concerns over its strong political overtones. Reverend Norman Bent claims that Miskitu pastors were preaching "liberation theology," though calling it by a different name. Although the Miskitu did not generally identify with the revolution, MISURASATA was still formally part of the revolutionary alliance. In contrast, influence of the "progressive" Moravian pastors notwithstanding, Creoles by this time already had turned oppositional. For a chronology of early Creole relations with the revolutionary government, see Edmund T. Gordon (1987).

46. Interviews with both brigadistas and students from the Sandy Bay area and elsewhere reveal unequivocally that education included promoting an awareness of Miskitu rights. Such goals ran parallel to those employed by brigadistas in western Nicaragua (known in Spanish by the term *concientización*) except that the political thrust of the education was different. Here and elsewhere, the parallels between the FSLN's and MISURASATA's organizing strategies is striking.

47. For a detailed analysis of this land question in relation to the broader process of ethnic conflict, see Hale (1991c).

48. A Freedom of Information Act inquiry to the CIA yielded very few documents dated before February 1981 and reams afterward that follow the escalating ethnic conflict in minute detail with undisguised satisfaction. But information from before 1981 would have been unlikely to be released because operations at

that time were more secret. The CIA declassified just enough to tantalize students of Nicaraguan ethnic politics. For example, one of the few released pre-1981 documents is a CIA intelligence report dated December 19, 1980, titled "Atlantic Coast Separatism," which describes the Miskitu as a "source of resistance to the Sandinistas." The following two (presumably crucial) paragraphs are blacked out by CIA censors. I am indebted to David Stoll for making these materials available to me.

49. Hazel Law, former MISURASATA leader, personal communication.

50. The possibility of CIA "penetration" often arises in regard to Steadman Fagoth, the most vociferous opponent of the government and by far the most influential leader among Miskitu townspeople. It is now broadly confirmed that Fagoth worked as an informer for the Somoza intelligence force, and it is widely alleged that he went on the CIA payroll soon after 1979. Regardless of how this question is resolved (and it will not be until the CIA documents are released), Fagoth's message resonated deeply among Miskitu townspeople who had no conceivable direct contact with CIA operatives.

51. Interview by the author with a former brigadista and former antigovernment combatant from that early period.

52. See the narrative from Sandy Bay presented in Chapter 3 for an example of this conclusion. Miskitu leaders from the Río Coco provided me with similar accounts.

53. Judging from the *Periodical Accounts* of the Moravian church, each time floods caused damage and loss in Miskitu communities—an almost yearly occurrence on the Atlantic Coast—donations from the United States helped the victims through until the next season. "We are grateful to friends in the United States who responded to our appeal for help and who supplied funds with which we were able to buy food to feed these hungry people," one report states. "This help," it continues, "strengthened the faith of our people and made them more appreciative and understanding in regard to our world wide Moravian Church" (1966, no. 174: 16). An important aspect of that "understanding," I suggest, was a pervasive awe of white people's wealth and eternal gratitude for their benevolence.

54. I heard such prefatory remarks more than once during church services in the Río Grande area, and I assume they were not the exception.

Chapter 6

1. Duran's case raises the intriguing possibility that the more well-off Miskitu community members were among the first, and most ardent, supporters of the incipient mobilization. Although there is some additional evidence for this hypothesis in Sandy Bay, it is far from conclusive. In any case, confirmation would require a systematic examination of communities throughout the coast.

2. Brooklyn Rivera, the MISURASATA leader, joined the governing board of ARDE in early 1983. He was entitled to a portion of the CIA funds and supplies that ARDE received at that time.

3. Of those 55, by the beginning of 1985, 11 had died, 17 had left the struggle to live outside Nicaragua (mostly Costa Rica), and the rest were still in the bush. Only after 1985 did these remaining 27 gradually began to return to the community. For more details, see Chapter 7.

4. She uses the term partly in jest and partly to emphasize her dissent from the majority in Sandy Bay. But outside the particular context of Miskitu politics in Sandy Bay, supporters of the revolution would never refer to the government as "Communist."

5. The cases of MISURASATA combatants' abuse is only one example. I also heard stories of young men not inclined to enter the bush, who succumbed to the urging of others in their peer group.

6. I received confirmation of this point from a former combatant, one of the 3,000 youths who fled, during lengthy discussions in Costa Rica in December 1987.

7. These comments came at a different phase in the war (1986–87), when bush people in the Sandy Bay area were reportedly hooked directly into the CIA supply line from Honduras. Yet the contrast must have been even greater in 1983, when the Masaya militiamen were stationed in Sandy Bay and the bush people began receiving shipments from Costa Rica via ARDE.

8. During two weeks in Costa Rica in 1987, I interviewed former MISURASATA combatants who expressed great bitterness that Brooklyn Rivera and other leaders had received ample resources from the United States and allegedly had put them to personal use.

9. In particular, they objected to the CIA's efforts to place the Miskitu combatants under the command of the Spanish-speaking contra organization and to postpone any discussion of autonomy until "after the victory." Anaya (1987), an adviser to MISURASATA, gives a graphic account of these internal politics. After conducting his research, Anaya, by his account, "met with U.S. government officials in Washington D.C. to report on my observations and to urge corrective action" (p. 2). These recommendations must have been gratefully received by the Reagan administration for Anaya's report leaves the distinct impression that, with a little less racism and ineptitude, the CIA could have prevented Miskitu disaffection and thereby advanced efforts to overthrow the Nicaraguan government.

10. Testimony from Robert Owen during the Iran-contra hearings confirms that Rivera received funds during his negotiations with the Nicaraguan government. These funds were clearly given with the intention of undermining the initial progress toward a settlement. See U.S. Congress (1987: 338–45).

11. Critics of the Nicaraguan government often describe state penetration as synonymous with the militarization of the Atlantic Coast. My evidence from Sandy Bay suggests that, though both factors are important contributing causes of the mobilization, equating the two is historically inaccurate.

12. Hazel Law, one of the original MISURASATA leaders, confirmed this in a 1982 interview.

13. From an interview with Philippe Bourgois, San José, Costa Rica (1984).

14. Rivera may well have exaggerated the case somewhat to justify his own

departure, but Hazel Law (1982), who chose not to leave, provides essentially the same account.

15. See, for example, Hale (1987) and Vilas (1989).

16. The notion of community rights implies the existence of an area between communities that belongs to the state, whereas according to the conception of territorial rights the entire area belongs to the Miskitu.

17. Leaders are defined as those who, between 1979 and 1987, held one of the following positions in the community: síndico (village headman), elected representative, pastor, lay pastor, teacher.

18. She met with them numerous times on behalf of the Autonomy Commission to discuss different versions of the autonomy proposal. In the autonomy workshop described in Chapter 7, she served as the discussion coordinator for the Río Grande delegates.

19. The percentages do not add up to 100 because "medium" responses are omitted. For more information on the interview methodology, see Appendix B.

20. Miskitu people are a phenotypic combination of African and Indian. When a Miskitu denigrates blackness, he or she is engaging in self-denigration.

21. I pursue this distinction and the implications for the land question further in a separate article (Hale 1991c). Essentially, I argue that before the post-1979 mobilization, Miskitu collective memories focused on political control rather than territorial rights. Currently, their notion of land rights is polysemic, combining an adherence to the previous notion of community lands with the more extensive territorial demands that came later.

22. A more difficult question is whether the leaders themselves spoke in these inflammatory terms. Law (1982) claims that soon after 1979 Fagoth began warning Miskitu community members about the imminent threat of "Communism." The others, including Law herself, probably took a more passive approach of merely omitting the United States altogether from their discourse.

23. Although Rivera's statements express his anguish over the discrepancies between his own position and the people's demands, he reports his resolution of the problem with greater self-confidence: "In the last analysis, I had to be on the side of the people." Hazel Law, who made the opposite decision to stay inside Nicaragua and work for her people through civic means, gives Rivera's solution a different gloss: "He was indecisive, without a political will of his own."

24. Manuel Rodriguez's statement in the epigraph to this chapter sums up the effect succinctly. Although he attributes the change to schools, which could not have made such an impact in two short years, the thrust of his perception coincides closely with my own argument.

25. The reader who shares the Miskitu belief that the Americans genuinely supported Miskitu rights need only examine subsequent U.S. policy to be convinced otherwise. By late 1985, the United States had made further military aid to the Miskitu contingent on their joining the Spanish-speaking contra organization the FDN. CIA operatives insisted that Miskitu contras abandon their concerns for ethnic rights and autonomy until after the Sandinista government had been overthrown. See Anaya (1987) and further discussion of this issue in Chapter 7.

26. The convergence is no coincidence. Analysts associated with this second position purport to convey the perspective of Miskitu exile leaders who oppose the Nicaraguan government. They are less forthcoming about their own substantial influence, as advisers, in shaping the analysis of these leaders. See, for example, the work of MacDonald (1988) and Nietschmann (1987 and, especially, 1989).

Chapter 7

1. Peter Ford, "Managua Gives Autonomy to East Coast—Hotbed of Dissent," *Christian Science Monitor*, April 27, 1987. The article quotes Borge in a slightly attenuated form: "If this is not democracy, what is?" Ford's original story also contained a more balanced selection of quotations from his interview with me, including my statement, based on observations in Sandy Bay, that the delegates to the assembly had been elected freely and democratically. The Washington editor eliminated those parts, which left me portrayed as an unrelenting skeptic.

2. Although I refer to them as officers (a translation of their own term, *oficial*), they were not professional soldiers. There were three men and one woman. Esteban Mora, a fiery and charismatic orator, held a top position in the national office of the Sandinista Workers' Syndicate. Mario Contrera, a lawyer, worked for the Ministry of Justice. Javier Chamorro was assistant dean at the National University. Elsa Duran developed school curricula for the Ministry of Education. She and her husband took turns in voluntary military duty; this time she had left him "in the rear guard" to mind their two children.

3. This role was especially evident during the days after the killing of Mildred Gomez, described in the Introduction.

4. By 1986, the FSLN had assigned a *secretario político* to the zone, resuming a policy that had been discontinued with the death of Tomás Hammond in May 1985. Two *secretarios* served during the period under question, both Creoles from Bluefields. Although their presence generally contributed to reconciliation between the state and Miskitu communities, relations were far from tension-free. Moreover, they made frequent and prolonged trips to Bluefields and, while in the zone, lived mainly in Karawala and made occasional visits to Sandy Bay. During the long interludes between these visits, *tropa* officers served as the de facto representatives of the state and party.

5. Examples of the first position include Vilas (1989) and Freeland (1988); the second is put forth by Anaya (1987), Nietschmann (1989), and others who have denounced the United States for depriving Miskitu combatants of adequate funding and thereby forcing them to negotiate with the Sandinistas.

6. In an internal work plan written in late 1986, for example, Sandinista cadres were exhorted to "continue perfecting the political organization of the FSLN, so as to more effectively confront the aggression and to achieve Sandinista hegemony." They also frequently used the term in informal or private political discussions. In public forums, however, they generally gave the term a negative inflection, as in references to "U.S. hegemony."

7. See for example, Brooklyn Rivera to Clem Chartier (president of the World Council of Indigenous Peoples), December 5, 1985, CIDCA-Managua Archives.

He refers disparagingly to Miskitu who support the Sandinistas as native stooges (*adictos elementos nativos*) and accuses the Sandinistas of "attempting to confuse [*enredar*] a few naive brother Indians and manipulate them into collaborating with the plan of disguised ethnocide [*etnocidio soplado*]."

8. For example, during the month of October 1985, tropa officers tried on a number of occasions to organize "workshops" and even informal discussions on the nascent autonomy process. People politely declined to attend, explaining that they had not received permission to do so from the bush people.

9. This information came from the Bluefields regional committee of the FSLN, whose members occasionally briefed CIDCA researchers on current events.

10. There was, of course, a "second track" that focused on "low-intensity" warfare rather than outright military victory. Ultimately more insidious and effective, this track involved greater emphasis on political-ideological struggle. The shift occurred, however, only after it became clear that military victory was impossible. For a useful analysis of these issues, see Klare and Kornbluh (1988).

11. See, for example, confidential memorandums to this effect cited by Sklar (1988: 274), in reference to MISURA, the other main Miskitu contra organization. Anaya (1987) portrays MISURASATA as being under similar pressures. For further information on the array of Coast organizations that opposed the revolution, see Appendix D.

12. See the interview with Uriel Vanegas in *Envio*. This also was confirmed in my interviews with Reynaldo Reyes (1988), who concluded that "the CIA was just playing with us," and with Nolan Escobar (1987).

13. As early as January 1985, community leaders in Sandy Bay had formed a peace commission intended specifically to mediate between bush people and tropa in hopes of keeping them from fighting each other. Interviews with Vanegas, Reyes, and Escobar, cited in note 12, also confirm that pressures from below were a factor in their decisions to negotiate.

14. Sources on the negotiations from the MISURASATA perspective include Lernoux (1985), MacDonald (1988), and Nietschmann (1989). To learn of the Sandinista perspective, I read and took notes from the documents they prepared for the fourth round and discussed the results with Sandinistas who were in a position to know what happened.

15. In a press conference afterward, he described his reasons for commencing the foray: "I am very aware of the danger that Sandinista policies toward KISAN [i.e., negotiations] are reducing my room for maneuver" (Unpublished mimeograph, CIDCA-Managua Archives). Among those who accompanied him were Russell Means, the noted American Indian leader, and Clem Chartier, the president of the World Council of Indigenous Peoples (WCIP). Chartier's decision to accompany Rivera caused a major controversy within the WCIP, which ended in his removal from the presidency.

16. For example, the "Documento Guía" affirmed an unconditional commitment to the revolution's broader objectives and referred to "Miskitu suffering at the hands of the counterrevolutionary traitors, and of imperialist agents, who have a vested interest in keeping them outside the country" (Untitled document,

mimeographed, emitted by MISATAN shortly after the July 1984 founding assembly, CIDCA-Managua Archives).

17. Undated MISATAN document entitled *Pliego de Peticiones*, CIDCA-Managua Archives.

18. A well-placed FSLN cadre in the north explained the outcome with reference to the MISATAN leaders' "childish opportunism" (*oportunismo político y infantilismo*) as well as an "absence of political-ideological education on our part" ("Consideraciones acerca del caracter del sujeto social," unpublished document, CIDCA–Puerto Cabezas Archives). The MISATAN leaders, in various conversations, characterized the FSLN representatives as authoritarian and intransigent.

19. Townspeople evacuated from the Río Coco had begun to return and resettle their communities, restrictions on freedom of movement were lifted, jailing of suspected "contra supporters" largely ceased, and most political prisoners had been set free. Most of these measures occurred after the autonomy announcement of November 1984, although the change in policy toward prisoners began a full year earlier.

20. Although "KISAN por la paz" (as they become known) officially formed part of the Sandinista armed forces, in practice they exerted military control over the Yulu area and enjoyed more autonomy than this institutional affiliation implied. For further information on Miskitu armed organizations, see Appendix D.

21. News of the event traveled quickly to Sandy Bay, where it was reported to me that the bush people had "taken over" Puerto Cabezas.

22. Chicha is a corn-based alcoholic drink produced and sold in Sandy Bay.

23. Manuel Rodriguez, who normally would have performed this function, was away in Bluefields. Dan Peters was Rodriguez's "second."

24. To my knowledge, marijuana was not grown locally. Townspeople frequently found it in large sacks washed up on the beach, apparently the result of mishaps in the Caribbean drug trade. In the last few years, many teenagers and some adults had taken to smoking and to selling it in neighboring communities.

25. About half of the 31 community members questioned on their feelings about Manuel Rodriguez's leadership in March 1986 responded with negative comments, focusing on his abuse of power. A typical response in that category: "He's a crook and he tells the community lies. When the government gave a chain saw for the community, he kept it for himself. Too much goes to the Rodriguez family. They are dictators, just like Somoza."

26. These also are classic tensions that emerge in any situation in which *caciques* or "bigmen" tend to dominate in community leadership: the leader needs to accumulate wealth and power to be an effective advocate for his community; the only way to achieve that end is to develop a certain alignment with the state; state officials are often willing to oblige and even to encourage this relationship because it helps them to secure loyalty; the question of whose interests the leader ends up serving becomes fundamentally ambiguous.

27. This document, dated September 1985, is an early version of what later would develop into a full-fledged proposal for a peace treaty (MISURASATA 1987). The thirteen points touch on all important aspects of the treaty but are stated generically rather than in legal language.

28. For additional information on the circumstances of this prohibition, see Chapter 6.

29. Although I was not permitted to observe the July workshop in Pearl Lagoon, it appears to have followed a similar course. The "military question" provoked a long debate that brought out all the unresolved differences with the government, yet the plenary issued a concluding statement of unqualified support for the current wording of the autonomy proposal.

30. The English word "promise" has been transliterated into Miskitu and depending on the context can have either a derogatory or a merely descriptive connotation.

31. "Proyecto piloto para el avance de la autonomía," undated mimeograph distributed around September 1986, CIDCA-Bluefield Archives.

32. In the neighboring community of Kara, townspeople refused to vote for reasons that combined principle (opposition to autonomía) with the more mundane objection that the CRA had not provided a green sea turtle as promised. Although irritated by Kara's intransigence, CRA and Sandinista cadres decided to give the community a second chance to be included. FSLN secretary Brian Smith reportedly delivered a stern warning to Kara, not unlike the one he had given Sandy Bay the previous May: if there were no elections they would be excluded from the benefits of autonomía. Within a few days, Kara had elected its autonomy headman, and the five-member council of the "autonomous zonal government" was complete.

33. Zonal autonomy immediately took on an air of seriousness in Sandy Bay because the government recently had provided the community with a generator and electric wire. In his first task as autonomía headman, Reyes set out to distribute wire to each home and to ensure the electric plant's successful operation.

34. Townspeople's main complaints centered on the insufficient distribution of basic consumer goods, especially foodstuffs, and the galloping inflation. They did not produce enough surplus to benefit much from the inflated prices of goods they sold in the regional market.

35. He gave particular emphasis to the literacy campaign, which drew my attention to tropa members' age. They would have been high school students in 1980, among the thousands of Pacific Coast Mestizo youth whose commitment to the revolution was forged in the euphoria and mobilization of those early days.

36. *Etnicista* is sometimes translated with the awkward-sounding neologism "etnicist." I prefer to retain the Spanish term, defined as a political orientation that gives primacy to ethnic identity, solidarity, and struggle to the exclusion of alternative or complementary forms of political affinity.

37. For example, a young man from the family with whom I lived returned from Honduras, having attended the meeting in which U.S. operatives made Miskitu combatants' alliance with the Spanish-speaking contras a condition for continued military aid. The organization that emerged from this meeting—FAUCAN—was short-lived (see Appendix D).

38. For further analysis of these contrasts, with reference to the post-1990 political scene, see Hale (1991b).

Chapter 8

1. An eloquent example of how this conflict reverberated outside Central America can be found in the Native American and Left-oriented periodical *Akwesasne Notes* and in statements of the international arm of the American Indian Movement during the period in question. The Miskitu question split these entities down the middle, along lines that were and are fundamental to their identity, political vision, and strategy.

2. Petition to the U.S. Department of State in 1924, quoted in Wunderich, von Oertzen, and Rossbach (1990: 449).

3. Anyone who relies heavily on Miskitu oral history finds ample justification for this neglect because one effect of Anglo affinity has been to induce a collective amnesia in relation to the conflictive conditions of its emergence. Historical evidence supports the contrary conclusion. The Moravian missionary *Periodical Accounts*, for example, are filled with evidence of Miskitu resistance to conversion, especially in the early twentieth century.

4. This explanation, of course, does not stand alone. A series of related causal factors include the Somoza state's successful efforts to co-opt Indian leaders and a growing crisis of leadership within the Miskitu organization that operated during that period. My argument, rather, is that consideration of the role of Anglo affinity in Miskitu people's consciousness provides the necessary context for the other factors to be properly understood.

5. For example, unusual historical conditions provided the basis for Miskitu people's uncanny receptivity to outsiders (at least outsiders who are white, non-Spanish-speaking, and willing to adopt Miskitu ways, very broadly defined). More substantively, Nicaragua's Atlantic Coast certainly is unusual in the extent to which state and civil society developed as two largely separate, and to some extent opposed, spheres.

6. This is the problem with much of the work of the Miskitu before 1979. For example, Mary Helms has conducted extensive and excellent ethnohistorical research on the Miskitu, placing the emergence and consolidation of Miskitu identity in the context of colonial and postcolonial relations (e.g., 1971, 1983a). Yet there is an odd disjuncture between this attentiveness to macrostructural inequities and her community-level ethnographic analysis, firmly grounded in the premise of bounded cultural production. For details see Chapter 2.

7. Handler claims that anthropological writings about ethnic/national groups and ethnic/national discourse tend to be mutually reinforcing because both embrace "the insistence on the boundedness of cultural differences" (1985: 177). Similar arguments have been made by Jonathan Spencer (1990) and Jean Jackson (1989).

8. Scott skirts this epistemological issue and claims that the task is merely to assess the discrepancy between the two "transcripts" and thereby "begin to judge the impact of domination on public discourse" (1990: 5). The tone and thrust of his argument, however, yield the distinct impression that people *always* have an autonomous realm of consciousness, free from the distorting influences of power, which expresses their profound and thorough critique of the existing order and

an elaborated vision of a future alternative. In short, disclaimers notwithstanding, the "hidden transcript" sounds much like an axiom regarding subordinate people's "true interests."

9. My use of the term "post-Marxist" is admittedly a gloss on a broad, heterogeneous, and contested category of social and cultural theory. I ask the reader's indulgence on the grounds that my purpose is not to engage systematically with this literature. Rather, I seek to specify my own conception of power and structural inequity in social analysis and to respond to prominent objections. I have chosen to contrast my position with post-Marxist theorists whose analysis is relatively close to my own—such as Ernesto Laclau, Chantal Mouffe, and Dorinne Kondo (as opposed to, say, Jean Baudrillard [1983])—because this, I reasoned, would require a sharper statement of where our paths part.

10. See, for example, the work of Stuart Hall et al. (1983, 1986) and Chantal Mouffe (1979).

11. For an example of the former, see Beverley and Zimmerman (1990); in regard to the latter, I am thinking especially of recent trends in the U.S. economy as documented by Phillips (1990), among many others.

12. The phrase comes from Rosaldo (1990) in the context of a plea for placing limits on the postmodern tendency to understand the consciousness and lived experiences of subordinated racial and ethnic groups as merely "constructed" or "imagined."

13. Kondo addresses my concern in a footnote (1990: 323, no. 11), associating it (accurately, I believe) with the call for a "foundational point" to avoid the "miasma of meaninglessness and nihilism, in which no political project can be undertaken." She considers this a "false dichotomy" that can be avoided by striking a middle course between "foundation" and "miasma" involving two steps. First, we use our values to make gross political distinctions (between just and unjust, oppressor and oppressed) and position ourselves as politically engaged analysts accordingly. Then we embark on analysis that eschews those very distinctions because they are simple-minded and reductionist, and we proceed instead guided by more sophisticated social theory. That solution, it seems to me, is predicated on an untenable dichotomy between a preanalytical moment of political positioning and the subsequent use of theory and production of knowledge. If our values are useful in making initial political distinctions, and if we believe the distinctions are valid and important, why not incorporate them into our analytical framework as well?

14. The term comes from Swedenburg's analysis of Palestinian nationalism (1990).

15. Indeed, historian James Dunkerley (1990) goes further, arguing that the revolution constituted the *birth* of the Nicaraguan nation.

16. To speak of a uniform orthodoxy is to simplify because important opposing currents coexisted within the Somoza establishment. The influential views of Pablo Antonio Cuadra, for example, did not coincide with those of the Somoza government's supporters and intellectual apologists. These complexities are beyond the scope of analysis here.

17. For example, a number of FSLN leaders were of peasant extraction, and

many others had spent years in the *montaña* among peasants. This imbued an understanding that surely helped them to keep similar tensions with disaffected peasants from developing into a comparable crisis. See, for example, the account of Omar Cabezas (1985 [1982]).

18. Consistent with this observation, I argued in Chapter 5 that the Sandinista leadership endorsed the formation of the Indian organization MISURASATA out of perplexity and expediency without a clear assessment of the political implications. Sandinistas intended for MISURASATA to represent Indians' cultural expression and for the other organizations (e.g., ATC, AMNLAE, CST) to represent them politically.

19. For example, the Sandinistas' allegedly rigid class framework had relatively little trouble adapting to the notion that peasant smallholders be granted a base of organizational power separate from agricultural wage laborers. Indeed, the rise of the National Union of Farmers (UNAG) in 1981, which entailed a split from the Association of Rural Workers (ATC), provides a telling contrast to the Miskitu case.

20. According to Weber, "a state is a human community that (successfully) claims the monopoly of the legitimate use of physical force within a given territory" (quoted in Corrigan and Sayer [1985: 210, n. 11]).

21. The thrust of Anderson's argument is that *criollo* nationalism, as described in his 1983 study, persists largely unchanged in countries like Nicaragua. There is an ambiguity in this claim; in an earlier sentence he refers to the Sandinistas as "unwitting heirs of *ladino* nationalism" (emphasis added). I take this to mean that, since he perceives no appreciable change in Latin American nationalism, he uses the modifiers "criollo" and "ladino" interchangeably.

22. The racial standard need not be "pure" in the sense of descended from a single racial stock, but it must be consistent with the assertion of homogeneity: Cuba's "Afro-latin people," Mexico's "raza cosmica," the North American myth of the melting pot.

23. Quoted in Nietschmann (1985: 30). In the wording of the autonomy law, the Sandinistas resisted referring to the Miskitu as a "people," for fear that the term would give them United Nations–endorsed rights to separation.

24. The prefix "proto-" is not meant to diminish their claim to rights; rather, it refers descriptively to the fact that they still live within the bounds of a dominant nation-state. Williams devotes scant attention to this category of people and does not even name them. She seems to assume that a rejection of the "invitation" and the protonationalism that results are neither historically significant nor politically viable. In this sense, she may exaggerate somewhat the omnipotence of the nation-state.

25. For an eloquent analysis of this point in reference to Maya Indians, see Smith (1988). Smith, however, leaves the ladino/Mestizo side of the argument advanced here largely untheorized.

26. For a more detailed statement of this comparative argument in reference to Central America, see Hale and Smith (n.d.). For further evidence of this pattern of conflict in relation to the antiquincentenary campaign, see Hale (n.d.).

27. That premise is not to be confused with the naive and utopian idea—

distressingly common in analysis of the Sandinista revolution—that "U.S. imperialism" was the sole cause of Nicaragua's internal problems. Rather, it is meant merely to specify the conditions under which the method can be applied. Although moving back and forth between conflicting worldviews could provide useful insights in cases in which structural commonalities are absent (e.g., between Blacks and Whites in apartheid South Africa), such an application would require substantial changes in the working premises, which are beyond the scope of my efforts here to specify.

28. This is not an assertion about the political impact of my work specifically; that is better left for another time and probably would be best evaluated by someone else. Regardless of the outcome of that evaluation, the parallel is valid and important.

29. Though Miskitu people certainly had the right to advance such demands, the long-term consequences would have been disastrous. The Central American region already suffers enormously from the abject powerlessness of being a "nation divided," and its people—Miskitu included—would become more powerless still with the further subdivision of already tiny nations.

30. For a more detailed account of these new, rather depressing political economic conditions, see Hale (1991b).

Bibliography

Abercrombie, Nicholas, Stephen Hill, and Bryan S. Turner. 1980. *The dominant ideology thesis*. London: Allen & Unwin.

Adams, Anna. 1987. Missionaries and revolutionaries: Moravian perceptions of U.S. foreign policy in Nicaragua, 1926–1933. *Missionology: An International Review* 15, 2: 50–60.

Adams, Richard N. 1981a. The Sandinistas and the Indians: The "problem" of Indians in Nicaragua. *Caribbean Review* 10, 1: 23–25.

––––––. 1981b. The dynamics of social diversity: Notes from Nicaragua for a sociology of survival. *American Ethnologist* 9: 6–69.

Adamson, Walter. 1980. *Hegemony and revolution: A study of Antonio Gramsci's political and cultural theory*. Berkeley: University of California Press.

Albo, Xavier. 1987. From MNRistas to Kataristas to Katari. In Steve Stern, ed., *Resistance, rebellion, and consciousness in the Andean peasant world, 18th to 20th centuries*. Madison: University of Wisconsin Press. 379–419.

Alonso, Ana. 1988. The effects of truth: Re-presentations of the past and the imagining of community. *Journal of Historical Sociology* 1, 1: 33–57.

Althusser, Louis. 1971. Ideology and ideological state apparatuses. In Louis Althusser, Leninism and philosophy and other essays. New York: Monthly Review Press. 127–86.

American Friends Service Committee (AFSC). 1987. Struggle over autonomy: A report on the Atlantic Coast of Nicaragua. Philadelphia: AFSC International Division.

Anaya, James. 1987. The CIA with the Honduran army in the Mosquitia: Taking the freedom out of the fight in the name of accountability. Unpublished report.

Anderson, Benedict. 1983. *Imagined communities: Reflections on the origins and spread of nationalism*. London: Verso.

––––––. 1988. Afterword. In Remo Guidieri et al., eds., *Ethnicities and nations*. Austin: University of Texas Press. 402–6.

Anderson, Perry. 1976. The antinomies of Antonio Gramsci. *New Left Review* 100, 29: 5–78.

Arce, Bayardo. 1988. *A donde va el FSLN*. Managua: Editorial Vanguardia.

Arias, Arturo. 1990. Changing Indian identity: Guatemala's violent transition to modernity. In Carol A. Smith, ed., *Guatemalan Indians and the state, 1540–1988*. 230–57.

Ashby, Maggie. 1976. *The Mosquitia of Honduras*. London: CIR Overseas Volunteers.

Austin, Diane. 1983. Culture and ideology in the English-speaking Caribbean: A view from Jamaica. *American Ethnologist* 10: 223–41.

Bahro, Rudolf. 1977. The alternative in Eastern Europe. *New Left Review* 106: 3–38.

Barre, Marie-Chantal. 1983. *Ideologias indigenistas y movimientos indios*. Mexico City: Siglo XXI.

Barrera, Mario. 1979. *Race and class in the Southwest*. Notre Dame: University of Notre Dame Press.

Barth, Fredrik. 1969. *Ethnic groups and boundaries*. Boston: Little, Brown.

Baudrillard, J. 1983. *Simulations*. Trans. P. Foss and P. Patton. New York: Semiotext(e).

Bell, Charles N. 1899. *Tangweera: Life and adventures among gentile savages*. London: E. Arnold.

Bentley, Carter. 1987. Ethnicity and practice. *Comparative Studies in Society and History* 29, 1: 24–55.

Beverley, John, and Marc Zimmerman. 1990. *Literature and politics in the Central American revolutions*. Austin: University of Texas Press.

Bonacich, Edna. 1976. Advanced capitalism and black/white race relations in the United States: A split labor market interpretation. *American Sociological Review* 41: 34–51.

———. 1979. The past, present and future of split labor market theory. *Research in Race and Ethnic Relations* 1: 17–64.

Booth, John. 1982. *The end and the beginning: The Nicaraguan revolution*. Boulder: Westview.

Borge, Tomás. 1984. El poder político (interview with Iosu Perales). In Iosu Perales, ed., *Nicaragua: Valientemente libre*. Madrid: Editorial Revolución.

Borgeson, Paul. 1984. *Hacia el hombre nuevo: Poesia y pensamiento de Ernesto Cardenal*. London: Tamesis Books.

Borhek, Mary Virginia. 1949. *Watchman on the walls*. Bethlehem: Society for Propagating the Gospel.

Bourgois, Philippe. 1981. Class, ethnicity and the state among the Miskitu Amerindians of northeastern Nicaragua. *Latin American Perspectives* 8, 2: 23–29.

———. 1982. Ethnic minorities. In Thomas Walker, ed., *Nicaragua: The first five years*. New York: Praeger.

———. 1985. Nicaragua's ethnic minorities in the revolution. *Monthly Review* 36, 8: 22–44.

———. 1988. Conjugated oppression: Class and ethnicity among Guaymi and Kuna banana workers on a corporate plantation. *American Ethnologist* 15, 2: 328–48.

———. 1989. *Ethnicity at work*. Baltimore: Johns Hopkins University Press.

———. N.d. Unpublished field notes.

Bourgois, Philippe, and Jorge Grunberg. 1980. La Mosquitia y la revolución: Informe de una investigación rural en la Costa Atlántica Norte. Unpublished report.

Bourgois, Philippe, and Charles R. Hale. 1989. The Atlantic Coast. In Neil Snarr, ed., *Sandinista Nicaragua*. Ann Arbor: Pierian Press. 135–64.

Brading, David. 1988. Manuel Gamio and official indigenismo in Mexico. *Bulletin of Latin American Research* 7, 1: 75–89.

Brautigam-Beer, Donavan. 1970. Apuntes para una historia de nuestra Costa Atlántica. *La Prensa*, April 19–June 17.

Brooks, David. 1989. U.S. Marines, Miskitos and the hunt for Sandino: The Rio Coco Patrol in 1928. *Journal of Latin American Studies* 21, 2: 311–42.

Brown, Doug. 1990. Sandinismo and the problem of democratic hegemony. *Latin American Perspectives* 17, 2: 32–61.

Buci-Glucksmann, Christine. 1980. *Gramsci and the state*. London: Lawrence and Wishart.

Burns, Bradford. 1980. *Poverty of progress*. Berkeley: University of California Press.

Cabezas, Omar. 1985 [1982]. *Fire from the mountain*. New York: Plume.

Calderon, Manuel. 1981. We have the job of forging a class consciousness. In Klaudine Ohland and Robin Schneider, eds., *National revolution and indigenous identity*. Copenhagen: IWGIA. 142–52.

Cardenal, Ernesto. 1973 [1970]. *Homage to the American Indians*. Baltimore: Johns Hopkins University Press.

Carr, Archie, Marjorie Carr, and Ann Borkau Meylan. 1978. The ecology and migrations of sea turtles, the west Caribbean green turtle colony. *Bulletin of the American Museum of Natural History* 162, 1: 1–46.

Carrion, Luis. 1983. La Costa Atlántica vista por el FSLN. *Pensamiento Propio*, January–February: 27–31.

Cattle, Dorothy. 1977. Dietary diversity and nutritional security in a Coastal Miskito Indian village, Eastern Nicaragua. Ph.D. dissertation, University of Arizona.

Chatterjee, Partha. 1985. *Nationalist thought and the colonial world—A derivative discourse*. London: Zed.

CIDCA. 1982. *Demografía costeña: Notas sobre la historia demográfica y población actual de los grupos étnicos de la Costa Atlántica nicaraguense*. Managua: CIDCA.

———. 1986. *Trabil Nani*. New York: Riverside.

CIERA. 1981. *La Mosquitía y la revolución*. Managua: Colección Blas Real Espinales.

COCADI, ed. 1989. *Cultura Maya y políticas de desarrollo*. Chimaltenango, Guatemala: COCADI.

Comaroff, Jean, and John Comaroff. 1991. *Of revelation and revolution: Christianity, colonialism, and consciousness in South Africa*. Chicago: University of Chicago Press.

Comisión Nacional de Autonomía (CNA). 1985. *Autonomía: Para unir, hermanar definivamente y para siempre a los nicaraguenses*. Managua: Dirección de Información y Prensa de la Presidencia de la Republica de Nicaragua.

———. 1986. *Memorias de un sueño: Autonomía de la Costa Atlántica*. Managua: Comisión Nacional de Autonomía.

———. 1987. *Autonomía: Rescate de la Unidad Nacional*. Managua: Comisión de Autonomía.

Comisión Regional de Autonomía (CRA). 1986. Anteproyecto de estatuto de autonomía. Bluefields: Mimeo.

Conzemius, Edward. 1932. *Ethnological survey of the Miskito and Sumu Indians of Honduras and Nicaragua.* Washington, D.C.: Smithsonian Institution, Bureau of American Ethnology.

Corrigan, Philip, and Derek Sayer. 1985. *The great arch: Cultural revolution, state formation and the rise of capitalism.* Oxford: Oxford University Press.

Crain, Mary. 1990. The social construction of national identity in highland Ecuador. *Anthropological Quarterly* 63, 1: 43–59.

Cudara Chamorro, Pedro. 1944. *La reincorporación de la Mosquitia.* Managua.

De Kalb, Courtney. 1893. Nicaragua: Studies on the Mosquito Shore in 1892. *Bulletin of the American Geographical Society* 25: 236–88.

de Ordal, Juan. 1948. *A orillas del Río Grande.* Barcelona: Editorial Franciscana.

Dennis, Philip. 1981a. Grisi siknis among the Miskito. *Medical Anthropology* 5, 4: 445–505.

———. 1981b. Costeños and the revolution in Nicaragua. *Journal of Interamerican Studies and World Affairs* 23, 3: 271–96.

Dennis, Philip, and Michael Olien. 1984. Kingship among the Miskito. *American Ethnologist* 11, 4: 718–37.

Denny, Harold N. 1980 [1929]. *Dollars for bullets.* Westport, Conn.: Greenwood Press.

Diaz-Polanco, Héctor. 1985. *La cuestión étnico-nacional.* Mexico: Editorial Linea.

Diaz-Polanco, Héctor, and Gilberto Lopez y Rivas, eds. 1986. *Nicaragua: Autonomía y revolución.* Mexico City: Juan Pablos.

Diskin, Martin, Thomas Bossert, Salamon Nahman, and Stefano Varese. 1986. *Peace and autonomy on the Atlantic Coast of Nicaragua: A report of the LASA Task Force on Human Rights and Academic Freedom.* Pittsburgh: LASA.

Douglas, James. 1869. Account of the attempt to form a settlement on the Mosquito Shore in 1823. *Transactions of the Literary and Historical Society of Quebec, Session of 1868–9.* 5–39.

Dozier, Craig. 1985. *Nicaragua's Mosquito Shore: The years of British and American presence.* Tuscaloosa, Ala.: University of Alabama Press.

Dunbar Ortiz, Roxanne. 1983. Covert action and indigenous groups: The Miskito case. *Covert Action* 18: 21–28.

———. 1986. *La cuestión miskita en la revolución nicaraguense.* Mexico City: Editorial Linea.

Dunkerley, James. 1990. Reflections on the Nicaraguan election. *New Left Review* 182: 53–61.

Enriquez, Laura, and Rose Spalding. 1987. Banking systems and revolutionary change: The politics of agricultural credit in Nicaragua. In Rose Spalding, ed., *The political economy of revolutionary Nicaragua.* Boston: Allen & Unwin. 105–26.

Fagen, Richard. 1986. The politics of transition. In Richard Fagen et al., eds., *Transition and development: Problems of Third World socialism.* New York: Monthly Review Press. 249–63.

Falla, Ricardo. 1982. El problema de los Miskitos en Nicaragua. *Estudios Centroamericanos* 401: 193–200.

Femia, Joseph. 1975. Hegemony and consciousness in the thought of Antonio Gramsci. *Political Studies* 23, 1: 29–48.

Field, Les. 1987. "I am content with my art": Two groups of artisans in revolutionary Nicaragua. Ph.D. dissertation, Duke University.

Floyd, Troy. 1967. *The Anglo-Spanish struggle for Mosquitia*. Albuquerque: University of New Mexico Press.

Food and Agriculture Organization (FAO). 1969. *Estudio de los recursos agrícolas y forestales del noreste de Nicaragua*. Managua: FAO.

Fordham, Signithia. 1988. Racelessness as a factor in Black students' school success: Pragmatic strategy or pyrrhic victory? *Harvard Educational Review* 58, 1: 54–84.

Fordham, Signithia, and John Ogbu. 1986. Black students' school success: Coping with the burden of "acting white." *Urban Review* 18: 54–84.

Freeland, Jane. 1988. *A special place in history: The Atlantic Coast in the Nicaraguan revolution*. London: Nicaragua Solidarity Campaign.

Friedlander, Judith. 1976. *Being Indian in Hueyapan*. New York: St. Martin's Press.

Gámez, José Dolores. 1939. *Historia de la Costa Mosquita hasta 1894*. Managua: Talleres Nacionales.

Geertz, Clifford. 1973. *The interpretation of cultures*. New York: Basic Books.

Giddens, Anthony. 1979. *Central problems in social theory: Action, structure and contradiction in social analysis*. Berkeley: University of California Press.

———. 1984. *The constitution of society*. Berkeley: University of California Press.

Gilroy, Paul. 1987. *There ain't no black in the Union Jack: The cultural politics of race and nation*. London: Hutchinson.

Gordon, David. 1972. *Theories of poverty and underdevelopment*. Lexington, Mass.: D.C. Heath.

Gordon, Edmund T. 1984. Aproximación teorica a la problemática de la Costa Atlántica nicaraguense. *Wani*, September–December: 11–17.

———. 1987. History, identity, consciousness and revolution: Afro-Nicaraguans and the Nicaraguan revolution. In CIDCA, ed., *Ethnic groups and the nation state: The case of the Atlantic Coast in Nicaragua*. Stockholm: Development Study Unit. 135–68.

———. 1991. Anthropology and liberation. In Faye V. Harrison, ed., *Decolonizing anthropology: Moving further toward an anthropology for liberation*. Washington, D.C.: American Anthropological Association. 149–67.

———. N.d. Afro-Caribbean Nicaraguans: Creoles and the Sandinista revolution. Unpublished manuscript.

Gordon, Edmund W. 1985. Social science knowledge production and minority experiences. *Journal of Negro Education* 54, 2: 117–33.

Gould, Jeffrey. 1990. *To lead as equals: Rural protest and political consciousness in Chinandega, Nicaragua, 1912–1979*. Chapel Hill: University of North Carolina Press.

————. 1991. Notes on peasant consciousness and revolutionary politics in Nicaragua, 1955–1990. *Radical History Review* 48: 65–87.

Gramsci, Antonio. 1971 [1929–35]. *Selections from the prison notebooks.* New York: International Publishers.

Gurdián, Galio. 1987. Autonomy rights, national unity and national liberation: The autonomy project of the Sandinista popular revolution on the Atlantic Caribbean Coast of Nicaragua. In CIDCA, ed., *Ethnic groups and the nation state: The case of the Atlantic Coast in Nicaragua.* Stockholm: Development Study Unit. 171–89.

Hale, Charles R. 1987. Inter-ethnic relations and class structure in Nicaragua's Atlantic Coast. In CIDCA, ed., *Ethnic groups and the nation state: The case of the Atlantic Coast in Nicaragua.* Stockholm: Development Study Unit. 33–57.

————. 1990. La conciencia política miskita: Hacia un análisis coyuntural. *Wani*, July–December: 80–93.

————. 1991a. Ethnic militancy and U.S. hegemony in the Miskitu political consciousness. In Faye V. Harrison, ed., *Decolonizing anthropology: Moving further toward an anthropology of liberation.* Washington, D.C.: American Anthropological Association. 127–48.

————. 1991b. Miskitu: Revolution in the revolution. NACLA 25, 3: 24–28.

————. 1991c. Wan Tasbaya Dukiara: Contested notions of land rights in Miskitu history. Working Paper from the Center for International Studies, Massachusetts Institute of Technology, 1991. Reprinted in *Wani*, June 1992: 1–19.

————. N.d. Between Che Guevara and the Pachamama: Mestizos, Indians and identity politics in the anti-quincentenary campaign. Unpublished manuscript.

Hale, Charles R., and C. A. Smith. N.d. Reframing the national question in Central America: The challenge from ethnic militancy of the 1980s. Unpublished manuscript.

Hale, Charles R., and Katherine Yih. 1983. El impacto socio-económico y ecológico del Proyecto Palma Africana, Kukra Hill. Unpublished report.

————. 1986. Mestizos, Creoles and Indians: The ethnic hierarchy of southern Zelaya. In Klaus Meschkat et al., eds., *Mosquitia: Die andere Halfte Nicaragua.* Hamburg: Junius Verlag. 189–204.

Hall, Stuart. 1980. Race, articulation and societies structured in dominance. In UNESCO, ed., *Sociological theories: Race and colonialism.* Geneva: UNESCO. 305–45.

————. 1983. The problem of ideology—Marxism without guarantees. In B. Mathews, ed., *Marx 100 Years On.* London: Lawrence and Wishart. 57–86.

————. 1986. Gramsci's relevance for the study of race and ethnicity. *Journal of Communication Inquiry* 10, 2: 5–27.

Handler, Richard. 1985. On dialogue and destructive analysis: Problems in narrating nationalism and ethnicity. *Journal of Anthropological Research* 41, 2: 171–82.

Haraway, Donna. 1988. Situated knowledges: The science question in feminism and the privilege of partial perspective. *Feminist Studies* 14, 3: 575–99.

Hechter, Michael. 1975. *Internal colonialism.* Berkeley: University of California Press.

————. 1986. Rational choice theory and the study of race and ethnic relations.

In John Rex and David Mason, eds., *Theories of race and ethnic relations.* Cambridge: Cambridge University Press. 264–79.

Helms, Mary. 1969. The purchase society: Adaptation to economic frontiers. *Anthropological Quarterly* 42, 4: 325–42.

———. 1971. *Asang, adaptation to culture contact in a Miskito community.* Gainesville: University of Florida Press.

———. 1977. Negro or Indian? The changing identity of a frontier population. In A. M. Pascatello, ed., *Old roots in new lands.* Westport, Conn.: Greenwood Press. 157–72.

———. 1983a. Miskito slaving and culture contact: Ethnicity and opportunity in an expanding population. *Journal of Anthropological Research* 39, 2: 76–84.

———. 1983b. Los indios miskitos de Nicaragua oriental: Aislamiento, integracion o destruccion? *Revista Occidental* 1, 1: 1–19.

———. 1986. Of kings and contexts: Ethnohistorical interpretations of Miskito political structure and function. *American Ethnologist* 13, 3: 506–52.

———. 1989. Symbols of ethnicity: Geo-politics and cosmography among the Miskitu of eastern central America. Paper presented at the Fifteenth International Congress of the Latin American Studies Association, San Juan, Puerto Rico, September 21–24, 1989.

Hewitt de Alcantara, Cynthia. 1984. *Anthropological perspectives on rural Mexico.* London: Routledge & Kegan Paul.

Hobsbawm, Eric, and Terence Ranger, eds. 1983. *The invention of tradition.* Cambridge: Cambridge University Press.

Holm, John. 1978. The English Creole of Nicaragua's Miskito Coast: Its sociolinguistic history and a comparative study of its lexicon and syntax. Ph.D. dissertation, University of London.

Horowitz, Donald. 1985. *Ethnic groups in conflict.* Berkeley: University of California Press.

Howell, Samuel. 1927. General George Hodgson: His life and achievements. Unpublished pamphlet.

Instituto Nicaraguense de la Costa Atlántica (INNICA). 1982. *Tasba Pri.* Managua, INNICA.

Jackson, Jean. 1989. Is there a way to talk about making culture without making enemies? *Dialectical Anthropology* 14, 2: 127–45.

Jenkins Molieri, Jorge. 1980. La Mosquitia nicaraguense: Articulación de una formación precapitalista, su historia. Parte 1. *Estudios Sociales Centroamericanos*, February–April: 9–53.

———. 1986. *El desafío indígena en Nicaragua: El caso de los Miskitos.* Managua: Editorial Vanguardia.

Karnes, Thomas L. 1977. La Standard Fruit y la Steamship Company en Nicaragua (los primeros anos). *Anuario de Estudios Centroamericanos* 3: 175–213.

———. 1978. *Tropical enterprise: The Standard Fruit and Steamship Company in Latin America.* Baton Rouge: Louisiana State University Press.

Keely, Robert N. 1894. Nicaragua and the Mosquito Coast. *Popular Science Monthly* 45, 6: 160–74.

Keyes, Charles. 1981. The dialectics of ethnic change. In Charles Keyes, ed., *Ethnic change*. Seattle: University of Washington Press. 4–30.

Klare, Michael T., and Peter Kornbluh, eds. 1988. *Low intensity warfare: Counterinsurgency, proinsurgency and antiterrorism in the eighties*. New York: Pantheon.

Kondo, Dorinne K. 1990. *Crafting selves: Power, gender, and discourses of identity in a Japanese workplace*. Chicago: University of Chicago Press.

Laclau, Ernesto, and Chantal Mouffe. 1985. *Hegemony and socialist strategy*. London: Verso.

Laird, Larry K. 1970. Origins of the Nicaraguan reincorporation of the Miskito coast. M.A. thesis, University of Kansas.

Laitin, David. 1986. *Hegemony and culture: Politics and religious change among the Yoruba*. Chicago: University of Chicago Press.

Law, Hazel. 1982. Interview with the author.

Lears, T. Jackson. 1985. The concept of cultural hegemony: Problems and possibilities. *American Historical Review* 90, 3: 567–93.

Lernoux, Penny. 1985. Sandinista treatment of Miskitos, a betrayal of revolution ideals. *National Catholic Reporter*, April 26: 39.

MacCaulay, Neil. 1967. *The Sandino Affair*. Chicago: Quadrangle.

MacDonald, Theodore. 1981. Nicaragua: National development and Atlantic Coast Indians. *Cultural Survival Newsletter* 5, 3: 9–11.

———. 1988. Moral economy of the Miskito Indians. In Remo Guidieri et al., eds., *Ethnicities and nations*. Austin: University of Texas Press. 107–53.

MacLeod, Jay. 1987. *Ain't no makin' it: Leveled aspirations in a low-income neighborhood*. Boulder: Westview.

Mallon, Florencia. 1987. Nationalist and antistate coalitions in the war of the Pacific: Junn and Cajamarca, 1879–1902. In Steve Stern, ed., *Resistance, rebellion and consciousness in the Andean peasant world*. Madison: University of Wisconsin Press. 232–79.

Marchetti, Peter. 1986. War, popular participation and transition to socialism: The case of Nicaragua. In Richard Fagen et al., eds., *Transition and development: Problems of Third World socialism*. New York: Monthly Review Press. 303–30.

Marcus, George, and Michael Fisher. 1986. *Anthropology as cultural critique*. Chicago: University of Chicago Press.

MIDINRA. 1985. Informe sobre los miskitos del noreste de Nicaragua. Unpublished report.

Ministry of Culture. 1982. *Hacia una política cultural de la Revolución Popular Sandinista*. Managua: Ministry of Culture.

MISURASATA. 1980. *Lineamientos generales: La unidad indígena de las tres étnias del Atlántico de Nicaragua*. Managua. Pamphlet.

———. 1985. Communique (September 12, 1985). *Akwesasne Notes*, Early Winter: 13.

———. 1987. Treaty of peace. *Akwesasne Notes*, Late Spring, 18–22.

Mohawk, John. 1982. The possibilities of uniting Indians and the Left for social change in Nicaragua. *Cultural Survival Quarterly* 6, 1: 9–11.

Mohawk, John, and Shelton Davis. 1982. Revolutionary contradictions: Miskito and Sandinistas in Nicaragua. *Akwesasne Notes*, Spring: 7–10.

Molyneux, Maxine. 1986. Mobilization without emancipation? Women's interests, state and revolution. In Richard Fagen et al., eds., *Transition and development: Problems of Third World socialism*. New York: Monthly Review Press. 280–302.

Morrow, R. L. 1930. A conflict between the commercial interests of the U.S. and its foreign policy. *Hispanic American Historical Review* 10, 1: 2–13.

Mouffe, Chantal. 1979. Hegemony and ideology in Gramsci. In Chantal Mouffe, ed., *Gramsci and Marxist Theory*. London: Routledge & Kegan Paul. 168–204.

———. 1988. Radical democracy: Modern or postmodern? In Andrew Ross, ed., *Universal abandon?* Minneapolis: University of Minnesota Press. 31–45.

Mueller, Karl A. 1932. *Among Creoles, Miskitos and Sumos: Eastern Nicaragua and its Moravian missions*. Bethlehem, Pa.: Comenius Press.

Nairn, Tom. 1975. The modern Janus. *New Left Review* 94: 329–63.

Naylor, Robert A. 1967. The mahogany trade as a factor in the British return to the Mosquito Shore in the second quarter of the 19th century. *Jamaican Historical Review* 7, 1–2: 40–66.

Neugebauer, Rhonda L. 1989. Augusto Cesar Sandino, 1895–1934. In Neil Snarr, ed., *Sandinista Nicaragua*. Ann Arbor: Perrian Press. 9–15.

Nietschmann, Bernard. 1969. The distribution of the Miskitos, Sumu and Rama Indians, eastern Nicaragua. *Bulletin of the International Committee on Urgent Anthropological and Ethnological Research* 11: 91–102.

———. 1973. *Between land and water: The subsistence ecology of the Miskito Indians, eastern Nicaragua*. New York: Seminar Press.

———. 1974. Cambio y continuidad: Los indígenas rama de Nicaragua. *America Indígena* 34, 4: 905–18.

———. 1979a. *Caribbean edge: The coming of modern times to isolated people and wildlife*. New York: Bobbs-Merrill Co.

———. 1979b. Ecological change, inflation, and migration in the far western Caribbean. *The Geographical Review* 69, 1: 1–24.

———. 1984. Nicaragua's other war: Indian warriors versus Sandinistas. *Coevolution Quarterly*, Summer: 41–47.

———. 1985. Sandinismo y lukanka india. *Vuelta* 107: 53–54.

———. 1987. The third world war: Militarization and indigenous peoples. *Cultural Survival Quarterly* 11, 3: 1–16.

———. 1989. *The unknown war: The Miskito Nation, Nicaragua and the United States*. Boston: University Press of America.

Nolan, David. 1984. *The ideology of the Sandinistas and the Nicaraguan revolution*. Coral Gables: Institute of Inter-American Studies.

Nuñez Soto, Orlando. 1981. The third social force in national liberation movements. *Latin American Perspectives* 8, 2: 5–21.

———. 1986. Ideology and revolutionary politics in transitional societies. In Richard Fagen et al., eds., *Transition and development: Problems of Third World socialism*. New York: Monthly Review Press. 249–63.

Nuñez Soto, Orlando, and Roger Burbach. 1987. *Fire in the Americas*. London: Verso.

Ohland, Klaudine, and Robin Schneider, eds. 1983. *National revolution and indigenous identity: The conflict between Sandinistas and Miskito Indians of Nicaragua's Atlantic Coast*. Copenhagen: IWGIA.

O'Laughlin, Bridget. N.d. The image of unlimited desires: Cultural interpretation, methological individualism and bourgeois ideology. Unpublished paper.

Olien, Michael. 1983. The Miskito kings and the line of succession. *Journal of Anthropological Research* 39, 2: 198–241.

Olzak, Susan. 1983. Contemporary ethnic mobilization. *American Review of Sociology* 9: 355–74.

Ortega, Marvin. 1986. Tierra y lucha de clases (con enfasis en el caso de Masaya). Unpublished paper.

Ortega Saavedra, Humberto. 1979. *50 años de lucha sandinista*. Mexico: Editorial Diogenes.

Ortner, Sherry. 1984. Theory in anthropology since the sixties. *Comparative Studies in Society and History* 26: 126–66.

Palmer, Steven. 1986. Carlos Fonseca and the construction of Sandinismo in Nicaragua. *Latin American Research Review* 13, 1: 91–109.

———. 1900. "A liberal discipline: Inventing nations in Guatemala and Costa Rica, 1870–1900. Ph.D. dissertation, Columbia University.

Pataky, Lászlo. 1956. *Nicaragua desconocida*. Managua: Editorial Universal.

Phillips, Kevin. 1990. *The politics of rich and poor: Wealth and the American electorate in the Reagan aftermath*. New York: Random House.

Popular Memory Group. 1982. Popular memory: Theory, politics, method. In Richard Johnson et al., eds., *Making histories: Studies in history-writing and politics*. Minneapolis: University of Minnesota Press.

Price, Richard. 1990. *Alabi's world*. Baltimore: Johns Hopkins University Press.

Proyecto Piloto. 1960. Proyecto Piloto de Educación Fundamental del Río Coco. Informe final sobre la labor realizada para la organización "Desarrollo de la Comunidad (Educación Fundamental)." CIDCA-Managua Archives.

Ragin, Charles. 1977. Class, status and "reactive ethnic cleavages": The social bases of political regionalism. *American Sociological Review* 42: 438–50.

Ramirez, William. 1983 [1981]. The imperialist threat and the indigenous problem in Nicaragua. In Klaudine Ohland and Robin Schneider, eds., *National revolution and indigenous identity: The conflict between Sandinistas and Miskito Indians of Nicaragua's Atlantic Coast*. Copenhagen: IWGIA. 218–34.

Reich, Michael. 1972. The economics of racism. In Michael Reich et al., eds., *The capitalist system*. Englewood Cliffs: Prentice-Hall. 313–21.

Rex, John. 1986. The role of class analysis in the study of race relations—a Weberian perspective. In John Rex and David Maxon, eds., *Theories of race and ethnic relations*. Cambridge: Cambridge University Press. 64–83.

Richter, Ernesto. 1986. El movimiento indígena en la Costa Atlántica de Nicaragua en la década del 70 y su contexto. Mimeo.

Rivera, Brooklyn. 1982. Miskito nation—Some further words. Interview with Brooklyn Rivera. *Akwesasne Notes*, Early Summer: 18–20.

Roberts, Orlando. 1965 [1827]. Narrative of voyages and excursions on the east coast and in the interior of Central America: Describing a journey up the River San Juan, and passage across the Lake of Nicaragua. Gainesville: University of Florida Press (facsimile).

Román, José. 1983. *Maldito Pais*. Managua: Editorial Union.

Rosaldo, Renato. 1990. Others of invention. Ethnicity and its discontents. *Times Literary Supplement*, February: 27–29.

Rossbach, Lioba. 1985. Ascenso y caida de Samuel Pitts (1894–1907). *Encuentro* 24–25: 55–64.

———. 1986. La evangelización protestante en la Costa Atlántica de Nicaragua: La Iglesia Morava de 1849 a 1894. Unpublished manuscript.

Rothschild, Joseph. 1981. *Ethnopolitics*. New York: Columbia University Press.

Ruchwarger, Gary. 1987. *People in power: Forging a grassroots democracy in Nicaragua*. South Hadley, Mass.: Bergin and Garvey.

Skocpol, Theda. 1979. *States and social revolutions: A comparative analysis of France, Russia and China*. Cambridge, Mass.: Harvard University Press.

Scott, James C. 1985. *Weapons of the weak: Everyday forms of peasant resistance*. New Haven: Yale University Press.

———. 1990. *Domination and the arts of resistance*. New Haven: Yale University Press.

Sewell, William H., Jr. 1985. Ideologies and social revolutions: Reflections on the French case. *Journal of Modern History* 57, 1: 57–85.

Sklar, Holly. 1988. *Washington's war on Nicaragua*. Boston: South End Press.

Sloan, William. 1979. Ethnicity or imperialism? A review article. *Comparative Studies of Society and History* 21: 113–25.

Smith, Carol A. 1987. Culture and community: The language of class in Guatemala. In Mike Davis et al., eds., *The year left 2: An American socialist yearbook*. London: Verso. 197–217.

———. 1990a. Origins of the national question in Guatemala: A hypothesis. In Carol A. Smith, ed., *Guatemalan Indians and the state, 1540–1988*. Austin: University of Texas Press. 72–95.

———. 1990b. Conclusion: History and revolution in Guatemala. In Carol A. Smith, ed., *Guatemalan Indians and the state, 1540–1988*. Austin: University of Texas Press. 258–87.

Smith, M. G. 1969. Institutional and political conditions of pluralism. In M. G. Smith and Leo Kuper, eds., *Pluralism in Africa*. Berkeley: University of California Press. 27–65.

———. 1982. The nature and variety of plural unity. In David Maybury-Lewis, ed., *The prospects for plural societies*. Washington, D.C.: American Ethnological Society.

Smutko, Gregorio. 1975. *Pastoral indígena*. Bogota: Editorial Paulinas.

———. 1980. *Los heroes y martires de Bluefields*. Bluefields: CEBIC.

Sorsby, William. 1969. The British superintendency of the Mosquito Shore, 1749–1800. Ph.D. dissertation, University of London.

———. 1972. Spanish colonization of the Mosquito Coast, 1787–1800. *Revista de Historia Americana* 72–74: 145–53.

Spencer, Jonathan. 1990. Anthropology, nationalism and culture in Sri Lanka. *Current Anthropology* 31, 3: 283–300.

Squier, Ephraim George [Samuel A. Bard, pseud.]. 1855. *Waikna, or Adventures on the Mosquito Shore.* New York: Harper and Brothers.

Stern, Steve J. 1983. The struggle for solidarity: Class, culture and community in highland Indian America. *Radical History Review* 27: 21–45.

———. 1987. The age of Andean insurrection, 1742–1782: A reappraisal. In Steve Stern, ed., *Resistance, rebellion, and consciousness in the Andean peasant world.* Madison: University of Wisconsin Press.

Swedenburg, Ted. 1990. The Palestinian peasant as national signifier. *Anthropological Quarterly* 18–30.

Taylor, James. 1968. Agricultural settlement and development in eastern Nicaragua. Ph.D. dissertation, University of Wisconsin.

Trinh, Minh-ha. 1989. *Women, native, other.* Bloomington: Indiana University Press.

U.S. Congress. 1987. *Joint Hearings Before the House Select Committee to Investigate Covert Arms Transactions with Iran and Senate Select Committee on Secret Military Assistance to Iran and the Nicaraguan Opposition.* 100th Cong., 1st sess.

U.S. Department of State (USDS). 1987. *Dispossessed: The Miskito Indians in Sandinista Nicaragua.* Washington, D.C.: Department of State Publication 9478.

Valenta, Jiri, and Virginia Valenta. 1987. The FSLN in power. In Jiri Valenta and Esperanza Duran, eds., *Conflict in Nicaragua: A multidimensional perspective.* Boston: Allen & Unwin. 3–40.

Vandermeer, John, and Peter Rosset, eds. 1986. *Nicaragua: Unfinished revolution.* New York: Grove Press.

Vanegas, Uriel. 1987. Interview. *Envio* 7, 87: 19–33.

Vilas, Carlos M. 1986. *The Sandinista revolution.* New York: Monthly Review Press.

———. 1987. Revolutionary change and multi-ethnic regions: The Sandinista revolution and the Atlantic Coast of Nicaragua. In CIDCA, ed., *Ethnic groups and the nation state.* Stockholm: Development Study Unit. 61–100.

———. 1989. *State, class, and ethnicity in Nicaragua: Capitalist modernization and revolutionary change on the Atlantic Coast.* Boulder: Lynne-Reinner.

Walton, John. 1992. *Western times and water wars: State, culture and rebellion in California.* Berkeley: University of California Press.

Wheelock, Jaime. 1974. *Raices indígenas de la lucha anti-colonialista en Nicaragua.* Mexico City: Siglo XXI.

Wickham, H. A. 1894. Notes on Soumoo or Wolwa Indians of the Bluefields River, Mosquito Territory. *Journal of the Anthropological Institute of Britain and Ireland* 24: 198–206.

Wiggins, Armstrong. 1981. Colonialism and revolution, Nicaraguan Sandinism and the liberation of the Miskito, Sumu and Rama peoples: An interview with Armstrong Wiggins. *Akwesasne Notes*, Autumn: 4–15.

Wilde, Margaret, 1981. The Sandinistas and the Costeños: Reconciliation or integration? *Caribbean Review* 10, 4: 8–11.

Williams, Brackette. 1989. A class act: Anthropology and the race to nation across ethnic terrain. *Annual Review of Anthropology* 18: 401–44.

———. 1991. *Stains on my name, war in my veins: Guyana and the politics of cultural struggle*. Durham: Duke University Press.

Williams, Raymond. 1977. *Marxism and literature*. Oxford: Oxford University Press.

Willis, Paul. 1981a. *Learning to labor*. New York: Columbia University Press.

———. 1981b. Cultural production is different from cultural reproduction is different from social reproduction is different from reproduction. *Interchange* 12, 2–3: 48–95.

———. 1983. Cultural production and theories of reproduction. In Len Barton and Stephen Walker, eds., *Race, class and education*. London: Croom Helm. 107–37.

Wilson, John. 1975. Obra morava en Nicaragua. San José, Costa Rica: Seminario Biblico Latinoamericano.

Woodward, Ralph Lee, Jr. 1985. *Central America: A nation divided*. New York: Oxford University Press.

———. 1986. Central America: The liberal era, c. 1870–1930. In Leslie Bethell, ed., *The Cambridge history of Latin America*. Cambridge: Cambridge University Press. 197–226.

Wunderich, Volker. 1989. *Sandino en la costa: De las segovias al litoral Atlántico*. Managua: Editorial Nueva Nicaragua.

Wunderich, Volker, and Lioba Rossbach. 1985. Derechos indígenas y estado nacional en Nicaragua: La convención Mosquita de 1894. *Encuentro* 24–25: 29–54.

Wunderich, Volker, Elenor von Oertzen, and Lioba Rossbach, eds. 1990. *The Nicaraguan Mosquitia in historical documents, 1844–1927*. Berlin: Dietrich Reimer Verlag.

Yih, Katherine. 1987. Nicaragua's Atlantic Coast dialogue: Autonomy and the revolution. *Against the Current*, November–December: 41–46.

Index

In this index an "f" after a number indicates a separate reference on the next page, and an "ff" indicates separate references on the next two pages. A continuous discussion over two or more pages is indicated by a span of page numbers, e.g., "57–59." *Passim* is used for a cluster of references in close but not consecutive sequence.

Library of Congress Cataloging-in-Publication Data

Hale, Charles R.
    Resistance and contradiction : Miskitu Indians and the Nicar-
aguan State, 1894–1987 / Charles R. Hale.
        p.   cm.
    Includes bibliographical references and index.
    ISBN 0-08047-2255-2 (cl.) : ISBN 0-08047-2800-3 (pbk.)
    1. Mosquito Indians—Government relations.   2. Mosquito
Indians—Wars.   3. Mosquito Indians—Politics and government.   4. Indians, Treatment of—Nicaragua.   5. Nicaragua—
Ethnic relations.   6. Nicaragua—Politics and government.
7. Nicaragua—History—20th century.   I. Title.
F1529.M9H37   1994
972.8505—dc20   93-17944
                                                                  CIP

⊗   This book is printed on acid-free paper.